ANNE CONWAY

This is the first intellectual biography of one of the very first English women philosophers. At a time when very few women received more than basic education, Lady Anne Conway wrote an original treatise of philosophy: her *Principles of the Most Ancient and Modern Philosophy*, which challenged the major philosophers of her day – Descartes, Hobbes and Spinoza. Sarah Hutton's study places Anne Conway in her historical and philosophical context by reconstructing her social and intellectual milieu. She traces her intellectual development in relation to friends and associates such as Henry More, Sir John Finch, F. M. van Helmont, Robert Boyle and George Keith. And she documents Conway's debt to Cambridge Platonism and her interest in religion – an interest which extended beyond Christian orthodoxy to Quakerism, Judaism and Islam. Her book offers an insight into both the personal life of a very private woman, and the richness of seventeenth-century intellectual culture.

SARAH HUTTON is Reader in Renaissance and Seventeenth Century Studies at the School of Arts, Middlesex University. Her publications include *The Conway Letters: The Correspondence of Anne, Viscountess Conway, Henry More and their Friends, 1642–1684* (1992, a revised edition of a collection originally edited by Marjorie Nicolson in 1930), *Ralph Cudworth: A Treatise Concerning Eternal and Immutable Morality* (Cambridge, 1996), *Henry More (1614–1687): Tercentenary Studies* (1990), and *Platonism and the English Imagination* (with Anna Baldwin, Cambridge, 1994).

ANNE CONWAY

A Woman Philosopher

SARAH HUTTON

Middlesex University

CAMBRIDGE
UNIVERSITY PRESS

PUBLISHED BY THE PRESS SYNDICATE OF THE UNIVERSITY OF CAMBRIDGE
The Pitt Building, Trumpington Street, Cambridge, United Kingdom

CAMBRIDGE UNIVERSITY PRESS
The Edinburgh Building, Cambridge, CB2 2RU, UK
40 West 20th Street, New York, NY 10011–4211, USA
477 Williamstown Road, Port Melbourne, VIC 3207, Australia
Ruiz de Alarcón 13, 28014 Madrid, Spain
Dock House, The Waterfront, Cape Town 8001, South Africa

http://www.cambridge.org

First published 2004

Printed in the United Kingdom at the University Press, Cambridge

Typeface Adobe Garamond 11/12.5 pt. *System* LaTeX 2ε [TB]

A catalogue record for this book is available from the British Library

Library of Congress Cataloguing in Publication data
Hutton, Sarah, 1948–
Anne Conway: A Woman Philosopher / by Sarah Hutton.
p. cm.
Includes bibliographical references and index.
ISBN 0 521 83547 X
1. Conway, Anne, 1631–1679. I. Title.
B1201.C5534H88 2004
192 – dc22 2004040786

ISBN 0 521 83547 X hardback

In memory of Rebecca

Contents

Acknowledgements

While writing this book I have benefited enormously from the help and encouragement of many people, among whom I would particularly like to thank Stuart Brown, Richard Popkin, John Rogers and the late Jan van den Berg, for their encouragement and support at different stages of the book's development. I thank Alan Gabbey for imparting his invaluable knowledge of the Conways and Northern Ireland. The shared interest of Susan James and Eileen O'Neill in seventeenth-century women philosophers has always been inspiring. I am very grateful to those who have read and commented on some or all of the typescript: Allison Coudert, Frances Harris, Anne Kelley, Margaret Osler and Jan Wocjick. Thanks also to the Cambridge University Press readers for their constructive suggestions, and to Benjamin Carter for assistance in checking the typescript. This book could not have been written without access to the rich collections of the Armagh Robinson Library, the British Library, the libraries of Christ's College, Cambridge, and Friends' House, London, the Herzog August Bibliothek, the Huntington Library, the Wellcome Institute Library, Dr Williams's Library and the Library of the Warburg Institute. I am grateful to the librarians and staff of them all for access to their collections. Thanks are also due to His Grace the late Marquis of Hertford for permission to inspect the collections at Ragley Hall. I thank the Huntington Library, California, for granting me a Mellon Fellowship to enable me to consult the Hastings papers, and for permission to quote from them. I am grateful to the British Library for permission to quote from the Additional Manuscripts, and to the Record Office for Leicestershire, Leicester and Rutland for permission to quote from the Finch papers. My thanks also to the Herzog August Bibliothek, Wolfenbüttel, for permission to quote from the correspondence of Knorr von Rosenroth, and to Oxford University Press for permission to quote from *The Conway Letters*. Last, but by no means least, I thank the British Academy for granting me an award under their Research Leave Scheme, which enabled me to do the major groundwork for this book.

Introduction

The year 1690 saw the appearance in Holland of an anonymous octavo volume entitled *Opuscula philosophica*.[1] The second of the three *opuscula* it contained was entitled *Principia philosophiae antiquissimae et recentissimae*.[2] Two years later, an English translation of this work was published, with the title *The Principles of the Most Ancient and Modern Philosophy: Concerning God, Christ, and the Creature; that is, concerning Spirit and Matter in General.* The preface to the book explains that it was a translation by one 'J. C.' of 'a little treatise published since the Author's Death', originally published in Latin in Amsterdam. No author is named, but the address to the reader explains that it 'was written not many Years ago, by a certain English countess, a Woman learned beyond her Sex'. The Latin edition, of which this is a translation, gives no further clues as to the identity of this erudite Countess, but her authorship treatise was not altogether a secret in the early Enlightenment. In his biography (1710) of Henry More, Richard Ward prints the preface originally prepared for publication with this treatise, and gives an account of its author, 'the Lady Viscountess Conway', whom he describes as the 'Heroine pupil' of the Cambridge Platonist, Henry More (1614–87). The unpublished preface speaks of her 'singular Quickness and Apprehensiveness of Understanding' and her 'marvellous Sagacity and Prudence in any Affairs of Moment'.[3] The most famous reader

[1] *Opuscula philosophica quibus continetur, principia philosophiae antiquissimae & recentissimae ac philosophia vulgaris refutata quibus junctur sunt C.C. problemata de revolutione animarum humanorum* (Amsterdam, 1690). (Note that primary sources are cited in full at first mention throughout; secondary sources are cited by author's name and date only.)

[2] *Principiae philosophiae antiquissimae & recentissimae de Deo, Christo & creatura id est de spiritu & materia in genere* (Amsterdam, 1690).

[3] Richard Ward, *The Life of the Pious and Learned Henry More* (London, 1710; rev. edn 2000), p. 123. Ward does not actually mention that Lady Conway's book had been published. He also erroneously attributes the unpublished preface to More, saying that it was written by him in Van Helmont's name. The content, however, indicates that the author was Van Helmont himself. The author states, 'I Can witness from these Seven or Eight Years Experience of her', which is consistent with Van Helmont's having resided at her home at Ragley Hall for most of the decade prior to Anne Conway's death.

of Lady Conway's *Principles* certainly knew her identity: Leibniz inscribed her name, 'La comtesse de Konnouay', on his copy of the Latin original, which is preserved among his collection of books at the Niedersächsische Landesbibliothek, Hanover.[4] Nevertheless, almost a century later her identity as the author of *The Principles* was not widely known in England, as may be seen in the correspondence published in *The Gentleman's Magazine* in 1784 answering a query about the name of the author, which was established as 'the illustrious Anne, Viscountess Conway'.[5] This did not redeem Anne Conway from obscurity, and it was not until Marjorie Nicolson published her correspondence with Henry More in *The Conway Letters* in 1930 that she was brought back into focus as a thinker connected with Henry More and the Cambridge Platonists.

Anne Conway's *Principia philosophiae* is a book that deserves the attention of historians of philosophy on many counts. Not only is it one of the earliest philosophical treatises by a woman to have seen print, but it is a treatise in dialogue with the philosophy of the seventeenth century. In the process of setting out an original system of metaphysics, Anne Conway engages in the critique of the philosophies of Descartes, Hobbes and Spinoza, as well as of her teacher, Henry More. Furthermore, the system she propounds has some striking similarities to the philosophy of Leibniz. She was also conversant with contemporary science and natural philosophy. Her treatise is a work of metaphysics, which, as its subtitle tells us, deals with 'spirit and matter in general' (*de spiritu & materia in genere*). It claims to be able to solve problems which neither scholasticism, nor Cartesianism, nor the philosophy of Hobbes or Spinoza have been able to solve: the benefit of her treatise will, she says, resolve all the problems which could not be solved by the scholastics, or the moderns, Descartes, Hobbes and Spinoza ('omnia problemata, quae nec per Philosophiam Scholasticam, nec per communem modernam, nec per Cartesianam, Hobbesianam, vel Spinosianam resolvi possunt'). Her distinctive solution to these problems is set out as tripartite ontology, deduced from the nature of God. In this Neoplatonic order of three species (as she calls them), the created world is derived from God via an intermediate species, Middle Nature, which is the

Moreover, he refers to More indirectly as a third party – 'that Party, who knew her from her Youth, and had the Honour of her Friendship to her Dying Day' – this is consistent with More's having been her friend for over twenty-five years.

[4] The book was probably presented to Leibniz by Francis Mercury van Helmont, mutual friend of Leibniz and Anne Conway. See Coudert (1995), Coudert (1999) and chapter 11 below.

[5] Since Anne Conway's reputation as a philosopher has been established under her married name, I shall normally refer to her by that, as a pen name rather than by her maiden name, Anne Finch.

first efficient cause through which all things come into being, and, as the imparter of God's providential design, the final cause of all things. In place of the dualism of soul and body, spirit and matter of Cartesianism, she posits a single created substance. Against the monistic materialists, Hobbes and Spinoza, she argues that body or matter itself belongs to a continuum of spirit-like substance. 'Spirit and body' she writes, 'are originally one and the same thing in the first substance'.[6] In opposition to new philosophies of the seventeenth century, which sought to explain all phenomena in the natural world in terms of matter in motion, matter being merely extension, differentiated by shape, size and position, Anne Conway argues that body is not 'dead matter', but a substance endued with life. Even where she differs from Descartes and More, Anne Conway remains philosophically indebted to them by virtue of the fact that, between them, they provided her starting point in philosophy. It was in response to them that she worked out her own system, which is in many ways a continuation of the process of cross-fertilisation of Cartesianism and Platonism initiated by Henry More.

Even after the first appearance of Marjorie Nicolson's magisterial edition of Anne Conway's correspondence in 1930, interest in her philosophy was slow to gather momentum. It is only within the last twenty-five years that there has been any appreciable study of it. The publication of a modern edition of both the Latin and the English versions of her philosophy, edited by Peter Loptson in 1982, and a new English translation of the Latin by Allison Coudert and Taylor Corse in 1996, have made her philosophy available to modern audiences as never before, while the revised edition of *The Conway Letters* (1992) has restored the philosophical content of her correspondence omitted in Marjorie Nicolson's 1930 edition.[7] In the wake of the women's movement and the new interest in women's history which it has generated, there is increasing interest in Anne Conway as a woman philosopher. This is registered in the inclusion of extracts from the *Principles* in recent anthologies of writings by female philosophers, and in

[6] Anne Conway, *The Principles of the Most Ancient and Modern Philosophy*, trans. Allison P. Coudert and Taylor Corse (Cambridge: Cambridge University Press, 1996), p. 63. Unless otherwise stated, all quotations from Conway's *Principles* are from the translation by Corse and Coudert. And unless the context requires the Latin version to be specified, I shall refer to the work by its English title.

[7] The story of the discovery and preservation of the Conway correspondence by Horace Walpole is told in the Prologue to *The Conway Letters. The Correspondence of Vicountess Anne Conway, Henry More and their Friends*, ed. S. Hutton and M. H. Nicolson (Oxford: Clarendon Press, 1992). However, Walpole's restricted idea of what constitutes a historical document led him to consign a good many of the papers he discovered to the flames (he regarded documents like bills and bonds as 'useless'). Horace Walpole, *The Yale Edition of Horace Walpole's Correspondence*, 41 vols. ed. W. S. Lewis (London: Oxford University Press, 1937–83), vol. IX, p. 17.

the appearance of entries on Anne Conway in philosophical dictionaries.[8] The growing interest is also evident from the fact that her treatise is being translated.[9]

Anne Conway lived at a time when only a minority of women received much by way of education, and when philosophy was considered a male preserve. It is therefore truly remarkable that she managed to become a philosopher in her own right. It is equally remarkable that we have as full a picture as we do of both her philosophy and her life. The major biographical work on Anne Conway was done by Marjorie Nicolson. Although this has been added to subsequently, the biographical framework established by Nicolson remains largely unchanged. What Marjorie Nicolson did not set out to provide was an intellectual biography which mapped her intellectual milieu and traced the development of her thought. In fact Professor Nicolson sidestepped philosophical questions altogether, by excising from her edition the letters which discuss Descartes, and by refraining from examining Conway's *Principles* in *The Conway Letters.* Nevertheless, from this correspondence we can learn something about Anne Finch's education, especially her relationship with her brother's university tutor, Henry More of Christ's College, Cambridge, who took her on as a kind of extra-mural pupil, since she, as a woman, was debarred from attending the university (I deal with the curriculum she followed with More in chapter 2). It is clear from the surviving letters from More's epistolary tutorials that Anne Conway's introduction to philosophy was through the new philosophy of René Descartes. It is therefore the more remarkable that Anne Conway's own *Principia philosophiae* entails a repudiation of Cartesian dualism. But apart from telling us something about her early philosophical education and about the circle surrounding Anne Conway, *The Conway Letters* gives few clues as to the evolution and writing of her *Principles.* Marjorie Nicolson's sidestepping of the philosophical life of her subject is understandable, for the letters reveal very little directly about Conway's philosophical life and the genesis of her treatise. Furthermore, the majority of the letters published in *The Conway Letters* are by Henry More. We therefore access Anne Conway indirectly through his replies to her no-longer-extant letters. But even here it is difficult to detect the developments in her thinking which resulted in the composition of her *Principles of Philosophy.* Her silence on this, together with the fact that one of the most important sources of information about her is indirect mediation, must give us pause. The compact

[8] For example, Atherton (1993), and *Women Philosophers*, ed. Mary Warnock (London: Dent, 1996). Also Craig (1998), see under 'Anne Conway'; Audi (1995), see under 'Conway, Anne'.

[9] At the time of writing, a Polish translation by Joanna Usakiewicz has just appeared, and a Spanish translation by Bernadino Orio de Miguel is being prepared.

self-consistency of her *Principles* and the relatively large amount of documentation of her life (large, that is, compared to most other women intellectuals of this period), belie the fact that our purchase on her life and thought is more fragile than it seems.

Aside from the anonymity of the published versions of her philosophy, we have to reckon with the fact that it is based on private notebooks, and does not, apparently, constitute everything she wrote. The unpublished preface by Van Helmont, printed in Ward's *Life* of Henry More describes the treatise as 'these broken Fragments': 'Thou art to understand, that they are only Writings abruptly and scatteredly, I may add also obscurely, written in a Paper Book, with a Black-lead Pen, towards the latter end of her long and tedious Pains and Sickness; which she never had Opportunity to revise, correct, or perfect.'[10] Her first editor tells us that her philosophical papers, originally written in English, were found among her effects after her death. They were never intended for publication but 'for her own use', and much of what she wrote was illegible. Nor do we have the original text. What we do have are two translations, one in Latin, and the other of that Latin into English: 'she wrote these few chapters for her own use, but in a very small and faint handwriting. When these were found after her death, part of them were transcribed (because the rest were hardly legible) and translated into Latin, so that the whole world might derive some profit from them.'[11] This translation was, the English version tells us, printed 'at Amsterdam, by M. Brown' in 1690, apparently at the behest of Anne Conway's erstwhile physician and friend Francis Mercury van Helmont.[12] The anonymous volume, *Opuscula philosophica*, in which the Latin version appeared, contains two other anonymously printed treatises, one by Van Helmont and the other by Jean Gironnet.[13] This means that, when Anne Conway's philosophical treatise was first published, it appeared in Latin translation. The subsequent English edition was a translation of a translation. The printed versions were, moreover, incomplete and published more than a decade after she died. And we cannot rule out the possibility that Van Helmont made some additions to the text.[14] Yet this is the fullest and most systematic work of philosophy by any woman writing in the English language in

[10] Ward, *The Life*, p. 123. [11] 'To the Reader', in *Principles*, p. 7. [12] See Coudert (1995).

[13] The two other works are Jean Gironnet's anti-scholastic discussion, *Philosophia vulgaris refutata* (Amsterdam, 1690) and *De revolutione animorum humanorum quanta stet istius doctrinae cum veritate. Christianae religionis conformitas problematum centuriae duae* which is a Latin translation of Van Helmont's *Two Hundred Queries Modestly Propounded Concerning the Doctrine of the Revolution of the Human Souls and its Conformity with the Truth of the Christian Religion* (London, 1684).

[14] At least some of the notes which give page references to the *Kabbalah denudata* must post-date the writing of the treatise, since they refer to the second volume, not published until 1684. See chapter 8 below.

the seventeenth century. It is an extraordinary chance that her treatise has survived. Without it, we would have, at best, only circumstantial evidence of her engagement in philosophy. Although there is sufficient surviving evidence of her writings for us to be able to identify her as a philosopher, her letters, like her treatise, are an imperfect record, since not many of them have come down to us, and those that have are reticent about her compilation of her philosophical notebook. The information to be obtained from these sources is therefore patchy. The best documentation we have gives us incomplete and indirect access to the nature and development of her philosophy.

PLACING ANNE CONWAY

The case of Anne Conway is in many ways emblematic of the anomalous position of women in history, and especially in the history of philosophy: they are visible like footprints in other people's lives, discernible largely by their impact on those around them. One notable example one might cite is Boyle's sister Lady Ranelagh, who by all accounts played a shaping role in the practical affairs of her time, but is only known from what others said about her. Another example is Elizabeth of Bohemia, who comes into view as a correspondent of Descartes. Common sense tells us that she did not stop doing philosophy when she stopped writing to Descartes. But she left no writings that confirm this. A further irony of Anne Conway's case is that, even at the point where her philosophy became known (the point of publication), its author had no name. Nor could she have enjoyed her anonymous fame, having predeceased the publication of her work by a decade. In recovering her as part of our philosophical heritage, we have to find a way of working with a record that seems, at times, more like a palimpsest.

Aside from the problems arising from discontinuities in the documentary record, there are other difficulties to overcome when recovering Anne Conway as a philosopher. These are in many respects the kinds of difficulty involved in reclaiming any forgotten female philosopher of the past. But each such philosopher is a special case, according to the character of her philosophy. And each has her own *fortuna* or lack of it in the history of philosophy. In Anne Conway's case, situating her as a philosopher in relation to philosophy as it is understood and practised today is not easy. Her treatise is a work of metaphysics, largely devoted to discussing the nature of substance and doing so in distinctly seventeenth-century terms. Moreover, the terms are not those familiar from the philosophical vocabulary of Descartes and Locke. Rather she employs the philosophical idiom of thinkers and philosophers no longer regarded as frontline, and in some cases considered definitively defunct. The philosophers with whom she was most closely associated were the group known now as the Cambridge Platonists. She also adopts terms from the language of alchemy and the kabbalah, while her vitalism has affinities with the biological thought of two figures not normally treated as philosophers, Jan Baptiste van Helmont and his son Francis Mercury van Helmont. Her very choice of title, 'Most Ancient and Modern', confounds the modern understanding of historical categories and our sense of the distinctness of one philosophical school from another. Her incorporation of religious and theological material in her treatise, in particular her use of kabbalistic and Origenist doctrines, runs counter to our sense of the modernity of seventeenth-century philosophy, and even our idea of philosophy. With her letters, as with her treatise, much of the intellectual subject matter is not recognisably philosophical – at least not philosophical discourse as we would understand it today. Many of the discussions consist of apparently abstruse topics with little direct bearing on philosophy – religious enthusiasm, millenarianism and kabbalism.

Not only does the example of Anne Conway aptly illustrate the general problem of the unfamiliar in philosophical history, but it highlights the particular case of the misfortunes of Platonism. Many of the non-canonical philosophers of the past worked within philosophical traditions that have since been declared suspect or unimportant. This is particularly the case with the Platonist philosophies with which Anne Conway was familiar through her contact with the so-called Cambridge Platonists. There has been a long history of hostility to Platonism ever since its recovery for the Western philosophical tradition in the Renaissance. This hostility manifests itself as a challenge to Platonism's status as real philosophy with Jacob Brucker and the German Enlightenment. It was Brucker who undermined the philosophical credentials of such figures as Plotinus, Iamblichus and Porphyry, by grouping them together under the heading *Neoplatonism*, separate from Plato, and associated with such dubious thinkers as Paracelsus.[15]

Recent attempts to place Anne Conway philosophically have tried to see her as a prototype of more familiar philosophical traditions or areas of philosophy. Jane Duran and Anne Becco, for example, have pointed out

[15] Jacob Brucker, *Historia critica philosophiae* (Lipsiae, 1742–67). Brucker's prejudices against Platonism are echoed by Johan Lorenz Mosheim in his Latin translation of the works of Cudworth, *Systema intellectualis huius universi* (Jena, 1733). During the Renaissance and the seventeenth century the main objections to Platonism were theological, often relating to the issue of the Trinity.

the parallels between her system and Leibniz's philosophy.[16] Peter Loptson, more boldly, detects anticipations of Wittgenstein, Kripke and others in the *de re* modality he discerns in her work.[17] Duran and Becco illustrate the problem of what may be called the 'coat-tail syndrome', that is a well-meaning attempt to recommend women philosophers (and other philosophers perceived as minor) by linking them to more famous canonical figures. This approach may have the advantage of bringing less familiar figures to the attention of established industries in philosophical scholarship, but it has the inbuilt danger of consigning such figures to permanent 'minor' status. Alternatively, we may, like Peter Loptson, read Anne Conway as a proto-modern, focusing on recognisable modern philosophical issues. This has the advantage of helping to give modern philosophers some sense of kinship with a remote figure from the past. But it is only possible by distortion and omission. On this kind of reading, much of the content of her book has to be consigned to the category of dross, or perhaps 'mysticism'. And in that category one will find her use of the kabbalah and of alchemical terminology, as well as such weird and wonderful concepts as 'vital extension'. Exceptionally among Conway studies, Coudert and Corse have tried to reverse this approach, and focus on Conway's use of the kabbalah as a key feature of her treatise. In doing so they lay themselves open to the charge that they have muddled mysticism with 'real' philosophy.[18] These apparently mystical features of *The Principles* mean it is difficult to accept the classification of Conway as 'a rationalist' according to the rationalist–empiricist opposition adopted in the twentieth century.[19] Of the few attempts to acknowledge Anne Conway's Platonism, Carolyn Merchant's study is limited by the fact that it is too narrow in its invocation of that context, with the result that she classes Conway's mentor, More, in the opposite philosophical camp from her own. Lois Frankel is another commentator who acknowledges a Platonist element in Conway's *Principles*. But her study illustrates precisely the ambivalent view of Platonism among contemporary analytic philosophers, in so far as she seems to regard Conway's Platonism as primarily a matter of *imagery* rather than conceptual framework.[20] More

[16] Becco (1978), Duran (1989). Also Merchant (1980).

[17] In *The Principles*, parallel text edition, ed. Peter Loptson (Delmar, NY: Scholar's Facsimiles and Reprints, 1998), pp. 10–11, 17, 146–9.

[18] Mary Warnock, in her review of the Corse and Coudert translation of Conway's *Principles*, in *The Times Literary Supplement*, October 1996.

[19] See, e.g., Duran (1989).

[20] Frankel (1991), p. 44. Loptson is another who sets the 'rationalism' of Conway in opposition to Platonism, as represented by the religious and poetic concerns of Henry More (*The Principles*, ed. Loptson, p. 16).

recently, by offering a historically nuanced analysis of informed feminist philosophy, Jacqueline Broad's study of early modern women philosophers signals a new departure in this area.

APPROACHING BIOGRAPHY

The discontinuous nature of the source material means that it is impossible to structure an intellectual biography of Anne Conway as a continuous chronological narrative of the kind that Marjorie Nicolson did when she packaged the letters as the story of a Platonic friendship, framing the correspondence with biographical commentary. In order to show that her philosophical treatise was the outcome of the philosophical concerns of a lifetime (or even to show that it was not), chronology is important, but the only philosophical text we have of Anne Conway's dates from her very last years, and there is no chronological lead-in from her letters. However, the letters do yield enough information about Anne Conway's conduct of her intellectual life to suggest an alternative approach, or rather to suggest ways of making the *indirect* access we have to her thinking into an asset. For this *The Conway Letters* gives us vital clues. Most importantly of all, they indicate that Anne Conway's philosophising was not confined to her treatise, even though that is the best evidence we have of what she thought. Her letters indicate that she was at the centre – the nerve centre perhaps – of continuous intellectual debate, in which she played the lead role in setting the agenda. As her letters show, it is she who asks the questions – questions which shape the answers emanating from her circle.[21] From the very beginning of her acquaintance with More right up to her last letters to him, it is she who poses questions that others answer. Nor does she simply initiate debate, but she conducts it, not so much as an interlocutor, but as an orchestrator. As we shall see in chapter 10, this is clearly the case when she involves Henry More in a debate with George Keith. This manner of proceeding raises the question of the authorship of treatises written in response to her or at her request. When Van Helmont tells us that *Two Hundred Queries* was put together at the request of 'a Person of quality', when we see her instructing More to respond to Keith's *Immediate Revelation*, or when we see echoes of Conway in the writings of Van Helmont and Keith, we ought to consider the possibility that her philosophical authorship is wider than the *Principia philosophiae antiquissimae et recentissimae*.

[21] A parallel (albeit a semi-fictional one) for this may be found in Castiglione's *Il Cortegiano*, where the duchess of Urbino presides over the dialogue of her courtiers and dictates the subject matter of their debate. However, she does not actually contribute a word to it.

Although Anne Conway's philosophy appears to have been conceived as a definitive system of metaphysics, when it is set in context we can see that it was the outcome of collective dialogue. In this respect (as well as others to be discussed later) she may be compared to Leibniz, whom Stuart Brown has described as 'a collaborative philosopher', a contributor to the debates of his time, and comfortable with a conception of metaphysics as open-ended, that is amenable to modification in the light of new problems.[22] A major difference between Anne Conway and Leibniz is the conditions under which they conducted their dialogues. As the employee of princes, and a full citizen of the republic of letters, Leibniz had privileged contact with the leading public minds of his day. As a woman and an invalid, Anne Conway's collaborative space was confined to what was possible within the social and physical constraints that circumscribed her intellectual activities.

Since *The Conway Letters* gives few obvious clues as to the evolution and writing of her *Principles*, the history of her philosophical activities has to be pieced together, by a process of what might be called reconstructive archaeology, from the intellectual circle she was fortunate enough to inhabit – a circle which included the chief mentors of her philosophical life: her brother John Finch, her teacher Henry More, and her physician Francis Mercury van Helmont. Given the dialogic nature of Anne Conway's conduct of her intellectual enquiries, the obvious means of access to the life of her mind is to examine those with whom she was in dialogue. This does not mean that hers was a reach-me-down package of disparate elements patch-worked into a whole. Far from it. We could not even begin to document her mental life without examining its traces in the mental lives of others, as recorded in their writings. To gain any insight into her intellecual activities, it is imperative to contextualise Anne Conway's thought by examining the personal, cultural and philosophical circumstances in which she lived, in so far as these can be reconstructed from her letters and the writings of those with whom she was in contact.

For this reason, the optimum starting point for an investigation of Anne Conway's philosophy is her starting point: Cambridge Platonism. When Marjorie Nicolson discovered and published More's correspondence with Anne Conway she confirmed the link with the Cambridge Platonists, especially with Henry More. Anne Conway became a philosopher not *in spite of* Cambridge Platonism, but *through* it. However, to underline the link between Conway and Cambridge Platonism is, again, to risk classifying her among the 'also-rans' of philosophy. But it is a risk that has to be

[22] Brown (1984), p. 8.

taken, since this is the group with which, historically and philosophically, she belongs. Among Platonists, the Cambridge Platonists have suffered the neglect and misinterpretation that is the lot of 'minor' figures, especially since, until recently, they have been considered a cul-de-sac in the history of philosophy – Platonists when the rest of the world was taking a modern turn with Descartes, Hobbes or Locke; theologians when philosophy had become self-confidently secular; in short 'mystical idealists, without a philosophical legacy'. This is a caricature view which, fortunately, is being revised, as the relevance of the Cambridge school to seventeenth-century and later philosophy has been recognised.[23] Their leading philosophical minds, Ralph Cudworth and Henry More, were, after all, two of the most important English thinkers after Locke and Hobbes. And their influence on English culture and European philosophy was wider and more long-lived than has often been supposed.[24] This is not to say that they were philosophers in the same league as Descartes and Hobbes. Nor does it mean that there are not important differences between Conway's philosophy and that of Cudworth and More (notably on dualism). Nevertheless, hers was, like theirs, a philosophy of spirit. Her critique of modern philosophy echoes theirs. She shared their moral and theological optimism. Their latitudinarianism is accentuated in her system where it manifests itself in an ecumenism which extends to Muslims and Jews as well as varieties of Christianity. In short, the only respect in which she does not qualify as a Cambridge Platonist is the fact that she was not educated or employed at the University of Cambridge, as they all were.

In her syncretic approach Anne Conway also shares with the Cambridge Platonists a view of philosophy which is no longer given credence, but one which was, nevertheless, widespread in their day and was enormously important in shaping her ideas. This was the view that all philosophies were part of a perennial philosophy (*philosophia perennis*), a view which was widely accepted in the Renaissance and the seventeenth century and involved conflating ancient and modern philosophy into one timeless system of thought. The title of her treatise adopts this picture of philosophy by placing ancient and modern on an equal footing. The way in which she cites authorities and deploys her arguments shows that she assumes equivalence across philosophical systems, being accustomed to viewing different

[23] Passmore (1951), Hutton (1990a), Hall (1990), Darwall (1995), Rogers et al. (1997). See also the introduction to my new edition of Ralph Cudworth, *A Treatise Concerning Eternal and Immutable Morality*, ed. S. Hutton (Cambridge: Cambridge University Press, 1996; first published 1731).

[24] Cassirer's seminal study treated the Cambridge Platonists as a cul-de-sac in the history of thought (Cassirer, 1953).

philosophies as variant pronouncements of the same single eternal wisdom. It is important to recognise this in order to understand what seem, to modern readers, to be unpardonable elisions of philosophy and theology, of Judaism and Christianity, and of different philosophical systems in *The Principles.*

In so far as it is loosely framed by Anne Conway's life, and discusses her thought in its intellectual and cultural context, what follows can be described as an intellectual biography. But my study is not a biographical one in the Nicolson sense. I do not aim to provide a continuous biographical narrative as such. The discontinuous nature of the material means that it is impossible to construct a continuous chronological story: the only philosophical text we have of Anne Conway's dates from her very last years, and there is no chronological lead-in from her letters. In order to cope with this problem, I have adopted a loosely chronological sequence within which to contextualise Anne Conway's thought by relating it to her biographical, cultural and philosophical circumstances in so far as these can be reconstructed from her letters, contacts and reading. I hope thereby to demonstrate that her philosophical treatise is the outcome of the philosophical concerns of a lifetime. My study is in many ways an essay in interconnections: connections between what is known about Anne Conway's philosophy and what is known about her life and contacts, between the tenets of her system and seventeenth-century philosophy, between philosophy and the social and religious priorities of its practitioners, between the known text and what that bespeaks of the unscripted. In the interests of clarification, it is necessary to separate out strands which were, in her life, closely intertwined, even though, paradoxically, such separations both illuminate and distort the picture. The area where this is most acute is Conway's simultaneous encounter with Helmontianism, Quakerism and kabbalism, which I discuss in separate chapters. The focus of my study is Anne Conway's philosophical formation, both in the sense of the constituent elements of her mature thought and in the sense of how she arrived at that position. A key question is how it was that she became a philosopher at a time when only a minority of her sex had any education, and when philosophy was very much the province of men. We can only hope to answer this question by examining in detail the intellectual personalities with whom she had contact, and the intellectual commerce they pursued. Space will therefore be given to her three chief mentors Henry More, John Finch and F. M. van Helmont, and others such as Robert Boyle and George Keith whom she encountered at different points in her life. In respect of methodology, my study perhaps has more in common with recent work in the history of science than with the history of philosophy as currently practised in the anglophone world.[25]

It is most certainly not my aim to reconstruct what Anne Conway might have said on modern issues, or to subject her arguments to analytic critique. My focus will be on the *nature* of her philosophy rather than the 'strength' or 'validity' of her arguments. In taking a historical approach, my purpose is contextual, not antiquarian. Nor does it signal a determination to privilege history over philosophy. Rather it is born of the recognition that, in order to familiarise ourselves with the forgotten names of philosophical history, we must return to origins and study their works within the philosophical conditions of their production. Before we can situate such figures within philosophy as we know it, we have to come to an understanding of the philosophical language they used and the circumstances which shaped their thought. We have, in other words, to reconstruct its context. Although historical in method, my aim here is ultimately philosophical: to enhance our understanding of Anne Conway's philosophy and to give her a meaningful philosophical identity.

The following study is premised on my view that the key to understanding Anne Conway's philosophy today lies, not in any putative proto-modernity but in its historicity, not in the ground shared with the present, but in its difference from the present. The nature of her contribution to philosophy and the measure of her achievement can only be grasped by positioning it historically in relation to the circumstances of its production. This is a process that enables us to see both the similarities and the differences between her system and that of her contemporaries. And it is only by examining that context that we can explain how, as a woman, she became a philosopher in circumstances where few women achieved even an education. By understanding the special conditions that applied in her case, we can gain a better understanding of why so few other women practised philosophy in her day. In so saying I do not mean that Anne Conway is a mere museum piece to be dusted down by the occasional historian. On the contrary, it is my hope that by reconstructing her milieu and suggesting a history of the production of her *Principles*, my study will widen interest in her as a philosopher.

[25] See especially Michael Hunter's useful remarks on the practice of intellectual history in Hunter (1995), p. 17.

CHAPTER 1

Anne Finch, Viscountess Conway

'Honoratissima atque illustrissima Domina'[1]

Anne Conway was born on 14 December 1631. She was the posthumous daughter of Sir Heneage Finch, younger son of Sir Moyle Finch, and Elizabeth Bennett, the daughter of William Cradock of Whickambrook in Staffordshire and widow of Sir John Bennett, a wealthy London merchant. Anne's parents were married on 16 April 1629 at St Dunstan's in the West in the City of London.[2] Her father was himself a widower, his first wife, Frances Bell, having died on 11 April 1627.[3] But he did not live long after his second marriage: he died on 5 December 1630, less than two weeks before the birth of his youngest daughter, Anne. When she married Sir Heneage Finch, Elizabeth Bennett already had at least one child, Simon Bennett, from her previous marriage.[4] By her marriage to Sir Heneage, she became stepmother to the four surviving children from his first marriage: Heneage, Frances, Elizabeth and John.[5] In her second marriage she had two children, both daughters, Francis and Anne. The future Lady Conway, then, was the youngest child of a large family of at least seven children raised in a fatherless household.

The Finch–Bennett match ensured their children belonged to a network of prosperous families, well on the road to social advancement: with roots in the City of London, a judicious combination of career and marriage alliances was to bring them connections in the law, government and the aristocracy. Elizabeth's first husband, the wealthy merchant Sir John Bennett, was the son of Sir Thomas Bennett, a member of the Mercer's

[1] Knorr von Rosenroth, addressing Anne Conway. Wolfenbüttel, MS Cod. Guelf Extrav. 30.4, fol. 8v.

[2] Unless otherwise indicated the following biographical details come from *Proceedings Especially in the County of Kent, in Connection with Parliaments Called in 1640*, ed. Lambert B. Larkin (London: Camden Society, 1862), and *Conway Letters*.

[3] She was the daughter of the judge, Sir Edmund Bell of Beaupré Hall in Norfolk.

[4] She also had two other sons by her first marriage, both named Thomas, who predeceased their father.

[5] Heneage Finch had other children who died in infancy. The old *DNB* mentions seven sons and four daughters. The only children mentioned in his will are Heneage, Francis, John and Elizabeth. Contrary to modern custom, the name Frances was given to a son and Francis to a daughter.

Company and one-time Lord Mayor of London. Her sister-in-law was married to Sir George Croke, MP, justice of the king's bench. Their daughter, Elizabeth's niece Mary, was to marry Sir Harbottle Grimstone, Master of the Rolls.[6] Her brother-in-law, Sir Simon Bennett, secured a baronetcy in 1627, and aristocratic marriage alliances for his three daughters. Her husband's great-uncle, Richard, was grandfather to Henry Bennet, Earl of Arlington, Secretary of State from 1662 to 1674, and member of the Cabal ministry of Charles II.[7] Lady Finch's cousin, Matthew Cradock, was one-time governor of the Massachusetts Bay Colony. In 1674 her grandaughter Elizabeth Bennett, daughter of her son Simon, married Edward, Viscount Latimer, son of Sir Thomas Osborne, Lord High Treasurer, and future Earl of Danby and chief minister of Charles II.[8]

By 1631 the Finch family was well established in the upper echelons of the legal class of the time, with developing aristocratic connections. The fourth son of Sir Moyle Finch, Sir Heneage Finch was named after his mother, Elizabeth Heneage, thereby continuing the family tradition of retaining the mother's maiden name as a forename (Sir Moyle had been so christened after his mother, Catherine Moyle). A barrister by training, Sir Heneage had already distinguished himself as a MP for Rye (1607), West Looe (1621) and the City of London (1623–6). He was Recorder of London in 1620 and Speaker of the House of Commons in 1626. His oldest brother Thomas inherited the title Earl of Winchilsea from their mother, who had been created Countess of Winchilsea in 1628 after her husband's premature death. Heneage's youngest daughter, Anne, may have been named after her aunt Anne Finch, who married William, first Baronet Twysden, father of the antiquary Sir Roger Twysden. The upward social trajectory of Heneage Finch's family was to continue through the seventeenth century, despite the early death of Sir Heneage and the political disruptions of the period. Anne herself married into the lower aristocracy. At least two of her brothers were to distinguish themselves in the world of public affairs in the next generation. Her half-brother, Heneage (1621–82), became a lawyer of distinction, who rose to become Lord Chancellor in Charles II's reign. He was created first Earl of Nottingham in 1681. His younger brother, John (1626–82), qualified as a physician, but lived abroad for much of his life in a diplomatic capacity.

[6] The Bennett–Finch connection was reinforced when Sir Harbottle's son, Samuel, married Anne Conway's niece, Elizabeth, daughter of her half-brother Heneage. *Conway Letters*, p. 353.

[7] *Proceedings in Kent*, p. xviii. There is also mention of a Mr R. Bennett and a Mr T. Bennett, and their children, as well as one Sarah Bennett. The precise relationship of these Bennetts to Anne Conway is unclear. *Conway Letters*, p. 150.

[8] *Conway Letters*, p. 364 n. and British Library MS Stowe 205, fol. 157.

Knighted in 1661, he was English Resident to the Court of Tuscany and subsequently succeeded his cousin Heneage, second Earl of Winchilsea, as English ambassador to the Ottoman Empire.

Although Anne Conway's social status is defined by the prominent men of her wider family, we should not overlook the presence in her immediate pedigree of two remarkable women. First was her grandmother, Elizabeth Finch (née Heneage), who achieved ennoblement in her own right, first as Viscountess Maidstone and then as Countess of Winchilsea.[9] While her elevation in status probably owed something to the memory of her husband, it is a comment on her personal standing that she achieved it in her own right as a woman. She must have played an important role in the upbringing of her grandchildren if she carried out the wishes of her son Heneage, who, recording their deep mutual bond of affection in his will, enjoined her to continue her 'love and true affection to mee and her good intencions towards mee may be continued and transferred unto my children'. From the little evidence available, it would seem that her daughter-in-law Elizabeth too was a woman of intelligence and strong character, whom Lady Wroth described as 'a good and wise woman'.[10] Elizabeth Bennett's handling of her suitors prior to her second marriage suggests a woman who knew her own mind, not easily pressured by male claims. The story of how this wealthy widow fended off fortune hunters to marry the man who had withdrawn from the competition is recorded by the leading candidate among the disappointed hopefuls, Sir Thomas Egerton.[11] Whatever her reasons for not remarrying a third time, her raising on her own of what was by then a large family is a tribute to her personal capabilities.[12] Her youngest daughter's deep affection for her mother is plain from the very few references to her in her surviving letters. Anne was deeply affected by her death in 1661.[13] A third outstanding woman in Anne Conway's immediate family was her husband's aunt, Lady Brilliana Harley (d. 1643), third wife of Sir Robert Harley and famous for her defence of her Brampton Bryan Castle when it was besieged by royalists during the English Civil War.[14]

[9] The Countess of Winchilsea's great-grandson, Heneage Finch, fourth Earl of Winchilsea, married Anne Haselwood better known as the poetess Anne Finch (1661–1720).

[10] *Proceedings in Kent*, p. xxv.

[11] Ibid., pp. xii ff.

[12] It is unlikely that the wealthy Lady Finch lacked suitors for her hand, even though widow Finch, with seven children, was perhaps less of a 'catch' than widow Bennett. Her not remarrying may be some indication of her affection for her second husband, or a desire to preserve some independence, or both.

[13] *Conway Letters*, pp. 136, 149, 196.

[14] Eales (1990). She was named Brilliana, because she was born in Brill while her father was governor there.

With two wealthy marriage partnerships behind her, Lady Elizabeth Finch and her family were well provided for.[15] The Finches possessed several rural properties and a recently acquired house in the rural London suburb of Kensington. It was here that Anne spent her childhood and the early years of her marriage. In 1666 John Evelyn describes it as 'standing to a very graceful avenue of trees; but 'tis an ordinary building, especially one part'.[16] It had been bequeathed to her half-brother John by their father. He sold it to his brother Heneage, who named it Nottingham House when he was elevated to the earldom of Nottingham. It was subsequently bought from his son Daniel Finch, second Earl of Nottingham, by William III, who extended it and renamed it Kensington Palace.

Since her father died before Anne was born, it was probably her mother, now Lady Elizabeth Finch, who was responsible for the upbringing and education of all her children and stepchildren. There is no record of Lady Finch's role in the education of her youngest daughter, but we must assume that she encouraged her intellectual development. Nor is there any documentation for Anne Conway's early education. She cannot have had the formal schooling that her brothers had – Heneage was sent to Westminster School, John to Eton. Her later education was certainly a 'spin-off' from her half-brother John's, for it was his Cambridge tutor, Henry More, who took Anne on as a pupil by correspondence. As will become apparent in later chapters, Anne's relationship with her brother, John Finch, was of key importance in enabling her to cultivate her mind. John and Anne Finch were extremely close as brother and sister, perhaps on account of the fact that their father died when they were infants.[17] They remained close in adult life and it is clear from the letters they exchanged during his travels that John Finch deeply respected Anne's mental abilities and encouraged her to engage in philosophical debate with him.[18]

We can infer that she was widely read before she was tutored by Henry More. Her 1651 exchange of letters with her father-in-law, the second

[15] Lady Finch was the main beneficiary of Sir Heneage's will, as she had been of her first husband's will, London custom being that she was entitled to two-thirds of her husband's property. *Proceedings in Kent*, p. xiv–xv. Sir Heneage left her £10,000 worth of land, in addition to other moneys, valuables and 'houshold stuffe'. London, PRO, PCC [1631] 132. St John. Prob 11/160 ff. 503–5.

[16] John Evelyn, *The Diary of John Evelyn*, ed. E. S. de Beer, 6 vols. (Oxford: Clarendon Press, 1955), vol. IV, p. 299. The Finch house was probably acquired by Sir Heneage Finch at the time of his marriage. According to Marjorie Nicolson the north wing and buildings surrounding the courtyard to the west are original. *Conway Letters*, p. 2, n. 1.

[17] John Finch's mother died when he was one year old and his father when he was five.

[18] *The Conway Letters* prints only those of topographical interest. Others on philosophical topics from John Finch and his companion Thomas Baines, are contained in British Library MS Additional 23,215.

Viscount Conway, discusses history, astronomy, botany and religion. In these letters Lord Conway refers to Lucan, Famianus Strada, Guido Bentivoglio and Dioscorides, as well as Ramus, Copernicus, Athanasius Kircher, Campanella and Descartes. His daughter-in-law cites Vitruvius, Sir Henry Wotton, George Hakewill and John Donne in her one extant reply. She also read the *Poems* of Henry More. At this stage in her life there is no confirmation that Anne Conway knew Latin, the lingua franca of intellectual exchange at that time, nor that she knew any other languages. She certainly learned Latin at some point, though we cannot be sure precisely when. In 1653 her brother thought it advisable to translate into English a treatise in Latin he had written, so that she could read it ('because I thinke it to be very true and worthy of your knowledge').[19] Later in life she learned Greek, and probably also Hebrew (for the purpose of studying the kabbalah).[20]

Anne Conway's social circumstances do not, of themselves, account for her educational advantages – many women of higher social status fared worse in educational terms. But it may not be irrelevant that she came from a family which could be described as members of the seventeenth-century meritocracy. The rise in status and power of the Finches derived in good part from their legal expertise. This is particularly the case with Anne's half-brother, Heneage, who scaled the heights of his profession, progressing from Solicitor General, Attorney General and Lord Keeper to Lord Chancellor. Their father prized learning sufficiently to direct, in his will, that his books should not be sold, but kept for his children. He also made substantial provision to pay for their education.[21] The family into which his youngest daughter married was distinguished by its possession of one of the finest private libraries in the country, thanks to the book-collecting activities of her father-in-law, the second Viscount Conway.[22] Clearly, the Conway–Finch clan was not one that despised cultivation of the intellect. Undoubtedly the second Viscount Conway had family advantage in mind when he arranged the match between his oldest son, Edward, and Elizabeth Finch's youngest daughter. But it is also clear from his letters to her that his idea of a suitable match for his son did not ignore the fact of her lively mind. The second Viscount Conway was a great bibliophile,

[19] *Conway Letters*, p. 78.

[20] According to her husband she was learning Greek in 1665 (*Conway Letters*, p. 266). See also p. 5. The editor of her *Principia* describes her in the preface to the reader as 'being very well skill'd in the Latin and Greek Tongues'.

[21] London, PRO, PCC [1631] 132. St John. Prob 11/160 ff. 503–5.

[22] See note 35 below.

and appreciated the wit and intelligence of his daughter-in-law, as his four surviving letters to her show.[23] These were written in 1651 and exchange opinions on books. 'Bycause I see your iudgment is good I will tell you some conceptions of mine concerning new bookes', he writes. Her learned responses prompted him to comment, 'you write like a man'.[24]

EDWARD CONWAY

On 11 February 1650, on Shrove Tuesday, Anne Finch married Colonel Edward Conway,[25] a man 'of great Honour and Generosity'.[26] The Conways were a family of Welsh descent who had advanced themselves across three generations through military, diplomatic and administrative services to the crown. Edward Conway's grandfather was rewarded for his services by elevation to the titles of Viscount Conway and Viscount Killultagh. This latter Irish title was accompanied by a grant of lands in County Antrim, in the north of Ireland. They also established themselves at Ragley in Warwickshire, which became their English seat.[27] In Ireland their estates bordered Loch Neagh at Portmore, near Lisburne (then called Lisnegarvey).

At the time of her marriage, the Conways, like most royalists, were a family diminished in both wealth and influence. The havoc wrought to their Irish estates was such that they could not hope to pay off their debts out of the peacetime proceeds therefrom. However, their preparedness to accommodate to changed circumstances in the aftermath of the Civil War enabled them to stabilise their position. Anne's father-in-law had commanded the King's Horse at Newcastle during the Scottish invasion of 1641, and was subsequently involved in the abortive Waller plot to secure London for the royalist cause. Faced, on the one hand, with the confiscation of his English property by parliament and the destruction of his Irish estates by the Irish rebels, on the other, he compromised his royalism in order to preserve his inheritance. The efforts of his son Edward in the English cause in Ireland – a cause which united would-be royalists behind Cromwell and the English

[23] *Conway Letters*, pp. xi and 29–38. [24] Ibid., p. 32.

[25] *The Parish Register of Kensington*, ed. F. N. Macnamara and A. Strong Maskelyne (London, 1890). Edward, first Viscount Conway, son of Sir John Conway, was created Baron Conway in 1625, Viscount Killultagh in 1626, and Viscount Conway in 1627. He was Secretary of State from 1623 to 1630. He also served as governor of Brill and of the Isle of Wight, and as envoy to Prague.

[26] George Rust, *A Funeral Sermon Preached at the Obsequies of the Right Reverend Father in God, Jeremy, Lord Bishop of Down* (London, 1670), p. 11.

[27] The Conway family acquired Ragley Hall, today the seat of the Marquis of Hertford, when Sir John Conway, great-grandfather of Anne Conway's husband, married Ellen, daughter of Sir Fulke Greville. *Conway Letters*, p. 6.

parliament – probably made it easier to negotiate a settlement with the English Republic.[28] As a result, the Conways appear to have survived the interregnum with their English and Irish estates more or less intact. At the time of Edward's marriage to Anne Finch, however, their financial future was still far from secure. Viscount Conway certainly had strong financial and political motives when negotiating the match: for the marriage alliance with the Finch clan linked the Conways to a family with good credentials in the House of Commons. He also ensured for his family the services of their legal acumen, an especially useful asset in the uncertain political times of the English Republic and in the perennially complicated problems of landowners in Ireland both then and in the Restoration.[29] The marriage alliance with the Finches proved particularly propitious at the Restoration when Heneage Finch became a pillar of the restored Stuart administration, having secured royal trust on account of his role in the prosecution of the regicides.[30] The immediate benefit of the match is clear from a letter which mentions that Lady Finch contributed to a £1,000 bond, and another that Edward Conway, junior, had been able to discharge a debt of £6,000 to Sir Gervais Elwes out of his wife's portion.[31] Although settling debts was a major concern for the Conways, there seems to have been more to the match than money. As Edward Conway put it to his future brother-in-law, George Rawdon, 'Having passed through the troubles of love, and now arrived to the condition of a married man . . . my father tells me if I can cleere the rest of the debts he had rather I should have maried M^{rs}. Anne Finche, then any other he knowes of, wth double her portion.'[32]

[28] Second Viscount Conway to his son Edward, 30 Dec. 1641, Huntington Library, Hastings MSS, HA 14366, and 'The Humble Petition of Colonel Edward Conway' to the 'Committee for the Affairs of Ireland at Derby House', Hastings MSS, HA 14345. His son took care to ensure his contribution to the war effort was well known. See [Edward Conway], *Exceeding Good Newes from Ireland* (London, 1646). In 1649 his father made his books and manuscripts over to his son, presumably in a bid to evade sequestration. *Calendar of State Papers, Domestic*, vol. III. The Calendar of the Proceedings of the Committee for Compounding in 1646 describes the second Viscount's sons as 'in arms for Parliament'. *Calendar of State Papers, Domestic*. The Conways also had a useful cross-party family alliance with Sir Robert Harley, who was married to Brilliana, sister of the second Viscount Conway. In 1643 Sir Robert Harley intervened to rescue Lord Conway's library. Historical Monuments Commission (HMC), *The Manuscripts of His Grace the Duke of Portland Preserved at Welbeck Abbey*, ed. F. H. B. Daniels, 3 vols. (London: HMSO, 1891–1923), vol. III, p. 120.

[29] Many of Edward Conway's letters in the early 1650s mention fear of sequestration. See Hastings MSS, HA 14352–57.

[30] The third Viscount Conway acknowledges the usefulness of his family alliance with Heneage Finch when he wrote of him in 1665 'he hath done me many friendly Offices, but none that I valew more, then his constant zeale to the good of or. affaires in Ireland'. Lord Conway to George Rawdon 26 Dec. 1665, Hastings MSS, HA 14433. The benefit was, it should be said, mutual: the Conways in return looked after Heneage Finch's affairs in Ireland.

[31] Hastings MSS, HA 14347 and HA 1439.

[32] Edward Conway to George Rawdon, 20 Feb. 1650, Hastings MSS, HA 14349.

Edward Conway was the eldest of a family of three children: his sister Dorothy married Major George Rawdon; his younger brother Francis (Frank) appears to have been the black sheep of the family, 'infinitely deboist and sencelesse', who ran away to France to take up soldiering.[33] Of Edward Conway's education we know little. He does not appear to have attended university, and there is no record of him having attended the Inns of Court.[34] The Civil War disrupted the tour of Europe on which he had embarked in 1640. From this we may conclude that he was not a man of learning. However, this does not mean that his cultural horizons were narrow. On the contrary, his father was a highly cultured man, abreast of new developments in philosophy and literature, with a large range of interests from 'chymistry' to writing plays. The second Viscount Conway was, furthermore, the foremost book collector in Stuart England, and he owned over 11,000 books. The library catalogue of his encyclopaedic collection gives us a glimpse of the richness of the literary and intellectual culture of the early Stuart courtier class.[35] With such a collection in the family, the younger Conways were better supplied with books than they could have been at any English university. The future third Viscount Conway was probably destined by his father for a military education, following the family tradition. This may have been part of the purpose of the continental tour on which he was sent.[36] Whatever his father's intentions or his own ambitions might have been, the exigencies of the Civil War dictated that he became a soldier – of fate rather than of fortune. The deteriorating political situation at home resulted in his being abruptly recalled from France in 1642. He was despatched to Ulster to defend the family estates at Portmore during the Irish rebellion. There he experienced real hardship in the gruelling conditions of the war.[37]

[33] Ibid., HA 14363.

[34] His father was educated at Queen's College, Oxford, but there is no record of his son going there.

[35] This library was a casualty of the Irish rebellion of 1641. The books which were not lost in the fire at Brookhill have since been dispersed. Two lists survive: one dating from 1641 in the Armagh Robinson Library (Armagh, Armagh Robinson Library MS g.III.15), which is divided into eighty-seven subject classes. The second is a list dating from 1643 of over 3,000 books sequestered during the Civil War (PRO SP 120/7). See Plomer (1904) and Roy (1968). Lord Conway knew of both Descartes and Campanella and recognised the originality of their thought. *Conway Letters*, p. 30. His book collection was well stocked with contemporary plays, including first quartos of Shakespeare. Freeman and Grinke (2002) and Birrell (1991).

[36] To judge by the arrangements he made for his nephews in the 1670s, Conway would have trained at one of the Protestant military academies in France. See Hastings MSS, HA 14525 and 14526. He was the descendant of a lineage of soldiers.

[37] 'The Humble Petition of Colonel Edward Conway' to the 'Committee for the Affairs of Ireland at Derby House', Hastings MSS, HA 14345.

Hardened soldier though he may have been, Edward Conway was nevertheless a man of intelligence and culture, who understood the value of education.[38] Whatever his own opportunities and experience, he certainly set education at a premium. This is revealed in his adverse comments on the lack of education of General Monk's son: he told his brother-in-law that he believed education paid dividends in social, economic and political terms: 'It is to be considered that Education is the greatest Estate one can give. What a sad creature is this yong Duke of Albemarle [son of General Monk] for want of education, and others of good Estate in yor. neighbourhood. But men of parts and education, seldome want Estate, and oft times arrive at the highest.'[39] On his own nephew and heir designate, Arthur Rawdon, he commented, 'he is a fine child, that if he liues, I am confident nothing can preiudice him but ill education'.[40] Gentlemanly attainment aside, Lord Conway's commitment to education is demonstrated by his preparedness to set up a free school in Lisburne, for which he offered to purchase the necessary land.[41] To judge by his own directions for the education of his nephews he believed that a training in philosophy, especially a grounding in Cartesianism, was a necessary part of a gentleman's education. He may of course have been guided by his wife on this, but it may indicate that his own education had been along these lines. Henry More recalls reading Descartes' *Passions of the Soul* with him in the Jardins de Luxembourg, during their visit to Paris in 1656.[42]

The third Viscount Conway shared his father's interest in acquiring books. For example, on the death of Henry Stubbe, who practised as a doctor at Stratford not far from Ragley, Lord Conway acted promptly to preserve his library with a view to buying it from his heirs.[43] But Lord Conway did not buy books solely for his private use. In 1671 he proposed acquiring the libraries of the Bishops of Downe and Dromore 'in order to

[38] Ibid., HA 14482. See also HA 14495, 14501, 14525. He was also interested in buying books when libraries came up for sale, among them George Rust's and Henry Stubbe's (HA 14501, 14505, 14550).

[39] Lord Conway to Sir George Rawdon, 28 March 1671, Hastings MSS, HA 14482. Founding of school at Coleraine/Lisburne. G. A. Jacobsen's assessment of Conway as ignorant is therefore absurd: Jacobsen (1932).

[40] Lord Conway to Sir George Rawdon 14 Oct. 1670. Hastings MSS, HA 14495.

[41] Lord Conway to Sir George Rawdon, 25 Feb. 1662–3, ibid., HA 14383.

[42] Henry More, Epistle Dedicatory (1659) to *Immortality of the Soul* (London and Cambridge, 1654). The high value that Lord Conway set on a training in philosophy is evident from a letter of 1674, in which he expressed disapproval at Sir George Rawdon's proposal to remove his sons from Cambridge before they had done any philosophy there. Hastings MSS, HA 14525. His expectation was that his nephews should spend at least a couple of years at Cambridge, then proceed to the Inns of Court for a year and then travel to France. See also HA 14501, HA 14526, HA 14482.

[43] Ibid., HA 14554.

the Library I intend to settle at Lisburne'.[44] And, to judge by the list of books redeemed from sequestration in 1647, Anne Conway had an impressive range of books at her disposal when she married.[45] She may indeed have had a personal library. She certainly had a library keeper – Sarah Bennet, who was with her as early as 1651, accompanied her to France in 1653 and was still with her when she died.[46]

For the first years of their marriage Edward Conway and his wife lived with her mother at the Finch home in Kensington. It was there in 1658 that their only child, Heneage Conway, was born. Conway noted this happy event as follows:

My sonne Heneage Conway was borne upon Sunday the sixth of February 1658, a quarter and halfe a quarter past one, in the afternoone, Baptized by M^r^. Daniell Whitby upon Thursday the 17. of the same Month the Earle of Winchilsea, and my brother Heneage Finch being his Godfather and my Lady Finch his Godmother.

Deus in Adiutorium, cui omnis honor, et gloria.

It is entred in the Church Book, in the Parish of Westminster, my Lady Finche's house, at Kensinton where he was borne, being in the s^d^. Parish, and I think M^r^. Whitby hath also entred it, in the Church Book, at Arrow in Com: Warwick.[47]

The surviving letters exchanged between Anne Conway and her husband are affectionate in tone, but reveal little about their relationship. The extant letters she wrote to him are largely of a mundane character and give little insight into their feelings for one another. Her letters show us, rather, her punctiliousness in carrying out her domestic duties and the responsibilities she assumed for day-to-day affairs during his absences in Ireland. But there is plenty of evidence to suggest that theirs was not merely a match of convenience.[48] While we should be cautious about making biographical inferences from Anne Conway's treatise, it is perhaps worthy of observation that sex and marriage are described in very positive terms in her *Principles* to illustrate the principle of love and unity that pervades the created world: 'we see in every species of animal that males and females love each other

44 Lord Conway to Sir George Rawdon, 21 March 1670–1, ibid., HA 14501.

45 The philosophy books in this collection included, among classical philosophers, works by Aristotle, Plato (in French and Italian), Iamblichus and Sextus Empiricus. The Renaissance philosophers listed include Jean Bodin, Giordano Bruno, Tommaso Campanella, Fortunius Licetus, Michel de Montaigne, Girolamo Cardano, Pierre de la Ramée and Francesco Patrizzi, as well as writings by Thomas Digges, Gilbert's *De Magnete* and Mersenne (PRO SP 120/7).

46 *Conway Letters*, pp. 57, 64, 78, 116, 359, 430, 480, 533. The fate of the Conway library at Ragley Hall is a mystery. I am grateful to the Marquis of Hertford for permission to inspect the present library at Ragley Hall. This library dates from the eighteenth century and contains none of the books that Anne Conway or her husband owned.

47 Hastings MSS, HA 14365, 6 Feb. 1658–9. The inscription says this was torn from 'ye great bible'.

48 See, for example, his letter of 20 Feb. 1650, to George Rawdon quoted at note 32 above.

and that in all their matings (which are not monstrous and against nature) they care for each other. This comes not only from the unity of their nature but also because of their remarkable similarity to each other.'[49]

For his part, Edward Conway appears to have been a caring husband and one who supported his wife's intellectual pursuits. As we shall see, he went to great lengths to obtain the best medical help he could for her. The best-documented example is his bringing the Irish Protestant healer Valentine Greatrakes over to England in 1665/6 to try his powers on Anne Conway's malady.[50] Lord Conway's procuring the medical services of Van Helmont is another example.[51] Even when his wife's interests developed in what was, for him, an unpalatable direction, namely towards Quakerism, Lord Conway used his influence at her behest to assist imprisoned Quakers.[52] His primary desire seems to have been his wife's happiness and well-being, as he told his brother-in-law in 1670, when he had obtained the services of Van Helmont: 'Wht benefit my Wife will receaue by it I cannot say yet, but I haue attained the satisfaction of doing that wch. is pleasing to my Wife in the highest degree. So I cannot regrett the expense of my money.'[53] Even when his relations with Van Helmont became strained to breaking point on account of the latter's Quakerism, Lord Conway was reluctant to act in any way that might hurt his wife. He confided in Sir George Rawdon, 'I am almost mad when I begin to write of this subject', but 'to injure Monsr. Van Helmont is to injure my wife in the sensiblest part'.[54] Even at this testing time, his letters to her are couched in terms of affection. Long before Van Helmont entered their lives, Conway did his utmost to enable his wife to enjoy the company of Henry More. Not only did he welcome More as a visitor to his homes in London and at Ragley Hall, but he attempted to induce him to live nearby, by offering him preferments either near Ragley in Worcestershire or in Ireland, so as to be close to his estates at Portmore,

49 Conway, *Principles*, p. 47. Anne Conway cites Genesis 2: 23 to demonstrate that 'the two foundations of love between men and women' are unity of nature and likeness to one another as created beings. Elsewhere she uses a gendered image of the interrelationship between the active and passive principles that make up the individual creature: 'In every visible creature there is body and spirit, or a more active and a more passive principle, which are appropriately called male and female because they are analogous to husband and wife', p. 38.

50 See *Conway Letters*, and chapters 5 and 6 below.

51 See chapter 7 below.

52 *Conway Letters*, pp. 443–4 and below, chapter 9. Privately, Lord Conway was deeply irritated by his wife's association with the Quakers, as he told his brother-in-law. See *Conway Letters*, pp. 439, 534.

53 Lord Conway to Sir George Rawdon, 15 Nov. 1670, Hastings MSS, HA 14496.

54 *Conway Letters*, p. 535. Conway's anger at the 'impertinencyes' of Van Helmont were sufficiently public, it seems, for him to have felt it necessary to scotch rumours of a breakdown in his marriage. He wrote to Rawdon in 1676, 'Much less shall I ever think of putting my Wife to an allowance, or anything else wch. lookes like a parting from her'. Hastings MSS, HA 14550.

County Antrim. More, however, declined all attempts to lure him away from Christ's College. More's was not the only intellectual company Lord Conway arranged for his wife: in 1665 he paid for George Rust's licence for absence from Ireland, 'because of his return hither on account of my Wife'.[55]

Edward Conway appears, therefore, to have been a man who cared about his wife and her interests sufficiently to have given her the support necessary to pursue these. To what extent he shared his wife's philosophical interests is impossible to say with any certainty. He certainly shared her intellectual pursuits to the extent that he studied Euclid with her. She told him in a letter of 1658: 'If your ambition in the study of Euclid be onely to exceed me, you have reason to be satisfied already, for I have not proceeded one proposition since you went, but I think before it be to long to try Elficks skill in it.'[56] Whether Conway's professed conviction that Cartesianism was important in the cultivation of a gentleman reflected any philosophical commitment on his part is impossible to say. But he does seem to have regarded reading philosophy as a worthwhile pastime.[57] Lord Conway also appears to have taken an interest in the views of people like More and Jeremy Taylor. On one occasion he asks Taylor and George Rust to give him their response to one of More's books.[58] On another occasion he reports that a reply to Taylor's *Dissuasive from Popery* is in press.[59] He was nominated one of the gentlemen founders of the Royal Society, though his participation in the affairs of the Society seems to have been negligible. On the other hand, through his brother-in-law Sir George Rawdon he was acquainted with the Hartlibians, Sir William Petty and Benjamin Worsley.[60] And, as we shall observe later, his brother-in-law John Finch deemed him a suitable confidant for his philosophical speculations.

In religious matters Conway could be described as broad church. He was certainly an Episcopalian, and loyal to the churches of England and Ireland after the Restoration. His patronage of Henry More, George Rust and Jeremy Taylor suggests that he was a man of latitude in his religious beliefs. This is borne out in his views on the toleration of dissenters, whose

[55] Lord Conway to Sir George Rawdon, 20 Sept. 1665, Hastings MSS, HA 14429.

[56] *Conway Letters*, p. 148. George Elfick or Elphicke was chaplain to the Conways at Ragley. He was recommended to them by Henry More. *Conway Letters*, pp. 144 ff.

[57] More, *Immortality*, Epistle Dedicatory.

[58] In 1664 he asks Major Rawdon to get Dean Rust to re-read a book of More's 'and then tell us what he thinks of it'. Lord Conway to George Rawdon 28 Feb. 1664–5, Hastings MSS, HA 14415.

[59] Lord Conway to Sir George Rawdon, 28 Feb. 1664–5, ibid., HA 14415.

[60] Mentioned in Hastings MSS, HA 14448, and Box 10, HA 14367.

economic value he recognised.[61] His patronage of Jeremy Taylor during the interregnum, a time when the Church of England had been abolished and when Taylor was regarded with suspicion by the English Republic, is a clear indicator of the nature and strength of his commitment to religious toleration. But he also understood the political value of discretion. When, in 1658, he brought Taylor to Ireland he asked him not to publicise his patronage of him.[62]

Whatever private interest Lord Conway had in philosophy, religion and learning, he cannot have had much leisure to pursue them. The picture that emerges from his correspondence is of a busy man of affairs, active in English and Irish politics, and therefore obliged to spend considerable time in both Dublin and London. His letters to his brother-in-law Sir George Rawdon show that he took an active part in running his estates in both countries.[63] And his wife's poor health meant that he was obliged to deal with some of the domestic affairs which would have been her province. For example, in 1665 he describes setting up house in London and furnishing it himself, in the absence of his wife, a task 'wch. did a little terrifie me'.[64] This private expression of doubt in his own competence is surprising in an astute business manager of his own affairs, who redeemed his family's fallen fortunes, and co-ordinated the running of his far-flung estates to financial advantage. His effectiveness as an estate manager was enhanced by a marriage alliance which secured him the services of a highly dependable agent: in 1654 he arranged for his sister Dorothy to marry Major George Rawdon (later Sir George), whose son Arthur was designated Conway's heir.[65] Major Rawdon had been the second Viscount Conway's agent in Ireland, where he fought in defence of the Conway estates against Irish rebels, during which time he had given the young Colonel Conway almost paternal support.[66] Until the Irish Cattle Bill in 1665 impeded the trade,

[61] Lord Conway to Sir George Rawdon, 27 Nov. 1666, Hastings MSS, HA 14448. That he was severe in his treatment of Catholics during his brief tenure as Secretary of State does not, itself, betoken religious narrowness on his part.

[62] In a letter to Taylor written in 1658, Conway enjoins him to think of him as one who has only done 'commonest civilities' in helping Taylor, and never to dedicate a book to him. See Stranks (1952), p. 185. On Jeremy Taylor going to Ireland, see Bolton (1958), pp. 24–30; 37 ff., 272 f. Writing to Rawdon in 1658, Conway claimed that his motive in sending Taylor to Ireland was to please his sister. Lord Conway to Major Rawdon, 17 Aug. 1658, Hastings MSS, HA 14363.

[63] Many of the letters written by Lord Conway to Sir George Rawdon are now among the Hastings MSS at the Huntingdon Library, San Marino, California. Replies from Rawdon are to be found in *Calendar of State Papers*. See also *The Rawdon Papers*, ed. E. Berwick (London, 1819).

[64] Lord Conway to Sir George Rawdon, 28 March 1665, Hastings MSS, HA 14419.

[65] Sir George Rawdon was, by all accounts an efficient manager and entrepreneur. The builder of Moira, he ensured that the Lisburne district had the best roads in Ireland. *Rawdon Papers*.

[66] *Calendar of State Papers, Ireland* 285,205.

a major source of the Conway income was raising cattle for the English beef market. Thereafter, he turned his hand to foreign trade. Although he seems to have been tight-fisted in financial matters, Lord Conway used his wealth to invest in the lifestyle of a *grand seigneur.* He embarked on an ambitious programme of house building: he rebuilt the mansion at Portmore, and planned to do the same at Ragley.[67] Portmore, with its 2,000-acre park beside Lough Neagh, is said to have been one of the most impressive houses rebuilt in Ireland after the Restoration.[68] In addition to his country estates in Warwickshire and County Antrim and the Somerset estates inherited from his mother Frances Popham, he owned houses in Dublin, London and Newmarket. This last is testimony to his promotion of the new sport of horse racing. His wife, however, was prevented by ill health from participating in the high-society lifestyle to which her husband aspired. She only visited Ireland once (1661–3), and played no role in his public career, since, for much of their marriage, she was confined at home by illness. It can have been only occasionally that Lord Conway had the leisure to read over the works of Descartes (as on the occasion in Paris recorded by More). And we may infer that, even if he was interested in philosophy, and even if he did read Euclid with her, he cannot have had a great deal of time to debate philosophical points with his wife. It was therefore as enabler rather than as partner that he played a part in her intellectual life.

ANNE CONWAY THROUGH HER LETTERS

Apart from what we can learn from her friends and family, little is known about Anne Conway as a person, unlike her contemporary Margaret Cavendish, who adopted a high-profile approach in her self-presentation

[67] Ragley Hall, designed by Robert Hooke, stands to this day. Building work started after the death of his wife Anne, and he made provision for its completion in his will. Lord Conway's choice of Hooke as architect may have been the result of a recommendation from the Boyle family. Equally, he was probably impressed by the celebrated Montagu House, designed by Hooke for Baron Montagu, and situated not far from his London house in Queen Street. Robert Hooke, Fellow of the Royal Society (1635–1703) is best known as an engineer and for his work on microscopes. On Hooke as architect, see Stoesser-Johnston (2000).

[68] *Conway Letters*, pp. 172–3. Lord Conway continued to embellish the house. A letter of 23 April 1667 mentions an order for '13000 Dutch Painted Tyles' to line the path to the church and a 'Volary betweene the Wildernesse and the Garden wall', and for a pigeon house. Hastings MSS, HA 14459. In 1671, 40 tons of marble were delivered for further building work. The architects and builders Lord Conway employed on his Irish building programme included John Darly, William Dodson and William Hurlbutt (or Hulbert) (Loeber, 1981). The stables at Portmore were modelled on Hugh May's classically inspired stables at Cornby (ibid., p. 71). The house at Portmore was demolished in the eighteenth century: all that remains are the ruined outer walls.

as a thinking woman.[69] Anne Conway pursued philosophy in the privacy of her own home. The space she made for philosophy in her life was very much a private space. One of the conditions she set for conducting a philosophical correspondence with Henry More was, as he restated it, 'the keeping of such letters secret to yourself that you shall receive from me'.[70] The main virtue of being in Ireland, she told More in 1661, was the chance of more personal privacy: 'the hopes that I shall be more at leisure then in England, to enjoy the privacy of my owne closett'.[71] Those who knew her testify to her reticence in public about her philosophical interests: Van Helmont reports Henry More saying: 'Nor could he ever observe while She could come abroad and Converse, that she would ever ostentate her Knowledge; or so much as make any Discovery of it, upon never so fair an Opportunity.'[72]

Her letters cover a range of subjects, including domestic matters. But household and even estate management are topics reserved for letters to her husband and Irish relatives. In two unpublished letters she writes of the difficulties of obtaining a lady's maid who can speak French and do her hair. On one occasion we glimpse her making new hangings for an apartment. But the most striking thing about her letter writing is its range: from domestic affairs to discussions of philosophy, of religious beliefs and of the apocalypse. Even as a young woman her ability to discuss a diversity of topics, from the poetry of John Donne to the origin of arts and sciences, prompted her father-in-law's comment, 'you write like a man'. The impression of Anne Conway that emerges directly from her letters, and indirectly from More's replies, is of an articulate and incisive mind, not afraid to challenge ideas, though always caring and considerate.

Nevertheless, in spite of the personal character of her correspondence, Anne Conway is surprisingly reticent about herself. When she does write about herself she appears constrained by external factors – factors which control the public domain of letters, even when they enter it in so private a corner. The constraints imposed by public self-image and social status, and the norms of propriety, are further complicated by the fact that she and her chief correspondent, Henry More, were of opposite sex. This 'gender factor' is further complicated by a difference of rank. In spite of the fact that, in respect of class, More was her social inferior, she defers to his superiority, belittling herself and 'so inconsiderable a friendship as mine'.

[69] On Margaret Cavendish, see chapter 5 below. Also Harris (1997) and Hutton (1997b and 1997d).
[70] *Conway Letters*, p. 53. By 'secret' she did not mean that others in her immediate circle should not know about it: for example, More often sends salutations to Lord Conway, and messages to others.
[71] Ibid., p. 191. [72] Ward, *Life*, p. 124.

More is always deferential, highly conscious of 'the great inequality of our persons', despite being her senior in age and knowledge.[73] At all times she exhibits modesty to the point of self-deprecation. For example, when she travelled to Ireland in 1661, she told More that if he wrote to her there it would be 'an argument that I am retained in your memory, in which I should be loath to lose a place, if I may hope you can continue your favour to one that so little knows to merit it'.[74] The Anne Conway described by both herself and her correspondent conforms to the stereotype of the good woman: modest, pious, self-effacing, self-censoring, eschewing the public domain in favour of the private. When she expresses herself as a woman, it is in conformity with the given model: unassuming, reluctant to be subjected to public gaze, self-deprecating. In response to More's dedication of a book to her, she writes, 'I could not read what you have published of me with out blushing . . . being conscious to my self of not deserving that commendation you would seem to give me there'.[75] The self-image she projects stands in vivid contrast to the incisive mind that could dissect Descartes and put Henry More to his 'plunges' for answers (to use his own expression). Nor does it tally with the comment by John Ward, vicar of Stratford upon Avon, that she 'was a right ffinch very proud'.[76] Henry More, who knew her better than anyone, gives us little insight into her psyche. When he writes about her, More emphasises her virtue, her piety, her intelligence. The Anne Conway complimented by More in his letters to her is the exceptional woman: a kind of secular saint, remarkable for her virtue and piety, not the equal of men but their superior. This is most fully expressed in the letter of dedication of his *Antidote against Atheism* to her in 1653. In this dedication he praises her 'singular wit and virtues' describing her as 'so noble, so wise and so pious a personage' in whom Plato might see 'Virtue become visible to his outward sight'. In essence this public portrait differs little from what private thoughts convey in the letters, the main difference being that it is more concentrated. In sum, what we can extract from these private statements are public stereotypes which belie the closeness of their acquaintance. They both employ pre-existing constructions of womanliness which filter out individual traits

[73] Of course, this may be more apparent than real since only a fraction of the total number of her letters has survived.

[74] *Conway Letters*, p. 191. [75] Ibid., pp. 70–1.

[76] John Ward, *Diary of the Reverend John Ward, A. M., Vicar of Stratford on Avon*, ed. C. Severn and, transcribed by D'Arcy Power (London, 1839), p. 551. Compare Glanvill's account of Lady Conway as 'a Person of so quick a wit, impartial judgement and sagacity': Joseph Glanvill, *Sadducismus Triumphatus* (London, 1688).

and transform the individual woman described into a generalised norm of praiseworthy femininity.

To discover what Anne Conway was like as a person from her letters, we have to read between the lines of the linguistic norms of social intercourse. The gulf between available patterns of self-expression and the experience they convey is particularly apparent when she writes about her personal condition and about the chief crisis of her personal life, the death of her only child. From her teens, Anne Conway suffered from bouts of inexplicable pain, the main symptom of which was an unrelievable headache. These 'fits' grew more intense, more frequent and more prolonged as she grew older. This medical condition was a major shaping factor in her life.[77] It was on this account that she and her husband devoted much time to seeking medical help far and wide (see chapter 6). As a result she spent long periods 'in physick', removed from social contact with the world. Finally, as her condition worsened during the last ten years of her life, she was confined by it to the Conway family home, Ragley Hall in Warwickshire. It is impossible to imagine the personal cost of the experience of continuous and unrelievable physical suffering which her condition imposed. In her desperation she travelled to France in 1656 with a view to undergoing the operation of trepanning.[78] On occasion the treatment was worse than the illness: in 1653 she nearly died of mercury poisoning at the hands of Frederick Clodius, son-in-law of Samuel Hartlib.[79] But to get an inkling of the intensity of the pain and the depth of the suffering she endured, it is her observers rather than she herself on whom we must rely. As early as 1652, her husband reported

> I am going this weeke wth my wife to Tunbridge, where she is sent by the Doctors under whos hands she hath been constantly in Phisick this 12 month, for the violentest paine in the head, that any one in the world was ever troubled with, and so frequently it comes upon her that no humane strength seemes to me able to beare it.[80]

Six years later, Lord Conway (as he had now become) found her suffering just as unbearable. He wrote to Rawdon:

[77] On Anne Conway's illness, see Owen (1937) and Critchley (1937), and below, chapter 6.

[78] See *Conway Letters*, chapter 4. [79] Ibid., pp. 88 ff.

[80] Edward Conway to Major Rawdon, 30 June 1652, Hastings MSS, HA 14355. Cf. Conway, 21 Oct. 1658, HA 14364: 'I am so taken up wth the thoughts, and perplexity of my wives condition, that I m not like to give you any perfect account of any thing I write to you, To relate the particulars of her sufferings, is not in my power, nor the resolution, and cheerefulnesse wth. wch. she encounters her great enemy, Paine, and Torment. I can only tell you, that I thinke it is impossible she should live many weekes, and that my trouble is very great.'

If I could have writ you any better news of my wife, than I did in my last, I should not have been negligent in doing it long before this. but it was seaven weekes last Sunday since she was confined to her chamber, and comes very little out of her bed^{m} being unable to set one leg before another, but as she is held up, by t[w]o persons, and this hath brought upon her other tortures, of paine in her bones and excoriation; I kept my horses heere two months to have gon to Ragley, and was forced to returne them last week, seeing no probablity of her amendment; she is so dismally melancholy; and her sighs, and grones come so deep from her, that I am terrifyed to come neere her. M^{r}. More hath continued in the house with us, since she fell into this condition.[81]

For someone so grievously afflicted by pain, Anne Conway complains astonishingly little about her suffering. She rarely mentions the pain that afflicted her so frequently, or if she does she is apologetic ('I am troubled my complaints should fill so great a part of my letter').[82] This does not mean that, stoically, she did not feel the pain. A rare expression of her appreciation of the sympathy of others comes in a letter to her brother-in-law written towards the end of her life. 'I could not read your letter', she writes, 'without being sensibly affected wth your kinde expressions and something astonishd, y^{t} notwithstanding my ten yeares exclusion from ye world, you should still retaine ye memory of mee, and a feeling concern for my sufferings'. She goes on to describe her experience with a remarkably unembittered comment on what it is like for other people to live with an invalid like herself: 'it commonly hapning y^{t} ye greatest afflictions by long continuance grows unregarded, and expectation of change beeing long frustrated, the patience is tired and then pitty ceases in persons unconcerned, tho^{gh} to those under ye pressure of great sufferings the weight is much augmented by continuance as our strength to beare does daily decrease'.[83] This patient self-effacement (her own pain here deflected through the experience of the observer rather than the sufferer) is at once admirable, yet unbearable to modern sensibilities. Her stance is more understandable in seventeenth-century terms, in a culture accustomed to the inability of medicine to provide a relief, and where pain was often unavoidable.

There is one occasion when the dictates of social propriety break down. The most personal of all of Anne Conway's surviving letters is the one she wrote to Henry More after the death of her son Heneage in 1660. The birth of Heneage Conway in 1658 ('your little son my pupil', as Henry More called him)[84] had been an injection of joy into the life of his mother, who by then had become accustomed to severe physical suffering during the

[81] 17 August 1658, Hastings MSS, HA 14363. Cf. HA 14425. [82] *Conway Letters*, p. 224.
[83] Ibid., pp. 533–4. [84] Ibid., p. 500.

bouts of illness that afflicted her throughout her life. The happiness that the birth of her child brought was short-lived. When he was only two years old little Heneage succumbed to smallpox. His mother was also afflicted with the disease, but survived.[85] The death of her infant is, however, one occasion when Anne Conway permits herself to articulate her suffering. In answer to an exhortation by More (standard for those times) not to give rein to her grief, but to exercise the control of reason, she replied:

the great sadness of perplexities I have suffered have rendered my thoughts so undigested and confused, that in reason I ought yet to have freed you longer from them. It hath pleased God to exercise me by divers afflictions and by one so sensible in the death of my child, that you must not wonder if I tell you it hath extorted from me a griefe proportionable to so great a losse.[86]

On her own account, the death of her child was the worst affliction of the many that had befallen her. Her response to such 'great sadnesse of perplexities' both acknowledges a duty of silence ('I ought yet to have freed you longer from them') and confesses to weakness and inability in exercising rational self-control:

I confess what you hinted at in your last [letter] is a thing very desirous, to gitt our reason so fortified by principles of philosophy and Religion as to be able to with stand all the calamities of fortune, but I find my proficiency in these so smale, and my weaknesse so great that though such considerations may enable me to bear lesser crosses, yet I lie open to receive the assaults of greater.[87]

At first sight this sounds like acquiescence in the role of the weaker sex: silent, submissive, irrational. But set against the advice to which Anne Conway here refers, we can see that it is more complicated. For we have here a tangential point beyond which the experience of the woman is untranslatable into male terms – a point philosophy cannot reach. Anne Conway's apparent acquiescence in the weak silent woman role is, in effect, a translation of her experience into words which cannot contain it. More than that it is, arguably, a refusal of the model. The letter is a reply in which More turned on all the wise tenderness he knew to counsel his friend not to be too indulgent in grief, because too much emotion is a bad thing ('exces of passion voluntarily yielded to, addes some soile to the soule').[88] But this is not just bad for her, it is bad for her husband: 'I cannot forbear to speak unto you also, and adjure you by all the power of Reason and Relligion not to indulge too much to unreasonable and

[85] Lord Conway to Major Rawdon, 5 Feb. 1661, Hastings MSS, HA 14373.
[86] *Conway Letters*, p. 181. [87] Ibid. [88] Ibid., p. 169.

unmeasurable affection, to hazard of your own safety, and the redoubling of sorrow and afflicion upon my Lord, your Husband, and upon all your dearest friends.'[89] To be fair to More, this formula of rational self-control of the emotions was one that he, very much the *homo philosophicus* and a Platonist to boot, attempted to practise himself.[90] Besides, social propriety no doubt required some gesture to the husband's superior interest in the matter over male outsider. The obvious model for More to adopt was that of priestly counsellor. Nonetheless, the social propriety here is undeniably patriarchal, and the priestly model very much that of the clergy*man*. Set against this, Anne Conway's 'confession' of weakness conceals a firm refusal of the model More proposes of rational self-discipline in which she should put her husband's feelings before her own. Instead, she insists she cannot do that, even if this has to be interpreted as the weak woman's excuse. Her reply to More highlights the limitations of formal comforting. It bespeaks the reaches of experience that social categories and rational discourse do not penetrate: an inarticulate realm of immediate emotion ('unreasonable and unmeasurable affection' in More's phrase, 'thoughts so undigested and confused' in Lady Conway's) that cannot be easily tidied into a rational moral order; the reactions of a mother which a childless bachelor don, for all his good intentions, cannot share. It is a letter which both reveals and conceals. But the surface of this letter uses the terminology and categories of an acceptable stereotype.

It might be argued that it was childlessness that gave Anne Conway leisure to philosophise. But we should remember that motherhood was not necessarily an impediment for women of her class who wished to cultivate their minds. It is true that several of the small band of female philosophers of her time were women who had no children, for example Princess Elizabeth, Margaret Cavendish and Queen Christina of Sweden. But being stepmother to nine children and the mother of one did not prevent Lady Masham from pursuing her philosophical interests. In Anne Conway's case, even if she was relieved of the burden of frequent pregnancy, and was unencumbered with the demands of motherhood, she still had to endure the impediment

[89] Ibid., p. 168.

[90] Writing to Anne Conway in 1651 after the sudden departure of her brother John Finch for Europe, More observes, 'that whatsoever is corporeall and personall proves a troublesome intanglement or an unexpected dodge and mocker to the affectionate minde of a man some time or other'. This Platonic/Christian distrust of the physical is translated into a resolution of solitude to protect himself against the repetition of the sorrow this has caused him by never again relying on someone else for happiness: 'For my own part I can excogitate no remedie nor revenge on this cross constitution of thinges, but by a solemn abjuration for the future from receiving any pleasure from any visible person whatsoever'. Ibid., pp. 52–3.

of chronic and, at times, incapacitating ill health. Moreover, the symptoms of her illness, especially the unrelievable headache which afflicted her, were particularly unfavourable in someone whose gifts were intellectual. Given her afflictions and the fact that the death of her infant son Heneage at the age of two was a loss which, understandably, she found hard to bear, the fact that she sustained a philosophically active life is itself extraordinary. It is the more remarkable when we realise that Anne Conway's *Principles* were written when her health was at its worst: the textual evidence is that *The Principles of the Most Ancient and Modern Philosophy* is, as I shall argue later, the product of the last two years of her life. By then she had been confined to Ragley Hall for nearly ten years, on occasion so ill that John Finch was told that she was 'incapable of reading what I write'.[91] In her last illness she was confined to her bed for several months.[92]

The isolation forced on her by illness meant that Anne Conway's pursuit of philosophy was very much a private and domestic activity. To judge by her request that More keep their correspondence private, this would have been the case if she had been able to lead a more active social life. However, her pursuit of philosophy was not a solipsistic activity. She was supremely fortunate in having contact with the intellectual currents of her day which enabled her to interact with contemporary philosophy. This was made possible largely through a select group of men – her brother John, the Cambridge Platonist Henry More, and her physician Francis Mercury van Helmont. Their writings are, therefore, indispensable for reconstructing Anne Conway's intellectual development. This does not mean that she was the passive absorber of their ideas. On the contrary, her contact with them was very much an interchange. Not only was the impact each made on Anne Conway reciprocated by hers on each of them, but More's letters make it clear that dialogue was at the centre of their philosophical activities. Letter writing, while a necessity given the geographical distances between them, was a written form of dialogue. Indeed their epistolary exchanges were conducted as a surrogate form of dialogue. In the ensuing chapters, I shall trace the course of Anne Conway's intellectual life through these friendships. But it was not as an untutored amateur or autodidact that Anne Conway pursued her interest in philosophy. She was more fortunate than most philosophically minded women of her day on account of the fact that she received a philosophical education. The discipline that this afforded and the questions on which it centred account, in no small measure, for

[91] Ibid., p. 362.
[92] In November 1678 she told her husband, 'I have not been able to have had my bed made for above these three moneths', ibid., p. 448.

both the character and content of her mature philosophy. Arguably, the dialogic nature of her philosophy tutorials helped to set the interlocutory manner in which she conducted her philosophical enquiries. No account of Anne Conway's intellectual milieu or the development of her philosophy would be possible without examining the role of John Finch, Henry More and Francis Mercury van Helmont. It is with her philosophical education under the guidance of Henry More that I shall begin.

CHAPTER 2

A philosophical education

'Conferences concerning Des Cartes philosophy'[1]

The question of what educational background any particular philosopher might have had is normally discussed in terms of shaping influences, be these positive or negative, that the individual concerned might have received – for example, Descartes' grounding in mathematics at the Jesuit College at La Flèche or Locke's encounter with academic scholasticism at Oxford. In the case of a woman philosopher living at a time when education for women was the exception rather than the norm, the question of educational background becomes part of the wider question of how she came to philosophy at all. This is a question which is not usually asked about male philosophers, even when the information about their education is quite full. Besides, the broad categories of school and university training do not fit the seventeenth-century female subject very comfortably. Nor are they especially illuminating in Conway's case, unless they are set in relation to other circumstances, in particular her social background, her personal relationships and the state of philosophy and philosophical education in the 1640s and 50s.

That Anne Conway was highly educated there can be no doubt. The address to the reader which prefaces her *Principles* describes her as 'a woman learned beyond her sex, most skilled in the Latin and Greek literature and especially well versed in every sort of philosophy'. However, the documentation of her education is patchy, consisting largely in the imperfect record that her surviving correspondence affords. Her exchange of letters with Henry More starts as a kind of seventeenth-century correspondence course in Cartesian philosophy and provides some important clues about Anne Conway's philosophical education. This chapter will attempt to reconstruct that education by reference to the letters, to show how it made possible her engagement with philosophy and the ways in which her original grounding in philosophy set her in the particular philosophical direction she took.

[1] *Conway Letters*, p. 53.

As we have already seen, there is no doubt that the privileged social circumstances into which Anne Conway was born were enormously important in making it possible for her to receive some education and to pursue her intellectual interests.[2] There are, broadly, two things to be said about Anne Conway's formal education: first, of her early education, we know nothing, beyond the fact that she was able to read. Of her university education we can be equally negative: she had none, for women were not admitted to Oxford or Cambridge in the seventeenth century. However, the picture is considerably more complex than these two negatives suggest, for, exceptionally for a woman of her time, she received the equivalent of university tuition.[3] Furthermore, before she embarked on this, she was already quite widely read in vernacular writing, with an interest in philosophical matters. Among contemporary writers she read John Donne, George Hakewill and Henry Wotton. Her view of philosophy was broadly in the Renaissance mould. Key evidence for this is her brief correspondence with her father-in-law, the second Viscount Conway, who traces the genealogy of learning in his first extant letter to her: 'Learning came to the Greekes from Aegipt, from Phoenicia, from the Jewes, and from the Indies. From Greece it came into Italy, from thence into France, Germany, and England.'[4] The second Viscount Conway also adds some light-hearted observations about the compatibility of Greek and Egyptian learning with Christianity, suggesting that the ancients 'madde themselves madde drunke' with philosophy.[5] The young Anne Conway's reply to this letter is an essay on the antiquity of learning, in which she retails the received view that Adam (who supposedly lived 900 years) was 'an excellent naturall philosopher as appeares by his giving names to every beast and bird according to their natures' and that Enoch inscribed two pillars with 'all the Learning [that] was then in Astronomy and naturall Philosophy'. She appears undecided as to whether ancient learning has the advantage over modern or vice versa. She observes, with wistful common sense, 'If I had a copy of these pillars I might then

[2] I do not mean to imply that all upper-class women of the seventeenth century had similar educational advantages. On the contrary, the limited education of most of them is well attested. But where the inclination to educate daughters existed, it was more likely to be put into practice where economic circumstances allowed. Although there are notable examples of erudite women among the middle classes (Bathsua Makin is one example), there was a stronger tradition of intellectual attainment among aristocratic and royal women (Lady Jane Grey and Elizabeth I are the outstanding examples).

[3] Anna Maria van Schurman is another example. She, however, was permitted to attend the scholastic lectures of Descartes' detractor, Voetius, by listening from behind a curtain. See de Baar (1996).

[4] *Conway Letters*, p. 35. [5] Ibid.

resolve when the World had more Learning, before or after the flood.'[6] This remark suggests both confidence in her own judgement and desire to know more – a wish that was soon to be fulfilled.

It was apparently her brother John who played a key role in enabling her to expand her educational horizons, for it was he who brought her into contact with Henry More, the man from whom she received her philosophical training, and who remained her life-long mentor. I shall deal with the broader aspects of the part played by these two men in her philosophical life in later chapters. For the present we shall be concerned with More's role in Anne Conway's philosophical education. Although Anne Conway did not attend university, the fact that she was taught by letter, rather than by an in-house tutor, means that there is some documentation of that education – possibly more, in fact, than if she had been able to attend a university.

Given that Anne Conway took an anti-Cartesian line in her mature philosophy it may sound contradictory to say that she was fortunate to have learned philosophy from one of the foremost English Cartesians. But, as I shall argue later, Cartesianism had (as it still has) distinct advantages as the basis of instruction in philosophy, especially for extra-mural study. For Cartesian method offered a way into philosophy that bypassed the highly technical introductory curriculum of university philosophy. Cartesianism, therefore, had a special appeal for a lay readership. This was a distinct recommendation for any woman lucky enough to come this far in pursuing her philosophical interests. Besides, Cartesianism was not freighted with the kind of misogynistic baggage that encumbered the Aristotelian philosophical legacy.[7] Furthermore, at this time, a grounding in Cartesianism meant an introduction to the new currents of thought that were displacing Aristotelianism as the framework of philosophy. Thus Anne Conway's Cartesian education gave her access to the most recent philosophical debates of the seventeenth century. She was, moreover, well equipped to treat philosophy as debate rather than a set of dogmas, because, as I shall show, she was taught by a man who was not uncritical of Descartes, and who imparted this critical approach to his pupil.

HENRY MORE AND DESCARTES

Henry More had been a Fellow of Christ's College, Cambridge since 1641. It was there that the young John Finch encountered him during his student

[6] Ibid., p. 37. [7] Maclean (1980).

years. Finch first came to Cambridge in 1645, before he had completed his studies at Balliol College, Oxford – his attendance there having probably been disrupted by the Civil War. After graduating BA at Oxford in 1647 he returned to Christ's College, where he graduated MA in 1649. At around this time he arranged for Henry More to give instruction to his sister who, as a woman, was debarred from enrolling at the university.

Henry More played a key role in Anne Conway's philosophical education. Not only was he willing to take her on as a pupil, but he appears to have done so without preconceptions about her intellectual capacities, or lack of them, as a woman. Far from deprecating her abilities, he was deeply impressed by them. His biographer Richard Ward reports that More told him 'that he scarce ever met with any Person, Man, or Woman, of better Natural Parts, than the Lady Conway'.[8] When dedicating his *An Antidote Against Atheisme* to her in 1653, More wrote that she was someone 'whose Genius I know to be so speculative, and Wit so penetrant, that in the knowledge of things as well Natural as Divine you have not onely out-gone all of your own Sex, but even of that other also, whose ages have not given them over-much the start of you'.[9] At the time when Anne Finch made his acquaintance, More had established his credentials as a Platonist in a series of philosophical poems, published in a collected edition in 1647.[10] He had not yet embarked on the series of philosophico-theological treatises which sustain his reputation as one of the main philosophers of the group since known as the Cambridge Platonists.[11] More's penchant for poetry and Platonism should not be allowed to obscure the fact that he was one of the brightest academic minds of his generation, and was to enjoy something of an international reputation as a philosopher. Like the other Cambridge Platonists, he emphasised the importance of reason in religion, and was widely read in philosophy, both modern and ancient. He was receptive to new developments in philosophy, and critical of those philosophies which he perceived as flawed (notably the philosophy of Hobbes and Spinoza

8 Ward, *Life*, p. 118.

9 'The Epistle Dedicatory', in Henry More, *An Antidote against Atheisme* (London: 1653).

10 Henry More, *Philosophical Poems* (Cambridge: R. Daniel, 1647). A separate title page after the dedicatory epistle lists the contents: *A Platonicall Song of the Soul; treating of the Life of the Soul, Her Immortalitie, The Sleep of the Soul, The Unitie of Souls, and Memorie after death*. It also contains 'Democritus Platonissans; or an Essay of the Infinity of Worlds out of Platonick Principles' and various shorter pieces.

11 On More see Hutton (1990a), which contains the best bibliography (by Robert Crocker). Also Hall (1990). The Cambridge Platonists were a loose grouping of like minds rather than a clearly defined school. They include Benjamin Whichcote, Nathaniel Culverwell, John Smith, Peter Sterry and More's friend, Ralph Cudworth. With the exception of More, all were educated at Emmanuel College, Cambridge. See Hutton (1996b and 2002).

which he repudiated as atheistic). His openness to new ideas is signalled by the fact that he was one of the earliest proponents of Cartesian philosophy in England. In the early history of the reception of Cartesianism in England, Henry More is a key figure who played an important role as publicist and teacher of Descartes' philosophy. His modest but enduring fame today probably owes more to his exchange of letters with Descartes than to anything else he wrote.[12] The More–Descartes letters, which date from 1648–9, testify to More's early admiration for Descartes, but they also show that More's acceptance of Cartesianism was never uncritical,[13] even at the time of his greatest enthusiasm for it.

Although the hold of Aristotle's philosophy was on the wane by the 1650s, Cartesianism had not established itself in the academies,[14] and the Cambridge curriculum was still underpinned by Aristotelianism.[15] Henry More was ahead of his time when he advocated the inclusion of Cartesianism in the university curriculum.[16] In 1662 he wrote the preface to *The Immortality of the Soul*, 'I think it is the most sober and faithful advice that can be offered to the Christian World, that they would encourage the reading of *Des-Cartes* in all publick schools or Universities'. Nevertheless, More insists on the limitations of Cartesian metaphysics even while commending Descartes as 'that admirable Master of Mechanicks'. Persuaded of the apologetic value of philosophy in the defence of religious belief, he argued that the study of Cartesianism would enable students to understand the limitations of philosophical mechanism, in order the better to utilise it in relation to religion. He recommended 'That the Students of Philosophy may be thoroughly exercised in the just extent of the *Mechanical Powers of Matter*, how farre they will reach, and where they fall short. Which will be the best assistance to Religion that Reason and the Knowledge of Nature can afford'.[17] Henry More's role in popularising Cartesianism is attested by his friend John Worthington, who observed to him in 1667:

[12] First published in René Descartes, *Lettres de Mr Descartes*, ed. Claude Clerselier, 2 vols. (Paris, 1657–9); modern edition in *Oeuvres de Descartes*, ed. C. Adam, P. Tannery and B. Rochot (Paris: Vrin, 1974), vol. V.

[13] Webster (1969), Gabbey (1982). Also Hall (1990).

[14] On the reception of Cartesianism in England, see Nicolson (1929), Lamprecht (1935), Laudan (1966), Pacchi, (1973), Gascoigne (1989) and Rogers (1985).

[15] Kearney (1959), Costello (1958), Gascoigne (1989).

[16] Henry More, *Immortality*, p. 13, in his *A Collection of Several Philosophical Writings* (London and Cambridge, 1662).

[17] Ibid., p. 12.

you have as highly recommended Des Cartes, as is possible, and as knowing no better method of Philosophy, you recommend it effectually in some parts of your books whereby you had so fired some to the study of it, that your letter to V.C. (which came long after) could not coole them, nor doth it yet: but they are enravisht with it.[18]

Henry More was not the first Englishman to take an interest in Descartes. Mention might be made of the Cavendish circle, which included Thomas Hobbes and the mathematician John Pell, as well as the aristocrats Sir Kenelm Digby and Charles and William Cavendish.[19] Sir Charles Cavendish exchanged letters with Descartes, through the good offices of Pell and Sir William Boswell.[20] He owned a copy of the *Principia*, as did Pell. Lord Herbert of Cherbury owned a copy of Descartes' *Meditationes*, given him by the author.[21] The first work by Descartes to be translated into English was the *Discours de la méthode*, which appeared as *A Discourse of a Method for the Well-guiding of Reason, and the Discovery of Truth in the Sciences* (London, 1649).[22] One of the attractions of Cartesianism for university education was that, at a time when scholastic Aristotelianism had been discredited as a plausible intellectual framework, Descartes' philosophy could supply an alternative scheme for the study of philosophy.[23] There were others besides More who proposed that Cartesianism should be introduced into the university curriculum. In 1654 John Webster's proposals for university reform suggested including Descartes in the curriculum.[24] Around 1655 Thomas Barlow recommended Descartes (together with Gassendi, Digby, White and Bacon) as a writer on natural philosophy suitable for inclusion in an academic library.[25] Joshua Barnes revised Holdsworth's 'Directions for a student at the universities' (originally written in the 1640s) to include Descartes.[26] The popularity of Cartesianism is attested by the fact that, in

[18] John Worthington, *The Diary and Correspondence of John Worthington*, ed. J. Crossley and R. C. Christie 3 vols. (Manchester: Chetham Society, 1847–86), vol. III, p. 254.

[19] Hervey (1952). For drafts of the Cavendish–Pell letters, see British Library, MSS Additional 4,280 and 4,278. For Hobbes and the Cavendish circle, see chapter 5 below.

[20] BL, MS Additional 4,280, fols. 118r–v, 131r. John Pell (1611–85) was a mathematician, resident during the 1640s in the Netherlands. Sir William Boswell (d. 1649) was English ambassador at The Hague.

[21] Fordyce and Knox (1936–9).

[22] The anonymous English translator expresses great admiration for Descartes, calling him, 'The great DES CARTES (who may justly challenge the first place among Philosophers of this Age'. It was printed without the *Dioptrique* or *Géometrie* and is based on the French original of 1637, not the Latin version (1644). The *Meditations* were not translated into English until 1680, when William Molyneux published his translation together with Hobbes' objections.

[23] Gascoigne (1989), p. 55.

[24] John Webster, *Vindiciae academiarum, or the Examination of the Academies* (London, 1654).

[25] Jordy and Fletcher (1961). [26] Printed in Fletcher (1956), pp. 623 ff.

1668, the vice-chancellor of Cambridge, Edmund Boldero, felt obliged to issue a decree forbidding undergraduates from basing their disputations on Descartes.[27]

In this climate Henry More's admiration for Descartes was bold, and his suggestion that Cartesianism be included on the university curriculum innovatory. But even at its beginning More's pro-Cartesian stance was not an uncritical one. In 1648, at the behest of Samuel Hartlib, he embarked on a correspondence with Descartes, which was cut off by Descartes' untimely death in 1650. The basic elements of More's critique of Descartes, which relates primarily to his *Principles of Philosophy*, are set out in his first letter, with further criticisms added in later letters. More sought to persuade Descartes that all substance, both corporeal and incorporeal, is extended, and indeed that God Himself is *res extensa*. Since both corporeal and incorporeal substance are extended, he argued, they are to be differentiated in terms of their defining properties, chiefly by solidity. More argues that body is extended and impenetrable, but that incorporeal substance (soul or spirit) is extended and penetrable. Likewise, bodies may be divided ('discerpible' is More's term for this), but spirits are indivisible (or 'indiscerpible'). In this way More gave prominence to the role of spiritual substance in the operations of nature, believing that he could give a more satisfactory account of the transmission of motion from one body to another. He also tried to persuade Descartes of the infinity of the universe, and he took issue with him over the existence of a vacuum, the importance of final causes, and animal souls, against the Cartesian view that animals are automata.

Descartes took More's objections sufficiently seriously to respond to them in some detail. But he evidently found More's arguments too anthropomorphic for his liking. More, whose perspective was founded in his Plotinian metaphysics and his own apologetic concerns, was dissatisfied with Descartes' replies. He continued to press the shortcomings of Cartesian physics in other writings, becoming more concerned with the atheistical implications of Cartesianism as time went by. For example, in *The Immortality of the Soul* (1659) he criticises Descartes' location of the soul in the pineal gland. He became convinced that, in spite of its explicit dualism and positing the existence of spiritual substance, Cartesianism could not actually demonstrate the existence of souls or spirits. In *Epistola H. Mori*

[27] In 1660 Gilbert Clarke published his disputation defending Descartes against Bacon, Hobbes and Seth Ward: *De plenitudine mundi* (London, 1660). By 1682, Cartesianism formed part of the undergraduate curriculum in natural philosophy, with a textbook published for the purpose, Joannes Schuler's *Exercitationes ad Principiarum Descarti primam partem* (Cambridge: Cambridge University Press, 1682, reprinted 1686). Information from Gascoigne (1989).

ad V.C. (1664) he argues that many of Descartes' cosmological ideas do not make sense even in his own terms: for example, on vortical theory, planets would be ovoid, not round. Something else must be adduced to account for phenomena not accounted for by Cartesianism. And that 'something' was, argued More, spirit or soul. Accordingly he coined the term 'nullibists' for the Cartesians, on account of the fact that they claimed that the soul exists, but could not show where it existed.

CARTESIANISM BY CORRESPONDENCE

Anne Conway's letters tell us little about her earliest education, but we can gather more about her later education in spite of the fact that there are only four letters which document it. These letters, dating from 1650, are all that remain of her correspondence course in Cartesian philosophy.[28] Three of these four Cartesian letters are by More, in reply to lost letters from his pupil. The fourth is Anne Conway's reply to the third letter of More's. There were clearly other letters which have not come down to us. And More's letter of 8 February (1658) suggests that they were still discussing Descartes eight years later. In addition to disclosing the curriculum of her studies, the early letters tell us something about how she was taught, that is, about More's pedagogical method. These letters are, therefore, a unique source: although they constitute only a fragment of the total number originally written, they give us a glimpse of the philosophical curriculum used by More, as well as his pedagogical approach, and philosophical comments on Descartes. Had Lady Conway been born male, she would, like her brother, have had the opportunity of attending a university and being taught, face to face, by a tutor like More. And there would in consequence be no record of the words that passed between them. These letters can, therefore, be seen as snatches of written tutorials, that is to say, of the kind of instruction that Anne Conway's brother John Finch might have had received from More when he was at Christ's College, Cambridge.[29] Later letters also show that More continued to teach Cartesianism long after he had publicly declared its 'ill consequence to religion'. They confirm that, for all his own primarily metaphysical interests, More was interested in Cartesianism as a body of natural philosophy rather than as metaphysics.

[28] On this group of letters, see Gabbey (1977).

[29] Another source for the teaching of Cartesianism in English universities at this time are student notebooks recording their Cartesian studies. These are listed and discussed in Kearney (1959), bibliography and pp. 166, 257–8. As far as I can tell from the ones which I have examined, it is not possible to reconstruct from these the method of instruction used.

These letters show that More used Cartesianism as the primary grounding in philosophy. The textbook in use was the *Principia philosophiae* (*Principles of Philosophy*), of which More made a translation especially for Lady Conway (a translation which is no longer in existence).[30] In 1651, her brother sent her a copy from France, and it may be this copy (the 1650 edition) to which More refers in his letter of 8 February 1658.[31] He also had her study the *Dioptrique*.[32] More took his pupil through the *Principia* section by section: the first letter, dated September 1650, discusses book I, section 4; the second, dated May 1651, discusses *Principia* book II, sections 18–21. The discussion is not confined rigidly to the specified sections – for example, his discussion of I.4 refers forward to II.30 in order to substantiate his point that Descartes did not 'in good earnest affirm that there is no meanes at all to distinguish waking from dreaming'. The first letter deals with the argument for the existence of God from the idea of a perfect being and with the question of whether we can distinguish between sleeping and waking. The second argues against Descartes for the existence of a vacuum: More does so by advancing arguments to demonstrate the existence of space as non-material extension. The third letter clarifies the difference between 'first and second notions'. The fourth letter, the one extant reply by Anne Conway, puts forward empirical evidence against the Cartesian view that colour is not a property of things but the result of the stimulus of the mind by light.

When, in 1650, More presented Lady Conway with his translation, he advised her how to approach the work:

> Onely lett me be bold to commend to you this rule, Though I would have you to habituate your self, compos'dly, and steddily to think of any thing that you think worth the thinking of, and to drive it on to as clear and distinct approbation as you can, yett do not think of anything anxiously and solicitously, to the vexing or troubling of you spiritts at all. What you would force at one time may happily offer it self at another.[33]

This echoes Descartes' advice to his reader in the preface to the French translation of the *Principles*, where he tells his reader to read 'without straining his attention too much or stopping at difficulties which may be encountered' and recommends his reader to read and re-read his text, without pausing over difficulties:

[30] *Conway Letters*, p. 51.
[31] *Conway Letters*, pp. 65 n. and 145. More gives page references which correspond to the 1650 edition.
[32] Ibid., p. 145. [33] *Conway Letters*, p. 52.

I should like the reader first of all to go quickly through the whole book like a novel, without straining his attention too much or stopping at the difficulties which may be encountered. The aim should be merely to ascertain in a general way which matters I have dealt with. After this, if he finds that these matters deserve to be examined and he has the curiosity to ascertain their causes, he may read the book a second time in order to observe how my arguments follow. But if he is not always able to see this fully, or if he does not understand all the arguments, he should not give up at once. He should merely mark with a pen the places where he finds the difficulties and continue to read on to the end without a break. If he then takes up the book for the third time, I venture to think he will now find the solutions to most of the difficulties he marked before; and if any still remain, he will discover their solution on a final re-reading.[34]

The approach recommended here underlines the appeal of Cartesianism to those without a formal academic training. It is, in a sense, philosophy for amateurs, requiring no more than literacy and common sense as prerequisites for study. This, combined with the fact that, in France at least, it was written in the vernacular, made it accessible to people outside the university system, especially women. Henry More, in his advice on reading quoted above, was evidently following Descartes' recommendations.

Confirmation of More's pedagogical method for philosophical instruction may be had from the Cartesian studies of Anne Conway's nephews, Edward and John Rawdon, in 1674. It was apparently the same diet of Cartesian philosophy which More provided when, at the behest of their uncle Lord Conway, they were sent to study at Christ's College, Cambridge. Although at that later date More declined to be tutor to the Rawdon boys on account of his age, he had promised to assist in their education, and sent regular reports of their progress to their aunt.[35] From these, it is evident that he took them through a programme of Cartesian studies, commencing with the *Principles*, then moving on to the *Dioptrics* and *Meteors*. And he appears to have used the same read-through approach which he used twenty years earlier when instructing Anne Conway. On 4 September 1674 he wrote: 'Mr Rawdon . . . comes diligently to his Cartesian lecture, we are just now gott through the 3 first parts of his *Principia*'.[36] On 19 October he reports:

[34] René Descartes, *Principles of Philosophy*, 'Preface to the French Edition', in *The Philosophical Writings of Descartes*, trans. J. Cottingham, R. Stoothoff and D. Murdoch, 3 vols. (Cambridge: Cambridge University Press, 1985), vol. I, pp. 184 and 185.

[35] Hastings MSS, HA 15371 and *Conway Letters*, pp. 393–9. More arranged for the Rawdon boys to be tutored by Mr Lovett, a relative of George Rust, but undertook to examine them five times per week 'upon the lectures which their Tutour shall have read to them. Which will contribute not a little to the claring things to them and to the fixing them in their minde'. Henry More to Sir George Rawdon, Hastings MSS, HA 15371.

[36] Ibid., p. 393.

'I have begun to read to him Des Cartes Dioptricks'.[37] In December 1674 he reports that he is about to embark on the *Meteors*, having completed the *Dioptricks*:

I have now gone quite thorough Des Cartes Dioptricks with Mr Rawdon, and made him understand them from the beginning to the end, the Machine for making glasses not excepted. I was thinking also to impart to him the Mathematicall Demonstrations how the rayes in a Parabolicall Speculum must necessary [*sic*] be reflected to one focus, as they are refracted to one focus in an Ellipsis or Hyperbola, but this being something harder then what concerns the Ellipsis and Hyperbola in Des Cartes, I think better to decline that whyle the young Gentleman is here, and I perceived by My Lord that he had a minde that Mr Rawdon should go quite thorough Des Cartes Philosophy, and his meteors is so little a part that we may likely goe thorough it before My Lords order come to transplant him to the Inns of Court.[38]

The subsequent letters (9 and 31 December 1674) report progress on the *Meteors*.[39]

More's earliest letters to Anne Conway show that his method of instruction was to encourage his pupil to evaluate arguments in a series of objections and replies with which he supplemented his programme of reading the text. These were not necessarily a standard set supplied by the teacher. Rather, he expected his pupil to raise queries or objections to the passages prescribed for reading, to which he would then respond. The first of More's letters to Anne Finch (as she then was, since it was written before her marriage) is a sequel to one (no longer extant) in which he had asked her to think of objections to Descartes' argument for the necessary existence of God from the idea of a fully perfect being. The objection she came up with (in the letter which is no longer extant), was, as quoted by More, 'That then the idea of a fully imperfect Being should emply the existence of a Being fully imperfect'. More replies by pointing out that this amounted to saying 'the idea . . . of what is fully imperfect, emplyes a necessary non-existence. And the idea of this fully imperfect, tells us that it is impossible for it to exist or be anything, as the idea of the fully perfect being tells that it dos necessarily exist'.[40]

37 Ibid., p. 395.

38 Ibid., p. 397. Another Christ's College student who apparently studied Descartes in this way was George Elphicke (or Uphicke), whom More recommended for service with the Conways, noting, 'I suspect he has not dived very deepe into Mathematicks yett, but he has read Des Cartes Principia over and over, and has a pretty dexterous mechanick wit'. More to Lady Conway, 8 Feb. [1658], *Conway Letters*, p. 145.

39 *Conway Letters*, p. 398.

40 *Conway Letters*, p. 484. cf. letter 22a (p. 489) where he criticises her argument that a vacuum is 'a reall subject'.

In the second letter of this group the discussion concerns Descartes' *Principles*, book II, section 18, where he denies the existence of a vacuum. His pupil had, apparently, preferred Descartes' view – 'Your Ladiship in courtesy seemes to take the strangers part', he writes, 'and lean towards his opinon that there can not be an empty space or any distance but by the interposition of a body or matter'. More then sets out six arguments in reply to her position, and asks her to tell him which are the best: 'But to win you over to my syde, I shall propound these arguments following. And your Ladiship in your next [letter] shall tell me your judgement wch of them is ye weakest. For I will not professe them all unconfutable.'[41] The six arguments that follow include one based on *consensus gentium* (consent of nations – that 'almost all men' hold that the world is finite), and one which turns on a scholastic axiom (that there is no motion in an instant). They also include arguments that More had put to Descartes, and arguments he was to repeat in his *An Antidote Against Atheism*, among them that if God annihilated the world and then made a new one, there would be a measurable distance of time between the two events, even though nothing existed then.[42] More then responds to three objections by Anne Conway to his own position on the existence of spatial extension separate from body. Her argument, 'that space is impenetrable as well as matter', is also to be found in Descartes' reply to More's first letter. Other points of disagreement which echo More's letters to Descartes include More's defence of the possibility of a vacuum and his rejection of Descartes' distinction between the terms 'indefinite' and 'infinite' in respect of the universe.[43] More also advances some of his own arguments in support of his concept of space.[44] Although many of the points he makes echo points he made to Descartes three years earlier, this is not always the case – partly for the pedagogical reason that he wants Anne Conway to identify the best out of six arguments which he puts.

Never in these Cartesian letters does More assume a thorough grounding in the technicalities of logical reasoning or non-Cartesian philosophical theory. Nor does he undertake to provide a grounding in logic, even if he uses the occasional technical term – for example, the term 'logicall notions' to categorise such properties as part and whole, subject and adjunct. But the one scholastic axiom he uses in this letter (that 'there is no motion in an instant') is used as an argument to be criticised. The only Latin tag he uses ('partem extra partem') in fact comes from Descartes.[45] His replies to Anne Conway, and indeed the arguments to which he provides the answers, are

[41] Ibid., p. 486. [42] Ibid., p. 487. [43] *Conway Letters*, pp. 486 and 489.
[44] Ibid., pp. 487–8. [45] Ibid., p. 486.

not devoid of formal philosophical reasoning. But the expertise in logic which they require is no more than what may be learned from Descartes himself. Nor does More expound Descartes solely through Descartes: on occasion he provides his own examples, often of a light-hearted or endearing kind. For example, when discussing the difference between sleeping and being awake, he recounts a dream he once had about finding a silver hat band.[46] On another occasion he refers back to his *Philosophical Poems*.[47] Furthermore, the approach to the text which he recommended suggests that Cartesianism offered not just a body of doctrine in the domain of natural philosophy, but a method for obtaining that knowledge – a method uncomplicated by formal exercises in logic or the need to absorb fixed dogma. This factor, combined with More's endorsement of the approach to the text recommended by Descartes, suggests that, from the pedagogical point of view, part of the attraction of Cartesian philosophy, especially the *Principles*, was that it addressed itself to the lay philosopher and did not require any more preparation than common sense. This would be particularly useful in the case of a female pupil with no formal academic training.

One significant conclusion about Anne Conway's education in philosophy to be drawn from the More–Conway letters on Descartes is that Henry More never encouraged his pupil to treat Cartesianism as a dogma, but argued against Descartes when he saw fit. While it would be too fanciful to speculate that the lost More–Conway correspondence on Cartesianism actually ghosts the More–Descartes correspondence, it is not too fanciful to suggest that the More–Conway letters show that the Cartesianism taught by More and studied by Anne Conway was a modified form of Cartesianism, consistent with More's earliest critique of Descartes. The More–Conway letters confirm that the Cartesianism taught by More was never uncritical of the master: his pupils may have been trained up in Cartesian philosophy, but they were armed with appropriate counter-arguments by a tutor who preserved a sceptical distance from the subject he taught. This would explain why – as in the case of the Rawdon boys – More continued to teach Cartesianism long after he had denounced it publicly as a pillar of atheism.

Furthermore, the fact that More was still teaching Cartesian philosophy long after he had publicly dissociated himself from Cartesianism underlines the point that the importance of Descartes for More was as a natural philosopher. Indeed Cartesianism was so important as a natural philosophy

[46] Ibid., p. 485.
[47] Ibid., p. 486, where he mentions his 'contending for a true infinite distance in space, in my Infinity of Worlds', i.e. 'Democritus Platonissans', stanzas 39–47.

that More's friend John Worthington thought that the only way to wean young scholars from Cartesianism with all the dangers it posed for religion was to substitute an alternative natural philosophy: 'there will be no way to take them [young scholars] off from idolizing the French Philosophy, and hurting themselves and others by some principles there, but by putting into their hands another Body of Natural Philosophy, which is like to be the most effectual antidote'.[48] Worthington looked to More to supply this 'new Phisiologie' as he called it. More, as we know, did no such thing. But the significance of Worthington's hope that he might underlines the appeal of Cartesianism as a substitute for Aristotelianism, especially Aristotelian natural philosophy. Furthermore, the fact that More continued to teach Cartesianism, even after he had publicly condemned it, can be explained by the fact that there was no suitable alternative system of natural philosophy. In respect of the new developments in astronomy and mechanics, Cartesianism was unquestionably superior to Aristotelianism. To some extent, therefore, More used it *faute de mieux*, as a framework for discussing issues in natural philosophy.[49] That this was not inconsistency or disingenuousness on his part is borne out by his early letters to Anne Conway, which show him teaching Cartesianism even though he did not agree with Descartes in all particulars.

ANNE CONWAY AND DESCARTES

Anne Conway's *Principles* differs significantly from both the philosophy of her teacher and the philosophy she studied with him. In relation to both, her book is strikingly independent: by no means the work of a dogmatic Cartesian, or Moreian for that matter.[50] Her divergence from Descartes clearly began with her very introduction to philosophy through Descartes. For, in her earliest correspondence with Henry More, we can see her being trained to be critical and to assess the relative strengths and weaknesses of arguments. And when instructing her More was himself prepared to argue against positions in the Cartesian text he has set her to read. In her responses to More we can observe her independence of mind and More being, as he put it, 'not a little putt to my plunges' for an answer.[51]

[48] Worthington, *Diary*, vol. III, p. 254.

[49] Charles Webster makes a similar point about Isaac Barrow, that 'even if the mechanical hypothesis was not acceptable as a comprehensive explanation of natural phenomena, it remained the most original and convincing theory to emerge during the recent revival of natural philosophy, providing the most convenient and best-informed source for the further consideration of scientific problems'. Webster (1975), p. 149. See also Gascoigne (1989), p. 55.

[50] For her critique of More, see chapter 4.

[51] *Conway Letters*, p. 489.

Even at this early stage, Anne Conway was prepared to side with Descartes against her teacher, for example on the question of the existence of the void.[52] But we also encounter her arguing strongly, on empirical grounds, against Descartes' theory of sense perception.[53] The critical spirit of the later chapters of Anne Conway's *Principles* may, therefore, be linked to the critical spirit with which she was introduced to philosophy. And elsewhere in her *Principles* she adopts an interrogative approach to argument. It is typical that she often makes her points as answers to questions ('If one asks . . . I answer . . .'),[54] or as anticipated objections ('If someone objects that our philosophy seems to be similar to that of Hobbes . . .', 'Let no one object that this philosophy is nothing but Cartesianism or Hobbesianism in a new guise').[55] Sometimes she answers objections by asking further questions ('I reply, how did the first body hold those spirits captive to such a degree? Was it because it was so hard and dense?')[56] On occasion she defends her position with a barrage of questions. This is what she does when arguing the nature of creatures from the divine attributes:

> since the goodness of God is a living goodness . . . how can any dead thing proceed from him or be created by him? . . . how can a dead thing come from him who is infinite life and love? Or how can any creature receive so vile and diminished an essence from him . . . that it does not share any life or perception and is not able to aspire to the least degree of these for all eternity? Did not God create his creatures to this end, namely, that they be blessed in him and enjoy his divine goodness in their various conditions and states? Moreover, how could this be possible without life or perception? How can anything lacking life enjoy divine goodness?[57]

Anne Conway's interrogative stance, her customary presentation of issues in terms of objections and replies, was clearly rooted in the induction to philosophy she received from Henry More. In its written form her philosophy combines the interrogative process of *quaestiones et responsiones* (questions and replies) with *apodeixis* (demonstration). Her *Principles* is the work of someone accustomed to the discipline of arguing *more geometrico* (in a geometric manner). Howsoever 'commonsensical' her induction into philosophy may have been, she was grounded by her tutor in the elements of logic and systematic analysis. The a priori character of her metaphysics and the underlying deductive framework of her exposition suggest that she remained faithful to the philosophical method in which she was trained.

Furthermore, the critical evaluation of Descartes which she learned from Henry More notwithstanding, she retained a strong measure of respect for Descartes, especially Cartesian natural philosophy. She shared More's

52. Ibid., p. 486. 53 Ibid., pp. 489 ff. 54 *Principles*, p. 60.
55 Ibid., pp. 64 and 63. 56 Ibid., p. 61. 57 Ibid., p. 45.

admiration for Descartes the 'master of mechanicks': 'it cannot be denied that Descartes taught many remarkable and ingenious things concerning the mechanical aspects of natural processes, and about how all motions proceed according to regular mechanical laws'.[58] Issues raised by Cartesianism recur in her *Principles*. This may be illustrated by the subject of corporeal motion, an issue fundamental to her critique of dualism and one which takes up a substantial portion of the treatise. It was a live issue in seventeenth-century philosophy, arising from Descartes' explanation of local motion as the transfer of motion from one body to another: 'motion is the transfer [*translatio*] of one piece of matter, or one body, from the vicinity of the other bodies which are in immediate contact with it, and which are regarded as being at rest, to the vicinity of other bodies'.[59] Anne Conway's discussion of this issue shows she is acutely aware that it is a matter of controversy.

it is a matter of great debate how motion can be transmitted from one body to another since it is certainly neither a substance nor a body. If it is only a mode of the body, how can this motion be transmitted from one body to another since the essence or being of a mode consists in this, namely that it inheres or exists in its own body.[60]

Her posing of the question is testimony not just to the importance of Cartesianism in setting much of the agenda in seventeenth-century philosophy, but also to her debt to More, who had raised the question when he wrote to Descartes in 1648. How, asked More, can movement be transmitted from one body to another if it is merely a mode of body? '[A]nother difficulty occurs to me concerning the nature of movement. For if movement is a mode of body, like figure [shape], the arrangement of the parts, etc., how is it possible that it passes from one body to another, rather than the other corporeal modes.'[61] Henry More proposed to Descartes a solution to the problem in terms of affect rather than impact: motion is not *transmitted* from one body to another, but *activated by* one body in the other. He believed that motion is brought about not by matter, but by spirit infusing the matter:

I claim that I am lead to believe that there is no communication of movement, except that by the mere impulse of one body, another body is woken, so to speak, from its state of indolence to enter into movement, just as the soul has one particular thought on account of such and such an occasion, and that the body does not so much receive motion, as put itself into motion, having been aroused by another.

58 Ibid., p. 64. 59 Descartes, *Principles*, vol. II, p. 25.
60 Conway, *Principles*, p. 69. 61 Descartes, *Lettres*, p. 179.

Anne Conway's answer to the same problem bears some striking similarities with More. She too agrees that motion, being a mode of body, cannot 'pass properly from one body to another'. She denies that 'motion is communicated from one body to another by local motion'. Rather it is propagated or activated in one body by another – by what she calls 'real production or creation' ('modus ergo istius propagationis est per realem roductionem vel creationem').[62]

'Engagement' is perhaps the word that best describes both More's interest in Cartesianism and Anne Conway's response to Descartes. Neither of them rejects Cartesianism outright, but nor do they adopt a fully Cartesian position. This was not contradictory on their part, but the result of participation in an on-going philosophical debate in which Descartes set the agenda, even for his opponents.[63] Although her philosophical studies were perforce extra-mural, Anne Conway came to philosophy at a time when philosophy flourished *outside* the academies. Hers might have been an unusual route to extra-mural philosophy, but it put her in good company with Descartes, Hobbes, Locke and Spinoza, none of whom had a university career in philosophy. There were other ways in which any disadvantage she had as a woman in not being able to attend a university worked out to her advantage as a philosopher. For she was spared negotiating the constraints imposed by career and the need for patronage and protection which a male university student would have faced. At all events, she could not have made the start she did without tutorial guidance from a philosopher who made his career within a university – Henry More. Before discussing her continuing philosophical dialogue with More and others, we need to examine another important shaping factor in her pursuit of philosophy, and that is the religious context.

[62] Conway, *Principles*, ed. Loptson, p. 144.

[63] Rogers (1985).

CHAPTER 3

Religion and Anne Conway

'So Noble, so Wise and so Pious a Personage'[1]

In the seventeenth century religion was central to people's lives and an essential component of the intellectual landscape. Anne Conway was no exception in this regard. Discussion of religious matters is a dominant theme in her letters, and the centrality of religion to her philosophy is beyond question, as the very title of her treatise makes plain. In this chapter I shall discuss her religious life from her early years until the period just prior to her encounter with Quakerism and kabbalism. After examining personal aspects of religion, this chapter will discuss the currents of non-conformist, millenialist and patristic theology which she encountered. One further aspect of Anne Conway's investigations of religion, her response to Islam, will be discussed in a later chapter, in relation to her brother John.

The fusion of theology and philosophy which Anne Conway achieves in her treatise entails a radical revision of her early view that philosophy is incompatible with Christianity. Writing to her father-in-law in 1651, she delivered herself of the opinion 'that Philosophy is fitted for the Religion of the Heathen and that it cannot agree with Christian Religion'.[2] By the time she wrote her *Principles*, however, she had found a way of reconciling religion and philosophy without compromising her Christian piety. This may be explained in part by the fact that her formal training in philosophy was predicated on the compatibilist position that philosophy was the handmaid of religion. She was, furthermore, schooled in philosophy by a teacher who devoted his philosophical talents to pious uses, and insisted 'That Piety is the only Key of true Knowledge'.[3] In his published writings More proclaimed his role as a philosopher to be that of religious apologist, whose aim was 'not to Theologize in Philosophy, but to draw an

[1] More, Dedication of *Antidote against Atheism*, Sig A2 in *A Collection*.

[2] Anne Conway's opinion, as summarised by the second Viscount Conway in a letter to her written 20 September 1651 (*Conway Letters*, p. 34).

[3] Cited in Ward (2000), p. 91.

Exoterick Fence or exteriour Fortification about Theologie'.[4] Early in his correspondence with Anne Conway he emphasises the subordination of philosophical study to the attainment of virtue and piety ('sett no price at all upon knowledge, but so far as it will make us vertuous, and obedient to God that made us').[5] But Anne Conway did not accept the possibility that philosophy and religion may be reconciled merely on the authority of her teacher. She worked out her own compatibilist solution, a *philosophia pia* or religious philosophy predicated upon the existence and nature of God.

The beginning of this process is signalled in a letter, written in 1652, which marks the point where her epistolary tutorials in Cartesianism develop into a more wide-ranging correspondence. In it she expresses a wish to broaden the scope of her philosophical discussions with Henry More beyond Cartesianism.

– *But I shall leave* Des-Cartes *for the present, and Propound some thing* new *to You. Sir, I do really think my self* infinitely *obliged to you in many Respects: But if you Please to deliver your* Opinion *freely and fully in Answer to those* Enquiries *I shall now make, you will more* particularly *Engage me than ever.*[6]

The queries she presented to More on this occasion derived from her reading of Henry More's poem 'Prae-existence of the Soul'. They all concern theological topics – the souls of men, animals and plants, the problem of evil, and salvation in general and the ancient theological question of whether the devils will be saved.

Upon the Reading of your Poem *of the* Prae-existence of the Soul, *and serious thinking of it, I desir'd to be satisfied in Four* Particulars, *which are* these.

First, Whether God did create the *Matter* for the *Enjoyment of Souls*, since they *fell* by it?

Secondly, Whether the *Soul* could Enjoy the *Matter* without being *Clothed* in Corporeity; and if it could not, how it can be the *Fall* of the *Soul* that makes it Assume a *Body*?

Thirdly, Upon Supposition most of the *Souls fell;* Why did not *all* Assume *Bodies* together: And how *Adam* can be said to be the *first Man*, and all Men to *Fall* in *him*, since they *Fell* before: And how the *Souls* of *Beasts* and *Plants* came into *Bodies*?

Fourthly, How *Man* can be *Restor'd*, to what he *Fell* from; And why the *Devils* that *Fell*; cannot? Why *Christ's* Death should Extend more to *One* than to the *Other*?[7]

Although these sound like obscure theological questions, the underlying issues nevertheless impinge directly on her philosophical investigations. The relationship of souls to bodies, the implications of this for salvation and the

[4] More, *Collection* (1662), Preface, p. vi.
[5] More to Anne Conway, 4 April [1653], *Conway Letters*, p. 76.
[6] Ward, *Life*, p. 169. [7] Ibid.

nature of goodness on which salvation is predicated are all fundamental in Anne Conway's mature philosophy. The questions she puts here to More in 1652 show her concern about the extent and limits of goodness, arising from its handling in Christian doctrine. Underlying them is the broader issue of the justice of God, especially of how to reconcile the existence of evil with the goodness and justice of God. As an answer to this perennial question, her treatise is centrally concerned with the problem of theodicy.

These themes are developed further in her *Principles*, which discusses the relationship of God to the created world and such issues as divine providence and salvation. Indeed the existence and nature of the deity is the primary principle from which her system unfolds. As in the *Enneads* of Plotinus, God is the one, the first cause and source of all being. But God is not just the philosopher's God – an abstract beginning point or first cause. The God of her *Principles* is a God of love, whose essential goodness pervades all His works. The created world reflects not just the goodness but the justice and wisdom of the creator. Her discussion has distinctively religious overtones, with an unmistakable emphasis on Christianity. The key communicator between the deity and creation is Middle Nature, also called Christ. Her treatment of metaphysical issues makes direct appeals to the teachings of the Bible. At the same time she sought to present religious truth as rationally deducible, so it might be accessible to both unbelievers and other faiths. She was clearly committed to defending religious truth against atheism, and expressing it in terms of the essential truth of Christianity. From a theological perspective, however, the result is highly unorthodox divinity. For not only does she subsume Christian doctrine within metaphysical categories, but her subordination of Christ to God, her explanation of the indwelling of Christ in created things by 'intimate presence', and her denial of the eternity of hell suggests the impact of radical religion of the mid-seventeenth century.

RELIGION AND ANNE CONWAY

Although Anne Conway was to all intents and purposes a practising Anglican prior to her conversion to Quakerism, her formative years were spent during a prolonged period when unified ecclesiastical authority was unknown.[8] The first ten years of her life were the period of the Laudian

8 Absence of central ecclesiastical authority was, of course, the common experience of English people in the interregnum, and should not be regarded as a determinant of non-conformity. After all, many of the leading figures of the post-Restoration high church lived through the same period of disestablishment, including the Archbishop of Canterbury's censor, Samuel Parker (1640–88) and the non-juror Thomas Ken (1637–1711).

ascendancy in the Church of England, a time when the institutional authority of the church and uniformity of creed seemed assured. However, the next decade of her life witnessed the collapse of the authority of Archbishop Laud and the distintegration of English Christian unity into a multiplicity of competing alternatives, ranging from Presbyterianism through to Fifth Monarchism. During the Civil War, the abolition of the Church of England (1644) completed the reversal of the fortunes of Laudianism, although Anglican traditions were kept alive by loyal ministers like Jeremy Taylor and John Hales, who found employment as private chaplains. The breakdown of central ecclesiastical authority during the Civil War and its aftermath had far-reaching consequences resulting, by default rather than design, in freedom to subscribe to beliefs that would have been judged heterodox, even heretical, under the Caroline regime. In this climate of religious freedom new sects emerged, such as Baptists, Behmenists, pre-Adamites and Quakers. A measure of the bewildering variety of unorthodox beliefs circulating in this period can be gauged from compilations like Thomas Edwards' *Gangrena* or Ephraim Paget's *Heresographie*, which provide catalogues of heresies old and new, including anti-Trinitarianism, Psychopannychism, pantheism and materialism. Although the English Republic and Protectorate never found a satisfactory means of reconciling the emergent varieties of Protestant beliefs into one national church, and although religious toleration was not looked on favourably by all the opponents of the Laudian church, the issue of toleration remained high on the political agenda.[9] The climate of intolerance fomented by some sectarians was countered by more moderate spirits, which included liberal Anglicans like Jeremy Taylor, who sought a modus vivendi for Anglicans after the disestablishment of their church. The Cambridge Platonists too propounded an inclusivist and tolerant approach to religious difference. The quest for religious toleration was supported by Cromwell himself, whose personal commitment to toleration extended to a willingness to allow Jews to settle in England.[10] The turbulent political events of the time fed an atmosphere of fervid millenarian expectation, which was not wholly dampened at the time of the restoration of the Stuart monarchy. English Protestantism remained fissured even after the re-establishment of the Church of England in 1660, in spite of the reimposition of ecclesiastical order and, with it, ecclesiastical control.

[9] On toleration, see Jordan (1936–40).

[10] On Cromwell and the re-admission of the Jews to England, see Kaplan et al. (1989).

We can only guess at the Finch family's religious allegiances during the 1630s and 1640s. If Anne Conway's mother shared the religious convictions of her cousin Matthew Cradock, one-time governor of Massachusetts, she would have had puritan leanings. On the other hand, to judge by the fact that they were certainly comfortable with the Restoration and its church, the Finch family were probably Anglicans at heart, but of a liberal stamp. John Finch's commitment to religious toleration was sufficiently strong to be incorporated in his philosophy.[11] And his acceptance of the restoration of the Church of England may, like More's, represent an easy transfer from liberal puritanism to Episcopalianism. Heneage Finch provides further evidence that the Finch family's loyalty to the Church of England after the Restoration was neither narrow nor intolerant. We know little of the personal beliefs of this pillar of the legal establishment beyond the fact that he shared his contemporaries' antipathy to Catholics and Quakers. Nevertheless, while he presided at the Court of Chancery, Finch's legal rulings were instrumental in making a legal space for dissent. By setting limits to the scope of the law, Finch drew a boundary between the business of public, judicial process and matters of private conscience, or, as he put it, that which 'is only between a man and his confessor'.[12] Finch's contribution was legal and practical, based not on agreement about what beliefs might be permissible, but on the principles of equity, which he believed might be studied as a science. In this way he 'delimited a judicial form of conscience that was not religious but "civic and political"', differentiating 'a conscience that was legal and procedural' from religious conscience that was personal and individual.[13] Heneage Finch's commitment to tolerant Anglicanism was continued in the next generation by two of his sons. Daniel Finch, second Earl of Nottingham, was to be instrumental in passing the Toleration Act of 1689, and prominent in moves to find an accommodation with religious dissenters through broad-based comprehension of differing groups within the church. Heneage Finch's second son, later first Earl of Aylesford, who was also called Heneage, and was, like his father, a prominent lawyer, was to act as leading counsel for the seven latitudinarian bishops imprisoned by James II in 1688, having himself been dismissed from the office of Solicitor General by James in 1686.

The Conways for their part never wavered in their Anglican loyalism, even if they were discreet about it during Cromwellian times. When Edward Conway brought Jeremy Taylor over to be lecturer at Portmore, his estate

[11] Leicestershire County Record Office, Finch papers MS DG 7 lit 9, fol. 331v. See p. 104 below.

[12] From 'Cook v. Fountain' (1676), cited in Saunders (1997).

[13] See Saunders (1997) for a full discussion of this issue. Also Yale (1957–71).

near Lisburne in Ulster in 1658, he enjoined Taylor not to make public acknowledgement of his patronage.[14] Had he not done so, Taylor would most probably have dedicated to him his *Ductor dubitantium, or the Rule of Conscience* (1660).[15] The churchmen whom the Conways patronised were latitudinarian in practice and liberals in theology, distinguished from the Calvinist predestinarians of mid-seventeenth-century Cambridge by their liberal theology of grace and their anti-voluntarism. More, Cudworth and their followers subscribed to an intellectualist view of the attributes of God, according to which God exercises his will in conformity to his supreme goodness and justice. So too did Jeremy Taylor, who like them placed emphasis on the role of reason in theology. Taylor's extreme liberalism regarding the doctrine of grace led him to assert the innocence of unbaptised infants. His anti-Calvinism is given most explicit statement in a work directed against Presbyterianism, his *Deus justificatus* (1656). Taylor became a trusted adviser to Lord Conway, on both ecclesiastical and Irish affairs. After the Restoration, probably at Lord Conway's instigation, Taylor was appointed Bishop of Down and Connor. He had personal contact with Anne Conway, whom he visited in London and at Ragley. She took a personal interest in his family affairs, and while she was in Ireland she valued his company. Indeed it has been suggested that he wrote his *Christian Consolations* for her.[16]

The theologians whom the Conways patronised were also proponents of religious toleration. Jeremy Taylor's *Liberty of Prophesying* (published in 1647) was a courageous defence of toleration which condemned the persecution of dissent as both wrong and unwise, and proposed religious comprehension based on subscription to a limited set of common beliefs.[17] More and Cudworth were distinct voices of moderation among the religious and political disputes of mid-seventeenth-century England, and were claimed by Gilbert Burnet as founding fathers of the tolerationist strand of liberal Anglicanism that has come to be called 'latitudinarianism'.[18] The eirenic stance of the Cambridge Platonists is exemplified in the sermons Ralph Cudworth published in the 1640s, which, at a critical moment during the English Civil War, appealed for a spirit of understanding among his

[14] Stranks (1952), pp. 184–5. It was Anne Conway who paid the £30 expenses for Taylor's removal to Ireland: ibid., p. 190.

[15] Ibid., p. 186. In the event, Taylor dedicated it to the newly restored king.

[16] *Conway Letters*, p. 176. [17] See Stranks (1952), pp. 70 ff.

[18] Gilbert Burnet, *History of My Own Time*, ed. O. Airy, 2 vols. (Oxford, 1897), vol. I, pp. 334–5. Most of the most prominent figures in this movement had some connection with the Cambridge school: Simon Patrick with John Smith, Edward Fowler with Henry More, Thomas Tenison with Cudworth, and Burnet himself.

hearers, arguing that the true Christian spirit was not a spirit of contention. 'Christ came not into the world', he said, 'to kindle a fire of wrangling and contentious dispute amongst us, and to warm our spirits against one another with nothing but angry & peevish debates, whilst in the mean time our hearts remain all ice within towards God, and have not the least spark of true heavenly fire to melt and thaw them'.[19] Henry More too sought to take a non-contentious line towards religious difference. His biographer, Richard Ward, reports of him that 'he was not either for Rancour of Persecution. He thought, that all Persons *making conscience* of their ways, and that were themselves *Peaceable*, and for granting of a *Liberty* unto *Others*, ought not to be severely us'd or prosecuted; but *born* with as befits Weak Members, till God shall give a *greater Light*.'[20]

Although More was less charitable towards Catholics and towards doctrinaire and factious sectarians, he never advocated persecution of dissent. In his most important statement of his theological position, his *An Explanation of the Grand Mystery of Godliness* published in 1660, he condemns forcible conversion and persecution of non-Christians as un-Christian. Persecution is behaviour which is not likely to win 'the Appretiation and high Value' which Christianity deserves. The truth of Christianity

> is not to be expressed as it usually is done, by vilifying and reproaching all other Religions, in damning the very best and most conscientious *Turks, Jews and Pagans* to the Pit of Hell, and then to double lock the Door upon them, or to stand there to watch with long Poles to beat them out again, if any of them should offer to emerge and endeavour to crawl out. This Fervour is but a false Zeal and of no service to the Gospel.[21]

Instead he advocates Christian eirenicism founded on the desire to recognise the good in other religions.

> Certainly it were far better and more becoming the Spirit of the Gospel to admit and commend what is laudable and Praise-worthy in either *Judaism, Turcism* or *Paganism*, and with Kindness and compassion to tell them wherein they are mistaken, and wherein they fall Short; than to fly in their faces and to exprobrate to them the most consummate Wickedness that Humane Nature is lapsable into in Matters of Religion, and thus from an immoderate Depression of all other Religions to magnifie a man's own.[22]

[19] Ralph Cudworth, *A Sermon Preached Before the Honourable House of Commons*, in C. A. Patrides (ed.), *The Cambridge Platonists* (Cambridge: Cambridge University Press, 1980), p. 96.

[20] Ward, *Life*, pp. 105–6.

[21] Henry More, *An Explanation of the Grand Mystery of Godliness* (London and Cambridge, 1660), p. 343.

[22] Ibid., p. 344.

The eirenicism of both Cudworth and More was founded in their understanding of the Christian message of love and underpinned by their intellectualist theology according to which goodness is the foundational attribute of God.

The Anglican loyalism of the Conways during the interregnum does not, however, denote strict doctrinal orthodoxy. The men whom they promoted within the church (or, in the case of More, attempted to promote) were theologians distinguished by a latitude of belief that extended, in some areas, to heterodoxy. Jeremy Taylor's almost Pelagian soteriology (for example, his belief in the innocence of unbaptised infants) probably cost him the chance of promotion to an English see at the Restoration. Conway was also the patron of More's friend, George Rust, for whom he secured the deanship of Connor. Rust is the putative author of an anonymously published defence of the heterodox Church Father, Origen, *A Letter of Resolution Concerning Origen* (London, 1661).[23] Rust had personal contact with Anne Conway in Ireland, and accompanied her back to England, remaining with her throughout the period of Valentine Greatrakes' visit. Another figure associated with the Conways is More's former tutor at Christ's College, Robert Gell, who has been described variously as an illuminist and a perfectionist. His house in Bow Lane was used as a postal address for letters between Anne Conway and Henry More. During More's struggle to retain his fellowship at Christ's College after the Restoration, he complained to Anne Conway, 'I am rayled and bluster'd for an Heretick' on account of his latitudinarian stance.[24] He too was an admirer of Origen, with the result that he experienced difficulties with the new Anglican hierarchy: the Archbishop of Canterbury's licenser, Samuel Parker, refused an imprimatur for the first volume of his *Divine Dialogues* until he had made changes to ensure that the doctrine of the pre-existence of souls was proposed merely as a hypothesis, not as an article of belief.[25] And Parker took it upon himself to attack both More and Cudworth for this and other things in his *Free and Impartial Censure of the Platonick Philosophie* and his *An Account of the Nature and Extent*

[23] The ascription of *A Letter of Resolution* to Rust is made by J. Crossley in Worthington, *Diary*. Marjorie Nicolson concurs: *Conway Letters*, p. 192 n. But Rust's authorship has recently been questioned by David Dockrill in a paper read at the Patristics Conference, Oxford, 1995. Dockrill has argued, not unpersuasively, that More may have been the author. More denied this, however. See his letters to Lady Conway in *Conway Letters*, pp. 192–7. Mullett (1938).

[24] *Conway Letters*, p. 220.

[25] More to Anne Conway, 12 May [1668], *Conway Letters*, p. 294. More told Anne Conway that the Vice Chancellor of the University of Cambridge (Theophilus Dillingham) regarded the *Letter of Resolution* as 'a dangerous booke, and therefore did in some sort censure it in the Consistory'. He singles out for mention the view that 'one of the unsound opinions of Origen was the Praeexistence of the soule'. More to Anne Conway, 26 October [1661], *Conway Letters*, p. 194.

of the Divine Dominion & Goodnesse.[26] More never renounced his belief in the pre-existence of souls, but he managed to reach an accommodation with his ecclesiastical superiors by bowing to their authority on matters of belief, but retaining a place for his heterodox view on pre-existence within philosophy.[27]

RELIGION IN THE LETTERS

Anne Conway's deep interest in religion is obvious in her correspondence with Henry More. This is formally predicated upon their mutual interest in religious questions. For when he agreed to continue to correspond with Anne Conway, after the departure of her brother John for Italy in 1651, More commended her 'pious and vertuous designe' and noted that God has 'touched your heart, as I conceive, with a generous desire after such knowledge as is of most concernment, I mean the right knowledge of Relligion'.[28] This justification may have served in part as a pretext to enable them to pursue their epistolary friendship in a socially acceptable way. But there is more than token piety in their correspondence. Far from dealing in mere pious platitudes, the letters convey a deep sense of the spirituality of both correspondents. They also discuss deep theological questions. It is not until a relatively late point in their correspondence that particular beliefs and sects feature as a topic of discussion.

Many of the religious topics in Anne Conway's correspondence arise from her interrogation of Henry More's beliefs and theories. Two motifs predominate. The first may be termed, broadly, dissent; the second, eirenicism. These may both, in general terms, also be said to characterise her philosophical writing, in which she draws on the unorthodox religious beliefs of her day. The issue of religious authority, and with it questions about the authenticity of religious teachings, recur in her correspondence in the discussion of religious enthusiasm. A related topic is millenarianism. Judaism is another important aspect of Anne Conway's study of religion (to be treated separately in chapter 8). The religious topics which caught her attention often had a philosophical dimension, for many of the unorthodox religious teachings she examined entailed concomitant natural philosophies. Questions about theories of substance underlie discussions of Behmenism

[26] Both published in Oxford in 1666. Parker cites Joseph Glanvill's, *Lux Orientalis*, but not Henry More. He does, however, express his esteem for 'Persons more than ordinarily learned' who held similar views (p. 94).

[27] More, *A Collection*, Preface, pp. xxv–xxvi.

[28] More to Anne Conway, 2 Nov. 1651, *Conway Letters*, p. 53.

as much as they do discussions of Hobbes and Spinoza. Her interest in dissent from received or orthodox religious opinion never dissolves into scepticism or denigration: rather the drive is towards the reconciliation of conflicting opinions through rational understanding. Furthermore, dissent makes its mark on Anne Conway's philosophy in the philosophical nonconformity of her system – that is, its divergence from the philosophy of her masters.

CONSOLATIONS OF FAITH

Throughout her correspondence, the most frequent occasion for expressions of religious conviction is Anne Conway's ill health. In letters where her health is mentioned, religion features as a consolation – the resort of one for whom human medical skill offers no remedy. I would add, however, that this provides an index for her spirituality and it also helps account for the presence and shape of the religious element in her philosophy. As a man of the cloth, it was natural that More should adopt the role of priestly counsellor, and exhort his pupil/friend to show 'Christian resolution and patience in bearing the present torture of your disease'.[29] His advice to her that she should endure her suffering by submitting herself to the will of God appears to have been accepted by her. In a rare admission of how she felt, she wrote to More, near the end of her life:

> should I adventure upon a presage concerning my owne condition, from the redoubling of my afflictions, the continuednesse of my great paines, increase of weaknesse, with additionall new distempers, I might fancy my release also not farr off, from these weighty sufferings I have groaned under . . . but life and death are in the hands of the Almighty, and what he designes for me, I desire, I may be enabled to give myself up to, willingly with out murmuring who onely knows what measure of sufferings are necessary for me.[30]

Just as Anne Conway sought, in her philosophy, to account for the fact that the mind suffers when the body is in pain, so also she had to explain how a good and loving God could allow His creatures to suffer. Henry More insisted that even when we suffer God's providence is arranging all for the best: mere humans cannot see beyond their immediate horizons to God's larger designs. On more than one occasion he held up the example of Christ's suffering as an example to be followed:

[29] More to Anne Conway, 16 Feb. 1666, ibid., p. 130.
[30] Anne Conway to Henry More, 4 Feb. 1675/6, ibid., p. 421.

And now for assuageing of present smart what an opportunity have we in our greatest paines to exercise that most lovely and most divine virtue of all virtues, patient Humility, that most eminent accomplishment of our blessed Lord and Master Christ Jesus. For how near is our behaviour to his, when through fayth and patience we decently undergoe those great trialls God layes upon us, not repining against, nor at all distrusting his providence in the World, we haveing so ample testimonies of it every where, both in the affairs of men and universally in the whole Creation. And the serious remembrance of those dreadfull agonies Christ underwent on the crosse which certainly transcended any that any one does ever bear in this life, methinkes the sense of his love in those great sufferings may something sweeten and mitigate our present torments, we endeavouring to conform ourselves to his patience, whyle we are under the rod of our heavenly Father as he then was. Thus I conceive a serious and fixt consyderation of that direfull passion of our dear Saviour on the crosse may be usefully enlarged even to the slaking of bodily paine, as the brasen serpent his type was to the Israelites.[31]

In 1655, to help her cope with her affliction, More recommended that Anne Conway read the *Theologia Germanica*, especially its account of Christ 'patiently bearing what ever it was his Fathers pleasure to inflict upon him'.[32] On several occasions he reminded her that 'that little German companion', as he called it, 'is at hand to converse with as often as your Ladiship has so much respite as to be able to read'. But he was careful to remind her to 'take the Christianity of it, but leave the Melancholy of it', lest it produce an imbalance of the mind towards 'enthusiasm', as it had done in the case of the self-styled prophet, Matthew Wyer.[33] Anne Conway accepted her lot of suffering right to the end. Five years before her death she expressed her 'desire to be humbled under His [God's] righteous hand and wholly resigned to His good pleasure'.[34] However, she may have drawn more comfort from the illuminism of the book which More commended as consolation than he intended. For *Theologia Germanica* was only one of a whole number of mystical and heterodox religious texts which she read, and her reading of them seems to have been far more sympathetic than More's.

ENTHUSIASTS AND SECTARIANS

Perhaps on account of his own heterodox leanings (in respect of the doctrine of pre-existence, his illuminism and perfectionism), Henry More

[31] More to Anne Conway, 18 June [1654], ibid., p. 103.

[32] More to Anne Conway, 7 May [1655], ibid., p. 109. An English translation by Giles Randall was published in 1646 and reprinted in 1648. Everard Digby also translated it. Smith (1989), p. 115.

[33] *Conway Letters*, pp. 280, 110 and 525.

[34] Anne Conway to Henry More, 25 Sept. 1674, ibid., p. 534.

was severely exercised by the problem of heterodoxy, especially during the 1650s. In his *Enthusiasmus triumphatus* (1656) he attempted to lay down criteria for distinguishing between true prophecy and false inspiration, giving as examples 'enthusiasts' like the Quakers, the Behmenists, the self-styled prophet David George (David Joris), and 'sundry Chymists and Theosophists' (including Paracelsus).[35] If More's discussion served as a source of information about the beliefs of his subjects, it also offered an explanatory framework for containing their excesses and discouraging converts to their beliefs. Lady Conway, by contrast, shows a preparedness to challenge More's strictures on 'enthusiasts', so much so that he found himself obliged to defend his adverse view of Socinianism and Familism in his letters to her.[36] His objections to these sects centred largely on their heterodox and heretical doctrines, which he explained as the result of psychological imbalance (or 'enthusiasm'). But, connected with their mistaken religious doctrines, were errors of a philosophical kind, such as materialism. When telling Anne Conway about a visit from the Socinian leader Christoph Crell in 1662, More attributed Socinian theological errors to their 'incapacity of conceiving any thing but Body or Matter'.[37] Not long after this, while Anne Conway was in Ireland, we find her discussing another heresy, Mortalism, or Psychopannychism, the central tenet of which is that after death the soul dies or sleeps until the resurrection. Among the Hastings manuscripts at the Huntington Library in California is a letter defending Psychopannychism against the arguments More had mounted in his *An Explanation of the Grand Mystery of Godliness* (1660).[38] The letter does not bear the name of the recipient, who is addressed as 'Madame' and referred to as 'Your Ladiship'. The name of the author has been torn off. Its presence

[35] The Behmenists were followers of the German mystic Jacob Boehme (1575–1624) (see pp. 65–6 below); David Joris (1501–56) was an Anabaptist leader in the Netherlands; Paracelsus, or Theophrastus Phillippus Aureolus Bombastus von Hohenheim (1493–1541), was a Swiss physician and iatro-chemist, controversial for his anti-Galenic medical theories.

[36] *Conway Letters*, pp. 204, 208, 505, and 503–15. The Socinians were an anti-Trinitarian sect which flourished in Poland, and named after their Italian founders, Lelio Sozzini (1525–62) and his nephew Fausto (1539–1604). The Familists were members of the Family of Love founded by the Dutch perfectionist Henrik Niclaes (*c.* 1502–80). They practised an interior spirituality, but concealed their allegiance to the Family of Love by conforming outwardly to the norms of prescribed religion. See Hamilton (1981) and Moss (1981).

[37] *Conway Letters*, p. 208. Another Socinian mentioned in More's letters is Christoph Sand (Sandius), author of *Bibliotheca antitrinitarorum* and *De origine animae*. *Conway Letters*, p. 342.

[38] The letter is listed as 'Psychopannychite's letter to a Lady refuting Dr Moor's lecture', dated *c.* 1674, and placed after HA 14537 among the Hastings MSS, but with no list number. More writes against mortalism in *Mystery of Godliness*, book 1, chapters v–xi. More also refutes Psychopannychism in his poem, 'Antipsychopannycchia', published in his *Philosophical Poems* (1647). On Psychopannychism see Burns (1972).

among the Rawdon family papers suggests that it may have been written to Lady Conway during her visit to Ireland between 1661 and 1664.[39] In 1670 Anne Conway sent More a copy of *Speculum justitiae* by the Familist leader, 'H. N.' (Hendrik Niclaes). More responded with a refutation of Niclaes as a bogus prophet, and attacks Niclaes' view that the externals of religious worship are *adiaphora* (unimportant).[40]

A prominent strand in Anne Conway's investigation of sectarian doctrines is the topic of Christology. Many of those who caught Anne Conway's attention were guilty of Trinitarian errors, notably the Socinians who denied the divinity of Christ. Although, in her *Principles*, she insists on the divinity of Christ and retains the idea of a triune deity, her proposed rewriting of the doctrine of the Trinity by removing any reference to three distinct persons, and her reinterpretation of it as a triplicity of God, divine wisdom and divine will savours of anti-Trinitarianism.[41] Another purveyor of heterodox Christology was the German mystic Jacob Boehme, known as the 'Prophet of Gorlitz' or 'Teutonic Philosopher',[42] who proposed an internalist Christology, a kind of Christ within, which More criticised as having affinities with both Familism and Quakerism. John Worthington mentions that there was intense interest in Boehme in Lady Conway's circle at Ragley in 1668.[43] The moving spirit in this may have been Elizabeth Foxcroft, the sister of Benjamin Whichcote, who was living with Lady Conway as her companion, while her husband George Foxcroft was absent in India between 1664 and 1672. Mrs Foxcroft's interest in Boehme is evident from the fact that her niece's husband, John Worthington, bequeathed her books on Behmenism and Familism when he died in 1671.[44] We know of Anne Conway's interest in Boehme at second hand, via More, who discusses him in letters to her between 1668 and 1670. More wrote a critique of Boehme, his *Philosophiae teutonicae censura*, which takes the form of a private letter ('epistola privata') which he published in his *Opera philosophica*. Although he regarded Boehme as an enthusiast, More did not question either his piety or his sincerity, regarding him as an honest, pious, but misguided fool. More's criticisms centre on the philosophical errors that accompany

39 Another possible recipient of the letter is Major Rawdon's wife, but there is no evidence of her having any interest in abstruse religious topics. In the Hastings collection, the letter is provisionally dated 1674, perhaps on account of where it was found among the papers. There is no internal evidence to support this date. The reference to More's *Mystery of Godliness*, suggests an earlier date.

40 *Conway Letters*, pp. 503–5. *Adiaphora*: literally 'things indifferent'.

41 Conway, *Principles*, p. 10.

42 Bailey (1914) and Thune (1948). Also Smith (1989).

43 Worthington, *Diary*, vol. III, pp. 287, 291–2, 302–3.

44 On Elizabeth Foxcroft, see new *DNB*, An indicator of Foxcroft's interest in Boehme is the fact that Worthington left her several Behmenist books in his will. Worthington, *Diary*. She seems to have taken some interest in Quakerism before the arrival of Van Helmont at Ragley.

his religious heterodoxy, in particular his single-substance monism,[45] which More regarded as a form of materialistic pantheism. Among the issues which exercised More in his 'censure' of Boehme, we can gather something of the attraction of Boehme for the Ragley set.[46] Whether or not Anne Conway agreed with More's criticisms, she would have found in Jacob Boehme's writings an attempt to formulate a pious philosophy. It is quite possible that the relative mildness of More's censure of Boehme may be attributed to the persuasiveness of the defence of him by Anne Conway and Elizabeth Foxcroft. The association of Boehme with Quakerism was not unprecedented in the seventeenth century,[47] but More was more generous than most when he made the connection, conceding that Boehme was better than both the Quakers and the Familists. If Lady Conway was attracted by Boehme's theory of substance and his inward Christianity – further recommended to her by his piety and naivety – it is also possible that Behmenism served as a propaedeutic to Quakerism. The chronology of her interests, as recorded in her letters, certainly suggests this. The spiritual quest of many other converts to Quakerism often took a similar route through sectarian heterodoxy. The Quaker Charles Lloyd, remarking on Anne Conway's interest in the same sects, observes that his own path to Quakerism lay through the Seekers, the Levellers and the Behmenists.[48]

As in the case of Boehme, every 'prophet' investigated by Anne Conway subscribed to a cluster of unorthodox beliefs, philosophical as well as religious. Among these were unorthodox teachings on the relation of soul and body. In many cases they held that all things are constituted of a single substance, a position their enemies interpreted as materialist. Among the Psychopannychites, for example, Richard Overton's denial of the immortality of the soul in *Man's Mortalitie* (1643) is set among a cluster of unorthodox teachings on the nature of the soul. The Mortalism of John Reeve and Lodowick Muggleton is founded on a combination of scriptural authority and a monistic account of substance. In *Joyful News from Heaven* they argue that soul and body are one and the same: 'the Soul . . . is so essentially one with its Body, being both produced by natural Generation, that it is utterly incapable of any Kind of Life without it'. One of the supporting arguments for their position is the observation that the soul suffers when pain is inflicted on the body. Anticipating Anne Conway, they observe:

[45] On Boehme's theory of substance, see Principe and Weeks (1989).

[46] For More's view of Boehme, see Hutton (1992). More also discusses Boehme in *Divine Dialogues* (London, 1668).

[47] See, for example, Lodowick Muggleton, *A Looking Glass for George Fox* (London, 1667).

[48] BL MS Additional 23,217, fol. 25.

Now, if the Body be under some extream Pain, is not all the Light or Life in Man sensible of it? Yea, doth it not participate of that very Misery, by being restless throughout, until the Extremity of its Pains be over. If this be so, as I am certain it is, what then is there in Man that can possible escape Death, when the Body returns to its Dust?[49]

The only sect named in Conway's *Principles* is the Ranters, though how deep her knowledge of their beliefs was we can only speculate. While she may have shared some ideas (for example, belief in animal souls),[50] she was strongly critical of them on two grounds: first, their pantheism, resulting from their claim that 'all things are one substance'. She charges them with the same error with which she charges Spinoza, namely that 'they confuse God with his creatures, as if these two notions were only one essential thing'.[51] Her second criticism is connected to this: their denial of Christ as mediator between God and creatures. This criticism underlines the fact that Anne Conway was alive to the pantheistic implications of her system, a problem which she addressed, as we shall see, by positing a Middle Nature between God and the world.

APOCALYPTICISM

Another aspect of Anne Conway's religious complexion which should be mentioned is millenarianism. Some of the longest and most fervent letters written to her by More concern interpretations of the apocalypse. More's deep interest in interpreting biblical prophecy is evident from the high proportion of books on the subject which he published between 1660 and 1687. His letters on apocalypticism were written in response to Anne Conway's questions, and he acknowledged that she was more widely read on the subject than he.[52] Given the breadth of apocalyptical scholarship which his own writings on the subject bespeak, his remark suggests that Anne Conway must have had a stupendous knowledge of the subject. If so, it does not show through in either her extant letters or her treatise. Nonetheless, an enormous and lively interest in prophecy and millenarianism is a fact of seventeenth-century life which is now hard to imagine, let alone understand. This was undoubtedly fired in part by the upheavals of civil war. It has been argued that, in the aftermath of sectarian excesses

[49] Lodowick Muggleton and John Reeve, *Joyful News from Heaven* [London, 1658], pp. 10–13.
[50] See Harrison (1993). Anne Conway mentions one Ranter, Rice (or Rhys) John, in a letter of 1675, in which she denies the Ranters are connected to the Quakers. *Conway Letters*, p. 408.
[51] Conway, *Principles*, p. 28. [52] *Conway Letters*, p. 515.

and the subversive political application of millenarianism during the interregnum, there was a concerted attempt to tone down, if not playdown, the role of prophecy in religion after the Restoration. This did not mean an end to it: on the contrary, the excitement generated by the appearance in the Ottoman Empire of a self-proclaimed Jewish Messiah, Sabbatai Sevi, is evidence of the continuing meaningfulness of millenarianism in seventeenth-century culture.[53]

Henry More's interest in prophecy was a bookish interest, founded in biblical exegesis, though with immediate application to practical Christianity. Indeed, part of his purpose in publishing on the subject was probably to rescue the prophetic as part of Church of England theology, at a time when it had fallen into disrepute because of the use made of it by sectarian republicans.[54] More had studied with the seventeenth-century Bible scholar, Joseph Mede (1586–1638), also a fellow of Christ's College, whose scheme for interpreting the book of Revelation was enormously influential in the seventeenth century. More was himself a follower of Mede, though he made various alterations to Mede's prophetic scheme.[55] His letters to Lady Conway largely consist in defences of his interpretations against objections raised by her to his synchronisation of the visions of St John – for example, whether the pouring out of the seven vials is synchronous with the sounding of the sixth trumpet. In 1671 he gives 'my answer to Your Ladiships Objections against my placing of the phialls within the seventh Trumpett'.[56] More indicates that she posed such questions as a diversion, a 'kinde and ingenious project for diverting me from my Melancholy'.[57]

The seriousness of his answers indicates that the subject was by no means purely recreational. Lady Conway's questions about the apocalypse overlap with her interest in Familism and Behmenism, and form part of her investigations of Quakerism. She may, therefore, have been investigating the truth claims of their religious leaders by examining biblical prediction. The Quakers, whom she encountered at around this time, certainly interpreted the Bible as predicting their own appearance on the stage of history.[58] Another reason for her interest was most likely the issue of the conversion of the Jews: her investigations of the Jewish mystical teachings contained in the kabbalah follow on from these enquiries about the shape of the end of time.

[53] Scholem (1973), Wall (1987a and b). [54] Hutton (1995a).
[55] Hutton (1994), Berg (1988). [56] *Conway Letters*, p. 527.
[57] Ibid., p. 521. [58] As did George Keith. See p. 192 below.

ORIGEN

Among the strands of heterodox Christianity to which Anne Conway was exposed through her association with Henry More, were the teachings of the Church Father, Origen, which enjoyed something of a renaissance in England between 1658 and 1662. It was during this time that William Spencer published his translation of *Contra Celsus*.[59] Origen was a particularly important figure in the theology of Cambridge Platonism, especially for Henry More who regarded him as the 'Miracle of the Christian World',[60] notwithstanding the fact that his championship of Origen was regarded with suspicion by the Restoration church establishment. It was through Origen's doctrine of the pre-existence of souls that More found a solution to the problem of how to reconcile God's justice, as manifest in his providential design, with the problem of sin and free will.[61] It was most likely Anne Conway's interest in the problem of evil which led More in 1661 to recommend to her the anonymously published summary of Origen's teachings, *Letter of Resolution Concerning Origen.* More offered to send a copy, believing that she 'might take some pleasure in persuing it' because he was 'persuaded it will please you better than any Romance'.[62] How detailed her knowledge of Origen was we cannot be sure. She certainly knew of More's championship of the doctrine of the pre-existence of souls in his poems, his *Immortality of the Soul* (1659) and his *Explanation of the Grand Mystery of Godliness* (1660). She also read Joseph Glanvill's Origenist *Lux orientalis* which she asked More to obtain for her in 1662. She may also have been familiar with William Spencer's edition of Origen's *Contra Celsus*, published in Cambridge in 1658. Anne Conway was under no illusions about the suspicion with which Origen was viewed in ecclesiastical circles, and she was well aware that *A Letter of Resolution* was considered 'a dangerous book' by the academic establishment, on account of its 'unsound opinions'.[63] And she knew very well the difficulties More encountered on account of his Origenism.

Lady Conway does not actually mention Origen's name, but he is the most important Christian authority for the doctrine of universal salvation (*apocotastasis*) to which she subscribed. This and other Origenist analogues

[59] Origen, *Origenes contra Celsus libri octo*, trans. William Spencer (Cambridge, 1658). Spencer incorporates the notes of David Hoeschelius. On Origen, see Walker (1964) and Baldi (1996).

[60] More, *A Collection*, Preface, p. xxi. More also praises Origen in section xvi of the *Praefatio generalis* of his *Opera philosophica, H. Mori Cantabrigiensis opera omnia* 3 vols. (London, 1675–9), vol. II.

[61] Hutton (1996a). He did not, apparently, subscribe to the Origenist doctrine of universal salvation. See Walker (1964).

[62] *Conway Letters*, pp. 192 and 195. [63] Ibid., p. 194.

in Anne Conway's system suggest she had direct knowledge of his work. Although she did not, apparently, share Henry More's belief in the Origenist doctrine of the pre-existence of souls, there are other aspects of her thinking which are strikingly Origenist, especially her denial of the eternity of hell and her argument for universal salvation. She bases her arguments for these on her conception of God as wise and good, and not upon the authority of the Fathers. Since God is 'charity and kindness itself', it is entirely *in*consistent with His nature to punish His creatures perpetually: 'For the common notion of God's justice, namely that whatever the sin, it is punished by hell fire, and this without end, has generated a horrible idea of God in all men, as if he were a cruel tyrant rather than a benign father to all his creatures.'[64] It is, likewise, entirely consistent with divine goodness that punishment for sin should be ameliorative, or, as Anne Conway puts it, 'medicinal': 'Just as all the punishments inflicted by God on his creatures are in proportion to their sins, so they tend, even the worst, to their good and to their restoration and they are so medicinal as to cure these sickly creatures and restore them to a better condition.'[65] She emphasises the salvific: 'all degrees and all kinds of sin have their appropriate punishments, and all these punishments tend toward the good of the creatures, so that the grace of God will prevail over judgment and judgment turn into victory for the salvation and restoration of the creatures'.[66] Other parallels with Origen's teachings include her view that the physicality of bodies, that is, the quasi-corporeal modes of the original substance, has a punitive function, and her idea that salvation entails refining the corporeality and reconstituting it in its original purity as spirit. Origen, like Anne Conway, proposes a principle of change running through all created things – change which can be both moral (from good to bad or bad to good) and ontological (from one level of being to another, up or down the ontological hierarchy). Furthermore, Origen's account of the transmigration of souls bears striking resemblance to Anne Conway's account of the correlation of moral and physical states, and the capacity for beings to ascend and descend the moral and ontological scale. In the Greek version of *Peri Archon* (*On First Principles*) book I, chapter viii, Origen invokes Plato's account of the soul in the *Phaedrus* when he writes of the soul having wings which it loses when it inclines to wickedness. He discusses the moral decline of the soul as *incorporation of the soul*, that is, the soul's acquisition of physical properties (principally weight) and its becoming attached to a body. Moreover, the greater the transgression of the

[64] Conway, *Principles*, p. 37. [65] Ibid., p. 38.

[66] Ibid., p. 37. In book III, chapter vi of *Peri Archon*, Origen regards the punishments of Hell as part of a process of purgation from sin.

soul, the lower in the ontological hierarchy it will be placed. In this way souls work their way down the scale of being:

> But by some inclination towards evil these souls lose their wings and come into bodies, first of men; then through their association with the irrational passions, after the allotted span of human life, they are changed into beasts; from which they sink to the level of insensate nature. Thus that which is by nature fine and mobile, namely the soul, first becomes heavy and weighed down, and because of its wickedness comes to dwell in a human body; after that, when the faculty of reason is extinguished, it lives the life of an irrational animal; and finally even the gracious gift of sensation is withdrawn and it changes into the insensate life of a plant.[67]

The reverse process is also possible, according to Origen. And in book II, chapter x, he explains how the 'natural body' will become a 'spiritual body' in the restorative process. In book III, chapter vi he argues that it is the same body that will be resurrected, with the difference that it will have been refined into a 'vessel of honour':

> we must understand that there is not one body which we now use in lowliness and corruption and weakness, and a different one which we are to use hereafter in incorruption and power and glory, but that this same body, having cast off the weaknesses of its present existence, will be transformed into a thing of glory and made spiritual, with the result that what was a vessel of dishonour shall itself be purified and become a vessel of honour and a habitation of blessedness.[68]

In so far as she can be said to be an Origenist in spirit, Anne Conway was, arguably, a more thorough-going Origenist than Henry More, who did not subscribe to Origen's doctrine of universal salvation or his denial of the eternity of hell. Conway's system tends towards pantheism, on the one hand, and, on the other, an ecumenism broader than even the average liberal churchman of those times was prepared to allow. There is, therefore, a real sense in which the resulting theological complexion of her treatise justifies the fears of Origen's opponents that his teachings opened the way to heterodoxy, if not heresy. Her familiarity with Origen's teachings, and her belief that they offered a better solution to problems of ethics and salvation than did orthodox Christian doctrine, undoubtedly predisposed her to Quakerism and kabbalism (which will be discussed in later chapters). In all likelihood her acquaintance with Origen's teachings, which predates her exposure to the kabbalah and Quakerism, predisposed her to regard them as different aspects of the same truth.

[67] Origen, *On First Principles* I.viii, trans. G. W. Butterworth (London, 1936), p. 73.
[68] Ibid. III.vi.

Anne Conway's investigations of different strands of religious belief was an on-going process which continued through the 1650s and 1660s, forming a backdrop to her philosophical studies, and which set the stage for her encounter with Quakerism in the 1670s. Prior to dealing with that, the next chapters will focus on her philosophical circle: Henry More, John Finch and Francis Mercury van Helmont.

CHAPTER 4

Anne Conway and Henry More

'Your Ladiships humbly-devoted Servant'

In Anne Conway's immediate circle three figures played an especially important part in her intellectual life: her brother John Finch, her teacher Henry More, and the companion of her last years, Francis Mercury van Helmont. Of these, it would be difficult to overestimate the significance for her of Henry More. Not only, as we have seen, was More responsible for her initial philosophical education, but he became and remained a personal friend for the rest of her life. This does not mean that they were of like mind in all things. On the contrary, in her religious life (by her sympathy with and ultimate conversion to Quakerism) and in her philosophy (especially her repudiation of dualism), Anne Conway would take a position independent of his. And at times she was directly critical of his theories. In her later years there is no doubt that Francis Mercury van Helmont came to be another strong influence. But in Henry More Anne Conway had a loyal intellectual companion, with whom she could discuss philosophical and religious issues, and who remained in close contact with her for longer than any other individual apart from her husband. The prolonged absence of John Finch in Italy, and later in Turkey, probably reinforced Anne Conway's reliance on More as a substitute intellectual companion. The length and depth of More's association with Anne Conway means that it is impossible to deal with all aspects of it within the confines of a single chapter. In this chapter I shall discuss the philosophical aspects of their relationship, as it developed alongside their personal friendship.

Their later philosophical differences notwithstanding, More's thought provided a viewing frame through which, initially, she engaged with the intellectual world. Since they first became acquainted as teacher and pupil, it seems natural to assume that their intellectual exchange would be dominated by More, who had more to impart to Lady Conway than the other way around. In fact, from the outset, he proposed the obverse, namely that she should set the agenda for discussion, and he would respond – 'As a friend I shall discuss with you what you shall be pleased to propound', he suggested at the beginning.[1] More's letters seem to bear this out: although most of her letters are lost, his extant replies often include responses to questions put by her. Even in the earliest stages of their correspondence, it is Anne Conway who poses the questions and objections and More who undertakes to comment on her 'ingenious proposalls' and to 'satisfy all your objections'.[2] When in 1651 More proposed continuing their correspondence, he asked her to set the topics of discussion: 'yourself must chuse according to the present Light of your own minde'.[3]

A PHILOSOPHICAL FRIENDSHIP

As a friendship between members of the opposite sex, the friendship of Anne Conway and Henry More was remarkable for its time. Friendships between men and women were not unknown in the seventeenth century – other examples are Descartes' friendship with Princess Elizabeth, and John Evelyn's with Margaret Godolphin.[4] But such friendships were unusual, as Jeremy Taylor acknowledged in his *Discourse of the Nature and Offices of Friendship* (first published 1657), where he defends his view that there can be friendship between men and women.[5] It was, moreover, a friendship across differences of age and class, which developed from a tutorial programme of philosophy and was continued, at More's express wish, as a dialogue of ideas. This transition occurred in 1651 when John Finch departed for Europe, and More, grieved by the loss of his young friend, proposed to Anne Conway the continuation of 'our intercourses and conferences concerning Des Cartes philosophy'. He did so as a compensation to both of them for the loss of Finch's company: 'Mr Finch's absence being as contrary to your Ladiships desires and myne. May this our common misery be mitigated by a remedy which will salve us both, viz. our intercourses and conferences concerning Des Cartes philosophy.'[6] He found that his hopes in this were anticipated by both Anne Conway and her brother:

[1] *Conway Letters*, p. 54. [2] Ibid., p. 489. Letter dated 1651.
[3] Ibid., p. 21. [4] Harris (2003).
[5] Jeremy Taylor, *The Whole Works*, ed. R. Heber, 10 vols. (London, 1856), vol. I. Taylor's *Discourse* was dedicated to the poet, Katherine Philips (1631–64) and published the year before he moved to the Rawdon–Conway household in Portmore. It is therefore probable that Katherine Philips and Anne Conway knew of each other.
[6] *Conway Letters*, p. 53.

What Mr Finch's letters and your own seem so earnestly to desire, is very easy to be obtain'd, it being the desire of a third party of us as well as you two, I mean of my selfe, to whom no such compensation for the absence of so dear a friend can be made, as the continuance of this intercourse of letters betwixt us.[7]

This compensation for the loss of John Finch entailed a substitution of sister for brother: More allowed himself direct expression of his admiration and affection for her by depicting her as John Finch's other self: 'For that candour, freeness and perspicacity of witt which I have observed in your brother is so eminent in yourself, that whyle I converse with you, the better part of him is still, present here in England, and will salute me at every arrivall of your letters to my hands.'[8] So the transition was made from a master–pupil relationship to a friendship between equals, by means of imagining sister as brother.

As the relationship developed, they were faced with a problem of definition – of finding a discursive space for their relationship. Friendship across the social divide between gentleman and aristocrat could not ignore inequalities of rank (as is evident from More's friendship with John Finch). But, even without the complicating factor of differential status, friendship across the gender divide confounded conventions of address and propriety. At the early stages of this new relationship, More was acutely aware of the problem of finding an appropriate language register, though, with time, this problem recedes. More's awkwardness may be illustrated from two letters written after his return from a visit to Anne Conway.[9] In the first of these letters he attempted to put his feelings into words, but, even as he does so, he appears embarrassed at his own temerity. Describing his conversation with her as 'the greatest enjoyment in this World ever afforded to me', he reaches for a model of affection combining Ciceronian friendship with Platonic idealism, while apologising for his directness:

I profess, Madame, I never knew what belonged to the sweetness of friendship before I met with so eminent an example of that virtue, though I be ashamed to use so familiar a phrase, there being that great inequality of our persons that there is, but I cannot command my self from most affectionately loving her, whom it is my duty aloof of to honour and adore. Nor is love itself, as it is a testimony of an honourable respect, and arises out of an opinion of eminency of worth in the party we love, incompetible to the highest Objects.[10]

[7] Ibid. [8] Ibid.

[9] These letters are printed as *Conway Letters* numbers 70 and 94a. Both are written in January, but neither is dated as to year. In my revised edition I conjectured that both date from 1658–9. Marjorie Nicolson proposed the earlier date of 1655–6.

[10] Ibid., p. 129.

At this point he stalls at his directness: 'But discretion bids me temper myself, and abstain from venturing far into so delicious a theme.' The problem is not just the social awkwardness of male writing to female, older man writing to younger person, don addressing countess. It is also the unease that language will misrepresent him, that such outright expressions of 'sincere affection' for her 'both as my fellow Christian and my choicest friend',[11] will be mistaken for mere compliment ('skill in courtship'). This is underlined in his reply to her (no longer extant) response: 'I profess Madame, there is no artifice in my carriage nor could any thing come from me to such as he does most entirely and affectionately love and honour.'[12] A decade after their first contact, the anxiety about where each stood in relation to the other appears to have receded. Their relationship is now well established and can be taken for granted, without the need of definition and its attendant dangers of misconstruction. There is no more discussion of the nature of their friendship. Statements of how much each values the other are less frequent but unselfconscious when they do arise. The formalities are simple Sir/Ladiship and each signs off as the other's 'affectionate and humble servant'. They discuss mutual interests without feeling the need to make overt references to each other's cleverness or gracious condescension. Their discussions of such topics as kabbalism, Quakerism and the book of Revelation are unimpeded by the formalities of social deference. In philosophy and theology they seem to have found common ground where the differences of sex, rank and age are dissolved into the minutiae of interpreting the significance of prophecies or unlocking the mysteries of the kabbalah. It is a meeting of minds for which More invokes the transcendent language of Platonic love:

But if the sense and meaning of my writings be the Picture of my soul, your soul when you read them is transformed into the same image, wch if I had timely consydered I should have been more carefull of what I writt, that the Picture of your minde yt my writings at any time transfigured it into, might bear the better proportion and subtleness with the beauty of your body.[13]

The claims of friendship are still invoked on occasion, however. Writing in May 1664, Anne Conway reports on 'the great increase of my distemper', and that she is subject of 'violent paines' and 'very little out of my bed'. She mentions her illness, confident that she can do so partly out of the right of friendship, 'because that freindship you are pleased to allow me seemes to give you some concerne in what befalls me'.[14] At her express request, More consented not to take her 'affliction so much to heart', understanding her

[11] Ibid., p. 131. [12] Ibid., p. 498. [13] Ibid., p. 499. [14] Ibid., p. 224.

wish as 'a great demonstration of your reall affection to me'.[15] Lady Conway's injunction did not stop More from offering comfort for her sufferings. He proved a devoted and loyal friend, who stood by her in periods of crisis. In 1658, reporting his wife's illness to his brother-in-law, Lord Conway told him, 'M^{r}. More hath continued in the house with us, since she fell into this condition.'[16] At times like this when he was not present in the Conway household, More wrote to her in order to cheer her spirits. On one occasion he describes his letter as 'children's prattle of mine to assuage your paines'.[17] More continued to write to her to the very end of her life – his last extant letter to her is dated January 1679 – even when he feared that, on account of her illness, 'it might be but a disturbance rather then a diversion'.[18]

Anne Conway valued More's friendship as much as he did hers. She enjoyed his company and was always solicitous about his personal well-being. This is particularly apparent from letters written during her trip to Ireland in 1662, when visits from him were out of the question, and where the courier service was irregular. She wrote to him in 1662:

> I have received yours of Nov. 22 which hath in some measure eased me of the great inquietude I was in before through the want of your letters, but nothing can comfort me for the want of your excellent company which though you seeme out of modesty to undervalue, were it to be purchased at any rate, I should soone make it appear how much it is esteemed by me, more than any thing either England or Ireland can afford, but there is no title to be had to your kindesse except that of your goodnesse and therefore with out that should encline you to favour me so much (which I cannot deserve) I must dispair of the happinesse of ever seeing you here.[19]

As might be expected, Anne Conway used her influence to try to get him 'some better preferment, more suitable to his deserts'.[20] He, however, declined all offers of preferment, though he undoubtedly benefited from the protection of the Conways.[21] His letters record touching examples of her generosity – such as when she bought him a set of laboratory equipment in 1675.[22]

Their extant correspondence contains no direct discussion of More's philosophy. This may be because so many of Anne Conway's letters have not survived. The topics of their epistolary discussions include a whole

[15] Ibid., p. 131.
[16] Lord Conway to Major Rawdon, 17 Aug. 1658, Hastings MSS, HA 14363.
[17] *Conway Letters*, p. 342. [18] Ibid., p. 447. [19] Ibid., pp. 208–9. [20] Ibid., p. 234.
[21] This was especially true shortly after the Restoration, when there were moves to try to oust More from his fellowship in Cambridge. See Nicolson (1929–30).
[22] *Conway Letters*, p. 405.

range of subjects whose relevance to philosophy appears remote today: the apocalypse, the kabbalah, religious enthusiasm (I deal with these aspects of Conway's interests in other chapters), as well as personal news. Although her side of the correspondence has largely been lost, we have More's testimony to Anne Conway's independence of mind. She was, according to More, strongly independent in her thinking: 'one that would not give up her judgement entirely unto any'.[23] The few letters of hers that do survive present a remarkably contrastive picture, since, as already noted in the first chapter, her self-presentation is so unassuming and self-deprecating – a stance matched only by the deferential tone of More's replies.

The paucity of discussion of More's writings in the correspondence does not mean that Anne Conway never ventured her opinions on his philosophy. As we have already noted, his letters indicate that she could be probing, putting him 'to my plunges' for answers. More's own writings too are a resource for reconstructing Anne Conway's intellectual life, especially since these writings probably owe more to his debates with her than might appear. For example, as will become apparent, the scholia added to later editions contain answers to objections raised to his arguments and ideas that must have formed part of his discussions with Lady Conway. I shall discuss identifiable examples later on.

THE PHILOSOPHY OF HENRY MORE

Since Henry More is nowadays regarded as a secondary figure in the history of philosophy, it is easy to dismiss him as inconsequential. But in his own time he came to be highly respected as a theologian and a philosopher. Along with his friend Ralph Cudworth, he was one of the leading intellectual lights of the University of Cambridge in the Commonwealth and Restoration period. Like Cudworth, he was abreast of contemporary developments in philosophy and science, although, again like Cudworth, his interest in these areas stemmed from clear religious priorities. More's function as a key enabling figure in Anne Conway's philosophical life should not obscure the fact that theirs was a two-way exchange, and that her impact on the shape and detail of his philosophy was significant, possibly formative. His career as a philosopher is practically co-terminous with his friendship with her. His first published philosophical works appeared during the first decade of their philosophical dialogue: *An Antidote Against Atheism* (1653), followed in 1655 by *Conjectura cabbalistica* and in 1659 by *Of the Immortality*

[23] Ward, *Life*, p. 121.

of the Soul. All three are linked to the Conways: *An Antidote* was dedicated to Anne Conway, *Of the Immortality* to her husband. According to More's biographer, Richard Ward, it was at her instigation that he wrote *Conjectura cabbalistica* and his critique of Jacob Boehme, *Philosophiae teutonicae censura*.[24] Marjorie Nicolson has suggested that More's *Divine Dialogues* records conversations at the Conway residence at Ragley.[25]

More first came to public attention as a poet: in the 1640s he published a series of lengthy allegorical poems which propound a philosophy of the soul framed in Plotinian terms. These poems and his later *Divine Dialogues* were directed at a popular philosophical audience. It may well have been through his poems that Anne Conway first became aware of his existence. Indeed, they may well have served as a propaedeutic to her later philosophical studies. She certainly valued them sufficiently to make presents of them to friends and acquaintances. More's correspondence with Descartes (1648–9), which immediately antedates his introduction to Anne Conway marks the debut of his career as a philosopher.[26] With the appearance of his *A Collection of Several Philosophical Writings* in 1662, his reputation as a philosopher was consolidated. It reached its apogee with the Latin translation of his *Opera omnia* in 1657–9. Throughout his life More was deeply interested in religious questions. His *An Explanation of the Grand Mystery of Godliness* (1660) sets out the grounds of his relatively tolerant Christianity (see chapter 3). Subsequently he published many studies on the interpretation of prophecy, and became involved in the study of the Jewish kabbalah.

More's philosophical formation belongs to the time when Aristotelianism, though still strong in the academies, was on the wane. The combination of the discoveries of Copernicus and the mechanics of Galileo, and the corrosive effects of scepticism had served to undermine Aristotle's philosophy as the framework of scientific and philosophical enquiry. Revolutionary proposals for new beginnings in these fields had been proposed by figures like Francis Bacon and Herbert of Cherbury, and the way was open for new contenders to propose new systems of thought, among whom Descartes and Hobbes were the most prominent. The impact of these developments on More is evident from his early admiration for Descartes, whom, as we have already noted, he held in high regard (initially, at any rate) as a philosopher capable of providing a coherent system of philosophy to replace scholastic

[24] Ibid., p. 122. Anne Conway's interest in Jacob Boehme was probably excited by her companion, Elizabeth Foxcroft. See p. 65 above. On More and Boehme, see Hutton (1990b).

[25] *Conway Letters*, p. 254.

[26] More's correspondence with Descartes was not published until 1657. Descartes, *Lettres*.

Aristotelianism. More also embraced Copernicanism and the atomistic physics revived by Gassendi. At the same time, like so many of his contemporaries, he abhorred the philosophy of Thomas Hobbes as materialist and determinist, and therefore atheistic.[27]

More's philosophical preference for Platonism has earned him and the other Cambridge Platonists their sobriquet. Assessing More's Platonism is not easy, because it runs counter to modern categories of philosophical history. His example amply illustrates the awkwardness of the ancient–modern distinction as a principle of classification in the history of philosophy. His recourse to the philosophy of Plato and his followers was born of the same dissatisfaction with Aristotelianism that fuelled the philosophical revolution of the seventeenth century. His Platonism, therefore, should not be seen as backward-looking nostalgia for antiquity, but must be set alongside his engagement with contemporary philosophical developments. Indeed, he regarded Platonism as compatible with Cartesianism, like the opposite sides of the same coin. More's appeal to ancient philosophy accorded with the Renaissance tradition of *philosophia perennis*, or perennial philosophy, according to which philosophical truth is the same for all times, though there is variation in the degree to which philosophers at different times have grasped it. The historical genealogy sustained by the perennial philosophy traced a line of transmission from the time of Adam through Moses, to the Egyptians, to the Greeks and thence to the rest of Europe. According to More, all true philosophy can be traced back to Pythagoras, who in turn derived his philosophy from 'the ancient Judaical Cabbala'. Platonism and Cartesianism are later manifestations of this ancient philosophy. In the preface to his *Collection of Several Philosophical Writings*, More traces 'the succession of the Pythagorick School' in the so-called 'Italick School', from Pherecydes through to Democritus and Epicurus. In the hands of Leucippus and Democritus, the 'Physical or Mechanical' part was separated from 'the Theological or Metaphysical', a development which had dire consequences in the atheistic philosophy of their successor, Epicurus.[28] Aristotle and Plato are just two philosophers among many, albeit very important ones, whose intellectual grasp exceeded that of others. More's admiration of Plato and his followers among the ancients was not, therefore, in conflict with his (albeit muted) respect for Aristotle, on the one hand, or his admiration for Descartes, on the other. Rather, the perennial-philosophy model accounts for why he regarded some contemporary philosophy as a revival of ancient

[27] More's assessment of Hobbes was not unusual for his time. See below chapter 5 and Mintz (1962).
[28] More, *A Collection*, Preface General, p. xvii.

theories. As he explained in his *A Collection of Philosophical Writings*, starting from separate points – Descartes from the philosophy of Democritus, More from the 'high and airey hills of Platonisme' – their philosophies combined to reconstitute the original philosophy compatible with the word of God. More's most extensive elaboration of the perennial philosophy comes in his *Conjectura cabbalistica* (1653), written at the behest of Anne Conway, in which he presents the true philosophy as a revived Pythagoreanism occulted in the symbolic language of the first chapter of Genesis. Familiarity with this concept contributed to Lady Conway's subsequent receptivity to kabbalism.

APOLOGETICS

As a philosopher, More dedicated his intellectual talents to the defence of religious belief in a rational and sceptical age. He presented himself as a 'fisher for philosophers', targeting those whose beliefs were, as he saw it, in danger of being undermined by the claims of reason. With the likes of Thomas Hobbes in mind, he invested much intellectual energy in arguing for the existence of spiritual substance, persuaded that materialism was the philosophical concomitant of atheism. As he put it in the preface of *Immortality of the Soul*, 'That saying is no less true in Politicks, *No Bishop, no King*, than this in metaphysicks, *No Spirit no God*'.[29] In formulating a rational apologetics, More attempted to frame his arguments in terms that would convince rational non-believers, basing his arguments on 'the eternal Characters of the Minde of Man, and the known *Phaenomena* of Nature'.[30] For example, he commences his *Of the Immortality of the Soul* with a series of axioms, adopting and adapting the Cartesian geometrical method of reasoning.

GOD

More, like his fellow Cambridge Platonists, was firmly convinced of the compatibility of reason and religious belief. Central to both his philosophy and his theology was his conception of God. In opposition to the voluntaristic theology of contemporary Calvinism, More took what is sometimes referred to as an intellectualist position. That is to say he emphasised the wisdom, goodness and justice of God. In his account of the divine attributes More adopts Descartes' argument for the existence of God from the idea of

[29] Ibid. More, *Antidote*, p. 142. [30] Ibid., Preface, p. 1.

a 'supremely perfect being' – God is, in More's words '*An Essence* or *Being fully and absolutely Perfect*'. The idea of such a being is innate to the human mind, although, More conceded, 'not alwayes acting, in the Soul of man'.[31] From the perfection of God, More derived not just his existence, but the divine attributes:

the perfections comprehended in this Notion of a *Being absolutely and fully Perfect*, I think I may securely nominate these; *Self-subsistency, Immateriality, Infinity as well of Duration as Essence, Immensity of Goodnesse, Omnisciency, Omnipotency*, and *Necessity of Existence*. Let this therefore be a Description of a Being absolutely Perfect, That it is a *Spirit, Eternall, Infinite in Essence and Goodnesse, Omniscient, Omnipotent, and of it self necessarily existent*. All which Attributes being Attributes of the *highest Perfection* that falls under the apprehension of man, and having no discoverable imperfection interwoven with them, must of necessity be attributed to that which we conceive *absolutely and full Perfect*.[32]

This definition encapsulates both his debt to Descartes and his difference from him. More's God is not conceived as an abstract *philosophers' god*, nor as a merely theistic supreme being. Rather, More's conception adapts Descartes' *ens perfectissimum* (most perfect being) to meet the requirements of a benign Christianity where God is above all a loving God, supremely concerned for the well-being of his creation. The perfection of God, best exemplified in the attributes of God's goodness, wisdom and justice, is reflected in the orderly constitution of the created world. More's anti-voluntarist emphasis on God's wisdom and justice sets him apart from Descartes every bit as much as from the Calvinist dogmatists of mid-seventeenth-century Cambridge.

SPIRIT AND MATTER

The central theme of More's philosophy is his philosophy of spirit, or pneumatology, in which spirit is conceived as incorporeal substance and efficient cause, and defined antithetically to the mechanical concept of body as extended substance. A major attraction of the mechanical philosophy of Descartes for More (as also for Cudworth) was precisely that it appeared to offer a solid foundation for demonstrating the existence of incorporeal agents. According to the mechanical hypothesis, matter is nothing but extension: inert, passive and devoid of properties. Matter cannot, therefore, initiate motion, nor yet provide the functions of life and mind. Dissatisfied with the Cartesian account of the interaction of soul and body, and therefore

[31] Ibid. [32] Ibid., p. 14.

of life itself, More proposed instead that the operations of nature, like the government of mind over body, be explained in terms of the action of spirit. In the *Immortality of the Soul*, More defines body and spirit in equivalent but converse terms.

I will define therefore *a Spirit* thus, *A Substance penetrable and indiscerpible.* The fitness of which Definition will be the better understood, if we divide *Substance* in generall into these first kindes, viz. *Body* and *Spirit*, and then define *Body* to be *A Substance impenetrable and discerpible.* Whence the contrary kind to this is fitly defined, *A Substance penetrable and indiscerpible.*[33]

What distinguishes material substance from other types of extended substance is what could be called its tactile quality: what Locke later called 'solidity', and for which More used the term, 'impenetrability'. Although analogous to body in respect of extension, spirit is to be distinguished from material substance by activity:

Now I appeal to any man that can set aside prejudice, and has the free use of his Faculties, whether every term in the Definition of a *Spirit* be not as intelligible and congruous to Reason, as in that of a *Body*, for the precise Notion of *Substance* is the same in both, in which, I conceive, is comprised *Extension* and *Activity*, either connate or communicated.[34]

More first proposed that spirit is extended substance in order to try to overcome a major difficulty in Cartesian dualism, namely that Descartes could not satisfactorily explain how spirit moves body. However, having defined body and spirit in mutually exclusive terms, he was confronted by the same problem as Descartes. Part of the solution he proposed was the one we noted in chapter 2 – that motion is communicated by *affect* rather than *impact*. Motion is brought about not by matter colliding with matter, but by spirit infusing the matter. Motion is *activated in* a body not *transmitted* to it from another body already in motion. But More also had to explain how incorporeal substance inheres in the corporeal substance which it activates. In order to do so he advanced his hypothesis of 'vital congruity', according to which both soul and body are predisposed to receive one another and be united in a kind of harmony rather than mechanically. In some respects More's concept of *vital congruity* could be described as proto-Leibnizian – an embryonic theory of the pre-established harmony of soul and body.

33 More, *Immortality*, p. 21, in *A Collection*.

34 Ibid. More restates his definition of spirit more fully in *Enchiridion metaphysicum* (London and Cambridge, 1671), chapters 27 and 28. These chapters were printed in English translation in the 1682 edition of Glanvill's *Sadducismus triumphatus*.

this *Union of the Soul with Matter* does not arise from any such gross *Mechanical* way, as when two Bodies stick one in another by reason of any toughness and viscosity, or streight commissure of parts; but from a *congruity* of another nature, which I know not better how to term then *Vital* . . . Not that there is any *Life* in the *Matter* with which this in the *Soul* should sympathize and unite; but it is termed *Vital* because it makes the *Matter* a *congruous* Subject for the Soul to reside in and exercise the functions of *life*.[35]

More further elaborates his hypothesis of vital congruity in the 'Appendix' to his *Antidote Against Atheism*, where he imputes to spirit a 'speciall faculty' which he names 'hylopathia'. In answer to the objection that if spirit is so pervious it cannot inhere in a solid body, never mind move it, More argues that spirits have the capacity to emit a quasi-corporeal filler which will attach it to the body it occupies. Hylopathia is

a power in a Spirit of offering so near to a corporeal emanation from the Center of life, that it will so perfectly fill the receptivity of matter into which it has penetrated, that it is very difficult or impossible for any other Spirit to possess the same; and therefore of becoming hereby so firmly and closely united to a Body as both to actuate and to be acted upon, to affect and be affected thereby.[36]

A central doctrine in More's pneumatic account of causality was his hypothesis of what he called the 'Hylarchic Principle' or 'Spirit of Nature'. He advanced this hypothesis principally to explain phenomena such as the sympathetic vibration of strings, gravitation and magnetic attraction, which could not be satisfactorily accounted for in terms of Cartesian science. More's 'Spirit of Nature', which is similar to Cudworth's 'Plastic Nature', is reminiscent of the Platonic World Soul, and includes among its functions those ascribed to the Aristotelian vegetable soul. As he explains in *Immortality of the Soul*,

The Spirit of Nature . . . is, A substance incorporeal, but without Sense and Animadversion, pervading the whole Matter of the Universe, and exercising a Plastical power therein according to the sundry predispositions and occasions in the parts it works upon, raising such Phaenomena in the World, by directing the

[35] More, *Immortality*, p. 120 in *A Collection*. More repeatedly invokes a principle of analogy by which the spirit is conceived in spatial, even material, terms.

[36] More, *Antidote*, p. 153. More's tendency to reify the immaterial or spiritual has been noted by D. P. Walker and John Henry who see it as a kind of materialism. See Henry (1986) and Walker (1964). But, as the latter points out, it is at best a weak form of materialism. In *Enchiridion metaphysicum*, More describes hylopathia as a quasi-material force emitted from created spirits ('ita ipsi spiritus creati materialem quasi quandam vim emittere possint'). And he underlines the analogy between soul and body: hylopathia is he says, 'Illud igitur quod in Anima has, quae dicuntur, corporeas proprietates imitatur', p. 327.

parts of the Matter and their Motion, as cannot be resolved into mere Mechanical powers.[37]

Although More conceives the Spirit of Nature as a fundamental component of the metaphysical order, it is open to criticism as a special theory designed to meet particular explanatory failures.[38] To a Platonist, accustomed to thinking in terms of hierarchies of spiritual agency, it made sense to posit intermediate causes of this kind to bridge divisions along the ontological scale. More's philosophy is characterised by other such special theories of the operations of spirit: other examples are his revival of the Platonist doctrine of the vehicle of the soul, according to which the soul inheres in a body so fine and diaphanous as to be almost immaterial. Another 'intermediate' between the divine and the creation is the concept for which he is most famous: infinite space. Indebted to Plotinus and to Plato's 'place of all things' (χωρα παντοῶ) *Timaeus* 52B and also to Plotinus' commentary on this passage in *Enneads* 2.4, More's conceives of space as analogous to God, possessed of similar attributes: unity, infinity, immobility, eternity, omnipresence, incorporeality, etc. Space is therefore an interface between God and the created world – or 'shadow' of God, as More put it in *Enchiridion Metaphysicum*. At the other end of the ontological scale, More posits an immaterial prototype of body, that he calls 'metaphysical hyle' in *Conjectura cabbalistica*, where he first describes it. 'Metaphysical hyle' is at most potential matter analogous to space – extended, incorporeal, but not infinite.

Finally, in putting the case for the existence of spiritual substance, More made extensive use of the design argument. He adduced observed phenomena in order to convince those, like Hobbes, who claimed that all knowledge derives from sense experience. The natural phenomena he cites include both standard design-argument details (such as the orderly structure of the internal organs of the human body) and occurrences which cannot be satisfactorily explained in mechanistic terms (for example, the sympathetic vibration of strings, and motion of the tides). But he also cites paranormal phenomena – well-attested sightings of poltergeists, witches and warlocks at work – as evidence of the activity of spirits. His accumulation of this kind of data has earned him ridicule for being credulous. Nevertheless, he was not an exception in his age for such beliefs. Indeed Anne Conway herself

[37] More, *Immortality of the Soul*, p. 193, in *A Collection*. In the scholia on the Preface to his *Enchiridion ethicum* in his *Opera philosophica*, More counterposes the 'vital motion' (*motus vitalis*) of the Spirit of Nature to 'mechanical and bodily motion' (*motui Mechanico & corporeo*), calling this vital motion 'magic' (*magia*). *Opera philosophica*, p. 10.

[38] A 'Spirit of the causal gaps', as Alan Gabbey has put it. Gabbey in Hutton (1990a), p. 24.

assisted him in compiling his taxonomy.[39] What is exceptional about More is that, like his admirer Joseph Glanvill, he attempted to compile the data on Baconian lines, in accordance with the observational principles of the Royal Society.[40]

MORE AND CONWAY'S *PRINCIPLES*

Apart from the record of her tutorials in philosophy, contained in their early correspondence, the main measure of More's impact on Anne Conway's philosophical formation is her *Principles*, composed at the very end of her life. Where her letters show her learning to think critically, the treatise is the product of critical thinking that extended to her original tutor in philosophy. The question inevitably arises whether her critique of More is the product of her late years, after her encounter with Van Helmont, or whether it can be traced back to an earlier point in her life. This is important for establishing the evolution of her philosophical system. But in order to answer it we must be careful not to overstate her repudiation of More. Before considering some of the detail of her attack on More, their common framework needs to be acknowledged. For the *Principles* is conceived within a broadly Platonic framework, and exhibits features associated with Cambridge Platonism in general. Much of the detail, especially the critical detail, can be linked to Henry More. I shall discuss this more fully in later chapters: in most cases it will be sufficient at this point to note More's input.

The centrality of the attributes of God, and her emphasis on divine perfection understood as consisting in goodness, wisdom and justice, places Anne Conway firmly among the Cambridge Platonists. Likewise, the philosophical model with which she operated was the Renaissance view of philosophy as a perennial philosophy which the Cambridge Platonists all shared. The 'most ancient and most modern' of her title, *Principia philosophiae antiquissimae et recentissimae*, invokes *philosophia perennis*. As already noted, it was at her behest that More wrote his fullest analysis of *philosophia perennis*, his *Defence of the Philosophick Cabbala* (1653). Like More, Conway was critical of modern philosophy: of Descartes, as well as of Hobbes and Spinoza. Partly to explain the operations of nature, and

[39] *Conway Letters*, p. 214. See also Glanvill's letter to More printed in *Sadducismus*, 'Relation XXVI', which mentions 'Lady Conway and other Persons of Quality' attending Jeremy Taylor's investigation of an apparition seen by one Francis Taverner.

[40] More published a compilation of data collected by his friend, Joseph Glanvill, together with some of his own, in his edition of Glanvill's *Sadducismus triumphatus*.

partly in vindication of divine providence, both More and Conway posit an intermediary cause between God and the world: in many ways Conway's *natura media* corresponds to More's Spirit of Nature. Within the framework of created nature, both posit an atomistic structure of created nature. Both refer to its constituent particles as monads. Conway, like More, conceived of all created substance as extended. As I showed in the previous chapter, she also shared More's admiration for Origen, and his advocacy of religious toleration. In some ways her differences from More were not so much radical divergences from his position, but result from a preparedness to go further than him on many issues.

ANNE CONWAY CONTRA HENRY MORE

Arguably, therefore, just as the ground was laid for her critique of Descartes by Henry More, so also Anne Conway's vitalistic monism can be seen to have been worked out in relation to More's philosophy of spirit, in particular as a critique of his dualism. This is clear in the *Principles*, where the arguments repudiating dualism (chapters VIII and IX) are framed in terms that indicate that their immediate object is Henry More not Descartes. More is not mentioned by name, but the terminology employed makes it quite clear that the object of her refutation is More's account of soul and body.[41] For Anne Conway centres her critique of dualism on those who attempt to define body and spirit as types of extension, differentiated by mutually exclusive properties: the impenetrability and divisibility of body and the penetrability and indivisibility of spirit. Her use of the terms 'discerpible' and 'indiscerpible' as synonyms for 'divisible' and 'indivisible' make the reference to More unmistakable.

According to the sense of those who maintain that body and spirit are so infinitely distant in nature that one cannot become the other, the attributes are the following: that a body is impenetrable by all other bodies, so that their parts cannot penetrate each other. Another attribute of body is that it is discerpible, or indivisible. The attributes of spirit, however, as these people define them, are penetrability and indiscerpibility, so that one spirit can penetrate another or a thousand spirits exist within each other, taking up no more space than one spirit.[42]

[41] Anne Conway actually refers to 'those doctors' (in the plural). The identity of the other 'doctors' is not clear. She may have had Cudworth in mind. At all events, it is evident from the detail that the chief figure to whom she refers is More.

[42] Conway, *Principles*, p. 48. Cf. also More, *Immortality*, I.ii.12, p. 20, in *A Collection*: 'Now then *Extended Substance* (and all Substances are extended) being of it self indifferent to *Penetrability* or *Impenetrability*, we finding one kind of Substance so *impenetrable*, that one part will not enter at

Other indicators that it is More's dualism that Anne Conway attacks in her *Principles* include her critique of his view that spirits can expand and contract, his explanation of soul–body interaction by his theory of 'vital congruity' (a theory which she dismisses as 'talking foolishly with vain words'), and his contention that spirits need bodies in order to act. Much of Anne Conway's critique of More consists of pointing up problems arising from his position and exposing inconsistencies in his argument. For example, she contends that More's attribution of impenetrability to corporeal extension and penetrability to spirit is arbitrary; and that it is inconsistent to ascribe impenetrability to one kind of extended substance (body), but not to another (spirit). It is similarly arbitrary to impute fixed limits to corporeal extension ('so that it is impossible for it to be extended more or less') but not to spiritual extension. Likewise, it is inconsistent to allow that spiritual extension may vary in extent ('be extended more or less'), yet to deny that bodily extension may vary. As a result More's account of body and spirit evades the problem it attempts to solve (it is, according to Anne Conway, 'but a begging the question'), because he and those who argue in this way 'have not yet proved that body and spirit are different substances'.[43]

For her part, Anne Conway denies that the attributes of impenetrability and divisibility pertain only to body, and that penetrability and indivisibility pertain only to spirit. On the contrary, these attributes apply to both. 'Spirits are no less discerpible than bodies' and 'Properly speaking, penetration pertains equally to bodies and souls'.[44] Bodies can expand and contract, just as spirits can.[45] Since spirits have dimensions, several spirits cannot occupy the same body without causing it to increase in size; a body, like spirit, is indiscerpible when it 'is understood as one single individual'.

all into another . . . I conceive, I say, from hence we may as easily admit that *some Substance* may be of it self *Indiscerpible*, as well as others *Impenetrable*; and that as there is one kind of *Substance*, which of its own nature is *Impenetrable* and *Discerpible*, so there may be another *Indiscerpible* and *Penetrable*.'

[43] Conway, *Principles*, pp. 50, 57. Even before her assault on More's dualistic account of soul and body, Anne Conway challenges More's account of the divisibility or discerpibility of bodies: she exposes as fallacious his argument that although bodies may in theory be infinitely divisible, in actual fact there is a limit to their divisibility – 'whatsoever is actually divisible is divisible into indiscerpible parts in as much as it is actually able to be divided'. More is guilty of the logical fallacy of 'joining words or terms which imply contradiction or absurdity, and this fallacy is hidden in this term "actually divisible" which denotes that one and the same thing is and is not divided . . . as if someone should say "visibly blind" or 'vivaciously dead"'. Ibid., p. 19. Cf. *Immortality*, pp. 3 and 19 in *A Collection*.

[44] Conway, *Principles*, pp. 52 and 53. I do not follow Coudert and Corse's translation of 'discerpibilitas' as 'divisibility', but have substituted the Morean term 'discerpibility', which is closer to the Latin and reveals that More is the object of Anne Conway's critique here.

[45] Conway, *Principles*, p. 52.

If discerpibility means 'that we can divide one body from another by placing a third between them . . . spirits are not less discerpible than bodies'.[46] So, Conway concludes, 'impenetrability and indiscerpibility are no more essential attributes of body than of spirit because in one sense these attributes apply to both and in another sense they apply to neither body nor spirit'.[47] Rather than being absolute and mutually exclusive characteristics, impenetrability and penetrability are simply the opposite ends of the same scale. After all, if bodies can vary in weight (lightness/heaviness) and density (being compact or rarefied), why should they not also vary in respect of porousness (penetrability and impenetrability). The same may be said of their relative cohesiveness (discerpibility and indiscerpibility). Treated as relative properties, the apparently irreconcilable differences between body and spirit actually turn out to be the opposite ends of a continuum of which soul and body are extremes. More's fundamental premise that matter and spirit are extended substances is actually an acknowledgement of their likeness rather than their difference. Indeed in framing his definition of spirit in terms an atheist materialist would understand, More himself acknowledged the likeness underlying the differences between matter and spirit in his account: he himself states, of the definitions of spirit and body in *The Immortality of the Soul* (quoted above), 'the precise Notion of *Substance* is the same in both'.[48]

Although Lady Conway highlights the inconsistencies and weaknesses of More's account of dualism, she nowhere challenges his basic premise that spirit is extended as well as body. Rather, her objections are to the way he develops his argument from that point. More has therefore failed to recognise that he has laid the foundation of a monistic concept of substance by demonstrating an affinity between soul and body: extension is that fundamental 'similarity or affinity' between soul and body.

> But if they alledge that the body and spirit agree in certain attributes, such as extension, motion and shape with the result that spirit has extension and is able to reach from one place to another move from one place to another, and also change itself into whatever shape it pleases, in such cases it agrees with body and body with it.[49]

Anne Conway's arguments against More are directed chiefly at his attempt to superimpose dualism on to his well-founded monistic intuition that body and spirit are both *res extensae* (extended things). The failure of his attempt may be measured by the number of questions his theory leaves

[46] Ibid. [47] Ibid., p. 53.
[48] More, *Immortality*, p. 21 in *A Collection*. [49] Conway, *Principles*, p. 49.

unanswered – questions which Anne Conway raises in her treatise: how soul and body are attracted to one another by what Conway calls the mutual love between them; how body and mind interact; why the soul suffers with the body when the latter is in pain. Dualism cannot explain how immaterial substance can move material substance for, on More's definition, spirit is so penetrable it will pass through body, leaving it behind. These are all problems which More attempts to solve in *Enchiridion metaphysicum*, chapter 28. Anne Conway was, evidently, not satisfied by his arguments. In her view, such problems can only be resolved when the 'similarity or affinity' between soul and body is acknowledged.

But if one admits that the soul is of one nature and substance with the body, although it surpasses the body by many degrees of life and spirituality, just as it does in swiftness and penetrability and various other perfections, then all the aforementioned difficulties vanish and one may easily understand how the soul and body are united together and how the soul moves the body and suffers with it and through it.[50]

VITAL CONGRUITY

What is not immediately apparent is whether Anne Conway was already thinking in non-dualist terms, or working out her arguments against dualism before she met Van Helmont and before she studied the kabbalah. An important clue to the answer to this comes from the discussion generated by the letter More wrote to Anne Conway in 1652, in answer to the queries she sent him which were quoted in the previous chapter. More's reply contains his first articulation of his theory of 'vital congruity'. And it is this topic which connects Anne Conway's later philosophy with her earlier philosophical discussions. Among the '*Four* Particulars' for which she requested answers in 1652 is the question, 'how the *Souls* of *Beasts* and *Plants* came into *Bodies*?' In response to this question, More proposed that souls conjoin with body by virtue of what he calls 'a vital Congruity betwixt the Soul and the Body'. This 'vital congruity' entails, on the one hand, that 'the very Nature of a Soul, is to have an Aptitude of vital Union with the Matter'. It also requires that matter, on the other hand, is 'prepared' for the reception of soul. He explains

There can be no Notion or Tenet either truer or fitter than this; that there is a *vital Congruity* betwixt the *Soul* and the *Body*: Which Congruity being in the prepar'd *Matter*, and it infecting of qualifying the *Air* and *Spirit* of the *World*, at a certain

50 Ibid., p. 58.

Distance round about . . . And it is these vital Rays of particular Congruity that fetch in Souls of Beasts and Plants . . . into rightly prepared *Matter*; whither when they have arrivd they straitway set upon the Efformation of that piece of corporeal Substance they are caught in, *naturally*, not *knowingly*.[51]

More mentions this theory of vital congruity in *Conjectura cabbalistica* (1652) and elaborates it further in *The Immortality of the Soul* (1659) and in the *Appendix* to *Antidote Against Atheism*, printed in 1662.[52] The latter was written, as More explains in the introduction, in answer to,

the chiefest and most material *Objections* I could meet with, whether raised by those that of themselves have excepted against any Argument I have made use of, or by such as have been invited more curiously to search and discover, where they could, any weakness or inconsequency in any Argumentation throughout the whole Treatise.[53]

More does not name the source of these 'most material *Objections*', but, given Anne Conway's singling out of 'vital congruity' for critique in her *Principles*, it is highly probable that she was one of the persons who raised objections or was invited to comment on More's arguments. This being so, More's elaborations of the theory of vital congruity in *Immortality of the Soul* as well as in the 1662 *Appendix* to *An Antidote* were also written in response to Anne Conway's comments.

Anne Conway cannot have been impressed by More's answers, either in his 1652 letter or later in the 1662 *Appendix*. For in chapter 8 of her *Principia* she discusses the doctrine of 'vital congruity' (*congruitas vitalis*) as part of her assault on soul–body dualism. She writes

If one says that the vital congruity of the soul for the body is the cause of this union [of soul and body] and that this vital congruity ceases with the corruption of the body, I answer that one must first ask in what this vital congruity consists? For if they cannot tell us in what this congruity consists, they are talking foolishly with inane words which have sound but not sense. For, surely, according to the sense in which they take body and spirit, there is no affinity whatsoever. For body is always dead matter lacking life and perception no less when spirit is in it than when spirit leaves it. Thus there is no congruity at all between them.[54]

Henry More is not named in this passage but here, as in her critique of dualism generally (discussed above), the terminology Conway uses identifies

51 Ward, *Life*, p. 174.

52 More, *Immortality*, book 2, chapter xv and book 3, chapter ii.

53 More, *Appendix to the Foregoing Antidote*, p. 145, in *A Collection*.

54 Conway, *Principles*, pp. 56–7. In the Corse/Coudert translation 'congruitas vitalis' is rendered as 'vital affinity', a term which renders the concept adequately, but loses the reference to More. To emphasise the point, I have modified their translation by substituting 'vital congruity'.

him as the primary target.[55] It would appear, therefore, that Anne Conway's critique of dualism can be traced back to her early interchanges with More, that is to at least 1652, when she identified flaws in his arguments such that he was obliged to shore up his position with his hypothesis of vital congruity. This does not mean that she abandoned soul–body dualism at this point. Nor does it mean that she had worked out an alternative. But she certainly had grounds for thinking that the philosophical basis of More's dualism was inadequate.

It would be a mistake, however, to represent Anne Conway as an opponent of More, and to conclude that her objections to More's dualism resulted in her rejection of his philosophy in its entirety. First of all, her rejection of dualism was itself entirely consistent with More's own arguments, in that she recognised and maintained the implicit monism of his argument that both spirit and body are extended substances differentiated only by certain attributes. In this respect her monism is the logical outcome of his attempt to spatialise the concept of spirit. On this view she looks like a more consistent Morean than he does. Secondly, as we have already noted, she owed much of her philosophical outlook to More, both in general framework and much of the detail. This is not to say that Conway followed More, but working within a similar philosophical framework, with a similar set of priorities, and contemplating the same problems, she developed her own system. More was, therefore, an important point of departure for Anne Conway and remained a presence behind even her mature philosophy. We shall continue to encounter him in every major aspect of her intellectual development. More, then, was a key interlocutor for Anne Conway – a witness to her spiritual and intellectual development. He was also a presence in her dialogues with the other important figures in her immediate circle, notably her brother John and Francis Mercury van Helmont.

Anne Conway's interest in philosophy did, of course, go far beyond her study of Cartesianism and her reading of Henry More. But More probably ensured that she was well read in other Platonist philosophers, particularly those for whom he professed admiration, including Ficino and Plotinus.[56] We have it on the authority of Van Helmont that she studied Plato and Plotinus, though we cannot be sure exactly when. Her discussion of the infinite and her concept of Middle Nature as mediator between God and the world in her *Principles* suggest she may have been aware of Nicholas of Cusa's

[55] For Anne Conway's critique of More, see Hutton (1995b).
[56] Ward, *Life*, p. 18.

philosophy of the infinite and his conception of a cosmic Christ. However, precisely when she might have encountered Nicholas of Cusa is uncertain. There was a copy of his works in the second Viscount Conway's library, while English translations of his *De visione dei* (1646) and *Idiota* (1650) by Giles Randall and John Everard show that there was some contemporary English interest in his philosophy at this time.[57] Another Christian Platonist whom she knew was the Master of Christ's College, Ralph Cudworth, who was a close friend of Henry More. She would have met him when she and her husband paid a visit to Christ's, and probably again when Cudworth brought his son to Ragley Hall in the hopes of being cured by Valentine Greatrakes. There are certainly parallels between his philosophy and hers, notwithstanding the humanist erudition in which it is steeped. But how much she knew of his philosophy we can only speculate, since his major work of philosophy, his *True Intellectual System of the Universe*, was not published until 1678. Unless she had access to his manuscripts (of which several survive unpublished to this day), his philosophy would not have had any formative impact on hers.[58] However, Anne Conway's philosophical horizons were not confined to Platonism: from an early point in her philosophical life, she was also exposed to philosophies antithetical to More's. Ironically, perhaps, even here More was not merely a presence in, but a point of access to, debates beyond her immediate circle. The next chapter will be concerned with the two figures who differed most emphatically from More: John Finch and Thomas Hobbes.

[57] Nicholas of Cusa, 'Οφαλμοσ 'Απλουσ, *or the Single Eye, Entitled the Vision of God*, trans. Giles Randall (London, 1646), and *The Idiot in Four Books*, trans. John Everard (London, 1650). See also Armagh, Armagh Robinson Library, Conway Catalogue, p. 30, item 29. On the translations of Nicholas of Cusa by Giles Randall and John Everard see Smith (1989), pp. 110–27. Nicholas of Cusa conceives of God as the sum of all perfection, and Christ as the medium and reason (*ratio*) of all things, who is a middle nature (*media natura*) between God and man. Created things are gradated according to their level of perfection, and each grade of perfection is called a 'species'. See Nicholas of Cusa, *De visione Dei*, in *Opera omnia*, 19 vols. (Hamburg: Meiner, 1932–) vol. VI, I.1–2, XX, XXII.

[58] John Covel, Cudworth's successor as Master, mentions Cudworth entertaining 'Lord & Lady Conway & their whole attendance . . . many days' at the Master's Lodge at Christ's College, in an undated 'Account of ye Master's Lodgings in ye College', BL MS Additional 22,911, fol. 228. There are intriguing parallels between the thought of another Cambridge Platonist, Richard Sterry (d. 1672) and that of Anne Conway, but there is no evidence of any contact between them. Sometime chaplain to Oliver Cromwell, Sterry is the author of one substantial work, his posthumously published *Discourse of the Freedom of the Will* (1675), which propounds a philosophy of love, universal salvation and shows a distinct debt to kabbalism, including the concept of Christ the Logos as Adam Kadmon, mediator between God and the world.

CHAPTER 5

John Finch, Thomas Hobbes and Margaret Cavendish

'the subtilest peeces of philosophy'[1]

Although it is impossible to be sure at what point Anne Conway's critique of dualism was fully formed, it is certain that she was well aware of contemporary non-dualist types of philosophy, and that she first encountered it at an early point in her life. This chapter will be largely concerned with two important examples: her brother, John Finch, and the most famous English philosopher of the mid-seventeenth century, Thomas Hobbes. It will also discuss Margaret Cavendish, who was connected with Hobbes's circle but staked out her territory in opposition to Descartes, Hobbes and More. Finch, like More, was a constant point of reference throughout Anne Conway's life. Hobbes achieved notoriety in the 1650s, at about the same time that Anne Conway embarked on her own philosophical career. Although she was not personally acquainted with him, Hobbes remained a force to be reckoned with throughout her philosophical life. Margaret Cavendish appears on the scene only briefly in 1665, after Anne Conway's return from Ireland, and just prior to her encounter with Valentine Greatrakes.

JOHN FINCH

After Henry More, the person with whom Anne Conway was in continuous philosophical dialogue for almost her whole life was her brother, John Finch. Despite their being separated for most of their adult lives because of Finch's residence abroad, they were very close as brother and sister. Finch maintained epistolary contact with his sister after he left for Europe in 1651, and throughout his long periods of residence abroad in Italy and in Turkey, where, from 1671 to 1681, he was ambassador to the Ottoman Empire. Although only a few letters survive from their life-long correspondence, these show that Finch found a match for his intellectual interests in his

[1] BL MS Additional, 23,215, fol. 31v.

sister, and that she was as important a figure in his personal as in his intellectual life. He undoubtedly fulfilled a reciprocal role for her.

John Finch's life was as cosmopolitan as Anne Conway's was confined.[2] After attending Eton College, he studied first at Balliol College, Oxford, and thereafter at Christ's College, Cambridge, where he proceeded MA in 1649. At Christ's College he made friends with two men who were to figure prominently in his life: first of all, Henry More with whom he studied; and, secondly, Thomas Baines (*c.* 1622/4–81), who proved to be the most significant figure in his life after his sister Anne. As in her case, Finch's original tutorial contact with More developed into a life-long friendship which survived Finch's peregrinations to Italy and, subsequently, Turkey. In all his travels Finch was accompanied by Thomas Baines who lived with him as his closest companion after he left Cambridge for the whole of his life.[3] Both Finch and Baines went to Italy in 1651 to study medicine at Padua. They both qualified as doctors of medicine there in 1657, and by proxy at Cambridge in 1661 – hence More's reference to them as 'the two Italian doctors'.[4] Finch does not appear to have practised as a physician, though he and Baines were, on occasion, consulted in that capacity by members of his family.

John Finch's life was very much that of the gentleman scientist, or *virtuoso*. In Italy, and later in Turkey, he was able to indulge both his scientific and his artistic interests, observing the phenomena of nature, collecting works of art and commissioning paintings. Finch was a link between the scientific communities of England and Italy. He was elected Fellow of the Royal Society in 1663, serving as a correspondent of the Society from his various postings abroad.[5] While in Florence he became a member of

[2] On Finch's life, see new *DNB*, under 'Finch, Sir John'. For his Italian sojourn, see T. Tozzetti (ed.), *Atti e memorie inedite dell' Accademia del Cimento* (Florence, 1780), Crino (1957); and for his embassy in Turkey see John Covel, *Extracts from the Diary of Dr. John Covel, 1670–1679*, in J. T. Bent (ed.), *Early Voyages and Travels in the Levant* (London: Hakluyt Society, 1893) and Abbott (1920).

[3] See Malloch (1917) for an idealised account of their friendship. Baines was knighted some time before 1672. He died at Constantinople in 1681. Finch had Baines' body embalmed, and brought it back to England with him in 1682 for burial in Christ's College chapel. Finch was buried in the same grave a year later. Together, in their wills, Finch and Baines left money to found two fellowships and two scholarships at Christ's College, Cambridge. Each contributed £2,000 for this purpose. A memorial commissioned from Joseph Cattens was erected in the Christ's chapel in 1684, with an encomium from Henry More celebrating the life-long friendship of the two men. See entry for Finch in the new *DNB*. The first incumbent of the Finch and Baines fellowship was Anne Conway's nephew, Henry Finch.

[4] *Conway Letters*, p. 164.

[5] Finch's Royal Society links antedate his election as Fellow. John Evelyn mentions a report on poisons that he sent from Italy in May 1661, and his presenting the Society with 'a piece of weaving Asbestos' from the Duke of Tuscany in September 1661. Evelyn, *Diary*, vol. III, p. 295.

the scientific circle surrounding Prince Leopoldo de' Medici in Florence, whom he counted as a personal friend. In 1665 he was appointed English Resident at the court of Florence. In 1669 he was closely involved with the visit to Britain by Prince Cosimo de' Medici.[6] In 1671 he was appointed ambassador to the Ottoman Empire, succeeding his cousin Heneage, Earl of Winchilsea. He resided for eight years in Pera, returning to England in 1681, shortly after the death of his companion Sir Thomas Baines. His visit to Ragley in September 1671, just prior to his departure for Turkey, was probably the last time that his sister Anne saw him, for she died shortly before his return.

Finch was a man of both science and culture. He was an anatomist of sufficient distinction to teach the subject at the University of Padua and to be accepted as a member of the Accademia del Cimento in Florence. He performed dissections and demonstrations at the Arcispedale of Santa Maria Novella in Florence, alongside such distinguished men of science as Nils Stensen, Francesco Redi and Marcello Malpighi.[7] To judge by his letters to Leopoldo de' Medici, Finch had a special interest in the anatomy of the brain. He introduced Leopoldo to the works of Thomas Willis,[8] and he conducted investigations of, among other things, the torpedo fish (which brought him into controversy with Giovanni Alphonso Borelli[9]) and vipers. His letters to his sister Anne and to Cardinal Leopoldo de' Medici, as well as his notebooks and diary, show that throughout his life he practised as a gentleman scientist or *virtuoso*, investigating and recording natural phenomena, theorising about them and commenting on the theories of others. He was also an art collector: he commissioned and collected some sixty paintings, including four by Carlo Dolci (1618–86), who painted his portrait and that of Baines. He also commissioned portraits from the Dutch artist Samuel van Hoogstraten (1627–78). The paintings Finch owned by Van Hoogstraten include a portrait of himself, a group portrait of his nephews, and the picture of a woman reading a letter that has been identified

[6] Crino (1968) and (1957).

[7] Nils Stensen (Nicolaus Steno), (1638–86), a Danish physician and anatomist and one-time friend of Spinoza, served as physician to Grand Duke Ferdinand of Florence in 1666, converted to Catholicism, took orders and was made a bishop. Francesco Redi (1626–97) was physician to Grand Duke Ferdinando II and Cosimo III of Florence. He demonstrated that the presence of maggots in rotting meat does not result from spontaneous generation but from eggs laid on the meat by flies. Marcello Malpighi (1628–79) was a physiologist who pioneered the use of the microscope in anatomy.

[8] On Willis, see next chapter.

[9] Giovanni Alphonso Borelli (1608–79), mathematician, astronomer and iatrophysicist, was a friend of Marcello Malpighi. Marcello Malpighi, *The Correspondence of Marcello Malpighi*, 5 vols. (Ithaca and London: Cornell University Press, 1975).

as Anne Conway.[10] Among the nephews in the group portrait, he had most dealings with Daniel Finch, son of his brother Heneage, and future Secretary of State under William III and Queen Anne. In 1662 John Finch supervised Daniel's tour of Italy.[11]

After departing for Italy in 1651, Finch wrote to his sister as often as he could. His letters, filled with vivid descriptions of places he visited on his travels, were for her a window on foreign cultures.[12] Letters to her took precedence over letters to others, including Henry More. He asks her to 'excuse my not writing to him . . . but I am resolv'd to lay aside all things in order to you'.[13] Once in Italy he apparently tried to write to her every week, but his intentions were not always carried out, as other business occupied him. In 1657 he apologises that pressure of business has forced him 'to break my Promise of writing to you constantly'. Again in 1658 he makes similar apologies.[14] By the time of his posting to Turkey, the frequency of their correspondence was much reduced: writing to his Dearest Dear ('DD') in 1674, Finch complains of the difficulty of maintaining his correspondence. He mentions 'my former unhappinesse' of not receiving her letters 'of late yeares'.[15]

In all his letters, Finch is given to expressing himself effusively, and nowhere more so than in his letters to his sister, where on one occasion he claims that he is 'so passionate a Lover of you Dearest that I would not for all the good in the world you should thinke I did not love you better then you and doe your selfe'.[16] His affection and admiration for her are expressed in unstinting terms.

> I vow and professe, having never in my life seen or heard of any person in whose breast there dwelt so much of reall worth and goodness; it would be a crime against the law of my Understanding not to represent the notions of worth and goodness by calling to minde your own person, which none shall so unfeignedly love as my selfe.[17]

This recourse to hyperbole overreaches itself on occasion, with the result that, as he admits, his expressions of affection for his sister exceed his extensive vocabulary of compliment – 'for the Idea of Worth by which I frame my admiration of you does as farr outgoe my expressions: as your Love exceeds my meritts'.[18] Finch's letters are full of fraternal solicitude for

[10] These paintings are reproduced in *Conway Letters*. The Dolci portraits of Finch and Baines are now in the Fitzwilliam Museum, Cambridge. The Hoogstraten painting of a woman reading a letter is in the Mauritshuis collection in The Hague. The identity of the subject is a matter of controversy.
[11] Horwitz (1968b). [12] *Conway Letters*, nos. 22, 23, 25, 26, 34, 37, 38.
[13] Ibid., p. 57. [14] BL MS Additional 23,215, fol. 39.
[15] BL MS Additional 38,855, fol. 108. [16] *Conway Letters*, p. 77.
[17] Ibid., p. 59. [18] Ibid., p. 58.

his sister's health, for which he offers her the informed advice of a medical expert. He visited her after the tragedy of the death of her child, and sent her books and presents from Italy – including a dog named Julietto.[19]

Finch's devotion to his sister found expression in other ways, and none more extraordinary than in his own attempt to cure her of her chronic illness. The evidence for this is scant – an entry in the notebooks of the vicar of Stratford, John Ward, who had become a clergyman after embarking on a career as physician. Ward's notebooks are a fascinating compilation of memoranda on such diverse subjects as medical receipts, reading and local places and people. The entries cannot be dated with great exactness, but the volume for the years 1663 to 1665 contains a note indicating that Anne Conway had recently undergone surgery: 'The Lady Conway hath great pains in her head her sutures open'. He adds, a few lines later, 'that shee came into this miserie by a Brother of hers who was a Traveller and had some skill in physick and chymistrie and tried experiments uppon her'.[20] Evidently John Ward did not know much about John Finch. But his notebook records enough other detail about activities at Ragley Hall to suggest that he was acquainted with the Conways (he reports on Valentine Greatrakes' visit, for example, and mentions Henry Stubbe). The reference to pain and open sutures does not give us enough information for establishing exactly what John Finch's intervention was. But the fact that he attempted to operate on her suggests that his studies of cerebral anatomy in Italy had been undertaken with the purpose of trying to help his beloved sister. The operation must have taken place after 1665, when he returned from Italy, and before 1666 when Greatrakes visited Lady Conway at Ragley (Ward's notes on Greatrakes are to be found later in the same volume). The fact that Thomas Willis did not mention it in his account of her also suggests that it took place after 1665 when Willis was her physician. There is no hint of Finch's intervention in any of the More–Conway correspondence. Anne Conway's courage in submitting to surgery in an age when there was no anaesthetic available is a measure of both her desperation for relief and her confidence in her brother. One can only imagine the pain she endured from the failure of the attempt. The additional burden of suffering that Finch's surgery caused may have been a precipitating factor in the Conways seeking out Valentine Greatrakes (discussed in the next chapter).

As this episode shows, Finch's relationship with his sister did not always run smoothly. A letter of 1674 contains a mysterious apology for hurting her: without giving any details, Finch refers to 'those Tears I made you shed'

[19] Ibid., pp. xxix, 147, 284. [20] Ward, *Diary*, pp. 549 and 551–2.

and 'the outrage you committed on yor selfe'.[21] And, like Edward Conway and Henry More, he found her conversion to Quakerism very hard to take. In 1678 he received from Henry More 'ye Transcript Verbatim' of a communication from her on this subject. He professed to be startled by the contents, which must have informed him of her final conversion to Quakerism with her adoption of the 'thee/thou' forms of address, for his reply of 18 November is a long argument seeking to persuade her to observe social decorum in the use of titles and styles of address. Given the length of time it would have taken for a letter to reach England from Constantinople, it is possible that Anne Conway never saw her brother's reply, for she died on 23 February 1679.

Finch's failed attempt to help his sister should not obscure the fact that the intellectual bond between them was as strong as the family ties that bound them together. The fragmentary remains of his correspondence with her show just how important each was to the other. The topics discussed in Finch's letters to Anne Conway, as well as those of his friend Baines, were philosophical in nature. Both John Finch and Thomas Baines' admiration for Anne's talents is abundantly clear. As Baines put it rather flatteringly in 1653,

> your ladyshippe passes through the subtilest peeces of philosophy, without making many difficultyes, and those difficultyes your ladyshippe moves are so apposite, so really intricate; so refined that I ver[il]y believe your ladyshippe understands what you do not question and understand[s] where ye difficulti (*sic*) lyes in those thinges your ladyshippe does not question.[22]

Hers was the judgement Finch held in the highest regard: writing to her in 1653 he declared, 'I doe not please my selfe in writing what I have not thought of more then once, nor certainly would any such writing be worthy of you reading.'[23] She was privileged to know about his writings – they were a secret with which he entrusted her: 'Pray, my dear, keep my writings from any eye but my Brother Conway for you two are one but I would not have my private thoughts made publique to any one else.'[24] Finch no doubt appreciated his sister's critical powers the more, given his view that there are 'so few persons y^{t} know how to Discourse'.[25]

To judge by a letter dated 1657, Finch relied on his sister to propose topics for their discussions. 'Would to God', he tells her, 'you would but

[21] BL MS Additional 23,215, fol. 51r.
[22] Thomas Baines to Lady Conway, 30 Nov./10 Dec. 1653, BL MS Additional 23,215, fol. 31v.
[23] *Conway Letters*, p. 77. [24] Ibid., p. 79.
[25] John Finch to Lady Conway, 15/25 Dec. 1667, BL MS Additional 23,215, fol. 51v.

begin to appoint me some subject of discourse that my letters besides my affection might impart something of knowledge to you'.[26] The knowledge he chose to impart included extensive discussions of his own ideas. In a letter written in 1653 he encloses a treatise of his own on an unspecified topic (the enclosure has not survived) and promises to send another 'concerning the Law of Nature'.[27] In 1657 he promises to explain 'all those phaenomena you putt me' in a projected treatise.[28] In the same letter he commends her for studying mathematics because it will assist her study of geography and astronomy, as well as 'Opticks or n[atu]ral Philosophy'. Among the Conway–Finch papers in the British Library there are papers in Finch's hand on the circulation of the blood and 'Of the Manner by which Tree Plants and all Vegetables are Nourished', and on the 'Flux and reflux of the sea', all of which were probably sent to Anne Conway.[29] His observation that she will learn geometry 'by the advice of Mr. More' confirms that Anne Conway continued to benefit from her intellectual exchange with More long after she had completed her Cartesian studies with him.[30] In the course of his travels, Finch also obtained books for his sister. In 1652 he sent her three copies of Descartes' *Principia philosophiae*.[31] In 1653 he sent her Copernicus, an anti-Copernican treatise by Fromond, and Descartes and Galileo on tides.[32] Doubtless he procured other books for her. John Finch and his sister, therefore, fulfilled an important role for each other as someone with whom each could exchange ideas. Finch's friend Thomas Baines also fulfilled this function for Lady Anne. Furthermore, Finch was also a useful source of information about the wider world and an important point of contact about developments in contemporary science. He was an eager observer of foreign customs and culture, and, for his time, a relatively unbiased one. Although a devout Protestant, he had a deep love of Italian culture, and even expressed admiration for the visual grandeur of the papacy. He was also impressed by aspects of Turkish culture, and shows both respect for Turkish power and fascination with cultural differences.

A *VIRTUOSO*'S PHILOSOPHY

Although for a time he practised as an anatomist, and although he spent much of his life observing the phenomena of nature, Finch never published anything. He did, however, plan to publish the fruits of his investigations:

[26] *Conway Letters*, p. 139. [27] Ibid., p. 79.

[28] John Finch to Lady Conway 3/13th Dec. 1657, BL MS Additional 23,215, fol. 32r.

[29] Ibid., fol. 14. [30] Ibid., 23,215, fol. 32r.

[31] *Conway Letters*, p. 65 n. It is not clear from the reference whether these were duplicate copies of the same version, or whether they were the Latin or French editions.

[32] Ibid., p. 78.

among the papers he left when he died was a lengthy manuscript treatise clearly prepared for publication, which sets out his own philosophy.[33] The content of this suggests that he gathered the materials for it during the course of his life and that it was completed sometime after 1675. It is unlikely, therefore, that Anne Conway ever saw it, since he was in Turkey at this time, and she had died before his return. However, his few extant letters to his sister show that he discussed many of his ideas with her as he developed them earlier in his life.

Finch's manuscript treatise is interesting in its own right, both for the *virtuoso* philosophy he expounds and as a source for the comparative social and cultural history of the seventeenth century. It is filled with observations on such diverse topics as music, astronomy, Italian and Turkish customs, as well as his thoughts on political theory, economics, theology and ethics. The treatise reflects Finch's activities as a physician and a diplomat, in the obvious sense that it discusses medicine, and uses examples taken from diplomacy. But a more accurate description might be that of a *virtuoso*'s philosophy: for it not only discusses natural philosophy at length but it contains a wide diversity of subject matter. Furthermore, it is not the work of a dilettante, but a systematically organised treatise, which places emphasis on drawing conclusions from observation. Since the 'Truth of Propositions' is 'nothing but the Congruity of Humane Conceptions with the Nature of those Reall Beings, wch the Omnipotent Authour of Truth has Unerringly assign'd them', 'the Nearest approach Human Discourse can make to the Discovery of Naturall Objects, being the History of their Actions and Passions faithfully Recorded from our own Observations; Or as Veridically convey'd to us by long and repeated Experiences of others.'[34]

Finch's treatise is not a scholarly work in the sense that it relies on the authority of books. It is evidently the work of a man who had leisure enough to write. While the non-bookish character of the treatise could mean that it is the work of someone who did not have a vast library to hand (on account of his peripatetic lifestyle), this is also consistent with it being, explicitly, the product of observation and experience. It is very much the work of the doctor/anatomist closely involved with new developments in observational science at the Royal Society and its sister institution, the Accademia del Cimento.

For present purposes, the special interest of his treatise is how Finch positions himself within the philosophical and scientific debates of his time and

[33] This manuscript survives among the Finch papers at the Leicester County Record Office, where it is erroneously listed as being by Daniel Finch, Earl of Nottingham. This mistake was noticed by Horwitz (1968a).

[34] Leicester County Record Office, Finch papers, MS, DG7 lit. 9, fol. 133.

where this puts him in relation to his sister's philosophy. Finch's treatise is critical of Cartesianism and remarkably positive about Hobbes. Its foundational premise is that experiment and observation of the external world are the basis of knowledge. Finch argued that since the only knowledge human beings can have is sense knowledge, human knowledge is confined to corporeal things. He therefore denies that we can have certain knowledge of incorporeal things, since these are inaccessible to sense perception. Since 'all knowledge arises from sense' and 'what is not Sensible is not Intelligible',[35] we cannot have knowledge of anything non-corporeal, such as immaterial substance. For this reason, speculation as to the nature of spirits, souls and God is futile. In contrast to his sister, and in accordance with his experimentalism, Finch was a materialist in his natural philosophy. But in so far as he allows that matter is endowed with the capacity for self-motion, he is better described as a hylozoist. Finch posits a corpuscularian theory of matter founded on the essential unity of the constituent particles. All things are aggregates of these insensible minima. He explains the appearance and properties of all things in terms of these constituent particles. However, since these are not accessible to the senses, it is idle to speculate on their shape or size. (He criticises Descartes for imputing the observable shape of the aggregates to the unobservable shape of constituent particles, and deriving their properties therefrom.) He adduces his own observations of the phenomena of nature to support his position, and he also invokes holy writ. Significantly, his main ecclesiastical authority is Tertullian.

Of particular relevance is the fact that Finch is critical of Henry More's philosophy of spirit and that his objections bear some resemblance to those of his sister. Although he describes More as someone 'the honour of being whose Pupill I reckon amongst the happy Circumstances of my life',[36] he devotes the third chapter of book 3 of his treatise to a confutation of the idea of spirit. It is clear from the terminology he uses and the supposed properties of spirit which he attacks that the target, in his discussion of spirit, was Henry More. As with Anne Conway's critique of More, Finch's use of terms like 'Indiscerpibility', 'Selfe-Penetrability' and 'Selfe Activity' make it plain that his refutation is aimed at Henry More. Like his sister, he argues that the properties that More attributes to spirit are just as applicable to matter. Like her, he notes the parallel between More's supposed 'distinct Notion of Incorporeall being' and the properties of body. However, unlike her, he argues that it is impossible for the human mind to form a conception of incorporeal things without using the terminology of

[35] Ibid. [36] Ibid., fol. 131.

corporealism: 'men make use of matter to expresse Immateriality'.[37] He denies More's claim that 'Spirit is Intelligible by Contrary Propriety's to Matter',[38] arguing that to impute properties to unobservable spirit is mere speculation. If these properties are observable, they must be apparent to the senses, and so corporeal. Furthermore, the properties More ascribes to spirit (self-unity, self-penetrability and self-activity) are self-contradictory. In particular, More's Spirit of Nature is a wholly unnecessary intermediate cause if spirits are able to move themselves. In this way, Finch demonstrates the *unintelligibility* of More's supposedly *intelligible* idea of spirit and argues that what More took to be the properties of immaterial spirit are in fact the properties of matter. His sister too turned More's argument into an argument for a single substance, which combined the properties of spirit and body in a single extended substance. But where Finch argued that the properties More imputes to spirit pertain to corporeal substance, and that therefore all substance is material, Anne Conway drew the obverse conclusion, namely that the single substance so defined is spirit, not body.

Finch does not in fact deny the existence of spirits and souls. He holds that souls and God exist, and even that they are non-corporeal. However, we have no direct knowledge of them, and know them only through their effects and from scripture.[39] He even devotes a chapter to witches and devils, in corroboration of More's axiom 'No Spirit No God'. But he denies the causal efficacy of spirit in the physical world, propounding instead a materialist theory of substance. He is, however, highly critical of those who try to demonstrate the existence of God and incorporeal substance through reason, claiming that their attempts have only served to advance the cause of atheism.[40]

Finch's is therefore a sceptical position that holds that we can know nothing about incorporeal substance, since knowledge of it cannot be obtained via the senses. Indeed he even denies that it is possible to gain certain knowledge of nature via the senses, since sensation varies with every individual. By admitting the existence of God and the soul, but at the same time denying that we can have any knowledge of divine or spiritual substance, Finch avoided the cardinal error of which Anne Conway accused Hobbes and Spinoza – the error of confounding God with created things. Finch is not, therefore, strictly a materialist. Although unexpected in someone tutored by Henry More, his dismissal of incorporeal substance as unintelligible allies him with Hobbes. It therefore comes as no surprise to find that he apparently had a high regard for Hobbes who, he says, 'justly deserves the

[37] Ibid., fol. 101. [38] Ibid., fol. 105. [39] Ibid., fol. 119. [40] Ibid., fol. 101.

name of a Person of Learning, hath given as good Evidence of His Poetry as of his Philosophy and Mathematicks'.[41] On the other hand, Finch's admission that incorporeal substances may exist, although we can have no direct knowledge of them, seems to place him closer to Locke than to Hobbes. It would be more accurate to describe him as a sceptic than a Hobbist – a sceptic, that is, in respect of metaphysical knowledge, and a mitigated sceptic in respect of the knowledge of nature, since experimentalism can only produce limited knowledge. Or, as he put it, 'Experiments may afford a good Sallad or a Good Sauce in Philosophy, but Never a good Meal.'[42]

John Finch's repudiation of metaphysics and his sense-based epistemology, therefore, set him in diametric opposition to his sister, for whom there is no matter distinct from spirit, and for whom everything is a mode of spirit. Nonetheless, brother and sister were offering alternative solutions to the same set of problems. They directed their arguments against the same dualistic framework within which they had been trained to philosophise, namely that supplied by Henry More. They were both responding to some of the same difficulties that More had encountered in prevailing philosophical debate, but they chose to deal with them differently from him.

These differences from More notwithstanding, John Finch, like his sister, nevertheless shared some of the same outlook with More. Although he argued that the finite human mind could not have true knowledge of an infinite God, Finch, like Henry More, held that the idea of God is innate, and that moral principles are internal to the mind. 'The Notion of a God & of Good seems to be as universally planted in Humane Nature as Life it selfe or any Naturall Facultys': there is, he argued, a 'Universall Inward Sense of Good and Evill Implanted in all Sonnes of Men, and Connaturall to Discourse and Right Reason'.[43] Finch also shares with More and his sister a deeply latitudinarian outlook: he argues strongly against forcing men's consciences and defends the freedom of every person to interpret the Bible for him/herself. He bases his argument on his conception of God as primarily a loving God.

God loving all things He created and hating nothing that He made, at the same Time that the Act of Being came from God to a living Creature, at y[e] same time Love was as necessarily implanted in the Creature. The Infinite Act of Creation being accompanyd with the Infinite Love of the Creatour, and as One was divided to succession, without w[ch] there could have been no continuation of Being or Existence in Creatures; so is the other perpetuated by the same Act, It being impossible yt there could have been succession of Animals without the Principle of Innate Love implanted in them, the providing for future generations depending

[41] Ibid., fol., 385. [42] Ibid., fol. 195 [43] Ibid., fols. 408 and 410.

upon the necessity of this Love, without wch there could be no prouision for offspring, wch require these strong Impressions of Love, from the very first Principle of Generation to nidification or preparing for Parturition, and the nourishm^t^ of what Animals were produced.[44]

Finch ascribes this observation to his 'most Dear and profoundly Judicious friend Sr Thomas Baines'. If it originates with Baines, it is a rare touch of Platonism in Baines' otherwise empiricist thinking. It is also a view that echoes Anne Conway's argument that the act of creation entails a communication of divine love to the world. One manifestation of this is the love all creatures have for one another. God is, she states, 'infinite life and love' and 'every creature shares certain attributes with God'. This love is manifest in 'that great love and desire which spirits or souls have for bodies', and also

We find examples of this among all animals which produce their own offspring in the same way as man. For they clearly love whatever they bring to birth. Thus even wicked men and women . . . love their own children and cherish them with natural affection . . . In addition to this particular love, there is also a certain universal love in all creatures for each other . . .[45]

Very possibly topics like divine and creaturely love were discussed by Anne Conway in her letters in the manner Baines called 'so apposite, so really intricate; so refined'.[46] One major difference between Finch and his sister on this point is that she uses it to support her view that all things are originally of one substance. Another major difference between them is that, for Anne Conway, so much hinges on the divine attributes. Her brother, by contrast, denies that we can have a clear idea of the attributes of God and rejects what he calls our 'anthropomorphite manner of discoursing about God and His Attributes'.[47]

Given that John Finch's rejection of More results in a very different philosophical position from that of his sister, it is unlikely that it was her influence that was decisive in the direction he took. She did not, after all, live to see his completed treatise. Nevertheless, Finch evidently discussed with her some of the topics contained in it, and sent her drafts over an extended period. In letters of 1653 and 1658 there is mention of various discourses he is sending. Again, in 1667, Finch mentions 'the continuation of my Discourse which by sheets I will constantly transmitt'.[48] Of particular

44 Ibid., fol. 331v. 45 Conway, *Principles*, p. 97. 46 See above at note 22.

47 Finch papers, MS DG7 lit 9, fols. 500 and 509.

48 John Finch to Anne Conway, 9 April 1653, *Conway Letters*, p. 78; John Finch to [Anne Conway] 1 Oct. 1658, BL MS Additional 23,215, fol. 38, and John Finch to Lord Conway, 18/28 March 1667, *Conway Letters*, p. 282. Finch asks his brother-in-law to keep the papers until Anne Conway is able to read them. He also indicates that the 'Discourse' is long.

significance here is Finch's letter of 1 October 1658,[49] because it gives some indication of the content of these early discourses, and therefore of the early date by which he had rejected More's dualistic philosophy. It is also evident from his comments that his sister had an important role for him in testing his arguments, and confirms a relationship between his early philosophical discussions and his later treatise. In this letter he thanks her for her objections to the arguments he had put to her in his previous letter, and promises to send her two more sheets of their discourse. This, he says, will put the case for a sense-based epistemology 'that it is absolutely impossible for any man to understand any thing but by a Corporall representation'. Finch was clearly already taking issue with More's philosophy of spirit and Cartesian dualism. He objects that the term 'incorporeall is nothing but meer negation in us, being the same as not Corporeall; and that when we say a thing is Incorporeall wee onely mean it is not either thick or thin body'. Furthermore he denies that Descartes ever convincingly demonstrated that mind ('Cogitative principle') is incorporeal ('void of Corporeity').[50] This argument is repeated in his treatise. Henry More was certainly aware of Finch's materialism by at least 1662, when he ascribes it to the influence of Thomas Baines, whose 'too corporeall interpretation . . . that can fancy nothing but matter'[51] he ridicules in the character of Hylobares in his *Divine Dialogues* (1668). In his 1662 letter, More still held that Cartesian philosophy was the 'best Engine' for defending religious truth. Although Anne Conway did not share her brother's materialism – at least not in her mature philosophy – these letters are evidence of the fact that she was debating the issue of dualism well before she encountered Van Helmont and kabbalism. We do not, unfortunately, have any means of telling what position she took in reply to her brother, or what alternatives she may have proposed to the shortcomings of dualistic arguments. But it is not beyond the bounds of possibility that she, like her brother, was already engaged in the process of working out her own philosophical system. This could be what Baines is referring to when he wrote to her from Italy that her philosophical replies 'will dispose me to receive your most elevated principles when I shall returne'.[52]

Anne Conway's continuous exchanges with her brother gave her the opportunity to keep abreast of and discuss contemporary developments in

[49] John Finch to [Anne Conway] 1 Oct. 1658, BL MS Additional 23,215, fol. 38. This letter does not name the recipient, but is addressed to 'DD', which is an abbreviation of 'Dearest Dear', the normal form of address used by Finch in other letters to Anne Conway. Sometimes he refers to her by the contraction 'D.D.': e.g. *Conway Letters*, p. 202.

[50] Ibid. [51] *Conway Letters*, p. 204. [52] BL MS Additional 23,215, fol. 31v.

philosophy and science, with direct access to the European dimension of those developments. Her contact with Finch, moreover, was contact with a mind whose openness is evident from his preparedness to criticise the philosophy of his tutor and his eagerness to participate in the developing science of the period. Thus, despite the privacy of the philosophical environment she inhabited, Anne Conway had opportunities to engage in philosophical discussion in an independent atmosphere. Through her brother's arguments she was exposed to a measure of scepticism about human capacities to understand the workings of the natural world and about received philosophical systems. However, her *Principles* shows no evidence that she adopted or accepted the physiology proposed by her brother. On the other hand, his *virtuoso*'s observational habits of mind may have contributed to her practice of appealing to experience – though this is also a characteristic of vitalists like Van Helmont. Her own critique of More certainly has points in common with Finch's, but she did not share his repudiation of metaphysics. Where he abandoned spirit as a conceptually viable category, she rejected matter as the basis of her substance monism. In all likelihood she would have been dissatisfied by his separation of God from the world, and would, in consequence, have regarded his account of causality as inadequate.

ISLAM

Although brother and sister diverged radically in the philosophical systems they propounded, they shared much in the way of general outlook. One area where Finch's Turkish sojourn may have been decisively influential on Anne Conway was in her awareness of Islam and in her developing an open mind towards Islamic culture. One of the striking features of Anne Conway's religious eirenicism is that it extended not just to Judaism, but also to Islam. She no doubt shared the tolerant view of Henry More who condemns the 'false Zeal' of those who attack non-Christians 'by vilifying and reproaching all other Religions, in damning the very best and most conscientious *Turks, Jews and Pagans* to the Pit of Hell'.[53] But Anne Conway goes beyond More in her concern to emphasise the common ground between faiths, and to remove Christian doctrines that non-Christians found offensive. In her *Principles* she singles out the doctrine of the Trinity as 'a stumbling block and offense to Jews, Turks, and other people'.[54] In an important respect

[53] More, *An Explanation of the Grand Mystery of Godliness*, p. 343.
[54] Conway, *Principles*, p. 10.

her *Principles* amounts to a reinterpretation of the doctrine of the Trinity, treating it as a metaphysical truth rather than as a tenet of faith. Her conviction that Islam was accessible to rational interpretation was probably encouraged by her reading of non-doctrinaire accounts of Islamic belief, such as the life of Ibn Yokdhan (Hayy ibn Yaqzan) by Abu Bakr ibn al-Tufail (Ibn Tufayl) translated into Latin by Edward Pocock as *Philosophus autodictatus* (1671) and into English by the Quaker leader George Keith, with the title *An Account of the Oriental Philosophy* (1674).[55] The 'wisedome of the East' which this purported to show was that the central tenets of Islam could be discovered by human reason. Keith gave a copy to Henry More in 1674.[56] But it may well be that Anne Conway knew it through her brother John, whose *virtuoso* curiosity about Turkish culture extended to religion. Significantly, in Anne Conway's treatise, Islam is represented by the Turks, a detail which suggests that a primary conduit of information about Islam was her brother, the ambassador to Turkey. Another possible source of information about Moslem beliefs was Henry Stubbe, who was physician to the Conways in the late 1660s. Stubbe's *An Account of the Rise and Progress of Mahometism*, which circulated in manuscript, is unusual for its time because it is free of common Christian prejudices that colour the accounts of his contemporaries. It also served as a vehicle for radical Christian views, such as denial of the divinity of Christ.[57] It is difficult to be sure how extensive her knowledge of Islam was, but through Baines and her brother Anne Conway had a window on Muslim culture that few of her contemporaries, and even fewer women, had.

The glimpse of Ottoman life which Finch and Baines provide exhibits a measure of cultural openness which is unusual among European travellers to Turkey at this time. While they never wavered in their Christian faith, he and his companion seem to have been interested in exploring common ground between Islam and Christianity, rather than highlighting their divergence. Evidence of Finch and Baines' latitudinarianism towards Islam comes from the diary of John Covel, who was chaplain to Finch's embassy. Covel reports a conversation between Baines and Vani Effendi, religious adviser to the Sultan. In the course of their dialogue, his interlocutor explained Turkish tolerance of Jews and Christians. In his reply Baines took a tolerant position towards Islam. He told Vani Effendi that

[55] Published in 1674, without place of publication mentioned, this translates the Latin as *Philosophus autodictatus sive epistola Abi Jaafar Ebn Tophail de Hai Ebn Yokdhan* (Oxford, 1671). Pocock first translated this from Arabic in 1671, dedicating it to Gilbert Sheldon. See Toomer (1996) and Russell (1994).

[56] *Conway Letters*, p. 392 and note.

[57] For Stubbe, see chapter 6.

he had read the Koran, and that he was aware that it was mistranslated and misunderstood among non-Muslims. In Covel's account, Baines presented his own Protestant beliefs as congruous with aspects of Islam:

> Sir Thomas told what kind of Christian he was viz he would rather dye than worship either crosse, Pictures, Images or the like. He adored only one true God, and lived in his fear onely: he believed a Mussulman, living up to the height of his law, may be undoubtedly saved. He thought himselfe obliged (though it was never so absolutely in his power to do it) not to touch a hair of a Mussulman's head for his difference of religion, but rather to help, assist, relieve, cherish them in every good office that he was able to doe for them. Here Sir Thomas Baines saies he wept, and said he could not believe any Christian came so near true Musselmen, but they had all been idolaters; and the standers by . . . cryed out *E Addam* – he was a *Good Man.*[58]

Baines was undoubtedly picking his ground with care during this interview, mindful of his position as a foreigner and a diplomat. But the passage is remarkable for the religious and cultural respect it expresses, and Baines' perception of common ground between Protestant practice and Islamic belief, and his sympathetic conviction that devout Muslims might be saved. Anne Conway makes no mention of Islamic doctrine in her *Principles* or her letters. But her few references to Islam are devoid of the kind of caricature condemnation that colours so many European perceptions. This may reflect the deeper knowledge of Islamic culture mediated to her by her brother. She certainly shared his rationalising approach to Turkish Islam.

THOMAS HOBBES

We can only guess at the kind of reception Finch's *virtuoso* philosophy would have received from his sister. However, one clue may be discerned in her response to one of the philosophers whom Finch mentions sympathetically, Thomas Hobbes. Finch's respect for Hobbes contrasts Henry More's antagonism towards him, of which Anne Conway was well aware. There were, as it happens, some links between the Finch family and Hobbes, who had in 1629 been tutor to Sir Clifford Clifton, son of Sir Gervase Clifton and brother-in-law to John Finch and Anne Conway. Sir Clifford's wife, Francis Clifton, was the sister to whom Anne Conway was closest. She was 'good chearfull company' for her, according to More.[59] She is the only one of Anne Conway's sisters to figure in her correspondence, and Anne Conway

[58] Covel, *Diary*, pp. 270–1. Besides his question about toleration, Baines asked Vani Effendi whether the souls of men, women and children were equal, and whether women could attain paradise.

[59] *Conway Letters*, p. 393.

left her £500 in her will.[60] The Cliftons were judged sufficiently interested or important to be given copies of More's *Antidote against Atheism* when it was published in 1652.[61]

With the publication of *Leviathan* in 1651, *De corpore* in 1653, and his controversy with Bramhall over free will in 1654–5, Hobbes rapidly acquired a reputation as a dangerous proponent of materialist, deterministic atheism.[62] As we have seen, Henry More took up the challenge of Hobbism in *Of the Immortality of the Soul*, published in 1659 with a dedication to Lord Conway. It is likely, therefore, that Anne Conway read Hobbes during the 1650s. And it is also likely that she read him through the critical lens supplied by More, who, in his *Antidote against Atheism* had already criticised the mechanical philosophy of Descartes for attributing too much to 'the blind fortuitous jumblings of the parts of the *Matter* one against another'.[63] This may also have been an implicit criticism of Hobbes. At all events, More's *Immortality* is explicitly aimed at Hobbes.

Given the anti-atheistical hysteria that met the work of Hobbes, and given that her chief philosophical mentor wrote a refutation of him, it is surprising that Anne Conway does not dismiss Hobbes out of hand. Critical of his philosophy she certainly is, but in her *Principles* she accords him a measure of recognition. This may owe something to her brother John, whose receptiveness to Hobbes is a remarkable exception to the antipathy towards Hobbes displayed by his English contemporaries.[64] Instead of rejecting Hobbes as the quintessential atheist, Anne Conway boldly concedes that there are parallels between her system and his: first of all the fact that both maintain that all creatures are of one substance, and secondly Hobbes's contention that 'all visible things can change into one another' so that 'nothing is so lowly that it cannot reach the highest level'.

> I concede that all creatures from the lowest to the highest were originally one substance and consequently could convert and change from one nature to another. And although Hobbes says the same thing, nevertheless this is not at all prejudicial to the truth; nor are other parts of that philosophy necessarily Hobbesian, where Hobbes says something true.[65]

Anne Conway was well aware that her acceptance of a principle of similitude between God and the physical universe laid her open to the charge that her

[60] Ibid., pp. 480.

[61] *Conway Letters*, pp. 69–70. Although More frequently sends his 'service' to Francis Clifton via Anne Conway, there is nothing in her letters to suggest that the sisters shared intellectual interests.

[62] Mintz (1962). [63] More, *Antidote*, p. 42 in *A Collection*.

[64] On the English reception of Hobbes, the classic study is still Mintz (1962).

[65] *Principles*, pp. 64–5.

rejection of dualism aligned her with Hobbes (and also with Spinoza). She therefore took care to underline the radical difference between her system and theirs on the matter of substance: 'as for Hobbesianism, it is even more contrary to our philosophy than Cartesianism. For . . . Hobbes claims that God is material and corporeal, indeed that he is nothing but matter and body. Thus he confounds God and creatures in their essences and denies that there is an essential difference between them.'[66]

Evidently Anne Conway regarded single-substance monism as a better basis for opposing Hobbes than arguments by those who took an Aristotelian or Cartesian/Morean position in order to deny the possibility of transformation of one thing into another. In her account, the problem with the Aristotelian argument is that transformation (e.g. of wood into flame and smoke) involves annihilation of one substance by the separation of matter and form, and the production of new substances by the recombination of prime matter with different substantial forms. Dualists like More fare no better when they argue that matter is inert and therefore that change is only possible via the agency of spirit, because they in effect appeal to something (invisible spirit) that is itself an unknown: 'If one asks from whence this spirit is sent or who sends it, and how a spirit of this sort and not another is sent there, they are in a quandary and open themselves up to their adversaries.'[67] This is an argument that echoes the critique of dualism to be found in John Finch's manuscript treatise. Finch's critique, as we have seen, contributed to his case for a sceptical materialist natural philosophy. Could it just be that he was one of the adversaries of dualism that Anne Conway had in mind when she derided 'the weak and false principles' of those who tried to refute Hobbes?[68] Finch's materialism does not fit Anne Conway's (reductive) account of Hobbism exactly, since he is careful to separate God from the world. To that extent, his philosophy would no doubt have met with the approval of his sister. However, Anne Conway's repudiation of materialism and her positing of a single universal spiritual substance sets her system at odds with her brother. Nevertheless, in her more receptive view of Hobbes she is closer to her brother than to Henry More whose opposition to Hobbes was unrelenting. John Finch's sympathetic appraisal of Hobbes may, therefore, have encouraged his sister to give Hobbes's arguments more consideration than most of his critics. And her brother's materialistic arguments against More may have contributed to her recognition that More's dualistic arguments were vulnerable to materialist critique. But John Finch's disavowal of More's metaphysics may have

[66] Ibid., p. 64. [67] Ibid., p. 65. [68] Ibid., p. 64.

persuaded her that More's arguments, far from holding the line against Hobbes, opened the way to a materialist natural philosophy (such as Finch's own).

MARGARET CAVENDISH

Another figure linking Anne Conway with Hobbes's circle is a woman, Margaret Cavendish. She is not the only female figure of whom we catch glimpses across the broken record of Anne Conway's correspondence. Besides her family (especially her sister Francis Clifton) and her maids, her female acquaintances included women with educated interests, among them Mistress Sarah, her library keeper; Elizabeth Foxcroft, sister to Benjamin Whichcote, the 'godfather' of the Cambridge Platonists; Mrs Somerville (or Summerfield); Lilias Skene (the Quaker poetess); Mrs Dury (Dorothy Moore); and the Countess of Dover[?] (described by More as 'really an understanding person').[69] She would have known of the poet Katherine Phillips through Jeremy Taylor and of the Quaker missionaries Katherine Evans and Sarah Cheevers through her Quaker maid, Priscilla Evans.[70] She probably also knew John Evelyn's wife Mary,[71] and, as we shall see, Lady Ranelagh (sister of Robert Boyle). Tantalising as these connections are, there is simply not enough information from which to examine their relations or to construct a female circle of acquaintances. An exception is, however, Margaret Cavendish, Duchess of Newcastle. Nevertheless, Anne Conway seems to have kept her at a firm distance.

Margaret Cavendish (née Lucas) was the wife of William Cavendish, Duke of Newcastle, who was one of Hobbes's chief patrons – the others being his brother Sir Charles Cavendish and their cousins the Earls of Devonshire.[72] In Restoration England the Duchess of Newcastle enjoyed a public reputation as a *femme savante*. She bears comparison with Anne

[69] *Conway Letters*, pp. 57, 61, 64, 78, 237, 349, 369, 435, 438.

[70] *Conway Letters*, p. 422 n. In their *Short Relation*, Evans and Cheevers recount their imprisonment in Malta while on a missionary voyage to convert the Turks in *A Short Relation of some of the Cruel Sufferings (for the truths sake) of K. E. and S. Chevers in the Inquisition in the Isle of Malta* (London, 1662).

[71] Although there is no record of contact between Anne Conway and Mary Evelyn, Mary's husband John Evelyn was a close friend of Jeremy Taylor. Mary Evelyn took an active interest in contemporary science and natural philosophy. See Harris (1997).

[72] Sir Charles Cavendish was a member of the Paris circle of Marin Mersenne, to which Descartes belonged. The Cavendish circle also included Walter Charleton. The Cavendish's European contacts included the Dutch physicist, Christiaan Huygens. Jacquot (1952). William Cavendish, third Earl of Devonshire, was married to Elizabeth Cecil, who was a friend of the second Viscount Conway. *Conway Letters*, pp. 9, 17.

Conway largely because she was, like her, a philosophically minded aristocratic wife. However, the parallel in social status belies sharp differences in educational experience and philosophical views. Unlike Anne Conway, Margaret Cavendish received no systematic education.[73] But she managed to make good her lack of schooling by reading the leading thinkers of her day, with whom Anne Conway too was acquainted: Hobbes, Descartes, More and Jan Baptiste van Helmont.[74] In contrast to Anne Conway, Cavendish was a prolific writer, author of many books besides her several volumes on natural philosophy. Her writings on natural philosophy range from her poetic *Poems and Fancies* (1654) and her Utopian romance, *The Description of a New World Called the Blazing World* (1666), to treatises such as her *The Grounds of Natural Philosophy* (1668) and *Observations on Experimental Philosophy* (1666). She also wrote plays, poems and occasional pieces. These were all published in expensive folio volumes, proudly announcing their female authorship. Where for Anne Conway philosophy was a private activity, Margaret Cavendish cultivated a histrionic self-image. Famed for the audacity of her dress, she made a virtue of eccentricity in order to make a public niche for her intellectual pursuits. She courted a philosophical readership, sending presentation copies of her books to the learned men of Europe, and she published their replies in 1670 as a public seal of approval in a collection entitled *Letters and Poems in Honour of the Incomparable Princess, Margaret Dutchess of Newcastle*. Margaret Cavendish earned recognition of a sort from the male scientific establishment of her day when on 30 May 1667 she was invited to visit the Royal Society.

Unlike Anne Conway, Margaret Cavendish declined to speculate about matters metaphysical, confining the scope of her enquiries to the physical world, or what she called 'Nature'. Like Francis Bacon, whose principle of the separation of theology from natural philosophy she adopted, she emphasised the utility of knowledge. Like Hobbes, she denied the existence of immaterial substance and postulated that everything in nature is corporeal, including the soul. Like both Hobbes and Descartes she accounted for all natural phenomena in terms of the properties of matter, that is in terms of the shape, size, position and movement of bodies. Her rejection of metaphysics and her materialism places her closer to Hobbes.[75] Nevertheless,

[73] Margaret Cavendish, *Philosophical and Physical Opinions* (London, 1663; first published 1655), sig. b2[5].

[74] This is evident from her *Philosophical Letters* (London, 1664), where she discusses the work of these men. On Cavendish's philosophy see Sarasohn (1984), Hutton (1997d) and James (1999). For a fuller comparative discussion of Conway and Cavendish, see Hutton (1997b).

[75] It is still widely believed that Cavendish's philosophy is the antithesis of that of Hobbes, but I believe there are greater affinities between them than is normally supposed. See Hutton (1997d).

she was unconvinced by the claims of the new physics to account for all phenomena, life and action in terms of the impact of moving bodies on one another. Unlike the mechanists, Cavendish took a hylozoist position, imputing life, motion and mental powers to body itself. To the extent that her natural philosophy combines modern views with more traditional doctrines, such as the Aristotelian doctrine of the four elements (air, fire, earth and water), it may be compared to Sir Kenelm Digby (1603–65) whose philosophy grafts new ideas on to old ones.[76]

There is no evidence that Anne Conway and Margaret Cavendish were personally acquainted. But Anne Conway certainly knew of the Duchess's existence, and of her reputation as *femme savante*, for in 1665 Margaret Cavendish sent Henry More a gift of some 'noble volumes' of her works, including her *Poems and Fancies* (1653) and her *Philosophical Letters* (1664). More thanked her with a letter of carefully crafted apology for his unpolished manner of writing (in his haste to thank her he had not 'as yet fitly polished and adorned my Stile'). At the same time, he reported his receipt of the gift to Anne Conway,[77] with the suggestion that it would be more appropriate for her to answer 'this great philosopher'. The text which Anne Conway might have read as a result of Cavendish's approach to More would have been her *Philosophical Letters*. This consists of a collection of epistolary critiques of some of the leading thinkers of the time, written to an unidentified and probably fictional lady. In the course of her critiques of Descartes, Hobbes, J. B. van Helmont and Henry More, Cavendish sets out her own theories, particularly her vitalist account of Nature as a composite of self-moving matter capable of thought and perception. Cavendish's 'Nature' combines the functions of Anne Conway's second and third species since, according to her, it is both the agency of order and the aggregate of material bodies that fill the world. Nature is the created world as well as the instrument of God. But where Conway's Middle Nature is invested with Christ-like attributes, Cavendish's Nature is separate from God and is entirely corporeal.

> First, that nature is infinite, and the eternal servant of God: Next that she is corporeal, and partly self-moving, dividable and composable; that all and every particular creature, as also perception and variety in nature, is made by corporeal self-motion, which I name sensitive and rational matter, which is life and knowledge, sense and reason.[78]

[76] Catholic courtier, diplomat and naval commander, Digby was a member of the Cavendish circle and served Queen Henrietta Maria in exile in Paris. His *Two Treatises* (Paris, 1644) deal with the nature of bodies and the immortality of the soul. See Dobbs (1973, 1974) and Henry (1982).

[77] *Conway Letters*, pp. 237 and 241.

[78] Cavendish, *Philosophical Letters*, sig. b4.

Cavendish denies the need for any such spiritual intermediary as the Spirit of Nature on the grounds that to posit such a causal agent is to impugn the omnipotence of God. With uncompromising common sense, she argues, 'God can surely just as well give power of motion to matter as to Incorporeal Substance'.[79] She also argues that to posit an intermediary spirit between God and creation is dangerously polytheistic.[80] She rejects any idea that Nature might be a manifestation of the divine, when she ridicules More's Spirit of Nature as the '*Quarter-master General of this Divine Providence*' (letter 28).

As far as we know, Anne Conway did not trouble herself to respond to the Duchess. Had she done so, her letter would undoubtedly have been included in Margaret Cavendish's collection, *Letters and Poems in Honour of the Incomparable Princess, Margaret Dutchess of Newcastle.* This act of self-publicity, not to say self-glorification, represents the opposite extreme to Anne Conway's very private mode of conducting her intellectual speculations. She would not have wished to be drawn into the glare of ambivalent publicity that surrounded the Duchess. In any case, by 1665 when More suggested she might undertake to answer Margaret Cavendish, Lady Conway, as we shall see in the next chapter, had other preoccupations. For the year 1665 was not only a low point for her health, it was also the year in which she became most closely acquainted with the new science of the Royal Society.

[79] Ibid., p. 195.

[80] This criticism of More's Spirit of Nature anticipates one of Pierre Bayle's criticisms of More's colleague, Ralph Cudworth, whose concept of Plastic Nature is very similar to More's Spirit of Nature. See Colie (1957).

CHAPTER 6

Experimental physick: Boyle, Greatrakes, Stubbe

For most of her life Anne Conway was afflicted by debilitating chronic illness for which no cure or palliative could be found. The crippling pain visited on her by her condition was an inescapable fact of her daily existence, and attempts to alleviate her suffering dominated her life. One consequence of this was that she had more than average contact with medical men.[1] As we shall see, it was through events supervening upon her consultation of the Irish healer, Valentine Greatrakes, that she became a front-row spectator of the debates about method and interpretation occasioned by the experimentalism of Robert Boyle (1627–91) and his defenders in the Royal Society. In this chapter I shall discuss links between Anne Conway's medical history and contemporary debates about theoretical and methodological issues. I shall also discuss some of the metaphysical issues raised by the competing explanatory claims of those who attempted to interpret natural phenomena, especially in the context of medicine.

Anne Conway's personal experience of unrelievable pain certainly impinges directly on her philosophy. It is more than likely that her own incontrovertible experience of bodily pain affecting her mind contributes to her refutation of mind–body dualism in the passage in her *Principles* where she asks,

> Why does the spirit or soul suffer so with bodily pain? For if when united to the body it has no corporeality or bodily nature, why is it wounded or grieved when the body is wounded, whose nature is so different? . . . But if one admits that the soul is of one nature and substance with the body, although it surpasses the body by many degrees of life and spirituality . . . then all the above mentioned difficulties

[1] On Anne Conway's malady, see Owen (1937) and Critchley (1937). It is likely that her domestic role as chief housekeeper required her to have the technical skills and practical knowledge necessary for producing medicines and household chemicals. This by itself would not mean that she would be conversant with the underlying theory, though having the enquiring mind she did, she would have undoubtedly investigated it. On the domestic origins of science and the domestic location for laboratories, see the articles by Lynette Hunter (1997a and b).

vanish; and one may easily understand how the soul and body are united together and how the soul moves the body and suffers with it and through it.[2]

The impact of contemporary natural philosophy is most evident in Anne Conway's 'third species' or created world, in chapters VI and VII of her *Principles* where she discusses the substance of body and the origins of life. As we shall see in the next chapter, the main source for this discussion are the theories of Jan Baptiste van Helmont and his son, Francis Mercury. This chapter will examine the extent to which she was conversant with both the theoretical and the practical science of her day.

Seventeenth-century medicine was more than a matter of therapeutics. On the one hand, as a body of applied knowledge, medicine entailed practical issues of investigative and curative methodology. On the other hand, as a mode of theoretical speculation seventeenth-century medicine raised metaphysical and epistemological issues that justified its claims to philosophical status. Although the new philosophies of the seventeenth century displaced the older Aristotelian framework, and repudiated the vitalistic theories of the Renaissance in favour of explanatory theories that accounted for all natural phenomena in terms of the movement of material particles possessed of no other properties than shape and size, the new mechanical philosophy did not succeed in displacing vitalist traditions in what would now be known as the life sciences, and also in chemical science. Older Aristotelian and Galenic medical traditions still retained adherents, while Platonism and natural magic continued to be accepted as providing cogent accounts of the phenomena of nature.[3] In iatrochemistry, biology, medicine and chemical philosophy, causal agency continued to be explained in terms of the action of spirits, emanations or the inherent properties of bodies and their constituent parts. In most cases the medical philosophies Anne Conway encountered explained the workings of nature in terms distinct from those of the philosophies she had studied in her youth (namely Cartesianism and the philosophy of Henry More). Contemporary medicine and natural philosophy offered alternatives to the mechanical philosophy of Gassendi, Hobbes and Descartes. However, medicine and the life sciences were not static, but in a state of continuous development, and receptive to new ideas. For example, a good number of them assimilated atomism, and developed corpuscular theories of matter.[4] But whereas the mechanical philosophers

[2] Conway, *Principles*, p. 58.

[3] The term 'magic' must be understood in its early modern sense. More, for example, defines it as a 'life force or vital motion' (*vim quandam vitae, motumve vitalem*) in opposition to 'mechanical and corporeal motion'. *Opera philosophica*, p. 10.

[4] Clericuzio (2001); Webster (1982); Debus (1977).

conceived of atoms as the inert constituents of body, chemical atomists imputed powers to these corporeal particles. The resulting vitalistic versions of atomism therefore blurred the distinction between soul and body. They thus represent a softening of the boundary between mechanism and vitalism. The seventeenth century also witnessed the development of new experimental methods in natural philosophy by, among others, members of the Royal Society. This new experimentalism had special relevance to a discipline like medicine with its own time-honoured investigative and diagnostic practices, founded in observation and experience.

To this we might add that, while seventeenth-century churchmen and metaphysicians, fearful of the atheistic implications of atomism, repudiated hylozoistic theories that imputed life to matter, early modern medical practitioners appear to have been willing to entertain the possibility that matter might be endowed with the powers of perception and thought: Francis Glisson and John Locke are the most famous examples.[5] Even when medical theorists explained change by imputing powers to the corporeal constituents of the natural world, their theories could not be readily identified as atheistic, while most natural philosophers insisted on the godliness of their enterprise. This was particularly true in the case of the experimenters associated with the Royal Society. Anne Conway had family connections with the Royal Society through her brother and husband, but it was her medical needs that brought her into closest contact with Royal Society science.

Anne Conway did, of course, encounter the biological and chemical theories of her day in other contexts besides the medical. Several people among her friends and family subscribed to vitalistic or chemical theories. An important instance is her father-in-law, the second Viscount Conway, whose personal interest in alchemy brought him into contact with the Arundel circle at Petworth, and with Sir Kenelm Digby. Lord Conway's book-collecting activities, which extended to books on alchemy and medicine, show that he must have had a high level of technical expertise.[6] But in contrast to what we know about his friend Sir Kenelm Digby's scientific interests,[7] we know little about the elder Lord Conway's alchemical views. Another chemical philosopher with whom Anne Conway had direct contact was Ezekiel Foxcroft, Fellow of King's College,

[5] Francis Glisson, *Tractatus de natura substantiae energetica* (London, 1672). See chapter 7, note 8 below. John Locke, *A Treatise Concerning Human Understanding* (London, 1690), IV.3.6.

[6] For example, in a letter to Theodore Turquet de Mayerne, Lord Conway mentions alchemical books by Timoteo Rosselli, Girolamo Ruscelli and Lionardo Fioravanti among others. *Conway Letters*, p. 539. The same letter mentions his own 'mercurial water'.

[7] On Digby see Petersson (1956) and Dobbs (1973, 1974).

Cambridge, where his uncle Benjamin Whichcote was Provost from 1645 to 1660.[8] Foxcroft was to be an important mediator of Rosicrucianism in England through his English translation of the Rosicrucian Johann Valentin Andreae's *Chymische Hochzeit* (1616), which was published posthumously as *The Hermetick Romance or the Chemical Wedding* (1690). He was present during the therapeutic sessions of Valentine Greatrakes at Ragley Hall, of which he gave an eye-witness account. Foxcroft functioned as an intermediary between Cambridge and Ragley, and as the handy local expert on whom Henry More called when he needed assistance in matters linguistic and chemical – for example, when Francis Mercury van Helmont first visited him in Cambridge in 1670, More invited Foxcroft to act as interpreter.[9]

AMONG THE PHYSICIANS

It is to one of the most eminent physicians of the Restoration period, Thomas Willis (1621–75), that we owe the fullest account of Anne Conway's condition.[10] Willis was an expert on the anatomy of the brain, and he may have been consulted by Lady Conway for the reason that one of the main symptoms of her disease was a violent headache. In his *De anima brutorum* ('On the soul of animals') (1672), Willis describes her symptoms and the cycle of pain that she endured.[11] He does not in fact name her in this account, and he omits any mention of the state of her blood that he gave to her husband. But there are compelling reasons to identify his patient as Lady Conway on account of his reference to her being 'skilled in the Liberal Arts, and in all sorts of Literature, beyond the condition of her sex', and to her having been 'sick with almost a continual headache' for a period of 'above twenty years'. Willis writes:

> Growing well of a Feavour before she was twelve years old, she became obnoxious to pains in the Head, which were wont to arise sometimes of their own accord, and more often upon every light occasion. This sickness being limited to no one

[8] Foxcroft's mother, Elizabeth (sister of Benjamin Whichcote) lived with Anne Conway as her companion between 1666 and 1670, while her husband, George Foxcroft, was absent in India.

[9] *Conway Letters*, p. 323.

[10] On Willis, see Isler (1968) and Frank (1980). Also, Thomas Willis, *Willis's Oxford Lectures*, ed. Kenneth Dewhurst (Oxford: Sandford, 1980), and Feindel's introduction to Thomas Willis, *The Anatomy of the Brain and Nerves*, ed. William Feindel (Montreal, 1965).

[11] Thomas Willis, *De anima brutorum* (London, 1672), pp. 203f and 207f. For an English version see 'The Prognostick and Cure of the Headach', in *Two Discourses concerning the Soul of Brutes*, pt. 2, ch. 1, in Thomas Willis, *The Remaining Medical Works of the Famous and Renowned Physician Dr. Thomas Willis* (London, 1683), pp. 121–2.

place of the Head, troubled her sometimes on one side, sometimes on the other, and often through the whole compass of the Head. During the fit (which rarely ended under a day and a night's space, and often held for two, three, or four days) she was impatient of light, speaking, noise, or of any motion, sitting up right in her Bed, the Chamber made dark, she would talk to no body, nor take any sleep, or sustenance. At length about the declination of the fit, she was wont to lie down with an heavy and disturbed sleep, from which awaking, she found her self better, and so by degrees grew well, and continued indifferently well till the time of the intermission. Formerly, the fits came not but occasionally, and seldom under twenty days or a month, but afterwards they came more often: and lately, she was seldom free. Moreover, upon sundry occasions, or evident causes (such as change of the Air, or the year, the great Aspects of the Sun and Moon, violent passions, and errors in diet) she was more cruelly tormented with them. But although this Distemper most grievously afflicting this noble lady, above twenty years (when I saw her) having pitched its tents near the confines of her brain, had so long beseiged its regal tower, yet it had not taken it. For the sick Lady being free from a Vertigo, swimming in the head, Convulsive Distempers, and any Soporiferous symptom, found the chief faculties of her soul sound enough.[12]

Lady Conway consulted Willis in 1665. Her husband reported to his brother-in-law, Sir George Rawdon:

D^{r}. Willis hath been with her lately, and doth not beleeue she hath any Ulcer growing there, though one may easily disserne a hard swelling, wch. he sayes is one of the kernells about the Messentery, inflamed, he did also let her blood, and discovered that all her blood is like arter[y] blood, hot, fiery, without serum, or black spotts, wch. he never saw in any one in his life, and attributes all her paines to this.[13]

From Willis, we learn something of the remedies Anne Conway tried on the recommendation of others. He tells us that she submitted to all manner of treatments, some of them pretty drastic: 'she tryed the Baths, and Spaw-waters almost every kind and nature; she admitted of frequent Blood-letting, and also once the opining of an Artery; she had also made about her several issues, sometimes in the hinder part of her Head, and sometimes in the forepart, and in other parts' and on one occasion, she 'endured from an oyntment of Quicksilver, a long and troublesome Salivation, so that she ran the hazard of her life'. This last is a reference to the near fatal treatment she received at the hands of Samuel Hartlib's son-in-law, Frederick Clodius.[14] According to her letters some of the other 'cures' she was recommended to try, included tobacco and coffee among modern novelties, as well as a

[12] Willis, *Two Discourses*, pp. 121–2.
[13] Lord Conway to Sir George Rawdon, 14 June 1665, Hastings MSS, HA 14425.
[14] *Conway Letters*, pp. 91, 94–7, 102, 104.

mysterious 'red powder' from Wales, and a 'blew powder' prescribed for 'the headache' by one Dr Johnson. In addition to the special treatment required by her illness, the ordinary medical needs mentioned in Anne Conway's correspondence range from common ailments to scurvy and pregnancy. When she was pregnant in 1658 she made provision to ease her pain in labour by obtaining an 'eagle stone' – 'a German stone, such as are commonly sold in London for 5 shillings apiece'. White in colour, with 'little black streaks in it', and 'about the bigness of an egg', it was to be worn on the arm like an amulet.[15] In 1661 both she and her child contracted smallpox, fatally in his case. She recovered, but was much disfigured, as her husband told his brother-in-law;

It hath quite spoyled her second Marriage as I often tell her, she is very much pitted, and they are deep, her right Eye is also a little sunk, and somwhat lesse then the other. It hath likewise made her complexion a great deale worse then it was. Yet I shall think it a good exchange, if she could recover as much in her health as she hath lost in her beautye.[16]

It was for advice on treating scurvy ('scorbuticall distempers') that she consulted Robert Boyle in 1664. However, her main reason for consulting such a wide range of medical expertise was, overwhelmingly, the acute pain of chronic illness.

In the course of her life the variety of medical practitioners whom Anne Conway consulted extended from royal physicians to faith healers, from Fellows of the Royal College of Physicians to self-taught lay practitioners. The latter included the healers Matthew Coker and Valentine Greatrakes. There is also mention of a woman healer whom she consulted in Ireland, to no avail.[17] The medical practitioners she consulted included Thomas and Luke Ridsley (or Ridgely), Frederick Clodius and the Warwickshire clergyman/physician, John Ward.[18] She also consulted some of the most eminent medical experts of her day: Theodore Turquet de Mayerne and Sir Francis Prujean, and her kinsman William Harvey, whom she consulted between 1651 and 1652.[19] Between 1664 and 1665 she consulted Thomas Willis. It is possible that the recommendation of Willis came

[15] Ibid., p. 154.

[16] Lord Conway to Major Rawdon 5 Feb. 1661, Hastings MSS, HA 14373.

[17] Anne Conway to Lady Dorothy Rawdon, 9 April 1662, Hastings MSS, HA 14430: 'if my Doctoresse shall make any enquiries after me you may Let her know y^{t} I have not found any benefitt from her prescriptions, they having neither kept off any fitts nor eased my ordinary paines'.

[18] Ward compared her ailment to 'an Irish ague'. *Diary*, p. 100. On Ward, see Frank (1974).

[19] *Conway Letters*, pp. 30 and 78. Harvey's niece, Elizabeth, was the wife of Anne Conway's half-brother, Heneage Finch. Malloch (1917), p. 7.

from another Warwickshire physician, Henry Stubbe, who had studied with Willis. The Conways certainly consulted Stubbe, though there is no documentary record of his having attended Lady Conway. He was certainly at Ragley in 1666 and again in 1667, when Lord Conway praises him as 'a very ingenious man, and an excellent Phisitian'.[20] The most prominent non-professional medical expert that Anne Conway consulted was Robert Boyle, whose assistance she sought in 1664. The Conways also sought medical help overseas, taking advantage of their contact with John Finch, to whom Lord Conway wrote as early as 1653 in the hope that he might be able to locate and establish contact with F. M. van Helmont. Finch obtained a recipe for 'a medicine made up of volatile salt of vipers' recommended by Otto Tackenius, who claimed to have cured thereby 'hundreds of headaches thought incurable'.[21] So desperate was Anne Conway to find relief from the pain she suffered that in 1656 she travelled to Paris with a view to undergoing the operation known as trepanning. Henry More accompanied her to Paris, and it seems that it was he who dissuaded her from going ahead with the operation.[22] On her way to Paris she stopped at Rouen in the hope of consulting Dr Bochart, but he was not in town.[23]

The period 1665–6 seems to have been one of particularly acute suffering for Anne Conway, so much so that it was feared that she might not last long. In June 1665 her husband told Sir George Rawdon: 'she had been in the dreadfullest condition, with paine in her right side, and that part of her body, that ever I saw in my life . . . being alwayes in so much paine in that side that she never rises out of her bed at present she is in one of her usuall fitts of the Headack'.[24] The acuteness of Anne Conway's condition at this time may account for the fact that she consulted a large number of experts in a relatively short space of time, including, besides her own brother, Thomas Willis, Robert Boyle, Valentine Greatrakes and, apparently, Henry Stubbe. It may also explain why John Finch persuaded her to submit to surgery at his hands (see previous chapter).

[20] Lord Conway to Sir George Rawdon, 8 Oct. 1667, Hastings MSS, HA 14464; Lord Conway was sufficiently well disposed towards Stubbe to intervene to protect his estate when he died in 1676. See Hastings MSS, HA 14550, 14551, 14553 14554. He was particularly interested in conserving Stubbe's books, describing his library as 'a very great Library and very choice', HA 14554. For the catalogue of Stubbe's books, see BL MS Sloane 35. The books remained unsold and were at Ragley when Robert Hooke visited the house in 1680. Robert Hooke, *The Diary of Robert Hooke*, ed. R. T. Gunther, in *Early Science in Oxford*, vol. X (n.p., 1935), p. 447.

[21] *Conway Letters*, p. 89.

[22] Ward, *Life*, p. 206.

[23] Henry Oldenburg, *The Correspondence of Henry Oldenburg*, ed. A. R. Hall and M. Boas Hall Madison, 13 vols. (Milwaukee and London, 1965–86) (1965–85), vol. I, p. 214.

[24] Lord Conway to Sir George Rawdon, 14 June 1665, Hastings MSS, HA 14425.

Anne Conway was a well-informed patient, who took an intelligent interest in the remedies she tried. It is notable that at least two of the doctors who attended her, Thomas Willis and John Ward, commented on her intellectual acumen. Ward, in his diary, called her 'a great phylosopher'.[25] She certainly consulted books to keep herself informed: for example, in 1664 she asked her husband to obtain for her Culpeper's translation of Riverius' *Practice of Physick*, as she had left her copy with Mr Brooks.[26] But she also made her own investigations. Here John Finch would have been a source of information about contemporary medicine, and the theoretical underpinnings of the treatments she received.[27] But her knowledge of medicine is best illustrated by her consultation of Robert Boyle.

ROBERT BOYLE

Although he was not a physician by training, Boyle possessed his own pharmacopoeia of cures derived from his expertise as a chemical philosopher.[28] In 1664 Anne Conway tried some of the 'Ens Veneris', which Boyle recommended, apparently, for 'an invetterate headache'. She obtained the preparation from one 'Dr Hearnshaw', who had in turn procured it from Boyle's Oxford landlord.[29] A note by John Ward confirms that she took quantities of *ens veneris*, but that it did not do her much good.[30] From the same Dr Hernshaw she borrowed Boyle's book on 'experimentall phylosophy' (*Some Considerations Touching the Usefulnesse of Experimental Naturall Philosophy*, 1663) so that she could read up on *ens veneris*. Her decision to sample Boyle's remedy was influenced by the opinion she formed of Boyle and the medicine from this book, whence she concluded that 'he is an ingenious person'. She asked her husband to see if he could obtain more *ens veneris* from Boyle himself.

[25] Ward, *Diary*, p. 100. Willis, *Remaining Medical Works*, p. 122. Another of Willis's patients was Sir Matthew Hale who appears to have shared his views on the nature and function of the souls of plants and animals. Like More and others he posited an immaterial force to account for life and motion. See Cromartie (1995), pp. 207 ff.

[26] *Conway Letters*, p. 230.

[27] For an account of the treatments to which she submitted, see Hutton (1996c).

[28] On Boyle's dispensing of medication, see Hunter (1996).

[29] *Conway Letters*, p. 225. Boyle says *ens veneris* is compounded of 'strongly calcin'd and well-dulcify'd colcothar of Dantzic vitriol and elevated with sal-armoniac into the form of a reddish sublimate'. Marjorie Nicolson suggests this Dr Hernshaw may be the Dublin physician whose name is spelled variously Ernshaw and Hernshaw, or possibly Thomas Henshaw, one of the founder members of the Royal Society. *Conway Letters*, p. 225, n. 1.

[30] Ward, *Diary*, p. 641.

Her letters about obtaining Boyle's remedy show that she was observant about the cures prescribed and motivated by practical considerations to investigate the make-up of the remedies she used. Her comments show that she was careful in her choice of treatments, experience having perhaps made her cautious. As she told her husband, she was wary of self-promoting purveyors of cures, and disinclined to try a remedy merely because it had worked for others: 'I shall not be forward to make tryall of any medison upon the report of a confident mountebank nor through others may have found releife by it, except our cases were perfectly the same.'[31] This suggests that she understood the relationship between the efficacy of medicines and the medical condition for which they might be recommended. She asked her husband to speak to Boyle personally about his remedy first, and to find out what he recommended. She was also careful to ask him to check the details of preparation with Boyle, asking him repeatedly to 'take his [Boyle's] directions . . . for the taking of it, both for the time he would have it to be continued and the quantity, as also what vehicle he thinks most proper to give it in'.[32] This indicates that she understood the importance of preparation and dosage. And her comment that she thought that 'sack may bee too hott' as a suspension for it, suggests that she had some practical knowledge of remedies.[33]

Anne Conway hoped that her husband might be able to obtain Boyle's preparation via his friend, Boyle's brother Roger, Lord Orrery.[34] In the event, Lord Conway proposed to collect the medicine in person.[35] Within three weeks he reported to Sir George Rawdon that 'she is taking a Medcine [*sic*] of Mr. Robert Boyles' and that her health had improved enough for him to bring her to London.[36] At the time of her initial request to her husband to obtain the *ens veneris* Anne Conway had been sufficiently impressed by Boyle's *Considerations Touching . . . Experimental Philosophy*, which she had borrowed from Hernshaw, that she asked her husband to buy a copy for her. In fact she was so impressed by the book that she asked her husband to buy her other recent publications of Boyle's.[37] This request suggests that Lady Conway's interest in Boyle was not solely medical, but extended to his

31 Ibid., p. 226. 32 Ibid., pp. 230. Cf. pp. 228, 229. 33 Ibid., p. 230.

34 In the Conway papers among the Hastings MSS in the Huntington Library, Orrery's name occurs frequently. Although Lord Conway describes him as a friend, their relationship did not always run smoothly. In 1670 Conway complains about the way Orrery's servants messed up his London home: 'threwe Glasses of wine, and wiped their greasy fingers upon my best hangings'. Lord Conway to Sir George Rawdon, 14 Oct. 1670, HA 14495.

35 *Conway Letters*, p. 230.

36 Lord Conway to Sir George Rawdon, 27 September, 1664, Hastings MSS, HA 14406.

37 *Conway Letters*, p. 226.

natural philosophy in general. The books her husband bought might have included, besides *Some Considerations*, Boyle's most recently published book at this date, *The History of Colours* (1663). But her husband might also have obtained for her other recent books by Boyle, such as *Specimens of Chymical Experiments* (1661), or *Some Specimens of an Attempt to make Chymical Experiments useful to Illustrate the Notions of the Corpuscular Philosophy* (1661), or even *The Sceptical Chymist* (1661). It is also most likely that Anne Conway's new interest led her to acquire subsequent publications of Boyle's: for example, *The Origine of Forms and Qualities* (1666) which sets out his most systematic matter theory, developing many of the ideas adumbrated in *Some Considerations*. She certainly owned Boyle's *Hydrostatical Paradoxes* (1666), which she lent to More.[38]

Anne Conway's request to her husband to obtain other books by Boyle is significant because it enables us to date her reading of Boyle. It is perhaps surprising that she had not read his writings before this, since the Conways and the Boyles were well known to each other through their Irish interests. Lord Conway was a friend and political ally of Boyle's older brother Roger, Earl of Orrery. Furthermore, her friend and mentor Henry More had had links with Robert Boyle through the Hartlib circle. More was also a Fellow of the Royal Society, albeit a less active one than Boyle, and had referred to Boyle's experiments in his published writings. The medical experts whom Anne Conway consulted included Frederick Clodius, son-in-law of Samuel Hartlib and close associate of Boyle. Boyle would have known of Anne Conway, since her visit to Rouen is mentioned in a letter to him by Henry Oldenburg in 1659.[39] Boyle also seems to have been acquainted with John Finch, whom he describes in his *Experimental History of Colours* as 'the deservedly famous Dr J. Finch'.[40] These personal links with the Boyles notwithstanding, Anne Conway's unsureness as to whether Boyle was living in London or Oxford in 1664 would seem to suggest that neither she nor Lord Conway knew Robert Boyle personally at this point in time. This situation was to change, however. In 1665 Boyle was witness to Valentine Greatrakes' healing sessions during the visit to England arranged by Lord

[38] Ibid., p. 269.

[39] Oldenburg to Boyle 11/21 April 1659, in Robert Boyle, *The Correspondence of Robert Boyle*, ed. Michael Hunter, Antonio Clericuzio and Lawrence M. Principe, 6 vols. (London: Pickering and Chatto, 2001), vol. I, p. 321. Henry Oldenburg (*c.* 1615–77) was appointed secretary of the Royal Society in 1663. He was closely associated with the Boyle family. He was also a friend of F. M. van Helmont.

[40] Robert Boyle, *The Works of the Honourable Robert Boyle*, 5 vols. (London, 1772), vol. II, p. 13. Finch and Baines met Robert Boyle's nephew, Roger, son of the Earl of Orrery, while he was in Florence in 1667. *Conway Letters*, p. 281.

Conway. If through no other means, Robert Boyle would have been made aware of Lady Conway and her illness by this episode. By 1675 the Boyle connection was sufficiently well established for his Pall Mall address to be used as a forwarding point for items being sent to Ragley.[41] In 1677 we find Lord Conway citing Boyle for a high opinion of the Warwickshire physician, Dr Johnson.[42]

EXPERIMENTAL PHILOSOPHY

The first book of Boyle's which Anne Conway obtained was the aforementioned *Some Considerations*. In this Boyle discusses in detail the three chemical medicines that he employed most: *flores colchotaris, balsamum sulphuris crassum* and *cornu cervini*. The remedy which interested Anne Conway, the *ens veneris*, is the one also known to Boyle as *flores colchotaris*. This Boyle recommends for treating fevers and persistent headaches. He also mentions the success his sister Lady Ranelagh had using it to treat children with rickets.[43] Of his three most favoured remedies, it is to *ens veneris* that Boyle gives most space in *Some Considerations*, adding an appendix explaining its preparation in great detail.[44] In addition to the therapeutic possibilities Boyle's book offered Anne Conway, she would also have found food for thought in its theoretical content. In the book Boyle defends medicine as a legitimate part of philosophy. Among other arguments, he claims that originally philosophers were also physicians. It was Hippocrates, he says, who was the first to separate physic from philosophy.[45] In this way he justifies the appropriateness of including a discussion of medicine in a treatise of philosophy. The book also propounds a corpuscular theory of substance, according to which the physical world is constituted of 'an innumerable multitude of very variously configur'd Corpuscles'. Boyle's corpuscular philosophy was, moreover, the product of an investigative method in which observation and experiment were central. Boyle's experimental philosophy is, furthermore, harnessed to pious uses, a recommendation, no doubt, as far as Anne Conway was concerned. The preface of *Some Considerations* emphasises that the study of natural philosophy has apologetic value against atheists, and promotes Christianity by cultivating both speculative and practical virtues.[46] In the first part of the book Boyle argues that the

[41] Ibid., p. 409.
[42] Lord Conway to Sir George Rawdon, 13 July 1677, Hastings MSS, HA 14555.
[43] Robert Boyle, *Some Considerations Touching the Usefulnesse of Experimental Naturall Philosophy* (London, 1663), p. 165.
[44] Ibid., pp. 164–5 and pp. 236 ff.
[45] Ibid., p. 236.
[46] Ibid., 'Publisher to the Reader'.

attributes of God, especially His power, wisdom and goodness, are displayed in the 'fabric of the World'. Since, therefore, study of natural philosophy leads us to an appreciation of God's glory, to forbid such study is to side with the enemies of religion.[47]

Robert Boyle is generally regarded as a proponent of the mechanical philosophy. It is certainly the case that he defended it as the most effective explanation of natural phenomena. For example, in *Some Considerations* he commends the value to medical science of 'those fertile and comprehensive Principles of Philosophy, the Motions, Shapes, Magnitudes and Textures of the Minute parts of Matter'.[48] However, his use of mechanical natural philosophy is, arguably, an adaptation, since his corpuscular philosophy accommodates the idea that matter has chemical properties. *Some Considerations* certainly recommends mechanical explanations as the simplest and most comprehensive. But it also testifies to Boyle's debt to Jan Baptiste Van Helmont (to be discussed in the next chapter). The second part of the book is devoted entirely to a discussion of Helmontian medicine. Boyle particularly recommends chemical philosophy as holding the key to improving both the theoretical and the therapeutic aspects of medicine. Finally, Boyle's modification of the mechanical philosophy, so as to allow the possibility of active powers in matter, accords with Anne Conway's own partial reception of Cartesianism – her acceptance of Descartes' analysis of the laws of motion and her rejection of his definition of body as inert extension.

Although Anne Conway's *Principles* is constructed on an a priori model, the central section of the treatise suggests that she did apply observational techniques in her thinking about the natural world. But it is unlikely that it was Boyle's *Some Considerations* that prompted her to use observational methods, since his was not the first experiential natural philosophy that she had encountered. Nevertheless, Boyle was certainly an important point of contact with the experimental science of the Royal Society. But he was not the only one – Anne Conway's brother John Finch was of course another. And, as we shall see, the basis of her observational practice could just as much have been Helmontian as inspired by the *virtuosi* of the Royal Society. One book we do know that was in the library at Ragley Hall was Thomas Sprat's *The History of the Royal Society of London* (1667).[49] Between 1665 and the early 1670s Anne Conway was made acutely aware of theoretical and methodological issues surrounding experimentalism. This came about

[47] Ibid., pp. 32, 60. [48] Ibid., p. 282.

[49] Stubbe mentions that he and More looked at copy of Sprat's book in Ragley library in 1670, and that More marked particular passages, 'as 'tis your custom'. Henry Stubbe, *A Letter to Dr Henry More in Answer to what he writ and printed in Mr Glanvil's Book* (Oxford, 1671), p. 63.

for two main reasons: first of all there was the heated debate occasioned by the visit of the healer Valentine Greatrakes and the debate about Royal Society science which it fuelled. Secondly, the issues concerning the proper conduct of experiments and the conclusions to be drawn from them were thrown sharply into focus by the controversy between Boyle and Henry More in the 1670s.

VALENTINE GREATRAKES

Anne Conway read Boyle against the background of the excitement and debate generated by the visit to England of the Irish Protestant healer, Valentine Greatrakes.[50] In January–February 1666, Greatrakes visited Ragley at the behest of Lord Conway, who used all his influence in Ireland, and his credit with the Boyle family, to persuade Greatrakes to travel to England in order to try his healing powers on his wife. Greatrakes' method involved the laying on of hands, whence his name 'the Stroker'. His visit was a sensation. As Marjorie Nicolson relates, crowds flocked to Ragley to see him perform and in the hope that he might work miracles on their ailing and paralysed relatives. To the great disappointment of the Conways his attempt to cure Anne Conway proved a failure. Nonetheless, he brought relief to others. 'My wife is not the better for him', Conway wrote to his brother-in-law, adding 'very few others have failed under his hands, of many hundreds that he hath touched in these parts'.[51] Greatrakes nevertheless made a favourable impression, as Lord Conway told Rawdon. He formed 'a very good opinion of him for an honest man, and we all think he deserves a better esteeme then he hath attained in his owne Country'.[52] Greatrakes, for his part, formed a high opinion of Anne Conway, whom he calls 'the incomparable Lady of the world (I believe) for worth, & sufferings'.[53] Among those whom he treated successfully was the son of Henry More's friend Ralph Cudworth. The witnesses to Greatrakes' cures were Lord Conway, Robert Boyle,[54] Ezekiel Foxcroft, Henry More, George Rust and Henry Stubbe. Foxcroft supplied a list of affidavits for the genuineness of Greatrakes' healing. These were appended to Stubbe's account of Greatrakes in his *Miraculous Conformist* (1666). After spending about a month at Ragley, Greatrakes went to London, where he demonstrated his

[50] On Greatrakes, see *Conway Letters*, chapter 5, Steneck (1982) and Kaplan (1982).

[51] *Rawdon Papers*, p. 212.

[52] Hastings MSS, HA 14436.

[53] Greatrakes to Boyle, 12 Sept. 1666, in Boyle, *Correspondence*, vol. IV, p. 98.

[54] A list of questions by Boyle regarding Greatrakes is printed in Maddison (1969). See also BL MS Additional 4,293 for Boyle on Greatrakes.

powers at court and to members of the Royal Society, and where, again, he was mobbed by the curious and the sick.[55]

Greatrakes' visit was the occasion of sharp controversy. There was speculation as to whether his cures were miraculous, or whether he performed them with the aid of the devil. He was accused by some of being a charlatan, but others offered naturalistic explanations for his successes.[56] Henry More explained Greatrakes' powers as a natural gift of healing given by God, and rendered the more efficacious by his piety. The process, however, was a physical one, whereby friction of his hand rendered the diseased matter subtle and drove it out through other parts of the body (e.g. fingers, feet, nose or tongue).[57] The efficacy of Greatrakes' cures was amenable to explanation in terms of a metaphysics of spirit, as opposed to medical theory. Henry More advanced just such an explanation in 1654, when he accounted for the healing powers of Matthew Coker, which he said were 'partly naturall and partly devotionall'. According to More, Coker worked his cures by a sort of transfusion of spirit:

> therefore he laying his hands upon diseased persons, his spiritts run out of his own body into the party diseased, and actuate and purify the blood and spiritts of the diseased party, which I conceive they do with more efficacy, if he add devotion to his laying on of his hands, for that setts his spiritts afloat the more copiously and animates them the more strongly, and they being no spiritts of a melancholy man but thus refin'd sublimated, they are the more feirce and strong in their motions, and more effectuall for the kindling of life and spiritt in such dead and diseased limbs as he is said to have healed.[58]

More defended Coker against the charge that he works 'by the power of the Devill', although he denied that Coker could perform miracles. He argued that Coker's healing powers were enhanced by his piety, his 'long temperance and devotion' which resulted in 'the blood and spirits' becoming 'sanative and healing . . . a true elixir'. His view was echoed by George Rust, who is reported by Joseph Glanvill as saying of Greatrakes 'I refer all his vertue to his particular Temper and Complexion, and I take his Spirits to be a kind of Elixir, and universal Ferment, and that he cures (as Dr M. expresseth it) by a sanative contagion.'[59] Lord Conway too echoed More in ascribing Greatrakes' healing powers to 'a sanative virtue and a

[55] Valentine Greatrakes, *A Brief Account of Mr Valentine Greatraks, and Divers of the Cures by him lately performed* (London, 1666). *Conway Letters*, pp. 246–50.

[56] See Jacob (1983).

[57] More, Scholium to *Enthusiasmus triumphatus*, section LVIII, in *Opera omnia*, vol. III, p. 224.

[58] *Conway Letters*, p. 101.

[59] Glanvill, *Sadducismus triumphatus*, cited in *Conway Letters*, p. 174.

natural efficiency'.[60] Whatever their explanatory theories, the several expertise of Willis, Boyle and Greatrakes did not achieve the desired outcome of curing Lady Conway. In October 1667, Lord Conway lamented to his brother-in-law: 'I leaue my wife in a weak Estate, she expects to dye evry hower but the Drs. think she will hold out till Spring, her condition is very lamentable.'[61] The failure in efficacy of their treatments did not mean there was a failure in theory. On the contrary, this episode led to important discussions of method and metaphysics in the Ragley circle, to which Anne Conway was privy. These discussions were conducted against a background of more public polemic, sparked initially by the involvement of the Warwickshire physician, Henry Stubbe.

HENRY STUBBE

Henry Stubbe was one of the local physicians consulted by the Conways.[62] He is best known today as a former radical and as a gadfly who attacked the experimental methods of the Royal Society and challenged the *virtuosi*'s claim to be practitioners of godly science.[63] Like Thomas Hobbes, Stubbe was an outsider to the Royal Society. At the time of Greatrakes' visit to Ragley, Stubbe had recently returned from a three-year sojourn in Jamaica (from 1662 to 1665).[64] Stubbe records Greatrakes' visit to Ragley in his *Miraculous Conformist* (1666), giving a closely observed account of Greatrakes' exercise of his healing powers, along with a balanced consideration of the possible explanation of his successes and failures. In the course of this discussion, Stubbe rejects the suggestion that Greatrakes was blessed with miraculous powers, and repudiates the concomitant imputation that he worked by the power of the devil. He offers an explanation of Greatrakes' cures partly in terms of the physical effect of massage, and partly in terms of the Helmontian doctrine of ferments, according to which 'our Life is but a Fermentation of the Blood, nervous Liquor, and innate constitution of the parts of our Body'.[65] Stubbe probably derived this Helmontian theory from his teacher, Thomas Willis. He did, however, concede that Greatrakes

[60] *Conway Letters*, p. 268. Daniel Coxe (FRS, 1640–1730) also accepted More's explanation of Greatrakes' healing powers, as he told Robert Boyle in March 1666. Boyle, *Correspondence*, vol. III, p. 82.

[61] Lord Conway to Sir George Rawdon, 8 Oct. 1667, Hastings MSS, HA 14464.

[62] Lord Conway had a high opinion of Stubbe. See ibid., HA 14464, 8 Oct. 1667.

[63] Henry Stubbe, *Legends No Histories* (London, 1670). See Jacob (1983).

[64] Jacob (1983).

[65] Henry Stubbe, *The Miraculous Conformist* (London, 1666), p. 14.

had received some kind of gift from God which had rendered his temperament particularly suitable to effect these cures by rubbing and chafing the affected parts of the patient's body. He concludes:

That God had bestowed upon Mr Greatarick a peculiar Temperament, or composed his Body of some particular Ferments, the Effluvia whereof, being introduced sometimes by a light, sometimes by a violent Friction, should restore the Temperament of the Debilitated parts, re-invigorate the Bloud, and dissipate all heterogenous Ferments out of the Bodies of the Diseased, by the Eyes, Nose, Mouth, Hand and feet.[66]

The God-given element notwithstanding, the explanation was a physical one. Stubbe went on: 'there may be given by God such a Natural Crassis and Effluvia consequential thereunto, that the stroaking with his hand for some space as to communicate the Virtue may restore the Blood and Spirits to that vigour and strength which is natural to them, and resuscitate the contracted imbecillity of any part'.[67] Stubbe insisted that the operation itself, the process by which the cure was effected, was a natural one:

It is Nature Cures the Diseases and distempers and infirmities, it is Nature makes them fly up and down the Body so as they do: they avoyd not his Hand, but his Touch and stroke so Invigorateth the parts that they refect the Heterogeneous Ferment, till it be outed the Body at some of these parts he is thought to stroke it out at.[68]

As 'partly naturall and partly devotionall', this explanation is not dissimilar to that offered by More. However, Stubbe's account of Greatrakes did not meet with the approval he had hoped. On 26 April 1666, More told Anne Conway that Boyle resented Stubbe's account.[69] Within three months Greatrakes felt obliged to protect himself by obtaining testimonials from worthy persons as to the integrity and innocence of his procedures.[70] He published these in *A Brief Account of Mr Valentine Greatraks, and Divers of the Cures by him Lately Performed* (1666), with a letter to his patron's brother, Robert Boyle.

CRITIQUING EXPERIMENT: UNGENTLEMANLY DISPUTE

The reasons for Boyle's resentment of Stubbe's *Miraculous Conformist* are not clear. He was apparently irritated by what he called Stubbe's 'medling with Theologicall matters' in his account of miracles.[71] But it may have

[66] Ibid., p. 10. [67] Ibid., pp. 12–13 [68] Ibid., p. 14.
[69] *Conway Letters*, p. 273. [70] Greatrakes' letter is dated 5 May 1666.
[71] [Boyle to Stubbe] 9 March 1666, in Boyle, *Correspondence*, vol. III, pp. 94–107.

been Stubbe's links with perceived opponents of the Royal Society that irked Boyle, rather than his account of Greatrakes. In 1670 Stubbe fired off the first three of a series of squibs against the Royal Society aimed at Thomas Sprat's *History of the Royal Society of London*, which had been published in 1667. Stubbe's *Legends no Histories, or, A Specimen of some Animadversions upon the History of the Royal Society* was followed by *Campanella Reviv'd: or, An Enquiry into the History of the Royal Society*, and *A Censure upon Certain Passages Contained in A History of the Royal Society*. In these provocatively entitled booklets, Stubbe struck at the heart of the Royal Society's presentational rhetoric (as exemplified by Sprat). He directly challenged the Society's claim that its members practised a Christian science, and the *virtuosi*'s claim to originality in their approach and their attempt to claim a monopoly on observational methods. In *A Censure* he supports his scepticism about the experimentalists' claim to be practising godly science by asserting Christian principles to be the criterion of true godliness, especially belief in Christ. Experiments, he points out, are no substitute for the study of scripture and striving for acceptance 'in and through the merits of Christ Jesus'. Science and philosophy (of whatever hue) are no substitute for religious faith: 'a devout Christian, will be better accepted than a *Cartesian Anthyme*, or a *Platonick* Canto of Dr *More*'.[72] As this quotation shows, Stubbe's critique of the Royal Society also took in Henry More. And he extended his critique to include the apology for the Royal Society by More's friend Joseph Glanvill, whose *Plus Ultra or, The Progress and Advancement of Knowledge Since the Days of Aristotle* (1668) had attacked Aristotelianism as obfuscatory nonsense. Stubbe's critique of Glanvill, *Plus Ultra Reduced to a Non-Plus, or a Specimen of some Animadversions upon the Plus Ultra of Mr Glanvill* (1670), was published with *Legends no Histories*. The ensuing exchange of polemics brought Henry More into the fray. Glanvill replied to Stubbe with a letter addressed to More – *A Praefatory Answer to Mr Henry Stubbe, the Doctor of Warwick. Wherein Malignity, Hypocrisie, Falshood of his Temper, Pretences, Reports, and the Impertinency of his Arguings & Quotations in his Animadversions on Plus Ultra, are Discovered* (1671). To Glanvill's riposte, Stubbe fired off his *A Reply unto the Letter Written to Mr Henry Stubbe in Defense of the History of the Royal Society* (Oxford, 1671). Stubbe's staunch defence of Aristotle was accompanied by the very modern claim that the medical tradition of Galen is to be credited with perfecting investigative procedures based on observation and experiment. Stubbe proposed his own

[72] Henry Stubbe, *A Censure upon Certain Passages Contained in A History of the Royal Society* (London, 1670), p. 27.

view of medical philosophy, as deriving not just from Hippocrates, but also from Aristotle and Galen, whose well-tried methods were based on reason and experience – principles put to the test in practice. Galenic medicine, he argues, is 'operative knowledge, guided by certain rules and observations to affect its end'.[73] Berating Glanvill for ignorance, dogmatism and suppression of evidence, he dismisses the idea that Galen's legacy was retrograde by instancing some of the best contemporary physicians, among them Mayerne. The Royal Society experimenters have no monopoly on experiment, since the principle of 'continual and diligent observation and reading' is an Aristotelian principle.

The Stubbe–Sprat–Glanvill spat was not directly connected to the Valentine Greatrakes affair. However, Stubbe's *Miraculous Conformist* was a demonstration of the cogency of his Galenic method – albeit with a Helmontian dimension in its application of the theory of ferments. But the presence of Stubbe at Ragley Hall ensured that the Royal Society view and Boyle's experimentalism did not go unchallenged in Anne Conway's circle. She studied Boyle against this background of detraction from Stubbe. Furthermore, it might be added that Stubbe had a high opinion of Hobbes – a factor which may have reinforced his scepticism about Sprat's claims, since Hobbes was excluded from the community of *virtuosi* at the Royal Society.

APPROPRIATING EXPERIMENTS: GENTLEMANLY CONTROVERSY

Stubbe's attack on Glanvill inevitably involved Glanvill's friend, Henry More, who found himself caught in the cross-fire of claim and counterclaim. In fact Stubbe said that he had discussed the atheism of the mechanical philosophy with More at Ragley Hall in 1666. On that occasion he had pointed out to More that they both shared the view that the mechanical philosophy was atheistic. More, for his part, struggled to keep faith with the experimenters, and to interpret their activities as commensurate with his own apologetic agenda. He felt constricted by the fact that Stubbe was a protégé of the Conways.[74] Angry that he was being used as 'a clod in the field to pelt the Royall Society with',[75] he wrote a letter of support to Glanvill, which the latter published along with his own answer to Stubbe.[76] In his *Enchiridion metaphysicum*, the proofs of which he was finalising at this time, More underlined his opposition to Cartesian mechanism, explaining

[73] Ibid., p. 41. [74] *Conway Letters*, p. 328. [75] Ibid., p. 507.
[76] Glanvill, *A Praefatory Answer* includes *A Letter from Dr More to J.G.*

to Lady Conway that this was 'as well a confutation of the Mechanick Philosophy as a Demonstration of Incorporeall Beings'.[77]

More saw no inconsistency between Royal Society claims to be practising godly science and his own application of that science to support his philosophy of spirit. To this end he had cited experiments from Boyle's *New Experiments Physico Mechanical touching the Spring of the Air, and its Effects* (1660) in the revised version of *An Antidote Against Atheism* published in his *A Collection of Several Philosophical Writings* in 1662.[78] Indeed, subsequently, he apparently conducted his own experiments, using equipment graciously supplied by Anne Conway.[79] In the 1662 *Antidote*, More drew on some of Boyle's experiments (numbers 2, 23 and 32), from which Boyle had originally concluded that natural phenomena may be explained by the 'mechanical affections of matter, without recourse to fuga vacui, or the anima mundi, or other unphysical principle'.[80] More, for his part, believed the experiments might be interpreted to support the existence of 'an All-Comprehensive and Eternal Counsel for the ordering and the guiding of the Motion of the Matter in the Universe to what is for the best' – in other words, confirmation of his hypothesis of the Spirit of Nature.[81]

Boyle did not take issue with More on this immediately. His public censure of More appears to have been sparked by More's repeated use of his experiments in *Enchiridion metaphysicum* published in 1671, at the time of Stubbe's *Censure* of the Royal Society. In his *An Hydrostatical Discourse occasioned by the Objections of the Learned Dr. Henry More* (1672),[82] Boyle objected to More's use of the experiments described to support his hypothesis of the Spirit of Nature. Perhaps the Stubbe controversies had made Boyle sensitive to the need to defend his experimental method and its rules of inference more closely. He professed to be motivated by his fear that, if he did not answer More, his position 'might pass for unanswerable, especially among those learned men, who, not being versed in hydrostaticks, would be apt to take his [More's] authority'. Boyle insisted on the limited scope of his experimental investigations, sticking by the mechanical explanation of the phenomena observed in his air-pump experiments: 'All that I have endeavoured to do . . . is to shew, that . . . the phaenomena, I strive to explicate, may be solved mechanically, that is by the mechanical

[77] Ibid.

[78] More, *Antidote*, pp. 43–47 in *A Collection* (*An Antidote* first appeared in 1653). For accounts of this controversy see Shapin and Schaffer (1985) pp. 207–23, Hall (1990). Also Henry (1990).

[79] *Conway Letters*, p. 405.

[80] Boyle, *Hydrostatical Discourse*, in *Works*, vol. III, p. 270.

[81] More, *Antidote*, p. 43, in *A Collection*.

[82] Boyle, *Works*, vol. III, p. 270.

affections of matter, without recourse to nature's abhorrence of a vacuum, to substantial forms, or to other incorporeal creatures.'[83] Boyle was careful to state his agnosticism towards alternative explanations, saying that he had not intended 'not to prove, that no angel or other immaterial creature could interpose in these cases'. There ensued a dignified exchange, which has been characterised as a model of gentlemanly civility.[84] More justified his position in a conciliatory letter to Boyle, in which he sought to explain that he was motivated by concerns about the atheistical implications of the mechanical philosophy, especially if physical phenomena are explained entirely in terms of the properties of matter. The thing he 'so much contends for', he tells Boyle, is 'that the phenomena of the world cannot be solved merely mechanically, but that there is the necessity of the assistance of a substance distinct from matter, that is, of a spirit, or being incorporeal'.[85] But their difference of opinion did not end there. As he explained in this letter to Boyle, his fears that Cartesian mechanism, by downplaying the agency of God, could encourage atheism, appeared to be confirmed in Spinoza's *Tractatus theologico-politicus* published in 1670.[86] Even while attempting to refute Spinoza,[87] More continued to defend the Spirit of Nature, and to voice reservations about the inferences Boyle drew from his experiments. Others entered the fray, among them the Chief Justice, Lord Hales, who took issue with Boyle in two essays published in 1673 and 1674. Although Hales rejected the idea of a universal spirit, his anti-mechanical position and his general sympathy with spirit theory encouraged More to invoke him as an ally. As late as 1676, in *Remarks upon Two Late Ingenious Discourses*, More targets Boyle's imputation of powers to matter, and most of all his imputation of elasticity to air – what More dubbed 'that monstrous spring of the ayre'.[88]

Boyle, for his part, was opposed to using metaphysical hypotheses as explanations for the observable phenomena of nature, especially where they simply duplicated other explanations. He had little time for appeals to intermediary causes, insisting on 'the generally owned rule about hypotheses,

[83] Ibid., p. 276. [84] Shapin and Schaffer (1985), p. 208. [85] *Conway Letters*, p. 520.

[86] The charges against Spinoza may have been something of an embarrassment to Boyle, who, between 1662 and 1663, through Henry Oldenburg, had conducted a correspondence with him about the nature of experiment. Oldenburg had maintained his correspondence with Spinoza until 1665. The correspondence was resumed in 1675, when Spinoza sent Oldenburg a copy of the *Tractatus*. One result of this was that Oldenburg considerably modified his initial enthusiasm for Spinoza. See Hutton (1995c). On More's refutation of Spinoza, see Colie (1957 and 1959), Hutton (1984).

[87] *Epistola altera*, More's refutation of the *Tractatus* was published in his *Opera omnia*, vol. II.

[88] Ibid., p. 423. Royal Society stalwarts who spoke up on Boyle's behalf included Henry Oldenburg, Robert Hooke and John Wallis. See Hall (1990) and Shapin and Schaffer (1985).

that *entia non sunt multiplicanda absque necessitate*' (entities should not be multiplied unnecessarily).[89] Although he was ready to accept that many natural processes could not be observed, because they involved the movement of corpuscles invisible to the human eye (for example, magnetic effects), Boyle was reluctant to put forward explanations which smacked of Aristotelian occultism. For example, in *Some Considerations* he rejects the Aristotelian denial of the void by the doctrine of *horror vacui* (the doctrine that nature abhors a vacuum) as an example of an explanatory hypothesis which 'supposes that there is a kinde of *Anima Mundi*, furnished with various Passions, which watchfully provides for the safety of the Universe'.[90] Henry More's 'Spirit of Nature', was, of course, just this kind of hypothesis. Boyle's own view of divine design obviated the need for any such intermediary agent, since the 'ordinary Concourse' of God's providence was sufficient to ensure that the 'innumerable multitude of very variously configur'd Corpuscles' produced the phenomena we observe as 'Bodies necessarily acting according to those Impressions or Law . . . as if each of those Creatures had a Design of Self-Preservation, and were furnish'd with Knowledge and Industry to prosecute it'.[91] Arguably, Boyle understood intermediate causes not merely as otiose and obfuscating, but as obstructive to the true enterprise of the Christian *virtuoso*. In his *A Free Enquiry into the Vulgarly Received Notion of Nature*, first drafted in 1665, but not published until 1686, Boyle takes up these themes, attacking the 'vulgar' notion of nature as unproven, unnecessary, obscure and un-Christian. Although Henry More's hypothesis of the Spirit of Nature is nowhere named, it is implicitly one of Boyle's targets. In particular Boyle's critique of the Platonic doctrine of the World Soul in section IV may be taken to be a veiled criticism of More's Hylarchic Principle. Here he castigates certain unnamed Christian philosophers for imputing to universal nature 'as many wonderful powers and prerogatives as the idolaters did to their adored mundane soul'.[92] In section V, he alludes more directly to More's hypothesis when he attacks those who conceive nature to be an immaterial substance which is 'the grand author of the motion of bodies'. The example he gives of 'the ascension of water in pumps' would seem to be a direct allusion to More's appropriation of his own experiments.[93]

[89] Boyle, *Hydrostatical Discourse*, in *Works*, vol. III, p. 276.

[90] Boyle, *Some Considerations*, p. 68. Boyle probably had in mind earlier chemical philosophers, like Duchesne and D'Espagnet, who accepted the existence of a universal spirit.

[91] Ibid., p. 71.

[92] Robert Boyle, *A Free Enquiry into the Vulgarly Conceived Notion of Nature* (London, 1686; modern edn, ed. E. B. Davis and M. Hunter, Cambridge: Cambridge University Press, 1996), p. 50.

[93] Ibid., p. 61.

Anne Conway was fully aware of More's controversy with Boyle. In 1671 she reported to More Boyle's opinion that he 'had better never have printed it, for you are mistaken in your experiments'.[94] This comment suggests that she thought the main shortcoming of More's position was his experimentalism, rather than his hypothesis of the Spirit of Nature. It is very likely that she was as fully engaged in the discussions of the issue as she was later over the matter of George Keith's 'new notion of Christ' (see below, chapter 9). We do not have a continuous exchange of letters to document any contribution she may have made to the More–Boyle controversy. But we do know that More asked her to point out to him his experimental mistakes. And her lending him a copy of Boyle's *Hydrostatical Paradoxes* in 1666, together with her buying for him 'hydrostatical knacks', suggest that she took a lively interest in the debate.

What her view of the controversy was we cannot be sure. But it is fair to infer that she did not think Boyle's objections convincingly disposed of the need for intermediary spiritual cause, since she herself postulated just such an intermediate cause between God and the world – the Middle Nature (*natura media*) of her philosophical system. More's vigorous defence of his hypothesis of the Spirit of Nature may have persuaded her of its value. Her own conception of Middle Nature certainly has much in common with More's Hylarchic Principle. Her *natura media* is not a sub-divine entity, like More's Spirit of Nature, but closely allied to God, as a manifestation of the divine in the created world. Middle Nature is not just a principle of causality, but the outgoing word of God (*logos prophorikos*), the son of God. While it is more than probable, therefore, that Anne Conway's high regard for Boyle's theories may have increased her confidence in his experimental methodology, the More–Boyle controversy, may have led Anne Conway to revisit her version of the Spirit of Nature. The divine character of Middle Nature implicitly meets Boyle's objection that this type of cause is un-Christian. At all events, Boyle's scepticism about metaphysical physics did not shake her confidence in metaphysical hypotheses. It may well be that her encounter with Spinoza's philosophy was a factor here – she certainly shared some of More's concerns about Spinozism. But by the time of More's defence of the Spirit of Nature against Boyle, she had encountered a champion of chemistry who was sympathetic to the metaphysical theories of More – Francis Mercury van Helmont.

[94] Ibid., p. 420. Also p. 358. See Henry (1990) and Hall (1990), pp. 181 ff.

KATHERINE RANELAGH

Before leaving the Boyle connection, some mention should be made of the outstanding woman in Boyle's circle, his sister Katherine Jones, Viscountess Ranelagh (1615–91). There is a strong possibility that Anne Conway became acquainted with her – though there is no mention of this in the surviving correspondence of either woman.[95] As intelligent women on the margins of intellectual life in the mid-seventeenth century, Lady Ranelagh and Anne Conway have much in common. Lady Ranelagh was a leading woman activist of her generation, closely involved with the Hartlib circle, deeply interested in educational, ethical, religious and scientific matters, and well known as a lady of 'vast Reach both of Kowledg and Apprehensions'.[96] Like Anne Conway, she had a distinguishing streak of non-conformist piety, and sufficient interest in Hebrew to set about learning it.[97] Unlike Anne Conway, she was active in contemporary politics, especially during the Commonwealth period. Also unlike Anne Conway, Lady Ranelagh left no writings from which we may form an impression of her thinking. Instead, she is visible largely by virtue of her association with others, most notably the circles of Samuel Hartlib, John Milton and her brother, Robert Boyle. As a member of one of the most important Protestant aristocratic families in Ireland, Lady Ranelagh and her brother Robert shared the same political interests as the Conways. And indeed Lord Conway was a close friend of her brother Roger Boyle, Earl of Orrery, and was well acquainted with her son Richard Jones in the 1670s.[98] In spite of this, and in spite of the fact that, as we have just seen, Lady Conway was in touch with her brother Robert Boyle, any links between the two women can only be guessed at, since there is no mention of their acquaintance in any correspondence. Nevertheless, there is enough to suggest that they must have at least been aware of one another. Valentine Greatrakes visited her when he was in London, after his visit to Ragley in 1666. On at least one occasion Lady Conway instructed More to send papers to her via Lady Ranelagh's house

95 Lady Ranelagh had her own collection of medical receipts (Hunter 1997b). Subsequently, Lord Conway became acquainted with her son, Arthur Jones, Viscount Ranelagh.

96 Burnet, *History*, p. 33.

97 See William Robertson's dedication to her of his *The Gate or Door to the Holy Tongue* (London, 1653).

98 Lynch (1965), p. 135. For Richard Jones, see *Conway Letters*, pp. 440, 463–5 and Hastings MSS, HA 14531, 14551, *Calendar of State Papers, Domestic, Car. II.* 412, 6, *Calendar of State Papers, Ireland, Car. II*, 339, 35. 14 September 1679. It was Lord Ranelagh who introduced him to Robert Hooke as architect for the proposed new Ragley Hall. Anne Conway may also have known Lady Ranelagh's sister, Mary Rich, Countess of Warwick, as an aristocratic neighbour. Her husband, the Earl of Warwick, was touched by Greatrakes in 1666 (Boyle, *Correspondence*, vol. III, p. 82).

in Pall Mall.[99] Lady Ranelagh was considerably older than Anne Conway, and the latter's ill health prevented her from having social relations with the ladies of London. But these factors need not have prevented them from being aware of one another as women of ideas. However, in the absence of documentary confirmation, it is impossible to decide the matter with certainty.

[99] This was in 1675, and the papers in question were More's reply to George Keith. *Conway Letters*, p. 409.

CHAPTER 7

Physic and philosophy: Van Helmont, father and son

Before the controversies between More, Stubbe and Boyle had played themselves out, a new figure entered Anne Conway's life. This was Francis Mercury van Helmont (1614–98), whom she first encountered in 1670. Physician, alchemist, inventor, diplomat, religious seeker, natural philosopher and Christian kabbalist, Francis Mercury van Helmont is a colourful figure who defies classification in modern terms.[1] Anne Conway's contact with him was to have a decisive impact on her thinking and outlook in her last years. The importance of Francis Mercury van Helmont for Anne Conway was, of course, not confined to medicine, and cannot be adequately covered in a single chapter. Like More, Van Helmont was someone who had a far-reaching impact on her thinking, as she did on his. His crucial importance in introducing her to Quakerism and kabbalism is too large a topic to discuss here and will be dealt with in later chapters. In this chapter we shall meet him in the capacity in which he first entered her life, namely as a physician. In that capacity he certainly had his own distinctive medical philosophy, but it originated from the natural philosophy of his famous father, Jan Baptiste van Helmont (1579–1646), whose legacy Francis Mercury had been responsible for collecting and publishing. Together, Jan Baptiste van Helmont and his son Francis Mercury were by far the most important of the many medical and natural philosophers whose chemical and biological theory forms the background to Lady Conway's treatise. This chapter will give some account of the elder Van Helmont before discussing his son. Since it was the latter who put Anne Conway in touch with Princess Elizabeth of Bohemia, it will close with a brief discussion of her.

Although, as we have seen, Anne Conway's acquaintance with medical and biological theory antedates her meeting with Van Helmont by many years, it was above all in the theories of the Van Helmonts that she found

[1] For a full account of Van Helmont, see Coudert (1999).

a theory of change on which to base her explanation of the workings of the created universe in terms other than those offered by the mechanical philosophy. It is a basic principle of her philosophy that the creation should be like its creator. In chapters VI and VII of her *Principles* she deduces the existence and properties of the third species (creation) a priori from the attributes of God. The idea that nature manifests the wisdom and goodness of God is a familiar *topos* of Christian philosophy, not least among the Cambridge Platonists. But where they rested their defence of religion on a natural philosophy which assumed that the constituent elements of created nature were active spirit and inert material substance, Anne Conway argued that, if God is 'life itself', his entire creation must be a living reflection of the vitality of the creator. Her account of created nature in chapters VI and VII is closer to vitalistic theories of her time than to the mechanical philosophy of Descartes, and the modified version of it proposed by More. Here she outlines a non-mechanistic account of life and action, using terminology familiar from the chemical philosophy of her day to describe the life processes of growth, change and transformation.[2] Her imputation of life and thought to the constituent particles of the physical world and her theory of the interchangeability of life forms have affinities with alchemical theories about the composition and transmutation of created things. She insists on the spirituality of 'every motion and action' and describes the interaction of bodies and particles in terms of 'emanation'. According to her theory of *vital action*, one body is able to communicate motion and life to another because 'it can extend itself through the subtle emanation of its parts'.[3] Her appeal to experience and observation is of a piece with the experimentalism of Paracelsian traditions, as is her frequent invocation of biblical texts in support of her theories. These general features of seventeenth-century chemical philosophy are also features of the iatrochemical theory developed by Jan Baptiste van Helmont and propagated by his son Francis Mercury van Helmont.

JAN BAPTISTE VAN HELMONT

Although he is critical of Paracelsus, the elder Van Helmont's own distinctive natural philosophy is derived from Paracelsianism. Van Helmont's collected writings, *Ortus medicinae*, were edited and published by his son,

[2] She invokes the theory of the transmutation of metals when she says Christ is an intermediary just as 'silver is a median between tin and gold', *Principles*, p. 25.

[3] Conway, *Principles*, p. 70.

Francis Mercury van Helmont, in 1648.[4] Couched in terms of mystical epistemology, this presents Van Helmont's wisdom as deriving from God. A critic of both Paracelsian and Galenic medicine, Van Helmont also repudiated Aristotelianism and contemporary atomistic natural philosophies. His methods of enquiry included observation and experiment to obtain quantifiable results. For this reason he is regarded as a forerunner of modern scientific method. His natural philosophy entails that all things are composed of non-corporeal entities, or monads, which contain a life principle. In place of the Aristotelian system of four elements and the Paracelsian three elements, he proposed a single element, water, as the basic substrate of all things. According to Van Helmont, the primary solid, *quellem* or quicksand, is precipitated from water to form the second of the two *elementa primagenia*, from which all natural things are constituted. There are two principles in nature, fire and water, the former warm and vivifying, the latter cool and rest-procuring. There are three types of fire: natural, solar and artificial. All things contain within them a male principle and a female one: fire being male and water female. The second principle, the 'watery essence', is a manifestation of soul. Van Helmont posits a universal motive power implanted in all living things by the creator. This he calls 'Blas' and he conceives of it as the impulse which directs and determines motion and change.[5]

Van Helmont's natural philosophy entailed a complex set of transformational mechanisms to explain the interaction of bodies and the growth and development of organisms. This process begins with water as the primary substrate, which is informed by the seeds (*semina*) and ferments. The *semina* are formative principles whence all natural bodies originate. These seeds are not physical agents, but operate according to the 'ferments' which they contain, ferments being formative spiritual agents. 'Fermentation' is the process by which bodies are refined and exalted, making them more like spirit. At the beginning the transmutational process produces 'gas' which constitutes the object's purest essence.[6] The metamorphoses effected through the transformational process result in a hierarchy of natural entities from simple substances to complex organisms.

[4] Jean Baptiste van Helmont, *Ortus medicinae, id est initia physicae inaudita, progressus medicinae novus in morborum ultionem ad vitam longam . . . edente authoris filio Francisco Mercurio van Helmont, cum ejus praefatio ex Belgico translata* (Amsterdam: Elzevir, 1648). This was translated into German by F. M. van Helmont's friend, Knorr von Rosenroth as *Aufgang der Artzeny-Kunst* (Sulzbach, 1683), into English by John Chandler as *Oriatrike, or Physick Refined* (London, 1664), and into French by Jean Leconte as *Les oeuvres de Jean Baptiste van Helmont* (Lyons, 1670). On J. B. van Helmont, see Pagel (1982), and Giglioni (1991a).

[5] Pagel (1982), pp. 87–95. [6] Ibid., p. 64.

The fundamental, vital principle, which serves as the blueprint of every individual thing, is the *archeus*. All creatures are composites of monadic particles or *archei insiti*. It is the image of the dominant spirit, the '*archeus influens*', which determines the form of any particular creature. Van Helmont's doctrine of the *archeus* forms the basis of his theory of imagination. The *archeus* operates via images, through the transmission of which Van Helmont accounts for a wide range of operations in nature. The process of growth and reproduction is effected by imaging – that is, through the transmission of an image or seed (*semen*) by the active principle and its retention by the passive principle. All interaction and communication between creatures or between their constituent elements involves the transmission of images, including the communication of thoughts and perceptions. Van Helmont's medical philosophy is based on his theory of imagination through which he explained both diseases and their cure. Since illness is caused by the interaction of the *archeus* of an intruding seed with that of its host, the imagination has a fundamental role in curing disease by restoring the image within the *archeus*.

Helmontianism had a wide diffusion in England in the second half of the seventeenth century. Initially promoted by members of the Hartlib circle, it was taken up in varying degrees by physicians and chemists alike. In 1650 Walter Charleton translated several tracts from *Ortus medicinae* in his *Ternary of Paradoxes*. In 1664 John Chandler translated *Ortus medicinae* as *Oriatrike, or Physick Refined*. During the 1660s many English iatrochemists combined Helmontian with corpuscular theories of substance.[7] Among the figures we have already discussed, Thomas Willis and Robert Boyle were, in different respects, indebted to J. B. van Helmont. Another important figure who was much indebted to Van Helmont was the most philosophical of the English physicians, Francis Glisson (*c.* 1597–1677), Regius Professor of Physic at Cambridge.[8] In his *Tractatus de natura substantiae energeticae seu vita naturae* ('Treatise on the energetic nature of substance, or the life of nature') of 1672, Glisson sets out to demonstrate the universal life of nature. Glisson drew not just on Van Helmont, but also on William Harvey's concept of irritability or natural perception, which emanates from the live tissue. Rejecting the idea that matter is devoid of life, his doctrine of *biusia*

[7] Clericuzio (2000). An earlier example is Walter Charleton's *Physiologia Epicuro-Gassendo-Charletoniana* (London, 1654), which propounds an atomistic natural philosophy based extensively on Gassendi, which propounds a theory of active matter that draws on Helmontian chemistry. On Helmontian medicine in England, see Grell (1996).

[8] Glisson is best known for his study of rickets (*De rachitide*, 1650) and the anatomy of the liver (*Anatomia hepatis*, 1654).

entails that all substance is possessed of some kind of life. Along a continuum, from lower to higher forms of living organism, 'Matter contains all forms, and consequently every kind of material life within itself potentially'.[9] He argued, further, that every substance is possessed of a principle of perception, appetite and motion. His book attacks Cartesian dualism, and especially Descartes' conception of body as inert extension. Anne Conway did not actually consult Glisson as a patient, but she was undoubtedly aware of his hylozoic theories because they were the subject of a critique by Henry More which was printed in 1679 as a scholium to his attack on Spinoza in the second volume of More's *Opera omnia*. More believed Glisson's theories to be dangerously reminiscent of Spinoza, although he did not suspect Glisson of atheism as he did Spinoza. Instead More ascribed the phenomena which Glisson believed to be evidence of hylozoism to the workings of the Spirit of Nature.[10]

Anne Conway makes no specific mention of Jan Baptiste van Helmont, but she was certainly aware of his work. As early as 1653 Van Helmont's name appears in Lord Conway's correspondence with John Finch, who mentions his treatise *Butler*, which recounts the cure of a woman who had suffered from a headache for some sixteen years. The key mediator of J. B. van Helmont's ideas was his son, Francis Mercury, who, as we shall see, drew heavily on his father's ideas in own theories. Whether Anne Conway had direct knowledge of the elder Van Helmont's theories from his writings, or was acquainted with them indirectly through his son, is impossible to say with certainty. In all probability she was indebted to both father and son for her knowledge of Helmontian life science. What is certain is that her explanation of the actual processes by which things change has a distinctly Helmontian ring, as does her account of the way creatures interact. Important among the recognisably Helmontian features of Anne Conway's philosophy is the doctrine that created substance was originally a form of spirit. She also accepts that solids take their origin from fluid. According to Anne Conway, individual creatures develop from 'universal seeds and principles' (*semina et principia*).[11] All creatures are composites of active and passive principles, denominated male and female respectively.[12] She draws on the Helmontian theory of imagination to explain the communication

[9] Francis Glisson, *Tractatus de natura substantiae energetica* (London, 1672), translation as quoted in Hall (1990). Glisson's concept of 'irritiability' is developed in his *Tractatus de ventriculo et intestine* (1662). On Glisson see Henry (1987) and Giglioni (1991b and 1996).

[10] Henry (1987). More's critique of Glisson is printed as a scholium to his attack on Spinoza, *Epistola altera* printed in *Opera philosophica*, vol. I. Cudworth's critique of hylozoism in his *The True Intellectual System of the Universe* (London, 1678), is also aimed at Glisson.

[11] *Principles*, p. 21. [12] Ibid., p. 38.

of thoughts and perceptions by the transmission of images. Her account of procreation also recalls Van Helmont's. Since all creatures are composites of monadic particles, it is the image of the dominant spirit that determines the form of any particular creature. Anne Conway does not employ Van Helmont's doctrine of the *archeus*. However, her conception of this dominant or 'ruling' spirit[13] recalls Van Helmont's '*archeus influens*'. And the 'multitude of spirits' in a creature seem to be versions of Van Helmont's subordinate *archei insiti*, while the external form of any creature is determined by the image of its dominant spirit.

FRANCIS MERCURY VAN HELMONT

Of all the medical practitioners with whom Anne Conway was acquainted, Francis Mercury van Helmont had by far the most far-reaching impact on her life. His father, Jan Baptiste van Helmont, took direct responsibility for his education because he distrusted the Galenic medicine which dominated medical faculties in this period. Thereafter, Francis Mercury pursued a career as physician, diplomat and courtier, giving counsel both practical and medical in the courts of Heidelberg, Mainz, Sulzbach and Hanover. In 1650s he became a close associate of the family of Frederick, the Elector Palatine, and his wife Elizabeth, sister of Charles I. Among other members of this family, he befriended the Elector's daughter, Princess Elizabeth, dedicatee of Descartes' *Principia philosophiae*, whom he was later (in 1658) to assist in securing the position of abbess of Herford in Westphalia. Van Helmont's success as a physician was confirmed in 1658, when he was rewarded for his services with the title of baron by the Emperor Leopold. The title was conferred at the behest of Johann Philipp von Shönborn, the Elector of Mainz (and subsequently patron of Leibniz). Van Helmont's career was not without its setbacks, however, for in 1662 he was arrested on suspicion of heresy and handed over to the Inquisition in Rome.[14] After spending two years in prison while charges of heresy were investigated, he was fortunate to be released without being prosecuted. The charges related to his Protestant leanings and philosemitic tendencies, both factors which were to shape the course of his intellectual life. Although born a Catholic, Van Helmont embarked on a personal spiritual quest which took him to Protestantism and philosemitism, and ended with his conversion to Quakerism.[15]

[13] Ibid., p. 55. [14] Coudert (1999), chapter 3.

[15] On Van Helmont's Quakerism see Coudert (1976), pp. 171–89; also Coudert (1992) and Hull (1941), p. 112.

As early as 1653, the Conways attempted to secure the medical services of Van Helmont. Edward Conway wrote to John Finch in Italy to ask him to enquire as to his whereabouts. The Conways were probably interested in Van Helmont on account of his knowledge of his father's cure for persistent headache described in his treatise *Butler*. Lord Conway believed he had the secret of a universal panacea which he hoped might cure his wife.[16] It may originally have been the second Viscount Conway who suggested that his son and daughter-in-law consult Francis Mercury van Helmont. John Finch had his doubts about the efficacy ascribed to any universal elixir, but he nonetheless attempted to discover the whereabouts of Van Helmont, consulting among others the Venetian professor of anatomy Molinetti and the mathematician Otto Tackenius. Finch suspected that the younger Van Helmont's fame as a doctor was more a matter of reputation than accomplishment, and his Italian contacts did nothing to allay his suspicions – perhaps on account of the professional jealousy of the Italians among whom Van Helmont had worked. Nonetheless, Finch was prepared to travel to Sarisburgh from Padua on hearing that Van Helmont was there with the Elector of Luneburg. But he does not appear to have succeeded in locating him. And it was not until Van Helmont arrived in England seventeen years later that the Conways managed to persuade him to visit them for a consultation. This came about thanks to the fortunate chance of his visiting Henry More when he came to England in 1670 on a mission for Princess Elizabeth of the Palatinate.[17] Van Helmont made contact with More in order to deliver letters from his friend and collaborator, the kabbalist scholar Christian Knorr von Rosenroth, who wished to consult More in connection with his project 'to bring into view again the old Judaical philosophy out of their own writings' – that is to say *Kabbala denudata* published in Germany in 1677.[18] More took the opportunity to persuade Van Helmont to offer Lady Conway his medical advice. Although Van Helmont would have preferred to visit Lady Conway for a personal consultation, lack of time prevented him from so doing at that point. So her first consultation was by letter with the aid of Doctors Ridsley and Howpert

[16] *Conway Letters*, pp. 494–7. See p. 122 above.

[17] Van Helmont came to England to claim arrears on the £400 p.a. pension that had been granted by Charles II to Princess Elizabeth in 1660 in lieu of two pensions formerly granted by Charles I. He was successful in obtaining the payments. See Weir (1941), who obtained this information from *Calendar of State Papers, Domestic*, vol. XII, and *Calendar of Treasury Books*, ed. W. A. Shaw (London, 1909), vol. IV. Van Helmont's fame as a physician had, however, gone before him by several years: the adoption of his methods by some physicians during the great plague in London in 1665 provoked attacks from the Galenists, recorded satirically in the ballad, 'London's Plague from Holland, or Inquiries after the Natural Causes of her Present Calamity'. See Coudert (1999), pp. 154–5. Also Grell (1996).

[18] See chapter 8.

(who gave an account of her illness) and Ezekiel Foxcroft (who undertook to relay Van Helmont's instructions). At some point shortly after this, Van Helmont did indeed pay a visit to Anne Conway at Ragley. He must have been very impressed by her as a person as well as a patient, for he returned to Ragley thereafter and lived as a more or less permanent member of her household until her death in 1679.[19]

By all accounts Van Helmont had an attractive personality. According to Henry More he was a good, kind person with a strong imagination. More found his conversation so engaging that on one occasion he was reduced to tears of joy. His 'phancy is strong enough in all conscience', he told Lady Conway in 1671,

> but he has a hearte so good, so kind, so officious, so plaine and simple and so desirous of the publick good, that the consideration of that in conjunction with something els, putt me into such a passion of joy and benignity, that I could not for my life keep my eyes from letting down teares, that morning in the parlour upon my converse with Mr Helmont.[20]

Van Helmont certainly seems to have made a deeply favourable impression on the Conways. Lord Conway described him to his brother-in-law as 'really an extraordinary person'. Ever the man of business, he estimated that his efforts to secure Van Helmont's help had cost him nearly £600. But he did not regret the expense: 'Wh^{t} benefit my Wife will receaue by it I cannot say yet, but I haue attained the satisfaction of doing that wch. is pleasing to my Wife in the highest degree. So I cannot regrett the expense of my money.'[21] Van Helmont assured Lord Conway that he would do all he could for his wife. Initially he appears to have given the Conways grounds for optimism that his medicines would bring her relief. Lord Conway told his brother-in-law, he 'gives us some hopes concerning my good Lady, in that he doeth not think hir incurable'.[22] But the relief Van Helmont brought Lady Conway proved only temporary and, ultimately, he failed to cure her. Nevertheless, she believed he had been more successful than the others whom she consulted, as she told her brother-in-law in 1674: 'yett I doubt not but I have had some releef (God be thanked) from his medicines, I am sure more then I ever had from ye endeavours of any person whatsoever else'.[23] We do not know in detail how Van Helmont treated Lady Conway, but the secret of even this limited success may have owed something to his

[19] He did make at least one foreign visit during this time. In July 1676 Lord Conway mentioned that 'Van Helmont is going over upon some frolick of his into Germany'. Hastings MSS, HA 14550.

[20] *Conway Letters*, p. 329.

[21] Lord Conway to Sir George Rawdon 15 Nov. 1670, Hastings MSS, HA 14496.

[22] Lord Conway to Sir George Rawdon 13 Feb. 1670–1, ibid., HA 14499.

[23] *Conway Letters*, p. 533.

own special approach to therapeutics, which is described in his *The Spirit of Diseases*. Here he argues that illnesses are psychosomatic in nature and 'that the Mind influenceth the Body in causing and curing of Diseases'. This is a view which derives from his father's account of disease and it is connected with the younger Van Helmont's own vitalist natural philosophy. With Van Helmont *fils* mind–body interaction becomes the basis of treatment of illness: the cure of bodily ailments is effected by altering the attitudes and feelings of the patient. Since diseases are the result of disordered passions (literally *dis*-tempers), they must be treated by bearing pain patiently and learning to love the disorder.[24] This was one feature of his clinical method which, according to him, did not meet with the approval of most doctors of his time.[25]

Another reason for Lady Conway's confidence in Van Helmont probably derives from the fact that he had more to offer his patient than mere medicines. Anne Conway's 1674 letter to her brother-in-law refers to the companionship Van Helmont gave her – 'yett I have had much more satisfaction in his company, he has yett ye patience to continue wt^h^ mee in my solitude wch makes it ye easier to mee'.[26] What her letter does not mention is that Van Helmont brought with him not just his own pharmacopoeia of cures, but a panoply of new ideas, religious and philosophical, which made a far greater impact on her than his medicines, and contributed profound changes to her religious and philosophical outlook. By the time he met Anne Conway, Van Helmont was deeply involved with Christian Knorr von Rosenroth's researches into the Jewish kabbalah and he had already embarked on the spiritual quest that would lead him to Quakerism. These interests brought a distinctive spiritual dimension to the Helmontian natural philosophy in which he was schooled by his father.

Van Helmont published no single comprehensive account of his ideas. Instead he published his thoughts piecemeal, usually with the aid of admirers and followers. Some of his books consist of records of their discussions with him which they published with his permission. One result of this is that his writings are sometimes attributed to others whose contributions to them were in effect no more than that of amanuensis.[27] Furthermore,

[24] In his 'Observations' in MS Sloane 530, van Helmont recounts how he acquired this insight into the treatment of pain and disease by loving them. See also Sherrer (1958).

[25] He says his method 'would oblige them to abandon their accustomed method, and to new-model the whole system of their practise', *Spirit of Diseases*, sig. A4^5^.

[26] *Conway Letters*, p. 534.

[27] The way his ideas came to be published is described in the preface of his *Paradoxal Discourses* (London, 1685), which recounts how two admirers sought him out, first in Amsterdam, then in London, and recorded their conversations with him when they found him. His *Observationes circa*

by all accounts, in the written versions (both published and unpublished) his ideas were rendered orderly by the compilers and amanuenses. The best evidence for this is his friend Leibniz, who complained that, although very interesting, Van Helmont's ideas were confused and hard to follow, and in need of being edited so as to render them comprehensible.[28] The problem of authorship surrounding Van Helmont's works is further complicated by the fact that his writings are sometimes confused with those of his father. This is not surprising in view of the fact that his philosophy incorporates much of his father's.[29] In addition to this, most of his writings were published after Anne Conway's death, and they were not published in the order of their composition. There is a good deal of overlap between them. Taken individually, they are a record of his thought in progress, amply illustrating the aural and dialogic pattern of communication which he seems to have preferred to the fixity of the printed word. No single book covers more than part of his thinking, but when taken together his books amount to a broadly consistent natural philosophy elaborated in conjunction with an equally consistent set of metaphysical and religious convictions.

Van Helmont's manuscript account of his theories, 'Some Observations of Francis Mer: Van Helmont', dated 1682, is probably the only one of his writings that can be dated with any exactness. It was written with the help of Daniel Foote three years after the death of Lady Conway.[30] There are other writings which date from Anne Conway's lifetime, but were not published until later – principally, *A Cabbalistical Dialogue* (1682), *Adumbratio cabbalae christianae* (1679) and *Two Hundred Queries* (1684), which will be discussed in later chapters. There are also writings published later still, which may date from the same period – *Paradoxal Discourses*

hominem eiusque morbos (Amsterdam, 1692) is described as 'per Paulum Buchium Med. Doct.', who is also credited with writing down van Helmont's *Het Godlyk Weezen* (Amsterdam, 1694) written 'naar de Gronden van Franciscus Mercurius van Helmont. In't Nederduytsch geschreven door Paulus Buchius Med: Doctr.', or, as the English version, *The Divine Being and its Attributes* (London, 1693) states on the title page, 'according to the Principles of M[onsieur] B[aron] of Helmont. Written in Low-Dutch by Paulus Buchius Dr of Physick'. Buchius also brought out another edition with the title, *De verduisterde waarheid aan het Ligt gebracht* (Amsterdam, 1695). *Het Godlyk Weezen* was translated into Latin by another medical acquaintance, Johannes Conrad Amman, author of two books on teaching the deaf to speak: J. C. Amman, *Surdus loquens, seu methodus, qua qui surdus natus est loqui dicere possit* (Amsterdam, 1692) – English translation by D[aniel] F[oote], *The Talking Deaf Man: or a Method Proposed, whereby he who is Born Deaf May Learn to Speak* (London, 1694) – and *Dissertatio de loquela* (Amsterdam, 1700).

[28] Gottfried Wilhelm von Leibniz, *Correspondance de Leibniz avec la Princesse Electrice Sophie de Brunswick-Lunebourg*, ed. O. Klopp, 3 vols. (Hanover, London and Paris, n.d.), vol. I, pp. 301, 306. Compare Sophie to Leibniz, ibid., vol. I, p. 306.

[29] This appears to be the case with his *One Hundred and Fifty Three Chymical Aphorisms* (London, 1688).

[30] BL, MS Sloane 530. This includes alchemical, religious, metaphysical and autobiographical topics.

(1685), *The Divine Being and its Attributes* (1693), *Seder Olam* (1694) and *The Spirit of Diseases* (1694). There are many parallels between these writings and Anne Conway's *Principia philosophiae*, especially on the subject of natural philosophy. And it is his post-1679 publications (such as *Seder Olam*) which exhibit the greatest number of similarities with her treatise.

Of all the younger Van Helmont's writings, the 1682 manuscript treatise, 'Some Observations', contains the earliest and most comprehensive account of his natural philosophy. It is therefore an important indicator of the closeness of his thought to hers and gives us some clues as to the kind of discussion to which Lady Conway may have been party during his residence at her home. 'Some Observations' expounds a natural philosophy that is closely allied to that of the older Van Helmont, especially in its evolutionary account of change. This is framed within a grand Neoplatonic hierarchy of spirit, in which God is the fountain of all being, and all things originate as emanations of spirit from the 'centre of All these beames or emanations', namely the son of God.[31] From this emanating spirit derive descending hierarchies of spirits, then visible light, the sun, moon and stars, and finally water, 'ye universall prime matter of all sensible, & corporeall space'. Van Helmont proposes as 'an universall maxime' that 'all bodies universally are transmutable one into another', and plots the course of natural evolution, from water to stones and minerals, to earth, vegetables, man and, finally 'to highest degree of spirituosity & immortality'.[32] Transmutation involves a cycle, or 'Rotation in Nature', according to which spirits are 'condensed' into bodies and bodies 'rarified and heightened to make spirits'. At the start of the treatise, he challenges 'moderne philosophers', to explain how a body may change 'without losing its originall & essentiall shape'.[33]

Many of the main tenets of his natural philosophy directly echo his father's. Like his father, he was a vitalist and a monist: a resounding theme of his writings is that 'whatever is, is a Spirit'.[34] While it is true that one source for the theory of transformation of substances common to both the Van Helmonts is the alchemical doctrine of transmutation, Francis Mercury develops this into a general principle of natural metamorphosis, 'That all bodies universally are transmutable one into another'.[35] All created things are in a state of continuous change, a 'Never-ceasing Revolution', as beings

[31] Ibid., fol. 18r. [32] Ibid., fol. 62r. [33] Ibid., fol. 5.

[34] Francis Mercury van Helmont, *A Cabbalistical Dialogue* (London, 1684), p. 13. Cf. ibid., p. 8: 'every Substance it self which appeareth under the form of *Matter* . . . was sometimes past a spirit, and as yet is fundamentally and radically such, and will sometime hereafter be such again formally'; and *Seder Olam* (London, 1694), sects. 32 and 33; 'Observations', BL, MS Sloane 530, fols. 62 and 94.

[35] Ibid., fol. 62r.

ascend and descend the ontological scale and 'work out themselves to their true perfection'. This constant state of transformation is possible because body and spirit, of which all things are constituted, are in fact one and the same substance:

spirit & matter differ only gradually, & by consequence are mutually convertible into one another . . . and so from Spirits condensed, ariseth light, and from light condensed ariseth Water, & from Water condensed ariseth other corporeall and sensible beings. But this ascent, y^{t} wh^{ch} is more immediate ariseth out of water is a certain stony concretion, wch vulgarly is termed ye quicksand etc.[36]

The references here to quicksand as the primary solid allude directly to his father's concept of *quellem*. He also subscribes to his father's theory that water is the primary substance. He does not, however, employ the conceptual vocabulary of his father (terms like 'gas', 'blas' and 'archeus').[37] One major difference between the younger Van Helmont's writings and those of his father is his invocation of kabbalist doctrine. He repudiates the mechanical philosophy ('our Modern Philosophers . . . who suppose that all bodies, as such are devoid of life').[38] And he rejects what he calls 'the moderne corpuscular Philosophy' as 'nothing else but a heap of Words'.[39] Like Anne Conway, Van Helmont emphasises the likeness of God and creation, and, like her, he uses this as an argument for rejecting the mechanical philosophy: 'mechanicall or like mechanicall or artificial motion or principles thereof: for ye workes of God are like himselfe permanent & no one naturall thing is moved so, or so along till it be annihilated, no, but rather changed, improved & enobled & ye utmost of y^{t} exaltation who is able to declare?'[40]

There are also obvious affinities between Helmontian theories and Lady Conway's account of change. According to Anne Conway change is the defining difference between creator and creatures: 'mutability is appropriate for a creature insofar as it is a creature . . . there is no other distinction between God and creatures'.[41] Change is therefore the condition of created existence. Furthermore, natural changes according to her philosophy are orderly, occurring by finite stages not arbitrary leaps. This itself is, she argues, a manifestation of divine wisdom. By change Anne Conway means not just the capacity for perfectibility, but natural processes such as digestion

[36] Ibid., fol. 94v.

[37] Francis Mercury van Helmont, *The Divine Being and its Attributes* (London, 1693), pp. 168ff. See *Paradoxal Discourses* for a more elaborate discussion of this.

[38] *Paradoxal Discourses*, p. 9. [39] *Divine Being*, sig. $a3^{6}$.

[40] Ibid., fol. 162v. [41] Ibid., p. 29.

and reproduction, or the evolution of one creature from another (e.g. worms and maggots from the carcasses of animals) and the precipitation of solids from liquids. This kind of change is non-destructive: it does not result in the annihilation of any species, but in its conservation and ultimate regeneration, if not evolution. The death of a creature is not its annihilation but a transmutation from one kind of life to another.[42]

As will become clear in later chapters there many further parallels between Anne Conway's *Principles* and Van Helmont's writings. However, judgements about influence and indebtedness are almost impossible, since the uncertain composition history of Van Helmont's writings means there is no means of dating them, and so of establishing priority, except in the case of those doctrines that occur also in his father's natural philosophy. Their presence in Francis Mercury's work gives us some means of isolating a Helmontian contribution to her thinking, for these antedate his son's encounter with Anne Conway. But they account for only part of the common stock of doctrines and ideas to be found in the younger Van Helmont's writings and Lady Conway's. Priority is, in any case, a crude yardstick against which to plot the evolution of ideas, or to assign authorship. In particular, the uni-directional linear model that it presupposes is inadequate to the task of representing discursive aspects of intellectual activity, or the role of milieu in the generation of ideas. As I shall argue in the next three chapters, the members of Lady Conway's circle at Ragley Hall in the late 1670s not only shared aims and outlook, but they were in intense dialogue with one another on topics of mutual interest. Parallels between Van Helmont's writings and Conway's *Principles* are therefore perhaps explicable as the result of an intellectual exchange which was not uni-directional. There is no doubt that their writings register the strong impact of each on the other. Besides which, important testimony of Lady Conway's impact on Van Helmont is the role he played in seeing her philosophy into print, and in disseminating her book. It would be pointless to speculate how Van Helmont's thinking might have developed had he not encountered Anne Conway, or how hers might have developed had she not encountered him. However, of two things we can be certain: first of all her dissatisfaction with dualism antedates her encounter with Francis Mercury van Helmont by many years, and her critique of More was probably complete by the time she met Van Helmont. Secondly, although the Helmontianism of chapters VI and VII of her treatise could have been derived from his father's writings, and exponents of his theories such as Francis Glisson, there was more

[42] Ibid., p. 62.

to Francis Mercury van Helmont's intellectual portmanteau than mystical biology. For it was he who introduced Anne Conway to the new horizons in Judaism and Quakerism, both of which had a decisive shaping impact on her philosophy.

In Helmontian science Anne Conway found a vitalistic account of created nature which had the advantage over Cartesianism, and even the modifications of it propounded by More and Boyle, that it met the requirement that the creation should express the vitality of its creator. However, the philosophical objection still remained that this kind of hylozoism implied pantheism, especially since the likeness between God and nature extends to the very substrate of creation, namely spirit. Helmontianism was, therefore, potentially open to the same imputations of Spinozism that More had levelled against Glisson. If Anne Conway found vitalist alternatives to the mechanical account of nature in the medical and chemical philosophies of her day, her final repudiation of dualism and materialism has a religious dimension. She needed to be satisfied not only that monism of spirit was philosophically workable, but that it was compatible with religious truth. This was not just a matter of pious intentions, but, as we shall see, her investigations of religious thought, especially of heterodox Christianity, proved persuasive in convincing her that, contrary to Henry More's opinion, single-substance monism was neither pantheistic nor atheistic. Part of the attraction of Francis Mercury's version of Helmontianism was that it was invested with far-reaching claims to theological authenticity. His writings show that kabbalism had an important function in corroborating those claims. Lady Conway too believed the kabbalah to be a repository of the essential truths of both religion and philosophy, and she found these to corroborate key elements of her own philosophy. If it was to be kabbalism that finally persuaded her of the truth of Helmontian vitalism, she was convinced by what was in effect an argument from authority. By introducing her to the kabbalah, and also by introducing her to the Quakers, Van Helmont's impact on Anne Conway's thinking was, as we shall see, decisive.

ELIZABETH OF BOHEMIA

Before examining the kabbalistic and Quaker consequences of Lady Conway's encounter with Van Helmont, one further outcome of Van Helmont's visit should be mentioned at this point: contact with Princess Elizabeth of the Palatinate (1618–80), on whose behalf Van Helmont made his fateful visit to London in 1670. Daughter of the 'Winter Queen', Elizabeth

Stuart, wife to the Elector Palatine, Elizabeth was the granddaughter of James I of England and cousin of Charles II. Princess Elizabeth was one of the foremost female philosophers of her generation, who enjoyed the distinction of having known Descartes personally. Descartes' regard for her philosophical acumen is clearly evident in both his letters to her, and in his dedication to her of the French translation of his *Principia philosophiae*. Born in Prague, Princess Elizabeth lived her entire life as an exile. She never married, and spent her last years as abbess of the Protestant nunnery at Herford, Westphalia.

Anne Conway would have known of Princess Elizabeth as the dedicatee of Descartes' *Principes de la philosophie*. She would also have known of her through his *Passions de l'âme*. There is a tantalising reference to a letter of hers and to Anne Conway's having had a role in 'intermediating' between her and More in 1659.[43] But it is not clear whether the letter in question was one sent by the Princess to Lady Conway, or a letter by the Princess that was circulating in the Dury–Hartlib circle. The key point of contact between Lady Conway and Princess Elizabeth was Van Helmont, whose links with her family went back as far as 1648. On various occasions he had performed services on her behalf, as for example in 1658, when he represented her to secure the dowry of 10,000 thalers from the Emperor, which had been accorded her under the terms of the Treaty of Westphalia. It was during a similar mission to England in 1670, to secure a pension from her cousin Charles II, that Van Helmont first met Anne Conway. For her part, the Princess certainly knew of Anne Conway. In 1671, presumably at the suggestion of Van Helmont, Anne Conway sent her a gift of books, including the works of Henry More. It is most unlikely that the Princess did not acknowledge this gift, and it is not improbable that some correspondence ensued, but no letters have survived. Elizabeth's personal contacts kept the memory of Anne Conway alive. Years later, Robert Barclay cited the example of Anne Conway to Elizabeth in the hope of converting her to Quakerism. Shortly after the death of Anne Conway, Van Helmont visited Princess Elizabeth in Herford.

For the Princess, as for Lady Conway, Cartesianism served as the propaedeutic to philosophy. But, unlike Anne Conway, Princess Elizabeth did not leave a treatise by which we may judge her philosophy.[44] Her correspondence with Descartes is the only surviving record of her activity as a

[43] *Conway Letters*, p. 158. But there is no further evidence to corroborate this. The first Viscount Conway had been a friend of Elizabeth's mother, Princess Elizabeth Stuart, sometime Queen of Bohemia. *Conway Letters*, p. 7.

[44] For an account of Elizabeth's philosophy, see Shapiro (1999) and the literature cited therein.

philosopher, so we have no means of knowing how her thought developed subsequently. The correspondence is, however, unique within the corpus of the Descartes correspondence: the letters are revealing about the correspondents, both personally and in respect of their philosophical development. Not only does Descartes adopt a more relaxed and self-revealing style when writing to her, but the letters document the background to the writing of his *Passions de l'âme*, a treatise which he wrote in response to questions by the Princess. She may therefore take credit for having persuaded Descartes to address ethical issues and, indeed, for his having completed a treatise on the subject of the passions, of which he sent her a draft in 1646. Elizabeth was not a passive admirer, but a perceptive critic of Descartes. Interestingly, the first objections she advances are not unlike those advanced by Anne Conway. Both women focus on the problem of soul–body interaction raised by the Cartesian conception of soul (mind) as thinking substance and body as extension. Both adduce the evidence of experience that the soul (mind) is affected by corporeal indisposition in order to challenge Descartes' radical separation of body and soul. A further common point between the two women is that both came into contact with Francis Mercury van Helmont. In the absence of further documentation, we have no means of knowing how Elizabeth's own philosophy developed. It would be especially interesting to know whether he inspired in her any of the interest in Helmontianism and in kabbalism that he did in the case of the English Viscountess.

CHAPTER 8

Kabbalistical dialogues

'the language of the learned Jews'

Francis Mercury van Helmont's first encounter with Anne Conway was as a physician, but he soon discovered that his patient was just as much interested in the arcane and exotic wisdom he purveyed as in his remedies. Having originally visited More in order to consult with him on behalf of his friend and collaborator, the Christian kabbalist Christian Knorr von Rosenroth (1636–89),[1] Van Helmont found a receptive audience not only in More, but in his friend Lady Conway.[2] This contact was to have a far-reaching impact on both of them.

FROM *CONJECTURA CABBALISTICA* TO *KABBALA DENUDATA*

Anne Conway's study of the kabbalah was unusual for her time. Prior to Knorr von Rosenroth's translation of kabbalistic texts, published in his *Kabbala denudata* in 1677, direct knowledge of Jewish mystical traditions among gentiles was extremely rare, particularly in England.[3] However, there had been a strong interest in the Christian variant on kabbalism, originating from the Christian kabbalism of Johannes Reuchlin in the sixteenth century, and continued in the seventeenth century by, among others, Henry More. Anne Conway's acquaintance with Christian kabbalism undoubtedly enhanced her receptivity towards genuine Jewish kabbalism which she first encountered when she met Francis Mercury van Helmont in 1670.

Anne Conway's interest in the kabbalah may have been stimulated by reports reaching Europe just prior to this that a Jewish Messiah had declared himself: the messianic movement surrounding the putative Messiah,

[1] For Knorr see Salecker (1931) and Coudert (1999).

[2] *Conway Letters*, chapter 6. In 1671, More refers to 'Cabalisticall papyrs' which they have received. Ibid., pp. 350 and 352.

[3] The main sources for gentile knowledge of the kabbalah at this time were Christian interpreters such as Reuchlin and Agrippa. See Secret (1964), Blau (1944).

Sabbatai Sevi, was greatly inspired by the teachings of the kabbalist Isaac Luria (1534–72).[4] Her interest may also have been sharpened by her investigations of millenarianism during the 1660s, but her awareness of the existence of kabbalism goes back to at least 1653, when Henry More published his *Conjectura cabbalistica*. According to Richard Ward, this was written 'expressly owing to her Desire or Instigation'.[5] More's *Conjectura cabbalistica* was, as he freely admitted, not a study of the actual Jewish kabbalah, but a Christian kabbalist reconstruction of what More took to be the essentials of the secret traditions of the Jews. It comprises a triple-layered interpretation of the first chapter of Genesis: literal, moral and philosophical. Among these, most space was given to the philosophical interpretation, for which More wrote a lengthy *Defence* as well as an *Appendix*, both printed in his *A Collection of Several Philosophical Writings* in 1662. The 'philosophy' set out in this amounts to a reconstructed neo-Pythagoreanism, since More bases his philosophical interpretation of Genesis 1 on the view that 'The one real Key for the Understanding of it in this first Chapter, will be those Pythagorical Mysteries of Numbers'.[6]

Although More insists that *Conjectura cabbalistica* is merely speculative, the book is predicated on and illustrates his idea of philosophy as perennial wisdom deriving from Moses via Pythagoras. In More's reconstruction, this Pythagorean legacy combines atomistic and vitalist natural philosophy with Platonic metaphysics. *Conjectura Cabbalistica* is also an indicator of the extent of his (and, by extension, of Anne Conway's) acquaintance with Jewish sources. Furthermore, it presents a view of the kabbalah which formed the receptive framework for More's later encounter with the Zohar and its Lurianic interpreters. With its conflation of ancient and modern into one seamless philosophical unity, *Conjectura cabbalistica* is a prime example of the Renaissance conception of philosophy as perennial philosophy (*philosophia perennis*). As in most formulations of this view, *Conjectura cabbalistica* is predicated on the idea that true philosophy is also *philosophia sacra* (sacred philosophy), incorporating religious truth (e.g. that there

[4] In the intense wave of messianism which peaked in 1665–6, Sabbatai Sevi (1616–76) of Smyrna was believed to be the messianic king prophesied by Nathan of Gaza. His conversion to Islam in 1666 put an end to the hopes of the Jewish diaspora that their exile would soon be over. See Scholem (1973). Whether or not the connection between the Jewish Messiah and the Lurianic kabbalah was known in England, among those who kept themselves informed on the Sabbatian movement was Henry Oldenburg, secretary of the Royal Society. See Hunter (1989). Important among Oldenburg's informants was his friend, the chiliast Pierre Serrurier (Petrus Serrarius). See Van der Wall (1987b).

[5] Ward, *Life*, p. 122. Shortly after this, in 1655, the Jewish leader, Menasseh ben Israel (1604–57) visited England from Amsterdam in the hope of persuading Cromwell to permit Jews to settle in England.

[6] *Conjectura cabbalistica*, p. 72, in *A Collection*.

is a God). The corollary of this view is that sacred texts (such as the book of Genesis or the mystical writings of the Jews) contain philosophical truth. Indeed, the neo-Pythagoreanism elaborated by More not only purported to contain aspects of contemporary natural philosophy (e.g. atomism, Cartesian vortices) but also a metaphysical endorsement of Christian doctrine. More's interpretation of Genesis as a repository of Cartesianism and atomism was new to the traditions of the Christian kabbalah. But his interpretation of the kabbalah as an adaptation of Pythagorean number symbolism was standard among Christian kabbalists of the Renaissance.[7]

It may well be that in the early days of their acquaintance Anne Conway pressed More for an opinion on the nature of ancient learning in the same way that she had discussed it with her father-in-law,[8] and that *Conjectura cabbalistica* was the result. More says that he wrote the book in response to Anne Conway's speculations on the allegorical significance of Adam and Eve.

> Onely I tell you, if you intimated, which I suspected before, that you looked for an Allegory of Adam and Eve, it has injected such a peremptory purpose in me of interpreting the 3 first Chapters of Genesis with a continuall paraphrase verse by verse according to a triple sense, Literal Philosophicall, and Morall, that I can not for my life sett my self about any thing but this till it be done.[9]

At all events, the massive erudition that More brought to bear on the subject far surpassed the exchange of authorities in Anne's letters to her father-in-law. In *The Defence of the Philosophical Cabbala*, which supplements *Conjectura cabbalistica*, he details 'the Authority of Auncient Philosophers and Fathers' in support of 'these births of my own braine', as he calls his kabbalistical conjectures.[10] He cites the Church Fathers and other theologians, and draws on a range of Platonist sources (including Plotinus, Proclus and Ficino). He also cites Jewish sources, though it is difficult to know how many of these are cited at first hand. In addition to Maimonides and Rabbis Schadiah, Abraham ben Ezra and Bechai, he mentions what he calls 'the most rational of the Jewish Doctors': Philo, Procopius Gazeus, the Schools of Hillel and Samai, and Menasseh ben Israel. There is nothing exclusively kabbalistic about this body of Jewish learning. Nonetheless, we might note that in the name of 'Cabbala' More advances a number of ideas that recur in his later kabbalistic speculations: among them his concept of the original matter as 'merely metaphysical' and that the original corporeal matter was something between 'fluid possibility' and 'seminal forms'. Among the

[7] Blau (1944), Secret (1964). See above, p. 81. [8] See above, pp. 18–19 and 37.
[9] *Conway Letters*, pp. 74–5. [10] *Conway Letters*, p. 83.

Pythagorean numbers, More cites the '*Monad* or *Unite*' as 'so fit a Symbole of the *Immaterial* nature'.[11] He glosses this claim in *The Defence*

> that as an *Unite* is *Indivisible* in Numbers, so is the nature of *Spirits* one piece of Corporeal Matter two, by actual division or severing them one piece from another. Wherefore what was truly and properly created the first day, was Immaterial, Indivisible, and Independent of the Matter, for the highest *Angel* to the meanest *Seminal Form*.[12]

More's sources here are Platonist, rather than kabbalist. As I shall explain later, this Platonist framework was to be important in his reception of actual kabbalist texts, on account of the Platonic element they contain. Nonetheless, in the 1650s More shared with Anne Conway an idea of 'cabbala' as a body of veiled wisdom. There is no evidence that at this time she had any direct knowledge of the Jewish kabbalah as such, never mind of Hebrew.

PHILO

More's *Conjectura cabbalistica* probably owed as much to Philo of Alexandria (*c.* 20 BC–AD 40) as it did to the Christian kabbalists of the Renaissance. Both Anne Conway and Henry More regarded Philo as an eminent example of ancient Jewish learning. In More's view Philo was confirmation that the Platonists and Pythagoreans derived their teachings 'from the Divine Traditions amongst the Jews'. Philo's philosophy consists of a synthesis of classical philosophy with the scriptures in which he offered a Platonised reading of the books of Moses. Philo's Platonist hierarchy of being is based on a fourfold interpretative scheme (literal, physical, ethical and mystical), not unlike the exegetical method later utilised by Christian commentators on the Bible (historical, allegorical, moral, anagogical). From Patristic times, Philo's authority among Christian interpreters derived partly from his contemporaneity with the origins of Christianity. It was above all his doctrine of the *logos* that recommended him to Christian interpreters, especially Trinitarians. The putative compatibility between Philo's concept of the *logos* and Trinitarian doctrine rested, in large measure, on his understanding of the *logos* as being dual-faceted. Philo differentiates between the *logos* as eternal archetype and the *logos* as first created being, between the *logos* as only begotten son and as first-born son of God. In this way the *logos*, as both bridge between and separator of God and creation, is the

[11] *Conjectura cabbalistica*, p. 17. [12] Ibid., p. 76.

mediator between God and the world.[13] For Philo, the hierarchy of *logos* functions was part of a descending hierarchy of being unfolding from the one (monad or beginning), through to the world of ideas, and thence to the sensible world.[14]

Henry More's threefold kabbalah matches the first three levels in Philo's scheme: literal, physical and ethical.[15] And the general principles of More's Pythagorean/Platonic reading of the first chapter of Genesis are also indebted to Philo. But a crucial aspect of Philo's teaching for More was its potential for defending belief in the Trinity. For More, the doctrine of the Trinity was an essential creed of Christianity: to deny the doctrine or to impugn it in any way was tantamount to rejecting the Christian faith. In his *Explanation of the Grand Mystery of Godliness* (1660) Henry More argued that Philo's *logos* theory confirmed that the 'Mystery of the Trinity' originated with the ancient Jews. More writes

> Philo the Jew speaks often of this Principle in the Godhead, calling it λογου Θεω [the Word of God], or το Θεου λογον [the Divine Word], or sometimes, ὁ Θεον [God], or other sometimes πρωτογενεν θεω λογον [the Firstborn Son of God] and attributes unto it the Creation of the World, as also the Healing of the Disease of our Minds, and the Purging of our Souls from Sins; in so much that this further might be a good Comentator upon this first Chapter of St John.[16]

More argued, furthermore, that the doctrine of the Trinity was an essential safeguard against the excesses of religious enthusiasts who believed that deification entailed direct, and therefore physical, union with God: 'that no less Union than Real and Physical Deification'. It was therefore necessary that there be a 'distinction and distance' between us and God, such that our union with Christ differed from Christ's union with God. The dual-faceted *logos* of Philo underpinned just such a distinction. Anne Conway too understood the *logos* as a mediator between God and the world, as the *logos prophorikos*, the outgoing word of God. The dual *logos* of Philo is important in her Christian reading of kabbalist texts.

KABBALA DENUDATA

In 1670 Anne Conway's conception of the 'language of the learned Jews' (to use an expression of More's)[17] was greatly enriched by her first direct

[13] See, for example, *Quaestiones et solutiones in Genesim*, I.4 and *Quaestiones et solutiones in Exodum* in *Philo in Ten Volumes*, ed. F. H. Colson and G. H. Whitaker (London and Cambridge MA: Harvard University Press, 1985), supplementary volume.

[14] *In Exodum*, I.68.

[15] On Philo, see *Philo*, and Runia (1986) and (1995). Also Wolfson (1948).

[16] More, *An Explanation*, p. 12. [17] *Ibid*, p. 8.

encounter with Jewish kabbalist sources. For it was in that year, on his visit to England, that Francis Mercury van Helmont met More and, subsequently, Lady Conway. He brought them both into contact with his friend, the German kabbalist scholar Christian Knorr von Rosenroth, who was at this time engaged upon a translation of a collection of texts from and about the Zohar that were published as *Kabbala denudata* in 1677–8 (with a second volume published in 1684). While in England in 1670 van Helmont consulted More on Knorr's behalf. Part of the mutual interest of Knorr and More was millenarian – the first letters which refer to Knorr mention his commentary on the apocalypse. But their mutual interest in kabbalism seems to have superseded this, and Van Helmont arranged for kabbalist manuscripts to be sent to More. The first of these arrived in 1671.[18] Further papers were sent in 1674 and 1675. These no doubt included texts published later in the *Kabbala denudata*.

The manuscripts sent in 1671 were probably those mentioned in Knorr's only extant letter to Lady Conway, in which, after gracious compliments on her learning, he sends her, via Van Helmont, 'a key to the more sublime ancient kabbalah'.[19] Knorr also refers to 'a certain small bundle of papers' relating to this, which Van Helmont has with him. He also offers to send her part of his Latin translation of the Zohar, if she wishes. Knorr explains to her that his kabbalistic researches were inspired by a desire to learn from Jewish traditions so that he might better interpret the gospel. He hoped to find 'a certain notion and explanation which might not be owing to the philosophy of the Gentiles', in order to 'throw some light on the terminology of Christ and the Apostles, who everywhere philosophise according to the Jewish manner'.[20] The same letter thanks Lady Conway for her kind invitation to him to pay her a visit. Knorr did not in fact visit England, but Lady Conway's invitation to him bespeaks her deep interest in his enterprise.[21] No further letters between Knorr and Lady Conway are extant. Even if they did not continue to correspond, Van Helmont would have been a go-between.

[18] *Conway Letters*, p. 352.

[19] 'clavem nempe sublimiorum antiquitarum Kabbalisticarum, quam ipsarum exhibitor Dominus de Helmont meo nomine Tibi offeres'. Knorr to Lady Conway, ?1672, Wolfenbüttel, Herzog August Bibliothek, Cod. Guelf Extrav. 30.4, fol. 8v.

[20] 'visusque mihi sum in atiquissimis Judaeorum scriptis simile quid invenisse quod terminis Christi & Apostolorum, qui Judaice ubique philosophant aliquam possit faenerare lucem'. Ibid.

[21] Ibid. The letter was accompanied by a letter to Anne Conway's husband (Herzog August Bibliothek, Cod. Guelf Extrav., 30.8), presumably in observance of social proprieties which would have prevented communication with his wife without the knowledge of her husband. The letter thanks Lord Conway for a present of books presented in his name, and for an offer of hospitality.

More too entered into direct correspondence with Knorr.[22] Although these letters are largely lost, Knorr published two of them in the second part of *Kabbala denudata* published in 1677–8. Knorr also published a clutch of commentaries and reflections by More in the 'Apparatus' printed in the second part of the first volume of *Kabbala denudata*.[23] Although Knorr did not wholly agree with More that kabbalistic texts preserved hidden nuggets of Christian truth, he greatly valued More's contributions to his enterprise – so much so that he even included a letter of More's in English in the 'Apparatus', presumably because he did not have time to have it translated into Latin in time for publication. The year 1675 was particularly hectic for More, for it was then that he was engaged on writing these letters and commentaries. To judge by references he makes in his letters to Lady Conway, he was in receipt of a number of treatises included in Knorr's collection: among them *Emek Hammelech* ('The Mystical Depths of the King') by Naphtali ben Jacob Bacharach and *Porta coelorum* by Abraham Cohen Herrera. It is safe to assume that he received copies of manuscripts of the Zohar itself, at least of those parts published by Knorr.[24] Just as Van Helmont served as a conduit for kabbalistic manuscripts to reach More, so More, in his turn, had them copied for Anne Conway. After Van Helmont had taken up residence at Ragley, she was able to study them there with his assistance. More was acutely aware that he was missing out on this, except when he was able to come to Ragley: 'I have been long detain'd from Ragley and the enjoyment of your Ladiships excellent converse, and the society of Monsieur Van Helmont and his Zo[h]aristicall Mss.'[25] This suggests that Anne Conway had an advantage over More in her study of the kabbalah because she had Van Helmont to hand for advice. Even so, like Knorr von Rosenroth, she regarded More as an expert, and she consulted him on points of interpretation. More was open about his limited knowledge of

[22] The Knorr archive at Wolfenbüttel includes autograph copies of More's correspondence with Knorr. These mention further letters which are not extant (Herzog August Bibliothek, Cod. Guelph Extrav. 30.4, fols. 9v, 23r, 27r, 30, 40r).

[23] The contributions from More were: (1) *Excerpta ex epistola quadam compilatoris, de utilitate versionis libri Sohar*, (2) *Tabulae duae synopticae kabbalisticae quarum altera est clavis sublimioris kabbalae*, (3) *Additus tentatus rationem reddendi Nominum & ordinis decem sepirotharum in duabus tabulis item cabbalisticis ex scriptura, platonismo, rationeque libera D. Henrici Mori Cantabrigiensis*, (4) *Quaestiones et considerationes in tract. I. libri Druschim D. Henrici Mori Cantabrigensis; cum ejusdem epistola*, (5) *Ulterior disquisitio de rebus in Amica responsione contentis D. Henrici Mori*, (6) *Visionis Ezechielis seu Mercavae expositio ejusdem*, (7) *Fundamenta philosophiae seu cabbalae aeto-paedo-melisseae ejusdem*. Knorr also prints a Latin version of *A Cabbalistical Dialogue*, though this is not listed in the table of contents: *Ad fundamenta cabbalae aëto-paedo-melisseae dialogus*.

[24] More tells Anne Conway his opinion that publication of the Zohar is desirable. *Conway Letters*, p. 390. This view is endorsed by Cudworth, Ibid., p. 406.

[25] *Conway Letters*, p. 401.

Hebrew, but undeterred by it. We cannot assume that Anne Conway had any knowledge of Hebrew, though it is possible that she studied it with Van Helmont. It is equally possible that her kabbalistic studies were based on Knorr's Latin translations. She certainly took her study of the kabbalah seriously, and pondered details of interpretation. This is evident from a long letter written in November 1675, where she asks More's opinion on the views of George Keith's interpretation of the *partsufim*, Zeir Anpin and Arikh-Anpin, in relation to his theory of the extended soul of Christ.[26]

In his capacity as kabbalistic consultant, More provided an interpretative framework for the materials Knorr sent him. He consistently maintained that the kabbalah was a corrupt form of Pythagoreanism, interpreting the ten *sepiroth* as a version of the Pythagorean decad. This in turn expressed the ancient wisdom of Adam, containing in encoded form fundamental doctrines of Christianity, including above all the Trinity: More regarded the first three *sepiroth* (*kether, binah, chomach*) as equivalent to Pythagoras' triad, and as symbols for the persons of the Trinity.[27] These and other intimations of Christian doctrine that he detected in kabbalism served to confirm his belief that kabbalistic texts preserved occulted truths of great profundity, immense antiquity and relevance far beyond Judaism. More was not, however, an uncritical enthusiast for kabbalistic learning. On the contrary, he was worried by the philosophical implications of many of the doctrines he found there. In particular, he regarded the doctrine of *tsimtsum* (the concentration and contraction of the divine nature that initiates the process of creation) as having profoundly materialistic implications.[28] Although he firmly believed that many of the truths of philosophy and religion were preserved in occulted form in kabbalistic writings, More was particularly critical of the version of kabbalism propounded by Isaac Luria. More's concerns in this regard are summarised in his *Ad fundamenta cabbalae aeto-paedo-melissae dialogus* which Knorr published in the second part of the first volume of *Kabbala denudata*. It was in response to this that Van Helmont composed his *A Cabbalistical Dialogue* which was first published in Latin in the second part of the first volume of *Kabbala denudata* which appeared in 1677. *A Cabbalistical Dialogue* was subsequently published in English in 1684. It proposes that all things are constituted of a single universal substance that emanates from God. As we have seen, the kabbalah was not the only possible source for Anne Conway's monism. The particular

[26] Ibid., p. 408. See below, pp. 190ff. [27] *Kabbala denudata*, p. 43.

[28] More's analysis of the materialistic implications of Luria's account of creation are contained in his *Fundamenta philosophiae seu cabbalae aeto-paedo-melisseae* published in *Kabbala denudata*, part 2, and in More's *Opera philosophica*, vol. II. See Coudert (1975).

importance of *A Cabbalistical Dialogue* is that it answers Henry More's charges that single-substance monism must necessarily be materialist and pantheistic.

The appeal of the kabbalah to More and Lady Conway, as to other Christian kabbalists, undoubtedly derived from its putative antiquity. For the kabbalah was believed to preserve the wisdom of an oral tradition originating with Moses. This combination of antiquity and divine sanction endowed it with enormous authority. Knorr calls it the 'highest theology of the Hebrews'. The subtitle of *Kabbala denudata* emphasises above all that it contains the metaphysical teachings of the Jews, as well as their theology, and that this corresponds to aspects of antique barbarian philosophy: *Kabbala denudata seu doctrina hebraeorum transcendentalis et metaphysica atque theologica opus antiquissimae philosophiae barbaricae variis speciminibus refertissimum.* Knorr explained to More that he was motivated to study the kabbalah in order to recover the philosophy of ancient times (gentile no less than Jewish) embodied therein:

In the kabbalistic writings of the Jews I hoped I would be able to discover what remains of the ancient Barbaric-Judaic philosophy . . . I scarcely hoped I would be able to catch sight of this light unless I followed the traces of that river and arrived at the spring itself. I believe that I will discover this spring in these very ancient books.[29]

The irony here is that the kabbalah is not as ancient as claims made on its behalf suggested. Indeed, the version of the kabbalah to which Anne Conway and Henry More were introduced by Knorr was the kabbalah of Isaac Luria, the 'Lion' of Safed (1534–72), which was of relatively recent origin. *Kabbala denudata* makes this clear in its description of Luria as 'Kabbala recentior'.[30] However, by the time of their contact with Knorr, the Lurianic kabbalah *was* the kabbalah, having superseded all other forms. By 1650 it was, according to Gershom Scholem, 'the one well-articulated and generally accepted form of Jewish theology at the time'.[31]

It is perhaps not surprising that Henry More and Anne Conway regarded the kabbalah as a source of ancient truth. Not only did they believe it to contain Mosaic, even Adamic, wisdom, but the version of the kabbalah with which Anne Conway and Henry More came into contact was heavily Neoplatonised. The influence of Plotinian strands of thought can be found among the earliest commentators. Azriel of Gerona, for example,

[29] 'Amica responsio' in *Kabbala denudata*, part 2, pp. 75–6. Translation by Corse and Coudert, as quoted in Conway, *Principles*, p. xix.

[30] This is clear on the title page.

[31] Scholem (1973), p. 25.

conflated Plotinus' hierarchy of hypostases with the last three *sepiroth*. But it was during the sixteenth century when Lurianic kabbalist thought was mediated to Europe from Safed that it acquired its heaviest accretions of Platonism, through the interpretations of his disciples such as Israel Sarug Hayim and Chaim Vital. Sarug played a key role in disseminating the Lurianic kabbalah in Italy, platonising Luria's interpretation in order to give it something of a philosophical basis. Naphtali ben Jacob Bacharach's *Emek-Hammelech* (*Mystical Depths of the King*, printed in 1648 and published in *Kabbala denudata*) relies heavily on Sarug's interpretation of Luria,[32] while *Porta coelorum* (*Gate of Heaven*) by Vital's pupil Abraham Cohen Herrera (1570?–1635) combines Renaissance Platonism with Sarug's interpretation.[33] Its subtitle in the Latin translation by Knorr von Rosenroth underlines its Platonist perspective: *in quo dogmata cabbalistica philosophice proponuntur et cum philosophia Platonica conferuntur*. Herrera's harmonisation of Neoplatonism and kabbalism equated the three highest levels of kabbalist transcendence (Aensoph, Adam Kadmon and created worlds) with the one, *nous* and *anima* of Plotinus' metaphysical hierarchy, citing a wide variety of non-Jewish sources, among them Plotinus, Boethius, Aquinas and Ficino. This rendered the metaphysical core of Lurianic kabbalism accessible to non-Jews acquainted with the Platonic tradition in philosophy. As a result Herrera's book played a key part in moulding the Christian view of the nature of kabbalism that prevailed in the seventeenth century, especially its putative pantheism. *Porta coelorum* is published in the third part of *Kabbala denudata* (in the volume published in 1677–8). It is the text most frequently cited in the notes accompanying Conway's *Principles*. As in the case of the Hermetic writings in the Renaissance, the familiarity of some of the doctrines contained in the kabbalah (familiar, that is, to those schooled in Platonism) appeared to confirm the supposed antiquity of the content of these texts: parallels with Platonic doctrines to be found in kabbalism were taken to indicate that both Neoplatonism and kabbalism had a common source, rather than that kabbalist texts were imbued with Neoplatonism.

In addition to this 'déjà vu' factor, the kabbalah provided endorsement for a theory of substance compatible with the nature of God, as Anne Conway understood it. Here Van Helmont's interpretations of the kabbalah were

[32] Scholem (1974), p. 257 and (1973), pp. 68–72.

[33] Scholem (1974), pp. 257–8 and (1973), p. 68. A Spanish Marrano who settled in Amsterdam, Herrera (d. 1635/9) wrote this in Spanish, with the title *Puerta del cielo*. It was translated into Hebrew as *Sh'ar ha Shamayim* (Amsterdam, 1655) by Isaac Aboab, who became one of the leading Sabbatian believers in Amsterdam. It was printed in abbreviated translation in the first volume of *Kabbala denudata*. For a brief summary, see Popkin (1999), pp. 215–17.

probably as important as the vitalistic theory of substance to which he subscribed. Van Helmont's Christian interpretation of the kabbalah, like Henry More's, offered a reading of kabbalistic doctrines which suggested that they were approximations of, or renditions of, basic Christian truths. In the kabbalah, moreover, Van Helmont found a precedent for the natural philosophy which he had learned from his father. There appeared to him to be striking parallels between the dynamic, monistic vitalism of Jan Baptiste van Helmont and the spiritual monism and regenerative cycles of change propounded in the Lurianic kabbalah. This parallel lent authority not less than divine to his monistic vitalism, according to which all substance consists of living monads of spirit. With Anne Conway, likewise, the spiritual monism of the kabbalah carried with it divine sanction for a non-dualistic metaphysic. For someone exposed to the orthodoxy that monism was symptomatic of atheism, and that a properly conceived dualism was essential to sustaining theism, the kabbalah was a vital means of endowing monism with theistic credentials.

KABBALISTIC FOOTNOTES

The references to the kabbalah in Anne Conway's treatise are one of the factors which indicate a late date for the work. When assessing the extent of the influence of Anne Conway's kabbalistic studies on her philosophy, it is necessary to address the problem that the kabbalistical notes included in her treatise apparently post-date Anne Conway's death. Indeed, many of these references are to sections of *Kabbala denudata* published in 1684, after her death. The fact that so many of these notes cite the *Adumbratio kabbalae christianae*, which was published at the end of the second volume of *Kabbala denudata*, would seem to support the view that the notes were added after Lady Conway died. If so, these, and possibly other references, must therefore have been added posthumously, possibly by Van Helmont when he prepared *Principia philosophiae* for publication. If this is the case, the kabbalistic notes in Anne Conway's *Principles* are no guide to the dating of the treatise. And the probability of Van Helmont's posthumous intervention raises, in turn, the possibility that there may have been more editorial interventions in the text than that registered by the presence of the notes. However, the kabbalistic notes are a guide to only a very limited part of the story. The impact of Anne Conway's study of the kabbalah in her *Principles* is far more extensive than mere footnotes.

The fact that the footnote references are to texts published after she died does not exclude the possibility that Anne Conway was familiar with the same texts in manuscript form. We do in fact know that she was in receipt of manuscripts from Knorr as early as 1671. Since some references are by section and volume number, with no page numbers given, they may refer to a manuscript version. If so, the notes in the *Principles* may be Anne Conway's own. This would mean that the *terminus ante quem* for the composition of the *Principles* might be earlier than 1677 (the year that the first part of *Kabbala denudata* was published). It is also possible that she had access to a manuscript copy of this compilation, as More evidently had. Another reason for ascribing the authorship of the notes to Anne Conway and not to Van Helmont is the fact that they do not always accompany doctrines that are exclusive to the kabbalah – for example, her argument that God is not subject to time and her denial of determinism, although supported by kabbalist references, are tenable in Christian terms, for which the authority of the kabbalah is redundant. Against this, it has to be acknowledged that there are instances where specifically kabbalist doctrines are referred to in *Kabbala denudata*: for example, the idea that suffering is redemptive (for which the note gives '*Kabbala denudata* ii, last tract p. 61, section 9; p. 69, sections 2 & 70, and tract 2, p. 15') or that all things are composed of spirit (for which the note gives '*Kabbala denudata* ii, last tract p. 613').[34] Furthermore, on a couple of occasions in the course of her discussion, Anne Conway uses kabbalistic terminology within the text of her discussion and without any notes: in chapter III she uses the term 'Aensoph', interpreting it as a Hebrew name for 'the infinite God' who 'is said to exist outside the place of the world because a creature could not comprehend the immensity of his light'. Later, in chapter V, in her discussion of Christ, she uses the kabbalist name 'Adam Kadmon, which she expounds as being the name used by 'the ancient Kabbalists' for 'the son of God . . . the celestial Adam, or the first man'.[35]

Footnotes and terminology aside, the impact of Anne Conway's study of the kabbalah is evident in the fabric of her arguments. Although she does not map her ontological hierarchy on to the ten *sepiroth*, she nevertheless adopts a hierarchy of species to describe the unfolding of the divine into the manifold of creation. Moreover, her deity is conceived as an immense light, and her second species, also known as Adam Kadmon, is presented as a mediator – not in the Christian sense of redeemer, but in a broadly ontological sense as a median between absolute, unchanging perfection, on the one hand, and the contingent condition of created things, on the other. In Lurianism, the son of God (or 'celestial Adam') is also conceived as an

[34] *Principles*, pp. 41, 42, 51 and 58. [35] Ibid., pp. 18 and 23.

emanation from the Aensoph. There are other specific examples of Lurianic doctrines in the *Principles*: first of all the doctrine of redemption (*tikkun*) which entails a process of restoration or purification, where suffering has a purgative function. Secondly, Conway's monistic concept of substance as entirely spirit echoes the Lurianic view that all created things are composed of spirit. Her discussion of this makes explicit reference within the main body of her text to the authority of the kabbalah.[36] Furthermore, in Lurianism, as in Conway's system, spiritual substances can, through the process of purgation, rise up the scale of being.[37] While Conway does not subscribe to the doctrine of the transmigration of souls that Luria held, her version of the redemptive process does entail the possibility of substance itself undergoing a periodic sequence of refinements. She also talks about souls as 'sparks' of the divine, using a kabbalistic term (*nizzuzuth*).[38]

Nevertheless, in general approach, Anne Conway's use of the kabbalah is strikingly free from the allegorical and symbolic interpretations that are the stock-in-trade of most commentators. Unlike most Christian kabbalists and many Jewish kabbalist scholars, she does not speculate upon or elaborate on the meanings of the ten *sepiroth*. On the contrary, her tripartite schema excludes the possibility of using the ten *sepiroth* as the basis of her hierarchy of being. She argues on logical grounds that it is not possible for there to be more than three species in the hierarchy.

> No argument can prove that there is a fourth species distinct from the other three . . . because the three aforementioned species exhaust all the specific differences in substances which can possibly be conceived by our minds, then that vast infinity of possible things is fulfilled in these three species. How could a place or space be found for a fourth, fifth, sixth, or seventh species?[39]

It is impossible, therefore, to map the ten *sepiroth* on to the order of being outlined in the *Principles*. This is a clear case where the mystical order of the kabbalah, as enshrined in the doctrine of the *sepiroth*, is at odds 'with sound reason and with the order of things'. Conway's ontological series cuts across kabbalist hierarchy and limits the applicability of kabbalist models to her philosophy. In her framing of a tripartite hierarchy of being, the requirements of logic and metaphysics, and possibly of Christian doctrine, take precedence over faithfulness to a mystical schema.

Furthermore, the identifiably kabbalistic elements of her system are subsumed within a framework, within which kabbalism can be seen as a particular example of a generic pattern of thought, with analogues elsewhere. Hers is, after all, a system that demonstrates the dependence of all things on

[36] Ibid., p. 51. [37] Ibid., p. 42. [38] Ibid., p. 39. [39] Ibid.

God, and argues that God is manifested, indirectly, in the works of creation, and is always present to that creation. Moreover, it is a system in which the nature of things is deducible from the idea of God as *ens perfectissimum*, the most perfect being. Essential to that perfection are the divine attributes of goodness and wisdom. The system of the world deriving thence is one framed providentially to ensure the restoration of the essential goodness of all creation. This metaphysical picture is not exclusively kabbalistic, but, as we have already seen, has analogues in Platonist and Christian thought, especially in the philosophical theology of the Cambridge Platonists. Likewise, Conway's radical soteriology, which denies the eternity of hell and holds out the hope of universal salvation, is not founded solely on kabbalistc idea of *tikkun* or restoration but, as we have already noted, owes something to the heterodox Christian theologian Origen, a figure much admired by Henry More.[40] Conway's anti-determinism is another position which she shares not only with kabbalists like Cordovero, but also with Henry More and Origen. Her doctrine of Middle Nature may owe as much to Philo as to kabbalism.

It is therefore difficult to pinpoint exclusively kabbalistic sources for her thinking. Rather, in any given instance, kabbalism can be said to provide one formulation among several possible alternatives. So, for example, redemption through spiritual regeneration and metempsychosis is a doctrine not just of Lurianism, but also Origenism. And the concept of substance as immaterial, so central in Lurianism, has an analogue in Plotinus' concept of incorporeal matter. This, as we have seen, was an idea revived by Henry More in his concept of 'metaphysical hyle', in the passage in *Conjectura cabbalistica* where he also invoked the idea of the monad as the 'most perfect parvitude' of substance.[41] Conway's use of the kabbalah is, therefore, best understood in the context of the idea of *philosophia perennis* (perennial philosophy), within which it figures as one repository of ancient truth among many. In that perspective, the truth contained in the supposedly ancient kabbalah is as valid and timeless as truth contained in any other system of thought, ancient or modern. She derived from the kabbalah a range of working concepts that she mustered within an overall metaphysical and moral framework that was not uniquely kabbalistic, though it had strong kabbalist overtones. This framework was one which might be endorsed by other philosophies, especially those of a Platonist variety. And

40 See pp. 69 and 87 above.

41 *Appendix* to *Defence*, p. 137 in *A Collection*, vol. II. '*Creation* is nothing else but an *Emanation* from God, as Aquinas hath determined; and I say, that this *position* and *Capacity* of things is the utmost *Projection* or *Emanation* from the *divine* Existence and would not be without Him', p. 138.

the working concepts it entailed had analogues in the philosophies that form part of the *philosophia perennis*.[42] In Conway's use of it, therefore, kabbalah is subordinated to a rational framework, where logical deduction takes precedence over doctrinal authority and decoding of symbolism as her preferred means of demonstration.

Arguably, therefore, her encounter with the kabbalah made available to Anne Conway a new conceptual vocabulary, which had the enormous recommendation that it was supposedly closer to original divine truth than any of the philosophical analogues that might be found in, say, Platonism or Cartesianism. On this reading, Conway's system could have been elaborated independently of her reading of the kabbalah. But the latter, by virtue of its supposed antiquity, and hence its presumed proximity to the divine original of all truth, served as invaluable confirmation of the truth of her philosophy.

Furthermore, for all her professed ecumenism in extending understanding to Jews, Turks and other 'infidels', Anne Conway Christianises her arguments through appeals to the Bible, including the gospels.[43] Notably, she retains – albeit in a radically modified reformulation – the doctrine of the Trinity, and a key role for Christ, the son of God, as mediator between God and the world. Arguably this Christian element is itself an aspect of Conway's religious ecumenism and philosophical syncretism. Besides, the analogy with Christianity lies at the heart of Knorr's project, and is epitomised in the last treatise included in his *Kabbala denudata*: that is, the *Adumbratio kabbalae christianae*. Thus, although the general outline of Anne Conway's system suggests a kabbalist framework, her use of the kabbalah is selective, and centres on areas of most significance to Christians (and Platonising Christians at that). However, by importing kabbalism into her system or, rather, by demonstrating its compatibility with kabbalist teaching, she believed she had a means of outreach to the Jews. For, if the kabbalah could serve as common ground between Christians and Jews, and if her system could offer an application of it that is at once compatible with Christianity and inoffensive to Jews, her philosophy would hold the key to conversion. Although a conversionist aim is not overtly stated in *Principles*, it is clear in her argument that if the role of Christ is correctly understood,

[42] At first sight it might seem improbable that arcane mystical wisdom could admit of philosophical interpretation. But this was exactly what happened. Scholem observes that 'mystical meditations, which are almost impenetrable to rational thought' (Scholem, 1974, p. 268). Yet the symbolic character of kabbalistic writing invited speculative interpretation: the Neoplatonising tendencies, among others, constituted a philosophical development of this speculative tendency in interpretation.

[43] On Conway's knowledge of Islam, see pp. 107–9 above.

and her theory of substance accepted, 'these matters . . . will contribute greatly to the propagation of the true faith and Christian religion among Jews and Turks and other infidel nations'.[44] Conway's system can thus, in one sense, be regarded as an exercise in ecumenical deism: a rational account of God and the world, with which non-Christians can engage. In respect of this apologetic purpose, the kabbalah functions essentially as theosophy. In another sense Conway's system is implicitly millenarian, since the conversion of the Jews, according to the Bible, is a necessary preliminary to the second coming. For this the kabbalah, 'rightly' applied and interpreted (that is, in a Christian manner), is the key. Anne Conway's use of kabbalism is far from comprehensive. Nor does it replace a broadly Christian agenda, even if the Christian doctrine propounded in her treatise is (as we shall see) of questionable orthodoxy.

MIDDLE NATURE

Nevertheless, if we consider the complex question of how the kabbalah informs the conceptual framework of her *Principles*, we have to recognise that Conway's philosophy exhibits a debt to kabbalism which runs far deeper than mere terminology or style, or kabbalistic footnotes. For all its religious overtones, hers was a fundamentally philosophical use of the kabbalah. Kabbalism furnishes her with both a general metaphysical framework and a conceptual vocabulary. The most important example of this is in her conception of the second species as mediator. Here the kabbalah contributed to her explanation of the interaction between the three species of her metaphysical system. Given that these three species are radically differentiated one from another, she is faced with the problem of how to explain their interconnections, especially the dependence of the third species, creatures, on the creator. This is particularly problematic in view of the fact that Conway's whole system presupposes an element of likeness between God and created things. There are no gaps in Conway's system. She deals with the problem by positing a second species, Middle Nature, known also as Christ and Adam Kadmon, which she conceives as a bridge between God and the world: a mediator both in a metaphysical sense and in a religious sense. By sharing both the attributes of God (such as immutability) and attributes of created things (mutability), Middle Nature

[44] Conway, *Principles*, p. 31. The same point is implicit in her earlier comment that the doctrine of the Trinity should be interpreted in such a way as not to be 'a stumbling block and offence to Jew, Turks, and other people', but should be interpreted in such a way that 'all could easily agree on this article', p. 10.

is the mediator between being and becoming, between the uncreated and the created, between the eternal and immutable deity and the temporal and changeable world.[45] Middle Nature participates in both divine and created being – though Anne Conway is at pains to stress that this mediation should not be understood simply physically or spatially, like 'the trunk of the body is between the head and feet'. Rather the median role of Middle Nature is ontological: 'as silver is a median between tin and gold, and water a median between air and earth'. (She is, however, careful to dissociate herself from the materialistic implications of these analogies – 'But these comparisons are quite gross in relation to the matter being discussed'.)[46] This second species (Middle Nature/Christ/the *logos* /Adam Kadmon) is an indispensable part of the hierarchy of being – with a primarily metaphysical function.

This metaphysical conception of Christ as Middle Nature has, to my knowledge, no parallel in Christian philosophy. There are certainly texts of the Bible which ascribe a significant role for the son of God in the creation of the world – and Anne Conway quotes some of these (e.g. Colossians 1: 15) to demonstrate that 'Christ is called the first of all creatures'.[47] Her conception of Christ has strong affinities with Philo's dual *logos*. But she quickly acknowledges that more needs to be said on the issue ('many things remain to be said about this matter which are necessary for the correct understanding of what follows')[48] and proceeds to devote chapter V to the topic ('hence for that reason we write this chapter'). It is at this point that she invokes 'the ancient kabbalists' as authorities on the coming into being of Christ/Adam Kadmon/'the celestial Adam', and his priority 'in the order of nature'. She goes on: 'This son of God, the first born of all creatures, namely this celestial Adam and great priest, as the most learned Jews call him, is, properly speaking, the mediator between God and the creatures.'[49] This mediator has an ontological function, not a purely redemptive one, a point underlined by the fact that its existence may be proved philosophically 'The existence of such a mediator is as demonstrable as the existence of God.'[50] The fundamental definition of Middle Nature as an intermediate being between God and created things, in combination with the idea that God's attributes may be differentiated according to whether they are 'communicable' or 'incommunicable', suggests that Conway owes more to kabbalism than to Christian theology for her conception of Middle Nature/Christ. Although, as we have seen, she insists that her Middle

[45] Ibid., p. 24. [46] Ibid., p. 25. The analogy with metals is alchemical.
[47] Ibid., p. 22. [48] Ibid., p. 23. [49] Ibid., p. 24. [50] Ibid.

Nature is compatible with Christian teaching, her philosophical concept of it as the intermediary between true being and contingent reality is largely formulated with the aid of kabbalism. The invocation of the kabbalah is obvious from the terminology she employs, particularly that of the kabbalistic commentary of Abraham Cohen Herrera, whose *Porta coelorum* was one of the texts included in the third part of *Kabbala denudata*. There are many references to it in the notes accompanying chapter V of Conway's *Principles*. According to Herrera, Adam Kadmon is 'the *medium* between Aensoph and the Aziluthic world' ('medium quid est inter Aen-soph & mundum Aziluthicum').[51] He explains the idea of a *medium* as the connector between extremes by virtue of the fact that it contains an analogy with either extreme ('omne autem medium in se habet analogum quid extremorum suorum'). Furthermore, Anne Conway's assertion that 'the Son of God comes into existence by generation or emanation from God rather than by creation strictly speaking'[52] is not a Christian view, but is found in kabbalism, where Adam Kadmon is conceived as emanating from the Aensoph. These details suggest that, in chapter V of the *Principles*, kabbalism is not simply a source of alternative terminology (as the name 'Adam Kadmon' might be used instead of 'Christ'), but contributes significantly to her conception of the second species as a 'middle' nature.

MATERIALISM AND SPINOZA

It was against the background of her kabbalistical studies that Anne Conway encountered the philosophy of Spinoza. The spectre of materialism and atheism her contemporaries perceived in the philosophy of Hobbes seemed to many to have reappeared in more potent pantheistic form in the writings of Spinoza. Where Hobbes had shocked Christendom by conceiving of the deity as infinite body, Spinoza's special infamy derived from his having proposed that all things are part of the body of God. His theory of a single universal substance was interpreted reductively as an unprecedented form of materialistic pantheism. Although Spinoza had initially been received favourably, the publication of his *Tractatus theologico politicus* in 1670 was greeted with horror by theologians across Europe for undermining revealed religion.[53] Among them, Henry More diagnosed Spinoza's materialist error

[51] *Kabbala denudata*, vol. I, part 3, p. 114.

[52] *Principles*, p. 25. The Latin reads, 'Deique Filius . . . ejusque productio potius est generatio vel emanatio a Deo, quam Creatio, si vox haec stricto accipiatur sensu' (*Principles*, Loptson edn, p. 124).

[53] On the reception of Spinoza, see Colie (1957); Colie (1963); Gründer and Schmidt-Biggemann (1984); Cristofolini (1995). For Spinoza's controversial impact on the Enlightenment, see Israel (2001).

as an atheistic cocktail of Judaism and Cartesianism.[54] The appearance of Spinoza's *Ethica* in *Opera posthuma* in 1677 confirmed his pious readers in their prejudices about his atheism, and panicked his well-wishers into dissociating themselves from him.[55]

In 1677, at precisely the same time as More was awaiting a copy of the first volume of *Kabbala denudata* (or 'the Apparatus to the Zoar', as he called it), he received from Van Helmont a copy of a refutation of Spinoza's *Tractatus theologico-politicus*. This was *Arcana atheismi refutata* by the Dutchman, Frans Kuyper. In order the better to understand Kuyper's case, More told Lady Conway, he decided to read *Tractatus theologico-politicus*, only to discover to his horror that it was 'such an impious work that I could not forbeare confuting him whyle a [*sic*] read him'.[56] The resulting critiques of Spinoza (*Epistola altera* and *Demonstrationum duarum propositionum . . . confutatio*) were published in More's *Opera philosophica* in 1679. More's extended demonstration of the atheistic errors of Spinoza was made partly in the light of his perception of the atheistical implications of the mechanical philosophy of Descartes. Spinozism confirmed his fears about Cartesian mechanism. In his letter of apology to Boyle for having misappropriated his experiments,[57] he expressed his belief that he felt obliged to offer 'invincible arguments' against those who tried to explain the phenomena of nature 'merely mechanically', because of the atheistical consequences of their position exemplified in Spinoza.[58] That More also read Spinoza in the context of his study of kabbalism is evident from his placing of his two refutations of Spinoza immediately after his critique of kabbalism in the 1679 volume of his *Opera omnia*. Henry More's critique of the Lurianic kabbalah in both *Cabbalistical Dialogue* and *Fundamenta philosophiae* centred on Luria's conception of substance as an emanation from the Godhead[59] – a cardinal error which he attributed to the failure of Jewish interpreters to understand that the *sepiroth* were not emanations but symbolic numbers (as in Pythagoreanism).[60] More was not the only one to interpret the Lurianic kabbalah as inherently pantheistic and materialistic. Even today Luria's

[54] More to Boyle, 4 December [1671], *Conway Letters*, p. 519.

[55] Henry Oldenburg, secretary of the Royal Society, was initially extremely interested in Spinoza, but his enthusiasm cooled significantly after 1670. See Hutton (1995c). For the reception of Spinoza in England, see Colie (1957 and 1959) and Hutton (1984).

[56] More to Anne Conway, 3 April [1677], *Conway Letters*, p. 429.

[57] See above, p. 135. [58] *Conway Letters*, p. 519.

[59] When discussing Luria's doctrine of emanation, Scholem notes the 'pantheistic implications of this doctrine'; 'its anthropomorphism, personalistic idea of God [of emanation]'; and the safeguards both Luria and later kabbalists had to import. Scholem (1973), pp. 272–3.

[60] See Hutton (1999a) and Coudert (1975).

system is regarded as deeply unorthodox in this regard.[61] In the seventeenth century Luria's interpretation of the kabbalah was widely criticised on the same grounds. Nor was More the only one among Spinoza's many critics who made a link between Spinozism and kabbalism.[62] His juxtaposing of his attack on Spinoza to his critique of Luria underlined the link.

Anne Conway's awareness of the dangers of materialism and pantheism was sharpened by the controversies surrounding the reception of the philosophy of Hobbes and Spinoza. This is evident from her critiques of both philosophers in book IX of her *Principles*: critiques which centre precisely on their failure to distinguish between the deity and created substance. In Conway's view the error of Hobbes, repeated by Spinoza, is that each 'confounds God and creatures in their essences and denies there is an essential difference between them'. Worse than Hobbes, Spinoza 'confounds God and creatures and makes one being of both'.[63] She follows More in her perception of Spinozism as an outgrowth of Hobbism and Cartesianism. However, she appears not to have shared More's view that Spinoza was a materialist – perhaps because her study of kabbalism made her more open to accepting spiritual substance as the single constitutive element of all things. In contrast to More, she recognises affinities between her own substance monism and Spinoza's. This was a courageous admission at a time when the prevailing view of Spinoza's philosophy was as the quintessence of atheism. While acknowledging similarities with Spinoza, she denies that, in her system, God and creatures are one substance. On the contrary, she argues that the hierarchy of species safeguards against any confusion of God with creation, because the species of her system (God, Christ/Aensoph and creatures) are radically differentiated one from another. One species cannot become another, although the lowest creatures within the third species may increase in perfection infinitely. She argues that, just as no polyhedron, by ever increasing the number of its sides, can become a circle, and no cube can become a sphere, so no creature can become God: 'Thus a creature is capable of a further and more perfect degree of life, ever greater to infinity, but it can never attain equality with God. For his figure is always more perfect than a creature in its highest elevation, just as a sphere is the most perfect of figures, which no other creature can approach.'[64] Nor can they be equal to Christ: 'the highest point they can reach is this, to be like him'.[65] Central to her own understanding of the relationship of God to the world is her concept of Middle Nature, through which she is able to

[61] Scholem (1974). [62] Most famously, by Georg Wachter. See pp. 236–7 below.
[63] Conway, *Principles*, p. 64. [64] Ibid., p. 66. [65] Ibid., p. 22.

explain the immanence of the divine in all things, but at the same time to preserve ontological distance between creation and creator. The second species of Conway's system is a 'stop' between the world and God: a barrier between creatures and God every bit as much as it is a bridge between God and the world. Anne Conway's system is thus designed to safeguard against imputations of pantheism and materialism of the kind that Christian interpreters saw in kabbalism, and Christian philosophers like More detected in Hobbism and Spinozism.[66] Her meticulous differentiation between the three species enabled her to deflect the charge that she confuses God with His creation, makes the world the body of God, or derives her monads from the divine essence. By this means she preserves her monadic vitalism of spirit from imputations of materialism and the charge of Spinozism.

In so far as it accommodates kabbalistic doctrines to Christian beliefs, Anne Conway's *Principles* certainly falls within the Christian kabbalist project of demonstrating the compatibility of Jewish thought with a Christian outlook (though not perhaps with mainstream Christian theology). However, Anne Conway's use of the kabbalah is more complex. Within the context of *philosophia perennis*, she focuses on aspects of kabbalism that are compatible with aspects of other systems of thought. In this perspective the kabbalah was only one repository of ancient wisdom among many. But, besides its authority as divinely sanctioned wisdom, kabbalism has a twofold function in Anne Conway's philosophy. On the one hand, it furnished an organisational framework for explaining aspects of her system. On the other hand, it was in its turn subject to modification through rigorous philosophical analysis. Anne Conway's encounter with kabbalism overlapped with her encounter with Quakerism. In so far as it was Van Helmont who introduced her to the Quakers, her kabbalistic studies may be regarded as a propaedeutic to Quakerism. At all events, Anne Conway's reading and interpretation of kabbalist texts cannot be understood in isolation from her reception of Quaker teachings. Just as her interpretation of kabbalism influenced her in her acceptance of Quakerism, so Quakerism served to confirm the authenticity of occulted truth in the kabbalah. Having examined Anne Conway's reception of kabbalism in this chapter, we shall now turn to her overlapping encounter with the Quakers, among whom George Keith was a key figure.

[66] See Hutton (1999c).

CHAPTER 9

Quakerism and George Keith

'this Light, Seed, Life, and Word'[1]

Probably the best-known fact about Anne Conway's personal spirituality is that she died a Quaker. Her conversion took place late in her life – sometime between 1677 and 1678. For a woman of her class, this was a momentous choice, made in direct opposition to the views of her immediate family and of her mentor, Henry More. Her 'convincement' followed that of her other key mentor, Francis Mercury van Helmont, who, as we have already noted, was instrumental in bringing her into contact with the Society of Friends. However, her conversion was not a sudden or unexpected event, but must be seen in relation to the religious route which extends back through her life to her earlier interest in religious dissent and illuminist spirituality. Her interest in Quakerism was most intense during the years 1674–9, and overlaps with her investigations of kabbalism, apocalypticism and heterodox Christianity. A rich texture of these religious topics fills her correspondence in the 1670s. If more letters of hers were extant, it would be easier to judge whether this represents a new intensity in her religious curiosity or a continuation of longer-term involvement with radical spirituality. These later letters are, of course, particularly important, because her philosophical treatise was written at the end of this period, against this background.

In this chapter, I shall focus particularly on the route that led her to Quakerism, and on the important role of the Scottish Quaker leader, George Keith. The path that led her to Quakerism was the same path which brought her into contact with Jewish mystical thought. Partly for this reason, it is very difficult to disentangle her interest in Quakerism from her interest in kabbalism. Her interest in both is contemporaneous, and, as I shall argue, her reception of each is integral to her interpretation of the other. Both Quakerism and kabbalism are crucial to our understanding of the way in which religion shaped her thinking and provided a medium for

[1] Robert Barclay, *Universal Love considered and established upon its Right Foundation* (n.p., 1677), p. 35.

expressing her ideas. In this chapter we shall see how the debates centring on George Keith contributed to the genesis of her *Principles*.

QUAKERISM: THE ROUTE TO CONVERSION

Anne Conway's leanings towards Quakerism ran counter to the negative attitude to Quakerism taken by Henry More and her own family. More had long since condemned the Quakers, whom he derided as deluded, melancholy fanatics.[2] More's negative attitude found a political and economic counterpart in Anne Conway's husband who had a landowner's view of the Quakers as troublemakers on a par with Anabaptists, 'whose design is only to turn out the landlords'.[3] More's own illuminism and perfectionist tendencies perhaps explain his zeal to distance himself from a group whose spirituality had much in common with his own.[4] And it is likely that Anne Conway's exposure to his illuminist religiosity made her more, not less, receptive to the spiritual interiority of early Quakers and their doctrine of the inner light.

Anne Conway's interest in Quakerism was undoubtedly stimulated by Van Helmont, who had first encountered Quakers at the court of the Elector Palatine in Heidelberg in 1659.[5] By 1675 he was a regular attender at Quaker meetings in England.[6] Lord Conway blamed Van Helmont for his wife's sympathy for Quakerism, but it is quite possible that the original motivator was Elizabeth Foxcroft, who was living at Ragley as Lady Conway's companion when the Quaker Thomas Bromley paid a visit there several years before Van Helmont arrived on the scene. Mrs Foxcroft also appears to have been the moving force behind discussions of Boehme and apocalypticism at Ragley.[7] However, she was no longer resident there when the Quaker leaders, Fox, Keith, Penn, Penington and Barclay, visited Anne Conway in the period from 1675 until her death.[8]

[2] More, *Mystery of Godliness*, p. 77, *Enthusiasmus triumphatus*, p. 19, in *A Collection. Mastix his Letter*, p. 306, 'A Continuation', in Glanvill, *Sadducismus*, p. 528.

[3] Lord Conway to Major Rawdon, 5 July 1659, *Conway Letters*, p. 161. According to Conway, the Quakers of Ulster were more troublesome than those Quakers he met in London. See Lord Conway to Sir George Rawdon 13 Feb. 1670/1, Hastings MSS, HA 14499.

[4] On the temper of More's spirituality, see especially Crocker (1990 and 2003). More's Cambridge tutor had been the perfectionist Robert Gell. He valued the perfectionist illuminism of the *Theologia germanica*, translated by Sebastian Castellio, another perfectionist whose writings he approved. *Conway Letters*, p. 155.

[5] On Van Helmont and the Quakers, see Coudert (1999), especially chapter 9, who dates Van Helmont's conversion to Quakerism to 1676.

[6] *Conway Letters*, p. 409. [7] See pp. 65–8 above.

[8] She also had contact with Charles Lloyd and Lilias Skene. *Conway Letters*, pp. 411 and 435.

The first record of contact between Anne Conway and the Quakers is a letter written by Henry Bromley to Elizabeth Foxcroft in 1666, in which he promises to send his brother Thomas to visit her. In 1671 she was visited by Charles Lloyd and Joseph Cooper.[9] George Keith visited her in 1675, deputising, apparently, for William Penn, whose letter to her dated 20 October 1675 indicates that the invitation came from her.[10] In June 1676 Lord Conway reported to Sir George Rawdon that six or seven Quakers had dined below stairs with Van Helmont at his house.[11] Robert Barclay visited in 1677, and George Fox was there twice in 1678.[12] Keith was at Ragley during one of George Fox's visits, and it was at Keith's behest that the Quakeress Lilias Skene visited Lady Conway in 1677. She also had contact with George Whitehead, Isaac Penington and William Penn.[13] In 1677, during this period of her closest contact with Quaker leaders, Penn made the first of his two missionary visits to Holland and Germany in the company of Keith and Fox. A manuscript copy of Penn's *Travels* was found among Anne Conway's effects when she died.[14]

SUFFERING AND THE QUAKERS

The attraction of Quakerism for Anne Conway may be explained, in part, by the fact that she recognised parallels between her own suffering and the sufferings and persecutions endured by early Friends. In this respect, therefore, Anne Conway's personal experience of unrelievable pain played a direct part in shaping her religious and intellectual life. In 1676, she explained to Henry More:

> They have been and are a suffering people and are taught from the consolation [that] has been experimentally felt by them under their great trials to administer comfort upon occasion to others in great distresse, and as Solomon sayes, a word in due season is like apples of gold in pictures of silver. The weight of my affliction lies so very heavy upon me, that it is incredible how very seldom I can endure anyone in my chamber . . . the particular acquaintance with such living examples of great patience under sundry heavy exercises, both of bodily sicknesse and other calamitys (as some of them have related to me) I find begetts a more lively fayth

[9] *Conway Letters*, p. 412, n. 21. See BL MS Additional 23,217, for letters from Lloyd and Cooper.

[10] William Penn to Anne Lady Conway, 20 Oct. 1675, *Conway Letters*, pp. 401–3.

[11] Lord Conway to Sir George Rawdon, 23 June 1676. Hastings MSS, HA 14549. A month later he expressed his relief that Van Helmont had gone away to Holland. Berwick, *Rawdon Papers*, vol. II, p. 385.

[12] George Fox, *The Short Journal and Itinerary of George Fox*, ed. N. Penny (Cambridge: Cambridge University Press, 1925), p. 267. George Fox (1624–91) was the founder of the Society of Friends, nicknamed Quakers.

[13] *Conway Letters*, chapter 7.

[14] Ibid., p. 453.

and uninterrupted desire of approaching to such a behaviour in like exigencyes then the most learned and Rhetorical discourses of resignation can doe, though such also are good and profitable in their season.[15]

To Lady Conway, the Quakers were, like Christ himself, a living model of suffering, fortitude, humility and patience. For their part, Quakers regarded her as an example of Christian patience and forbearing to be emulated by all. As the Quaker Henry Bromley told her companion, Elizabeth Foxcroft:

But the consideration of my Ladyes Wisdome and Christianity as it is a support to her selfe in her Great afflections [*sic*], so to her Ladyships frends that have the most exquisite sense of her sufferings. Being they beleeve she hath learnt to Glory in Tribulation also and to find that Great mystery and secret of Christianity that tribulation worketh patience.[16]

Quaker advice to Anne Conway on how to deal with her sufferings was not so very different from what More himself had to offer: patience in bearing the cross God had laid on her. The difference was both in the form their advice took and in the Quaker stress on interiority. Where More offered 'learned and Rhetorical discourses of resignation', as Lady Conway described them, the Quakers communicated by example. The cross they claimed to bear was not the outward, historical cross of the crucifixion, or the symbolic cross of Christian worship, but the 'inward yoak, burden, and cross' of Jesus working inwardly. Such is the consolation that William Penn offered Anne Conway in 1675.[17] In 1677 George Keith counselled her to 'wait upon the lord, in all possible patience, and quietness of mind', explaining to her that 'all thy afflictions that the lord hath laid upon thee, are the certain effects of the love of God, and ordered to come upon thee for thy good'.[18] Furthermore, the Quakers held out the prospect of future comfort through restoration to God. Joseph Cooper calls her 'affliction' a 'fiery tryall', but comforts her with the thought that 'the time is coming when your Ladyship will look back upon all the sufferings of this mortall

[15] Anne Conway to Henry More, 4 Feb. 1675/6, ibid., pp. 421–2. For all his reservations about the Quakers, More accepted Anne Conway's sympathy with them as an understandable reaction to her own intense suffering. He told her that he had read part of her letter to two friends, who, he said, 'could not blame your designe, but look'd upon it as a thing reasonable in your condition'. *Conway Letters*, p. 426.

[16] Henry Bromley to Elizabeth Foxcroft, 5 Nov. 1666, *Conway Letters*, p. 279.

[17] William Penn to Anne Conway, 20 Aug. 1675, *Conway Letters*, p. 403. 'This blessed inward yoak and burden, and cross has been my preservation, with thousands . . . This is more noble then crosses of silver or gold.' Lilias Skene likewise counselled patience. BL, MS Additional 23,217, fol. 23.

[18] George Keith to Lady Conway, 6 Mar. 1677, *Conway Letters*, p. 437. Compare Isaac Penington's letters to Anne Conway, written 1677–8. Isaac Penington, *Letters of Isaac Penington* (London, 1828), pp. 125–32, 252.

life, as shadow vanity and nothing compared with the glory to be revealed'.[19] Cooper interprets suffering as an indicator of goodness, and a preparative to the transcendent vision of divine beauty and the efficacious balm of divine love that will reward the afflicted soul:

> I beleeue that God is good, and that he doth not willingly afflict, but most naturally commiserate[s] the children of men, suiting his severities to blessed needs and the best Improuements. That partaking of chastisement may be a mean to participate in his holinesse, and that preparation for the vision of God. The pure in heart shal see God. And when we doe come to view yt Transcendent Beauty, we shal share as much wisedome as pulchritude and as much goodnesse as wisedome yea we that find that God is loue, an inexhaustible fountain of Immense sweetnesse; which pours itself into the soul when our measure of afflicitions is even to it[s] period.[20]

It was after her encounter with the Quakers that Anne Conway formulated her own explanation of suffering as spiritually medicinal. In so doing she was able to reconcile God's loving goodness with the miseries endured by created beings. In conformity with God's goodness, she wrote in her *Principles*, 'every creature must return toward the good, and the greater its suffering, the sooner its return and restoration':

> all pain and torment stimulates the life or spirit existing in everything which suffers. As we see from constant experience and as reason teaches us, this must necessarily happen because through pain and suffering whatever grossness or crassness is contracted by the spirit or body is diminished; and so the spirit imprisoned in such grossness or crassness is set free and becomes more spiritual and, consequently, more active and effective through pain.[21]

QUAKER PRINCIPLES

The appeal of Quakers for Anne Conway was more than as fellow sufferers. She was also attracted by their beliefs, especially their claim to have revived apostolic Christianity. Although the Society of Friends did not have a fixed catechism or creed, the post-Restoration period saw the consolidation of Quaker doctrine in the face of continued persecution, and the adoption of characteristic marks of dress and deportment. In both their convictions and their practices they believed they observed the original Christianity dating from apostolic times. The titles of their books make the claim that Quakerism was a revival of ancient Christianity: for example, William

[19] Joseph Cooper to Lady Conway, no date, BL, Additional MS 23,217, fol. 10v.
[20] Joseph Cooper to Lady Conway, 2 March [1671]. Ibid. fol. 4.
[21] Conway, *Principles*, p. 43.

Penn's *Primitive Christianity Revived . . . in the Faith and Practice of the People called Quakers* (1696) or Ambrose Rigge's *The Good Old Way*, and *The Truth which the Ancient Christians many Ages and Generations ago witnessed unto in the World from Age to Age; even from the Days of Christ unto this very time, wherein the same Doctrine, Life and Practice is witnessed unto us who are in contempt called Quakers* (1691).

Aside from the social dimension of their beliefs and practices (such as the egalitarianism of their mode of dress and address), the beliefs set out in the tracts produced by the Quakers of Anne Conway's acquaintance have many points in common with the theology of her own treatise. First of all they stressed the goodness and mercy of God, representing Him as spirit and light. In *Immediate Revelation* George Keith stresses the 'Goodness, Faithfulness, Righteousness, Power, and Wisdom of God'. God is, he says, '*an Infinite Being, of Infinite Goodness, Power, Wisdom, Holiness, Purity, Righteousness, . . . having no End or Limitation; an Infinite Ocean, Fountain, and Fulness of all that is Good, Excellent and Desirable*'. God is 'a Diffusive, Free, Communicative Light'.[22] Robert Barclay too calls God a spirit, adopting an almost Behemenist turn of phrase in calling him also 'Light', in whom there 'is no Darkness at all'.[23] Christ too is conceived in terms of light: Penn calls him 'the spiritual light of the world'. Both Barclay and Keith use the alchemical term 'seed' to describe God's working – 'this Light, Seed, Life, and Word'.[24] Keith employs a chemical analogy in his account of perfection achieved through suffering, 'as by calcination, melting in the fire, heating it, pounding and pressing it, bruising and squeezing, boyling and many such things, wel known to Chymists and Physicians'. The Warwickshire Quaker, Joseph Cooper, likewise couched his counsels in philosophico-theological language that recalls Henry More's *Mystery of Godliness*. In a letter which contrasts 'divine life' with 'animal life', he describes God as 'that Archetypall goodnesse' and our souls copies of his perfection, citing Hierocles, Nazianzen and Boethius.[25] The early Quakers believed in universal redemption as the signal mark of the mercifulness of God.[26] In their view, therefore, punishment for sin had an ameliorative function. They held that it was possible to reach a state of perfection: that is, likeness to God by becoming like unto Christ. It might also be added that their openness to

[22] George Keith, *Immediate Revelation* (1668), pp. 236–7.
[23] Barclay, *Universal Love*, pp. 35–6. [24] Ibid., p. 35.
[25] Joseph Cooper to Anne Conway 7 January 1671, BL, Additional MS 23,217, fol. 7.
[26] George Whitehead, *The Glory of Christ's Light within Expelling Darkness* (1669); George Whitehead, *The Way of Life and Perfection Livingly Demonstrated* (1676); Robert Barclay, *An Apology for the True Christian Divinity* (1678); Barclay, *Universal Love*.

the participation of women as equals with male Friends might have been attractive to Lady Conway, although this does not register in her treatise, and she does not mention it in her letters. Unlike most other sects, the Quakers accepted women as preachers,[27] and William Penn included a list of women of 'reputation, wisdom and virtue' in *No Cross No Crown*.[28]

Perhaps the most controversial doctrine of the Quakers was their Christology (or lack of it). To the horror of many seventeenth-century Christians, the Quaker doctrine of 'the light within', or the birth of Christ in the human soul, which laid emphasis on the presence and interior working of the holy spirit, ignored or at best downplayed the historical Christ. In 1677 Robert Barclay declared that 'the chief and first Principle' of Christianity was the 'inward sense . . . that there is somewhat of God, some Light, some Grace, some Power, some measure of the Spirit; some Divine, Spiritual, Heavenly, substantial Life and Virtue in all Men, which is a faithful Witness against all Unrighteousness and Ungodliness in the heart of Man'.[29] This was supported by the powerful doctrine of Christopresentism or celestial inhabitation, according to which Christ was literally present in the believer, and Christ revealed himself in the bodies of the saints. Thomas Wilson, for example, imputed to George Keith the view that Christ is the seed of God sown in the heart of man as 'a perfect substantial body of one Heavenly and incorruptible nature, which is Christ formed within, the Body of Christ, his Flesh and Blood, which cometh down from Heaven'.[30] Henry More ascribed the doctrine to Familist influences: 'they argue for the inhabitation of Christ in us not indeed through faith or spirit . . . but according to his human nature, that I know for certain is pure, unadulterated Familism'.[31] Quaker claims that when they preached they were the mouthpieces of God, that they were inspired by the inner light of Christ within, seemed to their contemporaries proof that they were, at best, mere enthusiasts. Quaker focus on the ever present light rather than Christ the man in history resulted in scripture itself being treated as secondary to personal witness. An anonymous anti-Quaker pamphlet

[27] Margaret Fell, *Women's Speaking Justified* (London, 1666). On female Quaker preaching, see Mack (1992) and Elaine Hobby, (1995), pp. 88–98. On women and early Quakerism, see Wilcox (1995).

[28] William Penn, *No Cross No Crown* (London, Society of Friends, 1930; first published 1669), chapter 19, section 4.

[29] Barclay, *Universal Love*, pp. 35–6.

[30] Thomas Wilson, *The Spirit of Delusion Reproved* (London, 1678), p. 7. According to Bailey, the doctrine of celestial inhabitation meant that the believer became the flesh and bone of the glorified Christ. Bailey (1992).

[31] 'Contendunt pro Inhabitatione Christi in nobis non quidem per fidem tantum aut per Spiritum . . . sed secundum humanam suam naturam, id certo certius scio purum putus Familismum'. More, *Opera philosophica*, vol. II, p. 746.

published in 1677 calls the doctrine of the inner light 'their alone Bible' and accuses Quakers of substituting an 'airy, abstract mystick notion of the Light and Spirit with every one' for the person of Christ.[32] Unsurprisingly, their downplaying of the historical basis of their faith was construed by their enemies as un-Christian. The heretical implications of the doctrine of the inner light were most vividly played out in the tragedy of James Nayler, and contributed to the hostile reception accorded to early Friends.

In the 1670s Quaker leaders set out to modify the more extreme Quaker beliefs, with the result that the doctrine of the light within was transformed from being a literal statement to a metaphorical expression of the workings of the spirit. Latterly, Quaker historians have placed Penn and Barclay at the centre of a move to tone down excesses in Quaker beliefs, and it has been suggested recently that Ragley Hall was the centre of Quaker revisionism in the 1670s.[33] However, whether this was revisionism of a moderating kind is not at all clear. It is certainly the case that Anne Conway had close contact with Penn and Barclay at this time. But her correspondence shows that the Quaker who excited her interest the most was one of the more intellectual leaders of the Society, George Keith. And in his case, if anything, the influence of the Conway circle ran counter to emergent Quaker orthodoxy, for one result of Keith's contact with Henry More, Anne Conway and Van Helmont was that he developed a theology which became increasingly incompatible with the milder, less intellectual strain of Quakerism promoted by Penn and Barclay. If this is the case, it could be argued that Anne Conway's unwitting legacy to the Society of Friends was schismatic.[34] Keith's aberrations in point of doctrine are, however, instructive in other ways: for his response to and assimilation of the intellectual culture of Ragley in the 1670s afford clues to the appeal of Quakerism for Anne Conway. As we shall see, Keith's interpretation of Quaker doctrine may have served to reinforce her perception that the spiritual essence of

[32] [Robert Fleming], *Survey of Quakerism* (London, 1677), pp. 12–13.

[33] The 'loose agenda' of Anne Conway and educated Quakers was 'to improve the image of the Quakers by "clarifying" the notion of the inner light and soliciting the approval of Henry More' who thereby 'played a role . . . in the transformation of Quakerism into a respectable mystical religion'. Bailey (1992), pp. 245 and 248. Barclay's *Apology* in effect codified Quaker doctrine, and ensured that a milder, less radical version of Quaker beliefs prevailed.

[34] While Bailey's thesis about the Quaker doctrine of Christopresentism is in many ways compelling, I think he has misunderstood the role of the Conway circle. The link between the Ragley Platonists and the Keithian schism is illustrated by the fact that Van Helmont and Keith subscribed to similar beliefs, especially the transmigration of souls, and Van Helmont was condemned by Fox, just as Keith was. The Quaker John Whiting attributed Keith's schism to the influence of Van Helmont in *Persecution Exposed* (1715). See Hull (1933); also Coudert (1976).

Quakerism was consistent not just with apostolic Christianity, but with Mosaic wisdom itself. For, by interpreting the Quaker doctrine of the inner light, or the presence of Christ in his believers, as enunciation of the truth hidden in the ancient wisdom of the Jews, namely the kabbalah, George Keith formulated Quaker theology in terms that appeared to confirm that the true, ancient root of the Quaker faith was the divine wisdom revealed to the most ancient Hebrews. The apparent compatibility of Quakerism and kabbalism meant that they could be understood as confirming one another: if Quakerism was consistent with the high theology of the Hebrews (that is, ancient religious truth deriving from Moses himself), this supported the Quakers' claim to be professors of true, unadulterated religious faith. If kabbalism was endorsed in important particulars by the teachings of such a pure sect, this underscored the Christian import of its teachings.

CONVINCEMENT

Anne Conway's acceptance of Quakerism seems to have been a gradual process. By 1677 she had adopted the Quaker style of address. In the same year, with the help of Lilias Skene, she employed Quaker women as her maidservants.[35] At first she had reservations about their 'rusticity'. But she changed her mind after reading their books. Meeting them in person helped to free her from 'former prejudicate opinions'.[36] Robert Barclay attests how difficult Anne Conway found it to adopt Quaker customs in speech. In 1677 he told Princess Elizabeth that she found that some things that had appeared 'small & Inconsiderable' at first turned out to present 'a great deal more difficulty than she apprehended & could not have believed to have found in herself so strong wrestlings before she could give up to obey', in spite of the fact that, being confined by the circumstances of poor health to her chamber, she was spared 'those affronts whom the like case might make others liable to'.[37]

Anne Conway tried to persuade her immediate family to take a more kindly view of the Quakers by providing them with Quaker books to

[35] *Conway Letters*, p. 438. [36] Ibid., p. 407.

[37] Barclay to Princess Elizabeth, 28 Dec. 1677, in Robert Barclay, *Reliquiae Barclaeanae. Correspondence of Col. David Barclay and Robert Barclay of Urie* (London: Winter and Bailey, 1870), pp. 31–2. Barclay cites the case of Lady Conway as an example of 'prejudice of the mind'. But he had entertained hopes that the conversion to Quakerism of 'that truly noble and virtuous Lady the vice Countess of Conoway' might inspire Princess Elizabeth to follow suit. The Princess responded by saying that she could not do so without sharing her convictions: 'I cannot submitt to the oppinion or practise of any others though I grant that they have more light than myself. The Countess of Conway doth well to go on the way which she thinks best, but I should not do well to follow her, unless I had the same conviction', ibid., p. 27.

read.[38] She gave copies of Quaker writings to her husband, to her brother-in-law Sir George Rawdon, and to Henry More, with the express purpose of persuading them to be more sympathetic to Quaker views.[39] She even persuaded Henry More to meet and debate with the Quaker leaders George Fox, William Penn, George Keith, George Whitehead and Isaac Penington.[40] Even before her own conversion her letters show that she took steps to persuade her friends and family to set aside their prejudices. She attempted to promote better understanding of Quakerism by encouraging dialogue. She herself acknowledged that 'their conversation doth much more reconcile me to them.'[41] She was convinced that dialogue would have the same effect on Henry More: 'I am glad, you had an opportunity of so free and full converse with severall of these Quakers . . . by which means you will be able to give a better judgment of their principles and practices, then you could doe upon the reports of others, who either through prejudice or ignorance had doubtlessly misrepresented them to you.'[42]

Her family, however, were not impressed. Rumours of her conversion scandalised her brothers. More told her how he had been harangued by her brother Heneage Finch, the Lord Chancellor: 'What a peal my Lord Chancellour rang in my eares about your being turned Quaker, and what a storme I bore with be too long to rehearse in this letter.'[43] By 1678 rumours of Anne Conway's Quakerism reached her brother John Finch in Turkey. He wrote to her upbraiding her for adopting the Quaker style of address (thee and thou).[44] Even though, at his wife's behest, Lord Conway used his influence to secure the release of imprisoned Ulster Quakers, he regarded them as 'a senseless, wilful, ridiculous generation of people'.[45] He did his utmost to conceal his wife's Quaker leanings, even to the extent of discouraging his brother-in-law from placing his daughters in neighbouring households.[46] In private, he made no secret of his antipathy to the sect: in 1679 he told his brother-in-law, 'all the woemen about my Wife are Quakers,

[38] *Conway Letters*, p. 407. [39] Ibid., p. 448.

[40] Ibid., pp. 391, 404, 414, 436. Fox's diary records that More went to Ragley in 1678 'to dispute with G.F.' Fox, *Short Journal*, p. 233, cited in *Conway Letters*, p. 436.

[41] *Conway Letters*, p. 407. [42] Ibid.

[43] More to Anne Conway, 3 Apr. [1677], *Conway Letters*, p. 430.

[44] John Finch to Anne Conway, 18 Nov. 1678, BL, MS Additional 23,214, fols. 94ff. See above, p. 99.

[45] *Calendar of State Papers, Domestic, Car. II.* 1 March–31 December 1678. *Conway Letters*, pp. 443–4.

[46] Lord Conway advised against placing his niece with Lady Puckering, 'for the consequence of that will be to divulge my Wife to be a Quaker wch. I have ever endeavoured to conceale'. Lord Conway to Sir George Rawdon, 1 Jan. 1678–9, Hastings MSS, HA 14558. This is a follow-up to a letter of 28 Dec. 1678, where he offers to place his niece with Lady Puckering. See *Conway Letters*, p. 440. Even at this late stage, Conway insisted, 'I doe not beleeue she is a Quaker' (HA 14558). Earlier, in 1676, he said he would take no action against his wife, 'wch looks like a parting from her'. HA 14550.

and she cares for no other society, and this little house is perpetually pesterd with a great number of them, whom I never see'.[47]

Opposition to the Ragley Quakers came not just from Anne Conway's family, but from the local parish: in 1678, Thomas Wilson, rector of Arrow, published a short tract entitled *The Spirit of Delusion Reproved*, in which he attempted to refute Quaker doctrines and to expose their appeals to scripture as misinterpretations. The book is aimed specifically at named Quaker leaders: Penn, Fox, Keith, Whitehead and Edward Burroughs. This suggests either that Wilson may have been invited to Ragley Hall to dispute with them, or that Lady Conway had given him Quaker books in a bid to persuade him to take a more tolerant line. Whatever the case, local controversy there certainly was. Keith responded in a short tract entitled *The Rector Corrected*, published after Lady Conway's death.[48]

Where her family were outraged and embarrassed by her association with Quakers, Henry More did his best to understand it and to counter Quaker influence. He met their leaders, Fox, Penn, Keith, Whitehead and Penington; he read their books and he wrote letters to them.[49] Fox's diary records that More went to Ragley in 1678 'to dispute with G.F.'[50] Personal acquaintance did not improve his view of Fox (whom he described as a man that turned his soul to brass)[51] or George Whitehead (whom he described as 'smug and plump . . . but the ayre of his countenance was more hard and opake, and I could not hit well in my converse with him').[52] Although More was not won over, one result of these dialogues was that he took a more moderate attitude to Quakerism, even when he did not agree with their views. A key document for his objections to Quakerism is the letter he wrote to William Penn in 1675. In this letter, written at Ragley Hall, More expresses joy at discovering that the writings of Penn which he had read contained many excellent and pious things. But he takes Penn to task for ignoring the importance of scripture, rejecting the sacraments of baptism and the Eucharist, and minimising the importance of the historical, 'outward' Christ.[53] More's discussions with Quaker leaders led him to revise his view of Penington, whom he now regarded as 'a down

[47] Lord Conway to Sir George Rawdon, 1 January 1678–9. Hastings MSS, HA 14558.

[48] Wilson, *Spirit* (imprimatur, 1 January 1677–8). George Keith, *The Rector Corrected* (London, 1680). This may be the response that Fox mentions in his journal.

[49] *Conway Letters*, pp. 391, 404, 414, 436. In 1676 More was disturbed by a rumour that he had converted to Quakerism, ibid., p. 425.

[50] Fox, *Short Journal*, p. 233, cited in *Conway Letters*, p. 436.

[51] Ward, *Life*, p. 120.

[52] *Conway Letters*, p. 404.

[53] The letter is printed in Ward, *Life*, pp. 180–99, without a date. A fuller version is printed in William Penn, *The Papers of William Penn*, ed. Mary Maples Dunn and Richard S. Dunn, 5 vols. (Philadelphia: University of Pennsylvania Press, 1981–7), vol. II, item 90. The editors suggest the date of 22 May 1675. This version mentions that it was sent to Penn via Van Helmont.

right good man', and to admit that 'There are some things which I hugely like in the Quakers'.[54] In particular he pronounced George Keith 'a good honest man according to his measure' and 'absolutely the best Quaker of them all'.[55]

GEORGE KEITH

Of all the Quaker leaders, George Keith played a pivotal role in Anne Conway's decision to convert. It was probably George Keith's visit in 1675 that was decisive in removing any prejudices and misconceptions she may have had about early Friends. Writing to Henry More after Keith's visit in November 1675, Anne Conway tells him of the better view she now held of George Fox, saying that she doubted whether there was any connection between Keith and Familism.[56] She also reports that she has been reading Quaker books. Keith brought with him a letter from William Penn, at whose behest he visited her, Penn being prevented from doing so. In it Penn explains that since he is unable to accept her 'perticuler kind invitations' on account of 'an unusual importancy of business', he has asked his 'innocent learned Christian Friend', George Keith, to visit her in his stead.[57] The encounter with Keith had momentous consequences for both Keith and Anne Conway, since it resulted in both of them discerning parallels between Quaker belief and kabbalism and had a shaping influence on Keith's ideas. Anne Conway was in close contact with Keith throughout the period immediately preceding her conversion to Quakerism. The interaction between them was more than a matter of shared beliefs. Not only did Keith subscribe to the general Quaker tenets just outlined, but in his formulation of them he echoes the terminology and ideas of the Ragley circle. By examining his writings and letters from this period, it is possible to track the influence of Lady Conway, Van Helmont and Henry More. Keith's writings, therefore, give us a valuable reference point for the development of her mature thought.

KEITH AND MORE

The period of closest contact between George Keith and Lady Conway's circle at Ragley occurred in the period 1674–8, that is between August 1674,

[54] *Conway Letters*, pp. 404, 418, 513. [55] Ibid., p. 513.
[56] Keith encouraged Barclay to visit in 1676. *Conway Letters*, p. 427.
[57] William Penn to Anne Lady Conway, 20 Oct. 1675, *Conway Letters*, pp. 401–3.

when Keith dined with Henry More in Cambridge, and 1678, when Keith's *A Way to the City of God* was published. It was also the period during which the first volume of *Kabbala denudata* was published. Keith had encountered Henry More through his works at an earlier date. Sometime around 1660 he had read More's *An Explanation of the Grand Mystery of Godliness.* According to More, there was a rumour that reading the book had been instrumental in Keith's conversion to Quakerism.[58] At all events, it was with a receptive frame of mind that he encountered More personally in the 1670s. An important cluster of letters from the period 1675–6 conserves a continuous exchange between Lady Conway and More and enables us to document the impact of Keith, as well as affording us some insight into Anne Conway's contribution to the discussions. In their turn, Keith's writings for this period register the impact of both kabbalism and Platonism on his thought. On the one hand, in the face of criticism by More, we see Keith obliged to give more attention to the historical Christ. On the other hand, we see Keith begin to articulate the key Quaker doctrines of perfectionism and of the light within in increasingly kabbalistic terms. In particular he seeks to provide an explanation of the Quaker doctrine of the inner light in terms of a divine pneumatology that draws on the kabbalah. We know that, at about the same time Keith was working out his Christology, he had been given More's *Enchiridion metaphysicum* and his *Philosophical Poems.* In his several meetings with More, he had had the opportunity to acquaint himself further with More's opinions.

In 1675, at the behest of Lady Conway, More met Keith. The result of their meeting was, first of all, that More reassessed his opinion of the Quakers: although he refused to change his view that Quakerism and Familism had much in common, he became more willing to admit that Quakerism exhibited some of the features of apostolic Christianity. At this time Keith was working out a new Christology, the details of which he discussed with Anne Conway and Henry More, and in letters to Knorr von Rosenroth, of which Anne Conway possessed copies.[59] The fruits of these conversations and correspondence were what Anne Conway called Keith's 'new notion' about Christ, in other words Keith's doctrine of the extension of the soul of Christ, first propounded in his *Immediate Revelation* (1668). More declared that Keith's book was 'the best book I had met with amongst the Writings

[58] More to Anne Conway, 14 July 1671, *Conway Letters*, p. 341.

[59] Some of the sources for Keith's views were his letters to Knorr, which he showed to More. *Conway Letters*, pp. 408 and 415–16. Keith's letters to Knorr are held at the Herzog August Bibliothek, Cod. Guelph Extrav., 30.4. I am most grateful to Allison Coudert for making available to me her translations of this correspondence.

of the Quakers'.[60] To the second edition, printed in 1675, Keith added 'An appendix containing an Answer to some new Objections and Questions upon some passages in the Book, Intituled Immediate Revelation not ceas'd'. The source of the 'Objections and Questions' is not named, but the answers are all directed to the kinds of criticism More had levelled against Keith and the Quakers in his correspondence with Lady Conway. In all probability they were a response to his conversations with More when they met in 1674. In this 'appendix' Keith sought to explain the Quaker doctrine of the inner light by drawing on the metaphysical language of kabbalism and Platonism, including Henry More's pneumatology. In answer to More, Keith writes of Christ as a living principle, a 'second Adam or Heavenly Man', the 'Divine birth', an incorruptible seed separate from our souls, but in which we partake.[61]

KEITH, KNORR AND MORE

Keith's Christology is elaborated further in two books dating from the period of his closest contact with Anne Conway: *The Way Cast Up* [1677] and *The Way to the City of God Described* (1678). These last two works register the impact of his reading of kabbalist texts and his contact with Knorr von Rosenroth, to whom he wrote, presumably on the advice of Lady Conway and Van Helmont. From a cluster of letters written between 1675 and 1676 we can track Keith's assimilation of kabbalism, and the development of the Christology propounded in these two books. Anne Conway, as the reader over his shoulder so to speak, was party to this exchange of letters. Her comments are important clues to the issues that attracted her attention. Further insight can be gained from More's rearguard action to counter the impact of Keith and kabbalism: this is registered not just in his letters but in the scholia he added to his *Opera philosophica*, which he was preparing for the press between 1676 and 1678.

The topic which dominates Keith's discussion with Lady Conway and Henry More is the nature of the soul of Christ. A lengthy letter from More to Penn in 1675 sets out the basis of his objections to Quaker Christology and lays the ground for his debate with Keith. More argues against the Quaker interpretation of John 1: 9 in support of their doctrine of the inner light by denying that the 'true light' here mentioned is 'the Eternal Logos'. Rather it is the soul of Christ *qua* man, 'the Soul of the Messias come in the Flesh'.[62]

60 Henry More to William Penn, printed in Ward, *Life*, p. 189.
61 Keith, *Immediate Revelation*, p. 250. 62 See Ward, *Life*, pp. 189–90.

Keith, for his part, explained the doctrine of the inner light by arguing that the soul of Christ is extended through the universe, believing that he had found evidence for this in the kabbalah. So, on 17 November 1675, he wrote to Knorr von Rosenroth in the hope of receiving confirmation of his view, ascribing his own interpretation of Christ as mediator to his reading of Knorr's interpretation of the gospel of St John: 'in a certain small MS of yours from our friend Van Helmont about the first part of the first chapters of St. John'.[63] In this letter, Keith sets out to explain the 'great mystery of piety' of how God in Christ is one with the uncreated *logos*, and how that *logos* is united with the soul and life of Christ extended through all men. He does this by expounding his doctrine of Christ the mediator, who bridges the gulf between infinite God and finite creatures:

> There is one God and one mediator between God and men, the man Jesus Christ, and indeed from the beginning of this world men have this mediator Jesus Christ, for without Christ as mediator, no man could come to God, wherefore in the time of Adam, Abel, Enoch, Abraham, etc. there was in any case this mediator the man Jesus Christ through whom they had access to the father and through whom they were able to enjoy divine communion with God, but before the time of these fathers, even from the first beginning, there existed our Lord Jesus Christ, through whom all creatures both visible and invisible were created as Paul once said to the Ephesians. Indeed he is our mediator since he takes part in both extremes, so to speak. He is both God and creature from the beginning, for since there is nothing more extreme than the infinite God and finite creatures, there must be some kind of medium to intercede between those two extremes, which medium is the man Jesus Christ, who is both God and creature – that is, he participates in the nature of both as a medium between two extremes.[64]

Keith supports his theory in kabbalistic terms. As 'the root of the creatures of the universe' ('radix est universae creaturae'), Christ is 'the first emanation of God' ('emanatio prima dei'), whom the kabbalists call Macroposopos ('the great man'), or Arikh Anpin, and Microposopos ('the small man') or Dseir Anpin. These, Keith claims, are manifestations of Christ, who is 'the great man' in so far as through him all things are made, and the 'small man' who could enter the womb of the virgin when he took on flesh. It is Christ 'the great man' whose soul extends to and illuminates every man. Keith also told Knorr that his doctrine of the mediator held the key to persuading the Jews and other non-Christians that the gospel account of the 'external' Christ is true:

[63] George Keith to Christian Knorr von Rosenroth, [November 1675], Herzog August Bibliothek, Cod. Guelph Extrav., 30.4, fol. 20.

[64] Ibid.

If the Jews can be led to believe that they are divinely illuminated through God by virtue of those human-like rays flowing from the Great Man [Macroposopos], whom their doctors and kabbalistical Rabbis call *Arikh Anpin*, then they may love that divine illumination and obey the same. And in this way they may feel Christ, that is, the divine soul live and move in them . . . For then, without trouble they would be led to believe those things which are true in the gospels concerning the external Christ . . . And this seem to me the best and most rational way to convert both the Jews and Mohamedans, and other infidels to the Christian faith, if they are first led to believe that pure life, light and divine virtue which everyone can experience in himself at any time.[65]

He also believed that Knorr's interpretation of the apocalypse showed that the Quaker movement had been prophesied in the book of Revelation.

If Knorr replied directly to Keith, the reply is no longer extant. In 1676 he asked Van Helmont to thank Keith for his 'most friendly letter, saying that he has had no response to 'his remarkable treatise'. Although he begs to differ about associating 'the anterior Adam' and 'Macroposopim or Arich Anpin' with Christ, he agrees with Keith's association of Microposopos and Neschama with Christ. 'Microposopim' is, he writes, the same as Dseir Anpin and that this is united with the Neschama of Christ.[66] Notwithstanding Knorr's reservations, Keith took his reply as an endorsement of his own interpretation. In his second extant letter to Knorr (1676), he continues to try to make his interpretation of Arikh Anpin and Dseir Anpin support his theory of the extended soul of Christ on which he attempted to found his doctrine of Christ as mediator. He agrees that Dseir Anpin refers to Christ, but insists that Arikh Anpin too must be interpreted as referring to Christ. Knorr's interpretation of Dseir Anpin as Christ still serves his purpose, namely to support his thesis that the soul of Christ is extended. No human soul, he writes, can reach God without mediation, and the mediation achieved by the extension of Christ's soul to all people. Keith insists that it is Christ's soul in his divine body that is extended and not his external body, because 'no body can be in many places at the same time'.[67] Keith claims that his assertion of the extension of the soul and divine body of Christ is consistent with the Christian kabbalists Guillaume Postel and Johann Reuchlin. His doctrine of Christ as mediator depends on singling out the apparently Christ-like properties of two of the five kabbalistic *partsufim* or manifestations of the deity, Arikh Anpin and Dseir Anpin. The first of these, Arikh Anpin, the 'Holy Ancient One', is a manifestation of divine love, and is the 'long suffering and merciful', while the fourth *partsuf*, Dseir Anpin is a manifestation of God as living Lord of the

[65] Ibid. [66] Knorr to Van Helmont, 17 Feb. 1676, ibid., fol. 16. [67] Ibid.

universe.[68] Keith's proposed interpretation of the *partsufim*, Arikh Anpin and Dseir Anpin appears to recapitulate Philo's theory of the dual-faceted *logos* (the *logos* as both eternal archetype and first created being). As with Philo, Keith's Christ is a mediator in the dual sense of both bridge between and separator of God and creation. One important difference between Keith and Philo is that Keith picks up on the kabbalistic attributes of the *partsufim* to endow the *logos*/mediator with palpably Christian attributes. Christ is not just the word (*logos*), but the merciful sufferer. Christ 'the heavenly man' ('homo coelestis') is the medium between us and the simple essence of God, which is remote from us.

On 29 November 1675, twelve days after Keith's first letter to Knorr, Anne Conway reported to More that she had just had a visit from George Keith on his way to Scotland.[69] She mentions having read Keith's letter to Knorr von Rosenroth, as well as a letter Keith had written to More. The main topic of Anne Conway's letter to More is Keith's Christology: the 'new notion of G. Keiths about Christ', that is to say, 'the extension of the soul of Christ' and his subscribing to 'the Jewes opinion, that there may be many soules in man, and that our sensitive soul is really distinct from that endued with understanding'. It is Keith's 'kabbalistic' doctrine of Christ the mediator to which Lady Conway refers when she told More that 'his opinion, if true, would facilitate the understanding of many places in Scripture, as well as it would make better sense of the Cabbalists Soir-Anpin and Arich Anpin'.[70] However, she had reservations about its 'seeming absurdities' – probably on account of Keith's obliviousness to the pantheistic consequences of his assertion that the soul of Christ is both united to God and contained in the extended body of Christ, which penetrates the whole created world.[71] Having heard of More's intention to refute Keith, she asked to have sight of the confutation, offering to send it on to Keith. She was particularly keen to see how he would answer More's criticisms:

> I could wish you would lett me see your answer to him, if you will send it hither, I know how to send it him, and I shall take great care of the conveyance of what you send, and now I am mentioning this, I would desire you to send me his answer to your Remarkes, for I have a mind to see all, he has to say for this opinion.[72]

More replied a month later.[73] He too had seen Keith's letter to Knorr. He was highly critical of Keith for what he regarded as his naive assimilation

[68] Scholem (1974). [69] *Conway Letters*, 407. [70] *Conway Letters*, p. 408.
[71] Herzog August Bibliothek, Cod. Guelf Extrav. 30.4, fol. 20.
[72] Anne Conway to Henry More, 29 Nov. 1675, *Conway Letters*, p. 407.
[73] Henry More to Anne Conway, 29 Dec. 1675, ibid., pp. 415–16.

of new ideas, especially 'this new opinion of his about the soul of Christ extended every way out of his body through the whole Creation is a haplesse and groundlesse conceit', he wrote.[74] Of Keith's debt to the kabbalah he commented that he 'seemes to catch at any thing to susteine himself in so weak a cause, and so maintaine one absurd theory with another'.[75] Keith's 'embracing the opinion of Jewes concerning Plurality of souls in one body' simply confirmed his gullibility.[76] Nearly two weeks later, on 10 January 1676, More despatched to Lady Conway his 'Examination or Confutation of G.K.'s opinion touching the extension of the soul of Christ'. This refutation of Keith, undertaken, More says, 'according to your Ladiships desire', has unfortunately not survived. But it is clear from the accompanying letter that chief among More's objections was Quaker denial of the historical Christ in favour of the interior and spiritual working of the Saviour. His concern was that 'they stick so much at the externall Mediation of our Savior and would have this Mediation of his performed within onely'. Keith's theory of the extended soul of Christ was the more 'scandalous' on account of his failure to adduce any sound reason for his opinions. His claim to be relying solely on 'illumination and Revelation' merely confirmed More's view that the Quakers were religious enthusiasts similar to the Familists.[77]

Anne Conway replied on 4 February 1676. Addressing More as 'Dear Doctor', she commends his arguments as 'considerable', containing 'very sober and usefull cautions'. She agrees with More that Keith's theory entails 'absurdities', but allows that, among his proofs, 'his 10th, 11, 12, 13, 14 makes the best shew for his assertion'. Unfortunately, neither Keith's defence nor More's confutation are extant, so we cannot make any kind of independent judgement of the case. But we may observe that Lady Conway's role in this exchange was not just as facilitator or spectator. She had her own independently formed views. She refers to an argument by Keith that involuntary pain and the experience of grief are proof of the presence of a living being in us, separate from our own souls, noting that 'it will be very hard for them to prove'. She was gratified to find that More agrees with her on some things:

[74] More to Anne Conway, 29 Dec. 1675, ibid., p. 415.

[75] More to Anne Conway, 10 Jan. 1675/6, ibid., p. 418.

[76] Ibid. In his own kabbalist studies More attacks the kabbalist view that the soul of the Messiah is extended throughout the world, and the Lurianic doctrine of the emanation of Adam Kadmon and the ten *sepiroth* from the Godhead (Aensoph), which he regarded as a root error that rendered kabbalism a materialist theosophy.

[77] More to Anne Conway, 10 Jan. 1676. *Conway Letters*, pp. 417–19.

I think it will not be easy for him to free his opinion from those seeming absurdities, you take notice, it is entangled with, many of *which I did apprehend it to be involved with before I read what you writt* and therefore was the better pleased to find them so fully insisted on and largely expressed to my hand by so judicious and able a pen.[78]

Significantly, she did not agree with More in all points. More had apparently interpreted Keith as meaning that the lower part of Christ's soul 'is onely plastical and not of the same nature with the souls of other men'. Anne Conway objects that this is a distorted interpretation, which 'I cannot think he would be understood to meane'. She continues: 'But I cannot imagine that he would be understood (which you seemed to suppose) that this farr extended soul of Christ did preceed the H. Ghost, for that being the life of the Deity, it is a contradiction to fancy the Deity ever destitute of.' More's replies are defensive. He insists on the care with which he had set out Keith's arguments: 'But as for that great soul [of Christ], I do not remember that I say he makes it preceed the Holy Ghost in time but in order of nature.'[79] Nor will he allow her commendation of some of Keith's arguments to stand without acknowledgement of the strength of his replies to them: 'What your Ladiship writes of G. Keiths 10, 11, 12, 13, 14th proofs, that they are the best, or make the best show, I agree to. But I think I have offer'd what is a sufficient answer to those that are unprejudiced.'[80]

There is a break in the continuity of the correspondence at this point, so we cannot see how the debate with Keith developed. Nevertheless, the issues surface again in other writings by More and Keith dating from the same period, in particular in the addenda, clarifications and answers to criticisms which More added to the last two volumes of his *Opera omnia*, published in 1679. The first volume of his *Opera omnia* had appeared in 1675; the second and third volumes (containing *Opera philosophica*) appeared in 1679. These volumes contain More's contributions to *Kabbala denudata*, which had been printed by Knorr in 1677.[81] The scholia which he added date from between 1677, when *Kabbala denudata* was published, and 1679 when the second volume of More's *Opera omnia* appeared. These volumes

78 Anne Conway to Henry More, 4 Feb. 1676, ibid., p. 421. My italics.

79 More to Anne Conway, 9 Feb. 1676, ibid., p. 423.

80 More to Anne Conway, 26 Feb. 1676, ibid., p. 424.

81 These More places between his critique of Jacob Boehme (*Philosophiae teutonicae censura*) and his refutation of Spinoza (*Demonstrationum duarum . . .* and *Epistola altera*). More also includes two items not printed in *Kabbalah denudata*, namely, *In visionem Ezechielis ex textu hebraico brevis et fidelis paraphrasis*; and *Explicatio tabulae visionis Ezechielis*. These contain a summary of Ezekiel chapters 1 and 10, with an illustration of Ezekiel's vision of the chariot and an explanation of it not in *Kabbala denudata*. See Hutton (1999a).

were being prepared for press at the same time as he was arguing against George Keith's interpretation of the kabbalah with Keith, Van Helmont and Lady Conway at Ragley Hall.[82] Among the scholia elaborating points made in his writings, those added to his commentaries on the kabbalah are especially important as a barometer of the intellectual climate at Ragley.

Of particular relevance to the Ragley debates is a long scholium which More adds to section 10 of his discussion of the second kabbalistic table. Almost as long as the original discussion, this scholium contains an attack on the kabbalist doctrine that the soul of the Messiah is extended throughout the world, and the Lurianic doctrine of the emanation of Adam Kadmon and the ten *sepiroth* from the Godhead (Aensoph). These are doctrines which More regarded as fundamental errors that rendered kabbalism a materialist pantheism. The scholium was clearly written with Keith in mind, for it includes the condemnation of doctrines ascribed to the Quakers: their repudiation ('striking dead' is his term) of the eternal *logos*, and their interpretation of Dseir Anpin as the incarnate soul of Christ extended through the world. This most abominable (*foedissimus*) error of Quakerism, writes More, smacks of Arianism, Sabellianism and paganism.[83] In a concerted effort to set limits to speculative interpretations of the kabbala, More also added to the scholia accompanying book I of his *Defence of the Philosophick Cabbala* five rules for establishing the compatibility of faith and reason, which had originally been published in his *Apology* of 1664.[84] These rules relate to the proper use of reason in matters of religion, and stipulate that the only acceptable philosophical tenets are those which are not repugnant to faith, and to the truth of scripture. He underlines the point in the ensuing discussion: he reminds his reader that he had always maintained that the contents of his *Conjectura cabbalistica* were to be taken as conjectural, not as true. He insists that we should indeed withhold our assent from all things that did not agree with, or were repugnant to, the established teachings of religion. We should never accept anything as mathematically certain against the wishes of our superiors. And, especially when interpreting the philosophical kabbalah, we should check its applicability to the text of Moses and always suspend judgement about the truth of its theorems.[85]

[82] In the 1670s More had been engaged in translating his works into Latin.

[83] More, *Opera omnia*, vol. II, p. 438.

[84] Ibid., pp. 534–7. More's earlier kabbalistic conjectures had incurred the criticism of at least one other English churchman, the future Bishop of Worcester, Edward Stillingfleet. See Hutton (1992).

[85] '*Assensum expresse suspendi ab omni re quae ullo modo videri possit dissona aut repugnans cum communio pervulgataque dogmatum Religionis nostrae intelligentia*', More *Opera omnia*, vol. II, p. 538.

THE WAY CAST UP AND *THE WAY TO THE CITY OF GOD*

While More was conducting a rearguard action against the excesses of Christian/Quaker kabbalism, Keith was busy modifying his theories in the light of his kabbalistic studies, no doubt with the active encouragement of Anne Conway. The continuing impact of Keith's encounter with her, as well as with Van Helmont and Henry More, reverberates through those of his writings which emanate from the same date as the first volume of *Kabbalah denudata*, and just prior to the publication of the second volume of More's *Opera omnia*. In *The Way Cast Up* [1677] and *The Way to the City of God* (1678) Keith continues to propound his doctrine that Christ's soul has infinite extension, a doctrine which he first expounded in *Immediate Revelation* ten years earlier. The increasing kabbalist–Neoplatonic emphasis which he gives to his theory reflects his reading of Henry More and Platonist sources, as well as his study of kabbalism. Keith, like More, conceives God as extended (More termed God *res extensa*, but Keith does not use this term), though More denied that Christ is in any way extended through the universe. Keith employs the Platonist terminology of emanation in his account of Christ's soul as 'a plenteous emanation of his spirituall and divine Body and Life, the proper vehicle and conduitt of the Holy Ghost and of God himself' in his disciples.[86] Keith also speaks of 'this wonderful extension of the Spirit of Christ as Man in his *Divine body* and *Seed*'.[87] These writings contain views which, at the very least, imply the compatibility of Quakerism and kabbalism: an important example, already cited, is Keith's spiritual monism, to which he subscribed as a result of his reading of kabbalistic texts. His account of Christ in *The Way Cast Up* directly recalls what he had written to Knorr von Rosenroth, with the difference that he does not cite the detailed kabbalistic interpretations he discussed with Knorr. *The Way to the City of God* expounds the 'kabbalistical' account of Christ, and the account of Christ as mediator, which Keith had outlined in

[86] George Keith, *The Way to the City of God Described* (1678), p. 127. cf. p. 103: Christ is in the saints as 'a ray or emanation of him'.

[87] George Keith, *The Way Cast Up* [1677], p. 142. Cf. Christ is '*a Seed of Life and Light in all*'. At the same time, Keith interweaves these kabbalistic strands with a scattering of epistemological doctrine, notably the Cartesian principle of clarity and distinctness as the criterion of certainty. He holds that the soul contains 'a self-evidencing power and vertue, whereby it can and doth sufficiently discover itself to be what indeed it is'. Keith, *Way to the City of God*, p. 166. Keith also attempts to account for the inner light in terms of epistemological certainty and that it is the clarity and distinctness of its impression on the soul which is the token of its divine origin. Keith speaks of the 'innate clearness and self-evidencing Power of the Divine Principle' which does 'sufficiently appear in every Soul of man and woman, upon the face of the earth with a sufficient clearness and self-evidence in some measure more or less . . . whereby to convince every Soul, that it proceeds from God and leads unto God'. Ibid., pp. 167 and 177.

his letters to Knorr. Keith explains the immediate presence of Christ to the soul of believers via the kabbalistic doctrine that the soul of Adam Kadmon extends through the world. The same book explains the union of God with the believer (or saint) and individual people in terms of the emanation of the soul of Christ or the extension of the soul of Christ through creation.[88] The 'universall presence' of Christ the mediator is the spirit of God which 'doth everywhere extend it self into all things'.[89] Keith makes the same distinction in the soul of Christ between 'Neschamah or Nischmah' (the divine spirit breathed by God into Adam) and 'Nephesch' (the soul of the incarnate Christ which He has in common with other men) that he had made in his letters to Knorr. Although he does not call Christ Adam Kadmon, he does use characteristically kabbalistic terms in describing Christ as a vessel or conduit for the dissemination of divine light from God to man.[90] He also proposes that regeneration entails a purification of substance, possible by virtue of the fact that the earthly and heavenly substance are like different modes of the same substance:

For *Earthly* and *Heavenly* are not so differing, but that remaining one in Substance: they may be changed into one another, so that as one and the same sinfull Soul may by the operation of the Mighty Power of God, be changed so as to be made heavenly and pure; even so one and the same Earthly body may by the same Power be made Heavenly, and thus in different respects they are one and the same, and yet not the same: *one* in Substance, and not *one*, but *another*, in the same manner of being.[91]

Most importantly, the kabbalistical Christology of these books has discernible affinities with Anne Conway's *Principles*. In *The Way Cast Up*, Keith describes God and Christ in terminology similar to that in which Anne Conway sets out her foundational concept of God in her *Principles*: he writes of the 'Spirit, Power, Light and Life of God, and his Divine Goodness, Love, Mercy, Kindness, and Compassion revealed to us in Christ Jesus'.[92] Christ, he writes, is a mediator, 'a certain mid[d]le nature, substance or being, betwixt the Godhead and Mankind'. Keith claims that, although received doctrine denies there is any such thing as an intermediate nature, this Middle Nature is in fact 'the heavenly or Divine Substance or Essence, of which the Divine birth was both conceived in Mary, and is inwardly conceived in the Saints'.[93] He explains that this Middle Nature is not the Godhead itself, nor a particle of it, but next to God in 'its excellency above

[88] Keith, *Way Cast Up*, pp. 126–27 and 132. [89] Ibid., pp. 159–60.
[90] Ibid., p. 137. [91] Ibid., pp. 131–2.
[92] Keith, *Way Cast Up*, 'To the Reader', sig. *4.
[93] Keith, *Way to the City of God*, p. 131.

other things'. This is 'the Heavenly Man' which links God and humankind: 'that wonderful nexus, tie, or bond betwixt God and him, through which he hath immediate union with him; yea it is, and may be called the *union*, viz., that by which *God* and *Man* is made *one*'.[94] Stressing the love and goodness of God, in *The Way Cast Up*, he maintains that Christ showed his love by suffering for mankind. He refuses to interpret Christ's sufferings as atonement for the wrath of God, but explains Christ's sufferings in perfectionist terms: 'it pleased the Father thus to try him, and make him *perfect* thus by *sufferings*, to the end he might overcome sin, and the spirit thereof, in the more glory, and might be the more fitted to help them, that are under Trials, as being *touched with the feeling of Our infirmitys*'.[95] George Keith, then, was rewriting Quaker doctrines in the light of his encounter with kabbalistic writings at exactly the same time that Anne Conway was finalising the details of her metaphysical system. The extent to which this and other doctrines were the result of Keith's direct reading of kabbalist texts, or whether he owes his view of kabbalism to Anne Conway, is hard to determine with any precision. Keith's more confused treatment of these doctrines would suggest that he owed more to her than the other way round.

ANNE CONWAY'S CHRISTOLOGY

The impact of the same Quaker–kabbalist discussions that led Keith to rework his theology is discernible in many striking verbal and conceptual parallels with Keith in Anne Conway's *Principles*, especially in her account of Middle Nature/Christ. Much of Keith's terminology is similar to Anne Conway's. Both regard Christ as a *mediator between extremes*.[96] Both account for the regenerative workings of Christ in the soul in terms of the 'intimate presence' of Christ to the soul. Both Keith and Anne Conway explain suffering in terms of love and regard suffering as a means to perfection. Anne Conway's discussion of Middle Nature (*natura media*) is far

[94] Ibid., p. 132. [95] Ibid., p. 146.

[96] Herzog August Bibliothek, Cod Guelph Extrav., 30.4 fols. 20 ff. See above, pp. 191–2. There is a parallel account of Christ as a mediator between extremes in Peter Sterry: 'The Lord Jesus then, as a Mediator of Union by Participation toucheth both the extremes of infiniteness and finiteness; of God and the Creature, comprehends both in *One* in himself; fills up the middle space between *both*; is the *way*, by which God descendeth into the Creature, and the Creature cometh forth from God; by which again God reascendeth together with the Creature, and the Creature returneth unto God'. Peter Sterry, *Discourse of the Freedom of the Will* (London, 1675, written prior to 1672). Sterry's sources possibly included kabbalist ones. To my knowledge there is no evidence of contact between him and either Keith or Anne Conway.

more extensive and metaphysical than Keith's. In Anne Conway's conception, Middle Nature has strong religious connotations, with distinct echoes of Trinitarian doctrine. Nevertheless, the Christological connotations of Middle Nature would appear to owe less to traditional Trinitarianism than to Quaker formulations of the inward operation of the inner light. But where Keith's concern was essentially theological, chiefly to apply kabbalist teachings to Quaker doctrines concerning Christ as son of God, Anne Conway uses her understanding of the relationship between God, Christ and the world to explain fundamental questions in philosophy. Her discussion of Christ as Middle Nature is not confined to the Christ as mediator between God and man in the spiritual sense. Middle Nature is the intermediary between God and the created world in a general, ontological sense, as the instrumental dimension of deity or first cause, which accounts for the omnipresence of God in the world and interaction between God and created beings. As 'Christ' or *logos prophorikos* (the outgoing word of God), Middle Nature is the deity, intimately present to all creatures, yet not 'confounded with them' ('cum ipsis non confundatur'). Through this idea of 'intimate presence', Anne Conway formulates her theory of vital action to explain life and movement in created things.

The analogies between Keith's Christology and Anne Conway's second species are clear. But so too are the differences between them. Where Keith's theory of the extended soul of Christ was an attempt to provide a theoretical underpinning for a central doctrine of Quakerism (the inner light), Anne Conway's Middle Nature is a key component of a philosophical system which explains life and motion in creatures in terms of the relationship between God and the world. She answers the thorny question that vexed the Cartesian generation of philosophers of how souls move bodies[97] in terms of the 'intimate presence' of Middle Nature and 'virtual extension' or 'vital action'. Distinguishing two forms of motion, local motion and 'vital action', she explains the latter as action at a distance, achieved through a suitable medium.

> vital action can proceed together with local motion from one thing to another when a fitting medium exists to transmit it, and this even at a great distance. Here one may observe a kind of divine spirituality or subtlety in every motion and in every action of life, which no created substance or body is capable of, namely through intimate presence.

[97] At the end of her treatise, she presents the conclusion of her discussion as the resolution of this contemporary philosophical question: 'it is a matter of great debate how motion can be transmitted from one body to another since it certainly is neither a substance nor a body', *Principles*, p. 69.

Arguing against Henry More's idea that motion and life in bodies is to be explained as the action of spirits which penetrate solid bodies, Anne Conway explains life and motion not in terms of penetrating spirit, but through the 'intimate presence' of the divine which serves as the medium of vital action. 'Intimate presence' is 'neither a substance nor a body', and the only being capable of it is God himself. 'Vital action' too is conceived as a kind of extension, which she calls 'virtual extension' (*extensio virtualis*). Derived 'immediately' from God, 'virtual extension' is a vital force ('vital virtue'/*vita virtualis*) proceeding from the 'inner being' of a creature and varying 'according to the kind or degree of life with which the creature is endowed'.[98]

Anne Conway's choice of the term 'vital extension' suggests that this vital action is to be understood spatially. This is consistent with the account of spirit she derives from the kabbalah.[99] But it also recalls Henry More's claim that extension is not a defining attribute of body, and that besides corporeal extension there is also spiritual and spatial extension. There are echoes, too, of More's view that God himself is *res extensa*. However, Anne Conway does not appear to hold that God is an extended being, since extension is an attribute of created things. She does, however, hold that Christ is an extended being, where More does not. This in turn recalls George Keith's conception of Christ as having an extended soul. In these important respects her account of the relationship of God to the created world, and, concomitantly, her discussion of the problem of motion, bear the traces of the philosophical and religious debates of her immediate circle. Her concept of Middle Nature is, in many respects, a divinised version of the intermediary causal principle posited by the Cambridge Platonists – More's 'Spirit of Nature' or Cudworth's 'Plastic Nature'. As a manifestation of God, Middle Nature is neither a subordinate deity nor an alternative deity, but God himself. Middle Nature is, furthermore, 'God with the Messiah in Creatures', enjoying a kind of consubstantial union with created things such that, although thereby united to God, they are not one with God. At the same time, by conceiving of Middle Nature as *logos*, Conway separates God and creation, thereby avoiding the need for occasionalism – the

[98] Ibid. By the term 'virtualis' Lady Conway probably meant some kind of non-physical power or force. The Latin word 'virtualis' is non-classical in origin, but has classical roots in the term 'vis' (power) and 'virtus' (excellence). The medieval coinage, 'virtualis' suggests both inherent properties and a capacity to exert influence through those properties. This survives in a pre-1680 meaning of the English term given in the *Oxford English Dictionary* – 'capable of producing a certain effect or result, effective, potent powerful'.

[99] Anne Conway follows the kabbalists and Neoplatonists in conceiving of Middle Nature as an emanative cause – the first emanation of God.

direct intervention of God in the world. The Trinitarian connotations of Middle Nature remove some of the difficulties associated with the Spirit of Nature and Plastic Nature of the Cambridge Platonists. Conway may be said to have both guarded against pantheism (as, for example, in the case of Spinoza) and anticipated Pierre Bayle's objection to Cudworth's concept of 'Plastic Nature' that by it Cudworth introduces polytheism – if not atheism.

Although both Conway and Keith were drawing on a common fund of kabbalistic doctrines at the same time, Keith certainly did not have a clear intellectual grasp of either the philosophical or the theological issues with which Lady Conway was concerned. His attempt to harness kabbalism to Quaker theology was piecemeal to say the least. As Henry More pointedly observed, 'those notions of the Cabbalists' were 'as sweet and pleasing to him as new milk to any Kittin'.[100] His importance in the biography of Anne Conway is not philosophical so much as historical. He was less a formative thinker or a source of ideas than a participant in an on-going debate with More, Anne Conway and Van Helmont. Keith's letters and books of this period are therefore important for the clues they afford about the immediate context in which Anne Conway wrote her *Principles* and in which she made her final commitment to Quakerism. They also show how the interpretation of kabbalism and Quakerism were intertwined in the Conway circle. The debate with Keith gives us a glimpse of the topics and tendencies of Ragley thinking at this time. But they are only one aspect of the on-going dialogue. For a more complete account of the discussions from which Conway's *Principles* emerged, the next chapter will examine their debates in the Ragley circle in the last years of her life.

[100] *Conway Letters*, p. 415.

CHAPTER 10

Last years

'though her Pains encreas'd, yet her Understanding diminish'd not'[1]

The last four years of Anne Conway's life were years of intense intellectual activity, crucial in the genesis of her philosophical system. From what we have seen of her investigations into kabbalism and Quakerism, she was at the centre of a lively interchange of ideas among the little group in contact with her at Ragley. Here her immediate circle of Henry More and Van Helmont had been enlarged by the entry of the Quaker leader George Keith. As we have seen, her correspondence of these last years documents an intense interchange between members of this group. The debates are also registered in what might be described as a penumbra of texts produced by Keith, More and Van Helmont, which supplement the epistolary record of her intellectual pursuits. The writings of Keith, the scholia assiduously added by More to his published writings, as well as the publications of Van Helmont, reverberate with these dialogues at Ragley. Far from being the passive spectator of the intellectual drama going on around her, Anne Conway was centrally involved as director of and participant in their debates. From these writings, we can gather more about the main issues under discussion, enabling us to register the impact that she made and providing us with some means of assessing her debt to her interlocutors. By this point of her life, Anne Conway's critique of More was fully formed, though we cannot be certain precisely when she took the decisive step towards positing a monism of spirit. But during the last four years of her life her encounter with the powerful combination of Helmontianism, kabbalism and Quakerism served to persuade her of the philosophical viability and religious authenticity of her alternative to dualism. Her *Principles of the Most Ancient and Modern Philosophy* was written against the background of these same debates. This chapter will reconstruct the last stages of those

[1] Van Helmont in Ward, *Life*, pp. 125–5.

debates by comparing the texts emanating from the Ragley circle in the period leading up to Anne Conway's death.

KABBALISTICAL DIALOGUES

The group of texts emanating from the kabbalistical debates at Ragley Hall during the last years of Anne Conway's life included, besides *Principles of the Most Ancient and Modern Philosophy,* one which we have already mentioned, *A Cabbalistical Dialogue* (1684), as well as *Adumbratio kabbalae christianae* (1677) and *Two Hundred Queries concerning the Revolution of Human Souls* (1684). The publishing chronology of these texts belies the fact that they emanate from the same period. *Two Hundred Queries* was published in Latin in 1690, in the same volume as Conway's *Principia*, with the title *CC problemata.* The prefaces of both these versions of *Two Hundred Queries* give us some clues to the fact that they emanate from the same earlier period. According to the preface of the English version of *Two Hundred Queries*, which was published in 1684, it was translated into English 'two years since', in other words in 1682. The same preface announces that it will be followed by two further treatises, including a hitherto unpublished 'Latine Tract' from the works of Rabbi Isaac Luria called 'De revolutione animarum tractatus'.[2] The English preface does not identify the other treatise, but the Latin version of *Two Hundred Queries*, printed in *Opuscula philosophica*, names it as *Adumbratio kabbalae christianae.*[3] Whatever the original publishing intentions, these kabbalistic treatises were in fact not published separately as a group. However, three of them appeared in *Kabbala denudata. A Cabbalistical Dialogue* was first published in Latin in the second part of the first volume of *Kabbala denudata* (1677–8), and both the Luria text and *Adumbratio* were included in the 1684 volume of the same work. Both *Adumbratio kabbalae christianae* and *A Cabbalistical Dialogue* were, therefore, intended as companion pieces to *Two Hundred Queries* (which will be discussed below), and they form the immediate interpretative backdrop to Anne Conway's *Principles.* To these may be added the scholia which More added to the Latin translation of his *Opera omnia* (discussed in the previous chapter). All these texts exhibit affinities in point of content: there are, furthermore, discernible parallels between *Two Hundred Queries*, Anne Conway's *Principles* and the letters

[2] Francis Mercury van Helmont, *Two Hundred Queries Modestly Propounded* (London, 1684), sigg. A3, A4r–v.

[3] *CC problemata,* preface, in *Opuscula philosophica.*

and writings of George Keith which date from the same period. Remarkably, the majority of these texts are dialogic in character. In almost all of them the other side of the debate is represented by Henry More, who was on the defensive. As we have seen, his letters and scholia show that he was deeply engaged in answering points put to him by Anne Conway, Van Helmont and Keith. *A Cabbalistical Dialogue*, as its title suggests, is the outcome of a dialogue between Henry More and Van Helmont, in which Van Helmont defended kabbalism against the objections of Henry More. *Adumbratio kabbalae christianae*, likewise, is a dialogue (between a learned Christian and a learned Jew), as is *Two Hundred Queries*. The dialogic character and context of these texts is suggestive of collective rather than single authorship. This being the case, it seems right to consider Anne Conway as co-author of at least some of them.

Adumbratio kabbalae christianae was printed at the end of the 1684 volume of *Kabbala denudata*. It is described in the preface of another book, *CC problemata* (*Two Hundred Queries*), as a hebraising manual for converting the Jews.[4] It takes the form of a dialogue between a Christian philosopher and a learned Jew. The Christian sets out to demonstrate to the Jew the compatibility of Jewish doctrines with Christian teachings. Among these he stresses the similarities between belief in Christ and the kabbalist account of Adam Kadmon. The Christian argues at length that the kabbalist conception of Adam Kadmon answers in every detail the biblical account of Christ the saviour.[5] The *Adumbratio* also, along the way, endorses More's view that the kabbalah contained an account of the Hylarchic Principle or Spirit of Nature (a view which Knorr too was inclined to accept).[6] It also justifies Van Helmont's belief in the transmigration of souls by arguing that it was a tenet of ancient judaic philosophy, as encapsulated in the kabbalah. *Adumbratio* is therefore a Christian kabbalist text, which endorses a fundamental element of More's philosophy of spirit, his Spirit of Nature. Together, both the *Adumbratio* and *Cabbalistical Dialogue* are not just examples of seventeenth-century Christian kabbalism but important indicators of the interests and concerns of Anne Conway's circle at Ragley in their reading of kabbalistic texts.

4 Ibid.

5 Francis Mercury van Helmont, *Adumbratio kabbalae christianae*, printed at the end of the final volume of *Kabbala denudata* (1684). It is not included in all copies. And the modern reprint does not contain it. The author was almost certainly Van Helmont.

6 Knorr obviously thought that More's hylarchic principle was a plausible hypothesis. See his letter to him, Herzog August Bibliothek, Cod. Guelph Extrav. 30.4, 9v.

TWO HUNDRED QUERIES

The dialogic character of the texts produced by the Ragley circle is best exemplified in a text not so far discussed, the anonymously printed *Two Hundred Queries Modestly Propounded Concerning the Doctrine of the Revolution of Human Souls and its Conformity with the Truth of the Christian Religion* (London, 1684).[7] This text has special claim on our attention because a Latin translation of it was printed in the same volume as the Latin translation of Anne Conway's treatise. Although both the English and Latin versions of this *Two Hundred Queries* were printed some years after Anne Conway's death, the internal evidence suggests that they are contemporaneous with her *Principles*. In his *Paradoxal Discourses* (1685), Van Helmont claims authorship of *Two Hundred Queries*, explaining that it was written 'upon the desire of a Person of Quality', and dictated to a friend who changed the 'method' and expanded it.[8] The person of quality was evidently Anne Conway and the friend in all likelihood George Keith. There are close parallels between *Two Hundred Queries* and others of Van Helmont's writings, such as *Seder Olam* and *Paradoxal Discourses*. But it seems clear from the content that Van Helmont was not the sole author of *Two Hundred Queries*. Rather, the book was the outcome of a triangular dialogue between him, Anne Conway and George Keith. In format the book exemplifies the question-driven approach which Anne Conway adopts in a good part of her *Principles*, and characterises George Keith's *Way to the City of God*. Like Conway's *Principles*, *Two Hundred Queries* is a theodicy: the central aim of the book is to defend the justice and providence of God, and to explain otherwise inexplicable passages of scripture. This aim is stated in the answer to the first query:

> to conduce unto the vindication of the Divine Justice, the clearing of the Divine Providence, and other the Divine Attributes of God, and finally to the satisfactory opening of the many portions of Sacred Writ; which have hitherto seemed, as it were altogether shut up from the understandings of most men, learned as well as unlearned.[9]

The book as a whole is devoted to demonstrating the doctrine of metempsychosis, or transmigration of souls, a favourite doctrine of Van Helmont's, and one for which he found endorsement in the kabbalistic doctrine of *tikkun*. Allison Coudert has demonstrated the profound influence of the

[7] The Latin version printed in *Opuscula philosophica*, is entitled *CC problemata de revolutione animarum humanarum*. This was translated into German as *Zweihundert Fragen betreffend die Lehre von der Widerkehr der Menschlichen Seelen* (1686).

[8] Van Helmont, *Paradoxal Discourses*, p. 185.

[9] Van Helmont, *Two Hundred Queries*, p. 2.

Lurianic doctrine of transmigration in the arguments propounded in *Two Hundred Queries*.[10] And she has also pointed out parallels between Anne Conway's *Principles* and the arguments contained in *Two Hundred Queries*. These points are beyond dispute. However, for present purposes I want to focus on what we can learn from *Two Hundred Queries* about the aims and evolution of Conway's philosophy, by noting further dimensions to the arguments and adding detail on the matter of collaboration.

Two Hundred Queries, as the title indicates, consists of a set of two hundred questions relating to the theologically unorthodox doctrine of the transmigration of souls. The underlying theological premises of the treatise are a liberal theology of grace – according to which Christ died to save all men, not just the elect few – and an emphasis on God's goodness and justice among the divine attributes. These are integral to the theodicical message of the work and the basic premises for a tolerationist and conversionist agenda. This theological liberalism echoes that of the Cambridge Platonists, and the Arminian opponents of predestinarian Calvinism, but the theological liberalism of the treatise is far more radical than theirs since it is argued that Christ died not just for all *men*, but for all *creatures*, including *animals*. The theory of transmigration also takes to a further extreme another doctrine dear to some of the Cambridge Platonists, the doctrine of the pre-existence of souls, to which Henry More and others subscribed as a means of vindicating the justice of divine providence. But where Henry More's theory of pre-existence entailed a previous 'life' for every soul prior to its conjunction with a body, transmigration entails the soul experiencing a succession of lives in different bodies. This theory has classical precedent in Pythagorean philosophy, and it was also taken up by Origen (both Pythagoras and Origen are cited in *Two Hundred Queries*). But the most important source was the Lurianic kabbala. However, *Two Hundred Queries* indicates that its scope is broader than a strictly kabbalist one, namely an argument from universal consent that this doctrine was part of true philosophy, sacred in origins, of which the kabbalah was taken to be a part. Luria is used as an important authority, but not by any means dogmatically. Furthermore, *Two Hundred Queries* deploys the theory of transmigration in the service of Christian doctrine, or, rather, what the authors believe to be an improved understanding of Christian doctrine. Though it is claimed that these doctrines date back to apostolic Christianity (according to query 90, transmigration of souls was believed in the time of Christ), and are mentioned in scripture, the beliefs in question were by no means mainstream in historical Christianity. Furthermore, the interpretative method applied is

[10] Coudert (1999), pp. 196 ff.

non-standard. The resulting interpretations are often breathtakingly heterodox, especially with regard to doctrines of damnation and the resurrection.

The main theological appeal of the theory of the transmigration of souls is that it explains punishment for sins, without impugning the justice of God. For, the argument goes, it would be unjust of God to punish us for sins we had not committed. However, if we have sinned in a previous life, punishment would not be unjust: 'we must all have formerly lived in the World, even before Christ' (query 29). This position is not unlike that taken by Henry More in his defence of his belief in the pre-existence of souls. Ultimately the theories of both transmigration and pre-existence were founded in the attributes of God: if God is just, then he does not punish unjustly. Since God does, evidently, punish people, it follows that they must have committed their offences previously, for God would not punish them undeservedly. Either way, transmigration is proposed in order to vindicate the justice of God. Furthermore, if Christ died for all men, how could he save those already dead, but for the possibility of their living again at the time of the gospel and beyond (query 30)?

The argument from God's attributes leads inexorably to scepticism about the existence and eternity of hell and to positing universal salvation.[11] Justice demands equity between crime and punishment: but infinite punishment for a finite crime is grossly inequitable (query 147). Since God is just, he does not punish sinners in this way. Besides, a good and just God must have as his end in view the good of his creatures: punishment should therefore be ameliorative (query 141). Another argument from the divine attributes is that since God is by definition loving and immutable, it would contradict the nature of God if he changed from loving to hating his creatures by consigning them to perdition (query 147).

Perhaps the most unorthodox interpretation of Christian dogma in *Two Hundred Queries* is the explanation of the doctrine of resurrection in terms of transmigration. The doctrine of the resurrection of the body is of course one Christian teaching with no analogue in Judaism. It was therefore a particularly contentious issue in conversionist attempts to accommodate Judaism and Christianity. That *Two Hundred Queries* focuses on the resurrection is a clear indicator that its agenda is primarily Christian and not kabbalist. But, by spiritualising body, the argument erodes Jewish objections to corporeal resurrection. A perhaps unexpected aspect of the transmigrationist argument is the argument for monism of substance: that there is no body, only spirit. The transmigrationist argument therefore

[11] Walker (1964) and Hutton (1996a).

offers a theological underpinning for monism – not by appeal to biblical authority or exegetical arguments, but on the grounds that transmigration is the only rational basis on which to make sense of the doctrine of the resurrection of the body. According to the authors of *Two Hundred Queries* one of the main objections to the doctrine of the resurrection of the body is that the body is not 'a living sensible Principle'. This objection is removed when it is understood that all creation is animate and all bodies are in fact alive in some sense (queries 125–33). The main argument for this is that God's creation is like God, and since God is living, his creation must be alive. In phraseology that echoes Conway's *Principles*, it is demanded, 'can any dead or unliving thing come from him, who is life itself?' (query 109).[12] The resurrection of the body is the resurrection of the same body, 'because that body . . . did partake with it, in its Sufferings and Afflictions'.[13]

Strictly, therefore, transmigration is not transmigration of *souls*, but a revolution of *bodies*, a cycle of corporeal regeneration, rather than metempsychosis. The neologism 'transcorporation' is coined to denote this (query 73, query 193). Another term employed for it is 'ensomatosis' (query 194). Ensomatosis, it is claimed, is the genuine form of transmigration to which Pythagoras and Plato, Plotinus, Hierocles and the Jews all subscribed. It was subsequently misinterpreted by many, among them Nicodemus, who took it to denote a physical process ('Corporal Transcorporation'), and the heathens, who corrupted it to metempsychosis. The 'new birth' preached by Christ to Nicodemus actually involves corporeal or bodily regeneration which 'is as true and real, as the inward is in its kind' (query 198). The body in ensomatosis is in fact a spiritual body, whose corruption will be purged away by punishment in repeated cycles of transmigration. The result of this will be that this spiritual body will be changed and will put on immortality. Ensomatosis is therefore a theory consistent with the true gospel message of the resurrection. This doctrine, however, needs to be purged of misinterpretation, 'to be corrected, reformed, and stripped of that disguise and deformed shape which many had put upon it'.[14] That done, ensomatosis 'will be very suitable to the Principles of the Christian Religion'.[15]

Two Hundred Queries ends with a call for the reform of philosophy, in order to make it consistent with the fundamentals of true belief. The inconsistencies of existing philosophies do no credit to Christians, and are an impediment to conversion. To the shame of Christians, non-Christians

[12] Compare *Principles*, p. 45. [13] Van Helmont, *Two Hundred Queries*, p. 98.
[14] Ibid., p. 163. [15] Ibid.

repudiate Christianity on the grounds that the philosophy practised by Christians is inconsistent with their creed: 'both *Heathens* and *Jews* . . . conclude the Divinity of the Modern Christians cannot be good, while their Philosophy is so bad'.[16] As things stand, non-Christians have a better philosophical understanding of religious matters: 'Infidels whether *Jews* or Heathens . . . have more wise and solid Notions, and Apprehensions of the Supream Being, than many called Christians.'[17] The treatise ends by making the case for the reform of philosophy in a series of insistent questions:

> Is it not then high time for all good and serious Christians, to be awakened, and to consider well how they lay Offences in the way of the weak, and concern themselves to remove them? And ought there not to shine forth among true Christians, a more solid and true Wisdom, and Light, to clear the blessed Attributes of God's Goodness, Wisdom, Justice, and Providence in all his Dispensations, and that much more abundantly than e[ver] Infidels, *Jews*, or Heathens, can offer?

The parallels between *Two Hundred Queries* and Anne Conway's *Principles* are manifold. Aside from receptivity to kabbalism and a theological liberalism that extends to heterodoxy (notably universal salvation and disbelief in hell) we might note that both advocate vitalism, both are concerned to vindicate the justice of God and both argue that punishment should be ameliorative. There are, furthermore, striking parallels in wording: for example the question whether a 'dead thing can come from God who is life itself' (query 109), the view that a God who damned sinners eternally would be a tyrant God, the view that punishment is medicinal in nature (query 141), and the use of the term 'stumbling blocks' for obstacles in the way of conversion.

The parallels notwithstanding, we should at the same time acknowledge the limits of overlap between Conway's *Principles* and *Two Hundred Queries*. A major difference is that in the latter the cyclical mode of ensomatosis (a term, in any case, not used by Lady Conway) is periodic and each cycle has a specific length. This comes closer to kabbalism and to Van Helmont's own adoption of the kabbalist cycles in *Seder Olam* and others of his writings. The demonstrative technique of both texts is sharply divergent: the rigorously deductive pattern of argument of the *Principles* stands in sharp contrast to the loose dialogic framework of *Two Hundred Queries*. In a work of collaborative authorship like the *Two Hundred Queries*, lack of agreement in all points is to be expected, especially in a treatise which is organised as a set of questions. Nonetheless, the similarities in the content

[16] Ibid., p. 164. [17] Ibid., p. 165.

and coincidence of date between it and Anne Conway's *Principles* are strong evidence that discussions from which *Two Hundred Queries* emerged was the discursive background to the *Principles of the Most Ancient and Modern Philosophy*.

One important piece of evidence to be derived from *Two Hundred Queries* is a rationale for Lady Conway's philosophy: *Two Hundred Queries* concludes with an appeal for the reform of philosophy so as to make it consistent with the truth of Christianity. Anne Conway's *Principles* is in many ways an attempt to do just that, for it amounts to a *philosophia pia* (religious philosophy), in which philosophical truth is compatible with the fundamental tenets of religion, and in which religious beliefs are presented in a philosophically satisfying way. The *Principles* is both a theodicy which 'conduce[s] to the Vindication of the Divine Justice' and a metaphysics where religious concepts contribute to the explanatory vocabulary of causality.

When we set Anne Conway's *Principles* into the context of the Ragley debates, alongside the writings of both Keith and Van Helmont generated by those debates, we can see that all these texts contain similar sets of questions, preferred answers and recurring arguments and doctrines. These are the key pressure points, so to speak, which shed light on the direction in which Anne Conway's philosophy developed. A consensus emerges on a number of common topics. There is general agreement that the basic 'stuff' of all created things is constituted from a single substance possessing the properties of spirit (principally life and action). With variations, all three conceive of Christ not merely in the conventional Christian sense of redeemer but as a mediator between extremes. All three agree that Christ is present in all creation, though there is no clear consensus on how. Van Helmont's doctrine of transmigration was not shared by Anne Conway or George Keith. Nevertheless, they were concerned with the same issues of sin, punishment and the justice of God to which Van Helmont proposed his doctrine as a solution. Transmigration of souls was one answer; transformation within the order of the third species, as proposed by Anne Conway, was another. The theory of ensomatosis or transcorporation of spiritual substance, as elaborated in *Two Hundred Queries* is in a sense a bridge between these two positions.

As we have already seen, the work of Keith which most deeply registers the impact of his discussions with Anne Conway and Knorr von Rosenroth is his *Way to the City of God*. Here, his greatest debt to his contact with the Ragley circle is his theory of the role and operation of Christ. Of particular relevance to the present discussion is the dialogic aspect of his treatment of this topic which introduces it through a set of questions, apparently posed from outside ('if it be asked . . .'). These are: whether the Godhead was conceived or born of the virgin; whether the seed of God is a particle of the Godhead; whether the birth is part of the Godhead; whether what is born is above the ordinary nature of man; and whether it is the Godhead itself. Keith's answers invoke, first of all, Henry More's concept of the indiscerpibility of spirits:

> I say then, that neither is the Godhead it self conceived or born in this birth, nor yet is it a particle or portion thereof. For I confess to say either of these two is very unsound, and is altogether contrary unto and inconsistent with the dignity and glory of God. And as for the *Godhead* (to speak properly) it is *not discerpible* into particles.[18]

He goes on to affirm that there is indeed 'something above the common nature of man' in the birth, that this is 'not the Godhead itself' but 'a certain . . . that is farr, yea and much farther transcendent in glory above the common nature of man, as the nature of man is above the nature of beasts; yea it is even above the nature of the angels'.[19] At key points in *Way to the City of God*, Keith presents his argument as sets of questions and answers. This dialogic presentation echoes the pattern of proposition and reply that fills Lady Conway's correspondence with More in the same period. Furthermore, Keith's way of posing the questions he asks implies strongly that the questions that shaped the debate were not his own. Keith's doctrines, therefore, appear to have been formulated against an immediate background of debate, queries, objections and replies. The fact that these writings of Keith's were the outcome of an on-going debate is an important clue to the question of the relationship of Anne Conway's ideas to those of her immediate circle. They are another example of the kind of question-driven discussion emanating from the Ragley circle, exemplified by *Two Hundred Queries . . . Concerning the Doctrine of the Revolution of the Human Souls.*

SEDER OLAM

Just as the after-echoes of the Ragley debates can be detected in the writings of George Keith, notably in his *Way to the City of God* and *Way Cast Up*, so also the Ragley debates find unmistakable echoes in the writings which Van Helmont published from the 1680s onwards. These writings constitute

[18] Keith, *Way to the City of God*, pp. 129–30. [19] Ibid., p. 130.

the main body of his published work. It was also during this spate of publications that Anne Conway's *Principles* was printed. To a greater or lesser degree, these texts bear the stamp of the Quaker–kabbalist conversations at Ragley. The work which contains the largest number of parallels with Conway's *Principia* is one entitled *Seder Olam sive ordo saecularum historica enarratio doctrinae* (1693), which, like so many of the texts associated with Van Helmont, was probably written under his direction rather than by him. It was translated into English by Dr John Clarke in 1694, on his recommendation. Although not structured as a dialogue, *Seder Olam* has enough in common with *Two Hundred Queries* to suggest that it too was the product of the same debates that occupied the Ragley circle in this period. The first thirty-three sections of it enumerate a large number of doctrines to be found in Anne Conway's treatise, and in the same order in which they are found in hers. According to *Seder Olam*, God, whose essential attribute is to be a creator, is the fountain of life; creation is the outcome of God's goodness and wisdom, and is eternal and continuous; God being loving by nature, His punishments are redemptive, not punitive; creatures are distinguished from God by their mutability. This capacity for change is, however, two-directional, either towards the good or away from the good towards evil. Christ is an *ens medium* or 'middle Being' between God and creation, partaking of the attributes of both, but only changeable in respect of the good. 'Spirit and Body' are not contrary essences, 'as many do vainly and falsely affirm'. All creatures have affinity with one another, 'from the highest to the lowest, and the lowest to the highest'. Body is not something 'wholly inanimate and void of Life'. Such an opinion 'borders on Atheism, and most grievously strikes at the Divine Goodness, Wisdom, and Power'. All bodies are endued with 'Life, Sense and Knowledge; or at leastwise [are] capable of those Attributes'.[20] The first part of *Seder Olam* thus reads like a paraphrase of Anne Conway's *Principles*. However, the later sections diverge from her treatise, especially the discussion of the pre-existence of souls, the transmigration of souls, and the second coming and the framework of kabbalistic worlds (Aziluth, Briah, Jezirah and Asiah).[21] The clearly kabbalistic traits in F. M. van Helmont's writings point to the fact that both he and Lady Conway engaged in deep discussion of the significance of the kabbalistic writings circulating among the Ragley circle.

The common ground between Conway, Keith and Van Helmont notwithstanding, there are important differences between *The Principles*

[20] Van Helmont, *Seder Olam*, sections 3.4, 4, 5, 6, 8, 10–14, 28.
[21] Ibid., sections 46, 72, 98, 41, 56.

of the Most Ancient and Modern Philosophy and the texts just discussed. For one thing, Anne Conway's treatise is philosophical, albeit with a religious dimension, whereas they have primarily religious concerns. Secondly, Anne Conway's mode of argument, by logical deduction, is very different from either Keith's or Van Helmont's. We can identify in all three key theological ideas which Anne Conway uses when she formulates details of her own philosophical system. Thus it would seem that in the conceptual vocabulary of her Christian kabbalist interlocutors she found the basis of an alternative to dualism which adequately filled the vacuum left by her critique of More. Combined with the theological premises she shared with them, she put together a *philosophia pia* which answered the call of *Two Hundred Queries* for a reform philosophy in accordance with the tenets of the truth of religion.

FAMILY TRAGEDY

Anne Conway's encounter with the Quakers and kabbalism was played out against a background of domestic tragedy. In 1670, reconciled to the probability that he would have no child to be his heir, Lord Conway had brought over to England from Ireland his sister's oldest son, his nephew Arthur Rawdon, to be raised in his own household as his heir. He also took a close interest in the education of his other nephews, John (Jack) and Edward (Ned) Rawdon, advising their father on their education at Cambridge where they studied at Christ's College in 1673. Lord Conway assisted Sir George Rawdon in both planning and financing their subsequent travels in Europe. His hopes for his nephews were, however, cruelly dashed by the deaths of Jack and Ned Rawdon while they were travelling in France. Jack died as the result of wounds sustained in a duel in France in 1675 and Ned of illness contracted there the following year. The depth of Lord Conway's affection for them may be gauged from his reaction to the news of their deaths, which was, he told their father, a worse affliction than losing his own son in infancy.[22] After the tragic loss of his nephews, Lord Conway agreed that Arthur Rawdon should return to live with his father Sir George Rawdon in Ireland, a humane decision which nonetheless was to have damaging consequences for Arthur Rawdon's position as heir designate to the Conway title and estates.

[22] Lord Conway to Sir George Rawdon, 19 Sept. 1676, Hastings MSS, HA 14553.

DEATH

These last years of Anne Conway's life were also a period of the most intense and debilitating ill health, as a result of which she was confined to Ragley Hall. Ill health had long since become the norm of her existence: in 1674 her husband reported to Sir George Rawdon, 'My Wife is as she uses to be, and she hath been these 10. yeeres past but how to giue you any particular relation of this doth exceed my skill.'[23] Throughout the 1670s her health continued to deteriorate. Already by 1675 she maintained her correspondence only with the help of a secretary, Charles Coke (or Cook). Sad custom did not make the pain she suffered any more bearable for her: on the contrary, she told her brother-in-law, 'My paines and weakness does certainely increase daily', and she hinted that her 'strength to beare' it was also failing.[24] So accustomed were her family to her condition by this time that they did not give her much support: as she told Sir George, 'ye greatest afflictions by long continuance grows unregarded'. By September 1678 she was so ill that she was confined more or less permanently to bed.[25] In view of her deteriorating health, it is truly remarkable that she sustained the debate with Van Helmont, Keith and More, and that she managed the feat of committing her philosophy to paper.

By February 1679 Anne Conway's 'extreme illness' was giving such cause for concern that Van Helmont and Charles Coke thought her husband, who was away in Ireland, should be informed. However, she forbade them to do so. On 18 February Coke started writing a letter which became a chronicle of her last days and hours, recording the 'continuall great paines and exceeding weaknesse' she suffered, and reporting how 'her violent paines having taken away her rest and stomach, which makes her groane and crye continually'. She endured this torment for another four days. Then, between 7 and 8 o'clock at night on 23 February, he recorded: 'My Lady parted this life, having her perfect understanding and senses to the last minute, giving up her Spirit very peaceably without any perceiveable motion and keeping a very sweet face, her paines have held her to the last, about Saturday at noone her leggs began to swell.'[26] Van Helmont was with her when she died. He too reported that she suffered agonies, but remained sound in mind to the very last: 'though her Pains encreas'd, yet her Understanding diminish'd not . . . she dyed without any Fever, merely of her Pains, drawing her Breath a while as one asleep, without throatling, and with

[23] Lord Conway to Sir George Rawdon, 31 March 1674, ibid. HA 14525.
[24] Anne Conway to Sir George Rawdon, 25 Sept 1674, *Conway Letters*, pp. 533–4.
[25] *Conway Letters*, p. 448. [26] Ibid., p. 451.

her Eyes open, and presently after giving up the Ghost'.[27] In order that her husband might see her body before it was buried, Van Helmont embalmed it and conserved it in a glass-fronted coffin. The embalming of her body was ordered by her brother Heneage Finch, by then Lord Chancellor, so 'that she might be decently buried and not according to the humours of the Quakers that were about her'.[28] In a codicil to her will, she had rescinded an earlier request to be buried according to the rites of the Church of England, requesting instead to be buried without 'pompous shewes and formalitys'. The Quaker origin of this request is indicated by her use of 'thy', and her statement that 'God Almighty having more enlightened my understanding . . . I find my self obliged to cleare my conscience in the sight of God to confesse to the truth'.[29] Her request for a Quaker funeral was not observed. She was interred with full Anglican rites in the parish church at Arrow, Warwickshire, on 17 April 1679.[30] Her husband described the funeral as being carried out 'with great decensy, though not in state, yet so as I should desire to be buryed my selfe'.[31] Henry More attended the funeral.

By her will (dated 1673), she left to her husband the estate she had inherited from her mother, requiring him to make a number of bequests from the proceeds. These included a legacy of £500 to her sister Francis Clifton, and the same amount to her brother Sir John Finch. She left £400 to Henry More and £300 to Francis Mercury van Helmont. She remembered her maid, Jane Wright, to whom she left an annuity of £20, and she left £20 to the poor of the parish of Arrow, where she was buried.[32] She also left £10 to the Quaker women's relief fund in London, known as the Box Meeting – though this is not mentioned in her will.[33]

The news of her death was conveyed to her brother John by their nephew, Daniel Finch, via Sir Thomas Baines. He was devastated, as he told Lord Conway:

[27] Ward, *Life*, pp. 125–6.

[28] *Conway Letters*, p. 451; Christopher Cratford to Lord Conway, April 1679, *Calendar of State Papers, Domestic, Car. II*, 411.119. Van Helmont's embalming of her body is recounted in the inscription on his portrait now in the Tate Gallery, London.

[29] *Conway Letters*, p. 481.

[30] 'Key to the Coffins in the Family Vault', Warwick, Warwickshire County Record Office, 114A/801. According to this document, the Conway coffins in the Seymour–Conway vault at Arrow church do not bear inscriptions. But one of these simple lead coffins (no. 13) has the words, 'Quaker Lady' scratched on it.

[31] Lord Conway to Sir George Rawdon, 22 April 1679, Hastings MSS, HA 15460.

[32] *Conway Letters*, pp. 480–1.

[33] London, Friends' House, Box Meeting Accounts, 1681–1750 records 'Lady Conaways legacy paid by van Helmott [*sic*] of £10 paid on 3rd February 1678/9'.

The Newes of my Dear Sisters Death, was and ever will be as afflicting to me that nothing this World has left, can be an Object worthy to divert that grief which I have for Her, of whom the World it selfe was not worthy . . . My Lord, I must never hope to see againe in this World, knowledge enough to have made a Man of Parts proud, in a more talkative Sexe to be possess'd without noise.[34]

After observing the decencies of mourning, Lord Conway revived his dynastic ambitions with urgent determination. In 1680 he remarried in the hopes of fathering a son and heir. The second Lady Conway was Elizabeth Booth, daughter of Lord Delamere. He also embarked on ambitious plans for rebuilding Ragley Hall, commissioning Robert Hooke to design a house to replace the one in which Anne Conway had lived. Not completed until after Earl Conway's death, Hooke's house stands to this day, with a rose garden on the site of the old hall.[35]

It was at this time that the Conway–Finch clan reached the peak of their political influence. In 1681 Lord Conway was appointed Secretary of State and was raised to an earldom. His brother-in-law Heneage Finch was made Earl of Nottingham shortly afterwards. But this latter-life upturn in personal and political fortune proved short-lived. Earl Conway's new wife died in childbirth in 1681. As soon as decently possible, he married a third time. But his marriage to Ursula Stawell in 1681 proved childless. His attainment of high political office proved brief, for within a short time, in January 1682, he was relieved of his office as Secretary of State,[36] though not before he had performed an act of support for the Quakers through his role in the founding of Pennsylvania. Between 1681 and 1683, as Secretary of State and Lord President of the Committee of Trade, Conway was involved with the granting of a patent to William Penn, and with signing a copy of the charter granting him the tract of land that was to be Pennsylvania.[37] Whether he was motivated by respect for his deceased wife, or whether this was an act of practical politics to deal with the intractable problem of Quaker separatism, or merely a routine signing by virtue of his being

[34] *Calendar of State Papers, Domestic, Car. II*, CCCXII, no. 90. Cited in *Conway Letters*, p. 457.

[35] Hooke, *Diary* (1935), pp. 447 ff. See chapter 1, note 67.

[36] The brevity of Lord Conway's career as Secretary of State has meant that he has been disregarded by historians, or treated as a mere cipher. Jacobsen (1932). Latterly this assessment has been considerably revised by Ronald Hutton, (1989), p. 405. As Secretary of State he presided over the aftermath of the Exclusion crisis and the arrest of Lord Shaftesbury.

[37] Now held by the Huntington Library, Hastings MSS, HM 3062, 'Charles the Second's Declaration to the Inhabitants of Pennsylvania commanding them to yeild obedience to William Penn as Proprietor and Governor of Pennsylvania Dated Whitehall, April 6, 1681 Signed by the King'. For other documents, see Penn, *Papers*, vol. II, documents 21 and 95. Another document relating to the granting of the Pennsylvania charter was signed by Anne Conway's nephew, Heneage Finch, Solicitor General and son of Heneage Finch, Earl of Nottingham. Ibid., document 22.

Secretary of State at the time, is unclear. At all events, he had gained closer awareness of the Quakers, their beliefs and practices through his first wife. It is to his credit that his personal antipathy to the Quakers did not undermine his own commitment to religious toleration in this connection.

Lord Conway's preoccupations with dynastic and political business had left no space for conserving or commemorating his first wife's intellectual achievements. In any case his undisguised impatience with Van Helmont, and what he called his 'frolicks', and his deep antipathy for her Quakerism, cannot have disposed him well towards perpetuating an intellectual legacy so intimately bound up with that of Van Helmont and George Keith.

Earl Conway died in August 1683, his dynastic ambitions blighted and his grandiose mansion unfinished. So far was he from controlling the Conway destiny that his original plans to leave his estates to his sister's family never came to fruition. For, exploiting the need to amend the Earl's will to make provision for his widow, his cousin Edward Seymour[38] took advantage of both the dying Earl Conway's collapsing sanity and Arthur Rawdon's distance in Ireland to redraft the will in favour of his own descendants. Arthur Rawdon, who had been unable to attend his uncle on his deathbed because of disturbances in Ireland, arrived at Ragley too late to pay his last respects to his uncle and too late to preserve his inheritance. He found himself cut out of the redrafted will Earl Conway had signed on his deathbed. The new will, naming Edward Seymour's younger son Popham Seymour as Conway's heir, had already been proved. The original will naming Arthur Rawdon as heir, and witnessed by John Finch and Henry More, had mysteriously disappeared into the hands of the Seymours.[39] A long drawn-out

[38] Edward Seymour was hardly a close relative of Lord Conway. He was married to Letitia Popham, daughter of Lord Conway's cousin, Francis Popham, who was brother to the Dowager Viscountess Conway, Lord Conway's mother. Twice chosen Speaker of the House of Commons, Seymour was a High Tory.

[39] The sorry story of the disinheriting of Arthur Rawdon can be pieced together from the Rawdon papers conserved among the Hastings manuscripts at the Huntington Library (Hastings MSS, boxes 13, 18, 27–32). Box 18, folder 4, 'The Case of Sr John Rawdon Bart', one of many drafts of Arthur Rawdon's case on behalf of his own son John, makes the point that the likelihood of Lord Conway's changing his will at the last moment, thereby disinheriting a relative previously named heir, for strangers, was too remote to be credible: 'It seems to be Morally impossible that any Man in his Senses should on a sudden change the Sedate Resolution of the Greatest part of his Life declared not man hours before and do an Injurious act in favour of meer Strangers against his own Relations and against his own Conscience'. He denies that Earl Conway was offended with the Rawdons, and states that he had never declared any intention of making Seymour's sons his heirs. The accusation of underhand dealing on the part of Seymour is blunt: 'yet by the Interest Sr. Edward Seymour had in the Late King James the Second's Reign he procured his pretended will to be Decreed by the High Court of Chancery'. The Rawdons managed to cast sufficient doubt on the Seymour claim to the Conway estates for an act of Parliament to be required 'for the settling of Lord Conway in his estates'. Arthur Rawdon was also prevented from claiming his uncle's title, in spite of his being his

legal battle ensued, but, bereft of powerful allies in England, the Rawdons were outmanoeuvred. In this unseemly wrangle the memory of the first Lady Conway quickly faded.

nearest male blood relative. And Popham Seymour-Conway became Lord Conway only after a fresh creation. He is nevertheless referred to as 'the first Lord Conway' by the incumbents of Ragley to this day. An anomaly in Earl Conway's will is that it provides generous portions for his Rawdon nieces, but makes no mention of their brother, Arthur. However, the legal disputes that ensued prevented them from claiming them until an agreement was arrived at many years later.

CHAPTER 11

Legacy

'l'histoire de cette Dame extraordinaire'[1]

The anonymous manuscript treatise that lay unpublished among Anne Conway's papers was the culmination of a lifetime's interest in philosophy. In its final form, it was most probably produced no more than a couple of years before she died. But it is the outcome of on-going philosophical discussions which, as we have seen, may be traced back to her earliest study of philosophy. Her youthful doubt as to whether philosophy and religion are compatible opened the way to central questions about the nature of God, the world, and God's relation to the world – questions she tackled using the philosophical tools of Platonism and Cartesianism, and in the light of her study of contemporary natural philosophy. Central to her investigations were the issues of how material reality can be produced by an immaterial God, and how the existence of pain and suffering can be reconciled with the perfection of God. The 'paper book' Van Helmont found among her papers contained the answers to these questions in the form of a synthesis which explains the nature of the world through its causes. The resulting *Principles* is both a philosophy of nature and a philosophy of religion, a cosmology and a theodicy, in which the ultimate origin of all things is God.

The centrality of God is not unusual in seventeenth-century philosophy, but for Anne Conway what matters is not simply the existence of God, but the nature of God, because her system is founded on an analogy between God and the created world.[2] In her account of the divine attributes, God as the most perfect being is self-existing, infinitely powerful, wise and good, eternal, immutable. She adds, further, that God is the creator of all things. This list of attributes is traditional for Christian theology and seventeenth-century philosophy. (It is, for example, comparable to the divine attributes

[1] Leibniz, cited in Coudert (1995), p. 38.

[2] Descartes, *Philosophical Writings*, vol. II, p. 28. Cf. Conway, 'It is impossible for a creature not to have some similarity to its creator or to agree with it in certain attributes and perfections', *Principles*, p. 48.

listed in Descartes' *Meditations*.)[3] But the list of divine attributes in Anne Conway's *Principles* is prefaced by the rather less traditional assertion that God is a 'spirit, life and light', probably deriving from kabbalism (though echoed later in Leibniz's definition of God as immaterial spirit).[4]

The ontological system which Anne Conway derives from her conception of God is premised on the claim that created things have some similarity to their originator through sharing the attributes and perfections of their cause. The same causal principle also assumes that any effect is less perfect than its cause. The basis of this is Platonic, because it is from their resemblance to the eternal and unchanging attributes of the highest order of being that things derive their properties and their existence. This causal principle is consistent with the traditional maxims invoked by Descartes in meditation 3 that any effect must be like its cause ('*effectus similis est causae*'), and also that the cause must be more perfect than the effect.

Since God is essentially a creator, he creates out of the necessity of his nature, and most freely. It is, therefore, inconceivable that he should ever not be creating. It follows that creation is a constant process, and that there is no *creatio ex nihilo* (creation from nothing), in the sense of bringing something into being from a previous state of nothingness. Nor is creation an event with a single beginning point in time; only from the perspective of created things can creation be seen as having a beginning. The creative process is a constant outgoing or diffusion of God's perfection, by emanation of his attributes. Anne Conway uses the term 'communication' to convey the idea that creation involves transmission of the attributes of God to the world of creation. Since created things are like God, they exhibit the perfections of God, and it follows that the created world is good, and wisely ordered. God's goodness and justice are manifested in the created world in the capacity of creatures to acquire greater perfection. Since God is living spirit, and God does not create that which is other from himself, created substance must be living spirit, like God.

The likeness between God and creatures notwithstanding, the created universe is unlike God in important particulars. Where God is one, infinite and unchanging, created substance is a plenum of an infinite multiplicity of individual particles or monads, each of which contains an infinity of infinitely divisible particles. But the key ontological difference between

[3] God, according to Descartes, is 'infinite, eternal, immutable, independent, supremely intelligent, supremely powerful, and which created both myself and everything else', *Philosophical Writings*, vol. II, p. 31.

[4] G. W. von Leibniz, *Discourse on Metaphysics*, section 36, in *Philosophical Papers and Letters*, trans. L. Loemker (Chicago: University of Chicago Press, 1956), pp. 503–4.

God and creatures is that God is unchanging and creatures are mutable – this fundamental difference of properties means that God and creatures do not share the same essence, but are ontologically distinct species. In one sense, the mutability of the created world can be understood as a negative expression of God's unchangingness, rather as the monads express divine singularity in an infinite multiplicity of single units. The mutability of creatures is, after all, essential to the perfectibility of the created world, for without it creatures could not increase in perfection. Mutability is therefore a necessary consequence of God's goodness. Change is, furthermore, the means by which the justice of God is expressed in creation, for change makes possible the restoration of creatures to their original perfection by means of appropriate rewards and punishments. However, mutability has negative consequences, because creatures may change for the worse. Even so, the dynamic of the created world is creatures' capacity for good. And the mutability of created nature also ensures that the system of the world is not deterministic, and that God is, therefore, not responsible for creatures falling away from good towards evil.

Although Anne Conway's account of the composition of created things is fully compatible with her conception of God, her system of nature is not deducible from divine nature in every particular. While the single-substance monism of created things derives from her account of God as a single universal spirit mirrored in creation, living creatures have properties which do not derive from God. Not only are they changeable, but they are extended, endowed with size, shape, solidity and motion. These, of course, are properties which mechanists like Descartes or Hobbes reserve for body, though in Anne Conway's philosophy all things possessed of these properties also have life and perception. Furthermore, although she posits a single common substance for all created things, this admits of differentiation and gradation such that some substance is 'dull', and therefore more like body, and some more refined, like spirit. As a result the monads may be combined in such a way that some groupings take on more corporeal attributes and some retain more spirit-like attributes. These clusters are in turn organised as souls and bodies. All created things are combinations of spirit-like and body-like particles. All things are living organisms, whether they be physical objects like dust and stones, or more complex beings like animals and humans. Every creature and particle in its make-up is capable of life and perception.

Although created nature is organised as composites of soul and body, the basic 'stuff' of creation is an infinity of monads (or living particles). Soul and body, therefore, are not radically distinct from one another, but exist as part of a continuum of substance. The difference between soul and body is therefore not essential, but merely modal. Within individual creatures, since body and soul are organised combinations of the same substance, there is no essential difference between soul (mind) and body. However, Conway's retention of a quasi-dualism of soul and body means that the laws of Cartesian mechanics still apply. Indeed, she would argue that the Cartesian account of matter and motion makes better sense in her system because she is able to account for soul–body interaction. For their being constituted of a common substance ensures the cohesion not just of soul and body within a particular creature, but also of all the constituent elements of each. At a micro-level, the common substance ensures the bonding of monadic particles to form organisms, souls and bodies, and the bonding of souls and bodies to form individual creatures. At a macro-level, the common substance of all created things ensures that the whole of creation is bound together in a single harmony. The attraction of like to like is the bond of love that unites all things with one another, and all creatures with God. Anne Conway also explains both the interaction of one organism with another, and the movement of bodies, through such emanations of spirit called vital extension, which may be likened to a field of force.

The essential similarity of all creatures (by virtue of their being constituted of the same substance), and their essential mutability, means that it is theoretically possible for one creature to transmute into another. Nevertheless, Anne Conway denies that individual created beings are interchangeable. Peter cannot transform into Paul because such a metamorphosis would contradict the divine order of nature, which is so organised as to ensure God's justice is reflected in creation. If one man (Judas) can become another man (Paul), this would contradict the moral order running through the universe, for neither would receive his due reward or punishment. Secondly, fluid interchangeability of creatures would destroy the objective truth of things conformable to the truth of ideas, guaranteed by God's wisdom. In this way Anne Conway argues for the integrity of the species (or categories) of created things. Nevertheless, she does allow for the possibility that particular creatures may, by successive changes in successive lives, move up or down the ontological scale: a horse might, by striving to perfect itself within the limits of its species, gradually, through successive incarnations, become a man. Likewise a man, by behaving in a bestial manner, may be reduced to the level of a beast. In both examples change is essentially a moral process, though it manifests itself in physical transformation. This exemplifies the way the moral imperative of a perfectionist universe accounts for the operations of nature.

A major problem attending any system of the world founded on an analogy with the divine is pantheism. This danger is the more acute because the perfectionist dynamic of Conway's system (according to which creatures may increase in perfection ad infinitum) implies that creatures are on a continuum with God. Another problem arising from the God–nature analogy is that the resemblance between nature and God contradicts the transcendence of God. A third problem is that on the God–nature analogy it is impossible to explain how God creates that which is unlike God. Anne Conway was, however, alive to these problems, and structured her system so as to avoid them by postulating a series of ontological separations between God and nature. First, her understanding of the divine attributes contains an inbuilt guard against pantheism. For, among the attributes of God, she distinguishes between what she calls 'incommunicable attributes' which belong to God alone, and 'communicable' attributes which are shared with created things. The former include his perfection, self-existence, immutability and infinity. The communicable attributes are 'spirit, light, life', goodness, holiness, justice, wisdom.[5] Although this particular division between the communicable and incommunicable attributes of God has theological justification, particularly in kabbalism, in philosophical terms it appears somewhat arbitrary. Nevertheless, the general principle that creatures do not share all the attributes of the creator is consistent with the causal premise that an effect is less perfect than its cause. The second inbuilt safeguard against pantheism rests on essential differences between God and creation, in particular the immutability of God and the mutability of created beings. Again this difference is, arguably, as arbitrary as the doctrine of communicable and incommunicable attributes.

The separation between God and nature achieved by assigning different attributes to each exacerbates the third problem of how God can be the cause of things unlike God. Her answer to this addresses not just the problem of transcendence but the problem of pantheism as well. She disposes of both by positing the existence of an intermediate species, Middle Nature, between God and the world. By sharing the properties of both God and creation, Middle Nature serves as the interface between them. Middle Nature is first in the order of creation, yet part of the creative process. It is both the efficient cause by which God creates things, and the final cause, by which nature is organised for the best. Like the *chora* of Plato's *Timaeus*, Middle Nature is 'the nurse' and 'receptacle' of all becoming,[6] for it is through Middle Nature that God creates the world and is present to the

[5] *Principles*, p. 45. [6] Plato, *Timaeus*, 52b–d.

world. And, like the *chora* of the *Timaeus*, it is also extended throughout the universe. As the presence of God to the world, Middle Nature makes life and movement possible. It is only through Middle Nature that things can increase in perfection, and it is through Middle Nature that God can be present to Creation. Conway explains: 'although God works immediately in everything, yet he nevertheless uses this same mediator as an instrument through which he works together with creatures, since that instrument is by its own nature closer to them'.[7] Thus Middle Nature bridges the gap between God and creation. Without such a mediating link, 'there would be an utter chasm and gap between God and creatures'.[8] However, Middle Nature also separates creation from God by obviating the need for the direct intervention of God in the world (i.e. occasionalism), and by forming an ontological barrier between nature and God. As the means by which the created world is both like and unlike God, Middle Nature is both bridge and buffer between God and the world.

PUBLICATION

More than a decade elapsed before *The Principles of the Most Ancient and Modern Philosophy* was published. This delay may be ascribed to a number of factors. First of all, it is more than likely that a patron could not be found: Lord Conway would have had no interest in advertising his first wife's Quaker leanings or having anything to do with a project that linked her with Van Helmont. He was, in any case, preoccupied with remarrying in order to beget an heir. Her half-brother, Heneage, would have had similar scruples. Her brother John Finch, who also disapproved of her Quakerism, was absent in Turkey when she died, and overwhelmed with his own sorrows (the death not just of his beloved sister but of his life-long companion Thomas Baines) after he returned thence in 1681.

It was left to Van Helmont and Henry More to rescue Anne Conway's manuscript remains: the original draft of her *Principles*, 'obscurely, written in a Paper Book, with a Black-lead Pen'. According to Richard Ward, they planned to have it published immediately after she died.[9] Evidence of Henry More's involvement comes from the 'Character of the Lady Conway' intended as a preface to the work but not printed until Richard Ward included it in his *Life* of More in 1710. Ward, writing several years after

[7] Ibid., p. 25. Conway explains movement in a similar way, as produced by the immediate presence of God. See *Principles*, pp. 57–8.
[8] Ibid., p. 26. [9] Ward, *Life*, p. 123.

More's death, misattributes the 'Character' to More. The content, however, makes it plain that the author was Van Helmont.[10] More's assistance in preparing this preface for the proposed publication must mean that he was aware of Anne Conway's critique of his position, and not afraid for her arguments to be aired. In addition to drafting the introduction subsequently printed by Richard Ward, Van Helmont also pressed ahead with publishing the other fruits of the Ragley exchanges between himself, George Keith, Lady Conway and Henry More: *A Cabbalistical Dialogue* appeared in 1682 and *Two Hundred Queries* in 1684. But any plans that he may have had to publish the *Principles* were probably overtaken by events in the history of his relations with the English Quakers.

Alarmed at the direction which George Keith's theological pronouncements were taking, the Quakers became suspicious of his associate, Van Helmont. In 1684 their leader, George Fox, proposed that there should be a meeting at which *A Cabbalistical Dialogue* and *Two Hundred Queries* should be subjected to scrutiny in order to determine whether Van Helmont was 'learned by ye Holy Ghost or ye unclean Ghost'.[11] There is no record of whether the proposed meeting took place, but Fox's proposal was linked to Quaker concerns about George Keith, whose pronouncements on doctrine appeared to be taking Quakerism in a direction that Fox and others could not countenance. The fortunes of Van Helmont in his relations with the English Quakers are therefore part of the course of development which resulted in the rupture known in the annals of Quaker history as 'the Keithian schism'.[12] Shortly after the 1684 scrutiny Van Helmont retired to the Netherlands. His break with Fox notwithstanding, he still moved in Dutch Quaker circles, where he was on friendly terms with, among others, the

[10] Although the 'Character', is attributed to More, it contrasts one person's 'Seven or Eight Years Experience of her' with 'Four times as long' of 'that other Party, whom I have so often mentioned'. This must correspond to Van Helmont's residence at Ragley, as against More's thirty years' acquaintance with Lady Conway. The narrator mentions being present when she died, which More was not. Also, the narrator uses Quaker forms of address ('And these things I have Communicated to thee, concerning our Friend'). Ward's misattribution of the 'Character' to More may be explained by the fact that it was probably in More's handwriting, because it was he who wrote it down on Van Helmont's behalf.

[11] Coudert (1975) and Coudert (1999), chapter 11. According to Gerard Croese, whose opinions about the Quakers must be accepted with caution, the Quakers regarded Van Helmont's theories as 'foolish Errors, and Distracted Notions', and Van Helmont broke with the Quakers in consequence. Gerard Croese, *The General History of the Quakers* (London, 1696), book 2, pp. 38–9. Some Quakers attributed Keith's apostasy to his having imbibed Helmontian ideas. Such was the view of John Whiting, *Persecution Expos'd* (London, 1715), p. 113. Besides the matter of transmigration, Keith's Christology was a key point at issue. W. Sewel, *The History of the Rise, Increase and Progress of the Christian People Called Quakers* (London, 1725), p. 640.

[12] Braithwaite (1919), pp. 482–7; see also Nicolson (1930) and Coudert (1976).

English Quaker merchant Benjamin Furly of Rotterdam.[13] Nevertheless, Van Helmont continued to meet opposition to his theories, especially the doctrine of the transmigration of souls.[14] The charge that Van Helmont's theory of transmigration underlay Keith's dispute with fellow Quakers is made by Gerard Croese in his *General History of the Quakers* (1696, first published in Latin in 1695), where he presents the doctrine of the transmigration of souls as Pythagoreanism embroidered by 'those pratling Jewish Masters call'd Rabbins', and revived by Van Helmont. He implicates 'a Noble Countess', whom he does not name, but who was evidently Anne Conway.

> This man living in England at the time conversing among the *Quakers* as one of their Society had occasion frequently to converse with a Noble countess that was a great admirer of knowledge and Learning, and to reason with her out of the Book of *Plato*, concerning this Platonical Doctrine, and come that length with her, that both he and she embrac'd the same opinion for a truth; and because *Keith* was oftimes present at their Conferences, they bring him in also to take share in the same opinion.[15]

Croese's association of Anne Conway (the 'Noble countess') with Van Helmont and Keith on the matter of transmigration probably derives from the fact that the Latin version of her *Principles* was published in the same volume as the Latin translation of *Two Hundred Queries* (that is, in *Opuscula philosophica* 1690). This volume appeared at around the same time as a spate of Dutch translations of writings by Van Helmont, all of which propound similar theories, including his theory of the transmigration of souls and other doctrines underpinned by his kabbalistical researches.[16] The English

[13] Benjamin Furly (1636–1714) was a Quaker and free thinker who lived in Rotterdam where his home was a stopping point for English travellers and political exiles, the most famous of whom was John Locke, who stayed with Furly during his exile in the Netherlands between 1686 and 1689. One of the attractions of Furly's house for religious and political radicals was his library of heterodox books. See Hull (1941).

[14] Croese, *History*, book 2, p. 39.

[15] Ibid., pp. 39–40.

[16] Books which Van Helmont published at about the same time as *Opuscula philosophica*, were Dutch, German and Latin translations of writings already published in English, and Dutch versions of works later published in English, namely *Zweyhudert Fragen betreffend die Lehre von der Widerkehr der menshclichen Seelen*, 1686 (i.e. *Two Hundred Queries*); *Eenige Gedagten . . . rakende de natur-kund* (Amsterdam, 1690) (i.e. *Paradoxal Discourses*); *Aanmerkingen . . . over den mens en desselfs Siektens* (Amsterdam, 1692) (i.e. *Spirit of Diseases*); *Seder Olam* (1693) (English translation, 1694); *Het godlyk weezen dezelfs eygenschappen* (Rotterdam, 1694) (i.e. *The Divine Being and its Attributes*); *Einige voor-bedagte en oeverwogene Bedengkigen over de vier eerste Kapitelen des eersten Boeks Moysis, Genesis* genaant (Rotterdam, 1698) (i.e. *Some premeditate and considerate Thoughts upon the four Chapters of the first Book of Mosis, called Genesis*). Also, *Een zeer korte Afbedeeling van het ware natuurlyke Hebreuwse A.B.C.* (Rotterdam, 1697) (i.e. *Alphabeti vere naturalis Hebraici*).

translation of the *Principia* appeared during a spate of English editions of Van Helmont's works. The first to be published were the English versions of *A Cabbalistical Dialogue* and *Two Hundred Queries*, which were followed by *Paradoxal Discourses* (1685), *The Divine Being and its Attributes* (1693), *Seder Olam* (1694) and *The Spirit of Diseases* (1694). It is quite possible, therefore, that Anne Conway's philosophy, in both its Latin and English translations, finally saw print as part of an attempt by Van Helmont to defend his position at a time when he was under renewed pressure on account of his subscription to unorthodox opinions.[17]

RECEPTION

Tracing the posthumous fortunes of Anne Conway's philosophy immediately after it was first published is made difficult by virtue of the anonymity of her book and the problem that very few copies of either *Opuscula philosophiae* or *Principles of the Most Ancient and Modern Philosophy* are still extant. A clue as to the readership of her treatise comes from the English translator who gives as a reason for translating the book his opinion that its subject matter would interest both learned and unlearned audiences:

> I did not doubt but that this little Treatise might happen into the Handes of some ingenious and well-disposed Persons, who (though not furnished with those artificial Helps and Advantages that Learning usually affords; yet nevertheless being qualified by a natural pregnancy of parts, by many serious Studies and deliberate Thoughts of this or the like Nature) might be competent judges of such Mysteries; or that it might fortunately light into the Hands of such whose eminency of Learning, and maturity of Judgement might render them either willing to approve it, or able to refute it, and that too with a better Salvo of Divine Attributes than is done in this Treatise.[18]

The few references that we do have suggest that Anne Conway's *Principles* attracted the attention in both readership groups anticipated by the translator: namely 'well-disposed Persons' who lacked 'artificial Helps and Advantages that Learning usually affords', and persons of 'eminency of Learning, and maturity of Judgement'. The former included radical pietistic Protestants, in particular the Philadelphians. Among persons of 'eminency

[17] Van Helmont certainly understood the value of noble patronage. In 1697 he sought the endorsement of the Electresses Sophie and Sophie Charlotte for his edition of Boethius' *Consolations* as a means of recommending it to readers. See Leibniz, *Correspondance avec la princesse*, vol. I, pp. 28–9.

[18] 'The Translater to the Reader'.

of Learning, and maturity of Judgement', Leibniz was its most famous reader. The connecting thread in both the philosophical and pietistic diffusion of Anne Conway's treatise is Francis Mercury van Helmont, who became an important agent of transmission when he resumed his peripatetic lifestyle as a 'wandering eremite' after Anne Conway's death. In the post-Ragley years, Van Helmont's name became indissolubly linked with the doctrine of the transmigration of souls among both his friends (like the Rotterdam merchant, Benjamin Furly, or Leibniz) and his detractors (like Croese). Van Helmont's theory as set out in *Two Hundred Queries* was available in Latin in *Opuscula philosophica*. The Latin diffusion of *Two Hundred Queries*, therefore, was a vehicle of the dissemination of Anne Conway's philosophy.

Prior to the publication of the *Principia* and the controversies that embroiled Keith and Helmont against Fox and Penn, Anne Conway's fame as a Quaker convert and learned lady was well known in Quaker circles, and was spread by Quaker missionaries and their associates abroad. Her conversion was known among Quaker women leaders like Margaret Fell Fox.[19] As we have seen, Penn, Barclay and Keith were most closely involved with the Ragley circle at the time of Penn's missionary trip to Holland and Germany in 1677, which is described in his *Travels*. Penn was accompanied by Keith, Fox and Barclay. Although Penn's *Travels* makes no mention of Van Helmont or Lady Conway, Van Helmont undoubtedly played a key role in ensuring that Penn received the warm welcome he describes from Princess Elizabeth at Herford, where she was, by then, abbess of the Lutheran convent. We know from Robert Barclay that Quaker missionaries cited Anne Conway as an example – as he himself did in his attempt to convert Princess Elizabeth.[20] Others who would have heard of Anne Conway, either from Quaker leaders or from Van Helmont included Benjamin Furly, at whose house in Rotterdam Penn's party stayed at the start of their trip, and who accompanied them during their tour. It was probably through Furly or Van Helmont that Adam Boreel heard about Anne Conway. He was sufficiently moved to compose a Latin poem on 'the Love of Pain' dedicated to her.[21] And, as we have just seen, the reference to the 'English Countess' by critics such as Croese confirms her link with the Quakers. No doubt George Keith kept the memory of Anne Conway alive in his later activities in both Britain and New England.

[19] Margaret (Fell) Fox to Katherine Evans, 3 June 1678. London, Friends' House, Spence MS 378, item 18.j.

[20] Barclay, *Reliquiae*, pp. 31–2.

[21] Oxford, Bodleian Library, MS Locke c. 17.

PIETISTS AND PHILADELPHIANS

After the publication of her *Principles*, interest in Anne Conway's work is to be found among other religious dissenters, in particular the German Pietists and English Philadelphians. A known reader of Anne Conway's *Principia* was the German pietist leader Johann Wilhelm Petersen, who had been obliged to leave his post as superintendent of Luneburg in 1692, as a result of the uproar caused by his support for the prophetess Rosamunde von der Asseburg.[22] Petersen eventually found patronage from Baron Freiherr von Knyphausen, a member of the court at Berlin, with the result that he was able to devote his time to his writings. Petersen also took a leading role in promoting English Philadelphian writings in Germany, since it was on the strength of his recommendation that his patron, Baron Knyphausen, commissioned German translations of the works of Mrs Lead.[23] Among Protestant visionaries, Petersen was an erudite man who cited a weight of learned opinion in support of his mystical and millenarian religious views. He was an acquaintance of Leibniz, who had defended his stand in the Rosamunde von der Asseburg affair, and encouraged him to write a Christian epic poem, *Uranias*, which, among other things, advocates universal salvation. It is quite possible that Petersen knew Van Helmont, as well as Leibniz. He certainly knew Van Helmont's writings, which he cites among the authorities he adduces to support his belief in the doctrine of universal salvation, in his book Μυστεριον 'Αποκαταστασεοσ Παντον, *Das ist, Das Geheimnisz der Wiederbringung aller Dinge* (1700–1). He also cites Conway's *Principia philosophiae*. In a later work, *Das Geheimnis des Erstgeborenen aller Creatur* (1711), Petersen also draws on Anne Conway and on Van Helmont's *Seder Olam* in his discussion of Christological doctrine. It may well have been through Petersen that Anne Conway's book attracted interest in Philadelphian circles in England. Evidence for this is an advertisement for the book which appeared in *Theosophical Transactions by the Philadelphian Society* in 1697.

ENGLAND

The earliest evidence of English interest in Anne Conway's book is the translation which appeared in 1692 with the title *The Principles of the Most Ancient and Modern Philosophy: Concerning God, Christ, and the Creature; that is, concerning Spirit and Matter in General.* The translation is signed by

[22] Aiton (1985), pp. 186–9; Walker (1964), chapter 14.
[23] Walker (1964), chapters 13 and 14.

'J.C. Medical Professor' who explains in his preface to the reader that it was Van Helmont who recommended the treatise to him for translation while he was visiting him in Amsterdam. The initials 'J.C.' have been taken to be those of Jodocus Crull, a Dutch physician who studied at Leyden and Cambridge and worked as a translator. Although he was medically qualified, there is no record of any contact between him and Van Helmont. I incline to Marjorie Nicolson's opinion that the translator was probably the English physician John Clarke, who translated Van Helmont's *Seder Olam* in 1694.

Among his English acquaintances to whom Van Helmont may have shown the *Principles* were John Locke and his close friend, Damaris, Lady Masham, the talented daughter of More's friend Ralph Cudworth, in whose house at Oates in Essex Locke spent his last years. Van Helmont first came into contact with Locke through their mutual friend Benjamin Furly, the English Quaker merchant at whose house in Rotterdam Locke spent part of his exile. Van Helmont was a visitor at Lady Masham's Essex home in 1693 when John Locke was in residence there.[24] Locke's papers include notes on Helmontian themes, as well as notes on the *Adumbratio cabbalae christianae* and extracts from the *Kabbala denudata*.[25] It is therefore possible that Van Helmont may have presented Locke and Lady Masham with a copy of *Opuscula philosophica* when he visited them at Oates in 1693. This possibility is strengthened by the fact that a copy of Adam Boreel's poem dedicated to Lady Conway is to be found among Locke's papers. However, there is no record of either Locke or Lady Masham reading her work.

The next mention of Anne Conway in English sources is Richard Ward's generous appraisal of her as Henry More's 'heroine pupil' in the biography of More which he published in 1710. Anne Conway's philosophical acumen receives high praise from Ward, while her involvement with the Quakers is singled out for apology. He mentions plans to publish her 'Remains' after her death, and prints the preface originally written by Van Helmont for the proposed edition.[26] But he does not mention either the 1690 Latin or the 1692 English printings of her treatise, perhaps out of ignorance of their existence, or maybe oversight. Thereafter Anne Conway survives as a footnote to the life of Henry More. In 1784 her authorship of the *Principia* became the subject of correspondence in *The Gentleman's Magazine*. Notwithstanding the curiosity about her that the *Opuscula philosophica* had occasioned,

[24] Anne Conway may have known something about Lady Masham. Lady Masham's mother was apparently a relative of Anne Conway on her mother's side. But since Lady Masham was considerably younger, and her philosophical writings post-date Anne Conway's death, it is unlikely that Lady Conway knew much about her interest in philosophy.

[25] Coudert (1999), pp. 278 ff. [26] Ward, *Life*, pp. 117 ff.

and the commendations of Leibniz cited by the correspondent, the treatise was summed up as 'A Singular Book, full of obscurities and paradoxes'.[27] The anonymity of the book meant that confusion continued to surround its authorship. Burke's *Peerage* attributes it to her husband. Not until Marjorie Nicolson's magisterial *Conway Letters* did Anne Conway resurface as the acknowledged author of the treatise.

PHILOSOPHERS AND THE *PRINCIPIA PHILOSOPHIAE*

The clearest part of the obscure *fortuna* of Lady Conway's book falls within the ambit of Leibniz in Hanover. Here Van Helmont played a key role, since he was a friend of Leibniz. It was undoubtedly he who presented Leibniz with his copy of her *Principia philosophiae.* The two had become friends when they first met in 1671. Van Helmont subsequently visited Leibniz at the Hanoverian court, where he also spent time with the latter's friend and patron, the Electress Sophie (1630–1714), to whom he may also have presented a copy of Anne Conway's book. The Electress was the sister of Van Helmont's friend and patron, Princess Elizabeth. She was married to Ernst August, Elector of Hanover, and was mother of the future George I of England. Van Helmont visited the Electress again in 1677 and was a visitor to the Hanoverian court in the 1690s. In 1694 he sent her two of his books, *Verhandeling van de Helle* and *Het Godlyk Wezen.*[28] In 1696, Leibniz reports conversations with the Electress Sophie and Van Helmont, in which Van Helmont told them 'l'histoire de cette Dame extraordinaire'.[29]

Through Van Helmont, Anne Conway's philosophy may also have become known to the two women with whom the Electress Sophie shared her intellectual interests: her daughter, Sophie Charlotte, Electress of Brandenburg, and her niece Elizabeth Charlotte, Duchess of Orleans. Leibniz too discussed Van Helmont's ideas with both women, so it is a reasonable assumption that he brought Anne Conway's philosophy to their attention as well.[30] It may well be that Leibniz also discussed Lady Conway with Caroline of Ansbach, Sophie's daughter-in-law and future queen consort of George II of England. But, in the absence of documentary confirmation, the extent of the knowledge of Anne Conway's philosophy in this circle of extraordinary women is a matter of speculation.

[27] The correspondence is printed in the Loptson edition of the *Principles.*

[28] Aiton (1985), p. 201.

[29] Leibniz, cited in Coudert (1995), p. 38. See also Aiton (1985), pp. 201–2. In a review in *Monatlicher Auzug aus aller hand neuherausgegeben nutlichen un artigen Büchern,* Leibniz mentions that Van Helmont has often told him about Lady Conway. Cited in Coudert (1995), p. 116.

[30] Aiton (1985), pp. 53–4 and Coudert (1995), p. 255.

LEIBNIZ

With Leibniz himself we are on more certain ground. He was a good friend of Van Helmont, whom he first met in 1671. They renewed their acquaintance at the deathbed of their mutual friend Princess Elizabeth of Bohemia in 1679, not long after the death of Lady Conway. The period of their greatest contact was during the 1690s, after the publication of her treatise. In the decade preceding Van Helmont's death in 1698, Leibniz wrote commentaries on Van Helmont's books. In 1694 his *Tagebuch* records discussions of Van Helmont's *Seder Olam*, which Leibniz had previously read and criticised.[31] In 1696, Leibniz saw Van Helmont frequently in the company of the Electress Sophie. Although he regarded a good many of Van Helmont's opinions as eccentric and extreme, he found much of value in his conversations with him. Leibniz was also, like Van Helmont and Lady Conway, acquainted with Christian Knorr von Rosenroth, whom he had visited in 1681 shortly after the publication of *Kabbala denudata*.

Leibniz's copy of *Principia philosophiae*, inscribed 'La comtesse de Konnouay', is preserved among his collection of books at the Niedersächsische Landesbibliothek, Hanover. Leibniz certainly read the book, to which he refers on several occasions. And he was impressed by what he read. He evidently regarded its author as a Platonist and a vitalist. In his *New Essays* he mentions 'the late Platonist Countess of Conway' as one of 'those who put life and perception into everything'.[32] He also aligned her philosophical approach with his own, as one that offered a middle way, drawing on both the mechanical philosophy and Platonism. In so doing he recognised Anne Conway's departure from Henry More:

> My philosophical views approach somewhat closely those of the late Countess Conway, and hold a middle position between Plato and Democritus, because I hold that all things take place mechanically as Democritus and Descartes argue against the views of Henry More and his followers, and [I] also hold that everything takes place according to a living principle and according to final causes – all things are full of life and consciousness, contrary to the views of the atomists.[33]

[31] Coudert (1995), p. 58.

[32] Gottfried Wilhelm von Leibniz, *New Essays on Human Understanding*, ed. P. Remnant and J. Bennett (Cambridge: Cambridge University Press, 1981), p. 72. See Coudert (1995), chapter 6. On Conway and Leibniz see Brown (1990). A case for her direct influence on Leibniz is argued by Becco (1978) and Merchant (1979).

[33] Gottfried Wilhelm von Leibniz, *Die Philosophischen Schriften von G. W. Leibniz*, ed. C. I. Gerhardt, 7 vols. (Berlin, 1875), vol. III, p. 217. We can deduce further details of what Leibniz approved in Anne Conway's philosophy from his comments on Van Helmont's *Het Godelyk Wesen* in a letter to Electress Sophie, dated September 1694. According to Leibniz, he agreed with Van Helmont's

In 1701 he quoted from her *Principia* in a review of Petersen's *Mysterion* in *Monatlicher Auszug*.[34]

In broad terms Anne Conway's philosophy has many affinities with that of Leibniz. There are, of course, differences of scope and detail, but in general terms the affinities are particularly striking in Leibniz's late treatises, the *Theodicy* and *Monadology*. Both Leibniz and Lady Conway were deeply interested in contemporary philosophy, but neither was satisfied that it lived up to its claims. Both attempted to reconcile the old and the new, and the philosophy of each recasts new developments (notably the mechanical philosophy) within the context of time-honoured principles (e.g. final causes). As synthesisers both viewed their own and other philosophy as examples of a perennial philosophy. Both were motivated by a profound ecumenical impulse. Both can be characterised as idealists in so far as they both regarded the substantial constituents of nature as immaterial spirit (historically speaking, Platonist would be a better designation).

For Leibniz, as for Anne Conway, a principle of likeness holds between God and the created universe, most evident in the view that the perfection, wisdom and goodness of God is manifest in the created world. Both understood creation as the communication of divine perfection, and both propose emanationist accounts of the production of created substance. Like Leibniz, Anne Conway sought to reconcile the apparent imperfections of created existence with the perfection of God. And, like Leibniz, she underpinned her theodicy with a metaphysics of substance. Anne Conway like Leibniz was a vitalist, and, like him, she elaborated her vitalism as a monadology. Each postulates monads as simple entities expressive of the unity and infinity of God through the simplicity of the individual monad and the infinite multiplicity of the monads in their ontological class. For both, monads are subject to change, their mutability being both that which distinguishes them from God, and the grounds of amelioration – the means of achieving greater goodness. Both conceive of bodies as aggregates of monads, unified by a dominant monad. Both sought to define body in terms of force rather than extension, but both held that the mechanical account of bodies was compatible with a metaphysics which located the principle of action in substance itself. Some of the parallels are implicit rather than overt – for example, Anne Conway formulates no principle of

critique of Cartesian mechanism for trying to explain all things in terms of matter or extension, noting that he himself has proposed a principle of force. He agrees that substance never perishes and accepts the doctrine of transformation, but not metempsychosis. Above all, he says, he agrees with Van Helmont's conception of the infinity of all things. Leibniz *Correspondance*, vol. I, p. 305.

[34] Gottfried Wilhelm von Leibniz, *Monatlicher Auszug aus allerhand neuherausgegeben nütlichen und artigen Büchern, April 1701.* Reprinted in Fichant (1991), pp. 94–7.

sufficient reason, but, like Leibniz, she assumes that ontological reality is intelligible and she applied rigorous deductive argument to the problems with which she deals. And while she does not explicitly state a principle of contradiction, her arguments treat contradiction as a criterion of disproof.

Thus stated, the similarities between Conway and Leibniz indicate clear generic similarities in the type of philosophy each propounds, and a good deal of shared conceptual detail. This may be explained by the fact that both brought similar considerations to bear on a common set of philosophical issues. For example, they shared profound dissatisfaction with Cartesianism and they both adopted a synthesising approach which led them to investigate the same currents of vitalist and mystical thought, namely Helmontianism and kabbalism. Nevertheless, the similarities between them should not be overstated, for the differences between them are important. Some of these derive from the fact that Anne Conway's system is simply shorter: her monadology is not elaborated to anything like the same extent as Leibniz's. This is not to say that Anne Conway was a primitive or undeveloped Leibniz. In comparing their philosophies, it is important to bear in mind that there may have been more to her philosophy than what has come down to us. But the differences between them are not simply a matter of scale. For one thing, Leibniz was not a substance monist, since he posited an infinite variety of substances (albeit all of them soul-like). Another extremely important difference is their theory of causality, by which they sought to preserve both efficient and final causality. Where Leibniz denied that substances could interact, and explained the smooth functioning and providential organisation of the universe in terms of larger design – that is, by the law of pre-established harmony – Anne Conway proposes an intermediate causal agent, 'Middle Nature', which is less a law of nature than a substance. This she postulated as the interface between God and the world, a principle of divine immanence and the medium for activity in the created cosmos. In so doing she holds to her Cambridge-Platonist roots, notably More's Hylarchic Principle. No doubt on this point Lady Conway would have come in for the same criticism that Leibniz made of More and other Platonists that his Spirit of Nature was an unnecessary and merely speculative hypothesis. He writes in *New Essays*: 'The late Henry More, the Anglican theologian, brilliant as he was, was a little too quick to fabricate inscrutable and implausible hypotheses – for instance, his hylarchic principle which explains the weight and elasticity of matter and other wonders that are found in it.'[35]

[35] Leibniz, *New Essays*, p. 343.

GEORG WACHTER

While the question of whether Anne Conway influenced Leibniz is open for debate, there is also evidence that her *Principia* had an impact in the controversies sparked by the philosophy of Spinoza. For her book was, it seems, read by Georg Wachter (1673–1757). In the history of the reception of Spinoza's philosophy, Wachter is chiefly known as an anti-Spinozist whose influential anti-Spinozist *Der Spinozismus im Judentum* (1699) argues, notoriously, that Judaism was responsible for Spinoza's monstrous errors, and in particular that Spinoza derived his pernicious doctrines from the Jewish kabbalah.[36] This book was an attack on Johann Peter Speeth (or Späth), one-time assistant of Knorr von Rosenroth in the preparation of *Kabbalah denudata*. Speeth was a Behmenist who, through his study of kabbalism, became persuaded that Judaism was the true religion and, to the scandal of Christian Europe, converted to Judaism, taking the name Moses Germanus.[37] Through Knorr, Speeth was acquainted with Van Helmont, and he too appears to have read Anne Conway's *Principia*.

In *Der Spinozismus im Judentum*, Wachter, citing the authority of Henry More, argued that Spinoza's pantheism (*Deus sive natura*) derived from the kabbalah which, he claimed, taught that the created world was an emanation of God, that the created world is God, and that stones, plants, animals and human beings can transmute into one another, and into God. Wachter's thesis about the Jewish origins of Spinozism had popular take-up, but was condemned by the more discerning for its misrepresentation of kabbalism.[38] Subsequently Wachter changed his evaluation of both Spinoza and the kabbalah. His *Elucidarius cabbalisticus* (1706), retains the Spinozism–kabbalism thesis, but reverses his assessment of it. This time he interprets both Spinozism and kabbalism in a positive light, making a distinction between earlier kabbalism and that of Isaac Luria and Abraham Cohen Herrera. There are several possible explanations for Wachter's change of view, including the fact that he had further discussions with Moses Germanus. But it is clear from other unpublished writings that his further reading included Anne Conway's *Principia philosophiae*. In his unpublished manuscript, 'Theologia martyrum', which rehabilitates Spinoza, Wachter cites the author of *Principia philosophiae* in support of his own kabbalistical interpretation of Christ as the first-born son of God.[39]

[36] Scholem (1984). [37] Coudert (forthcoming). [38] Israel (2001), pp. 644–51.

[39] See Martin Mulsow's forthcoming paper in a collection edited by Christopher Ligota and Jean-Louis Quantin in the Oxford-Warburg Studies. Also his forthcoming edition of 'Theologia martyrum'. I am most grateful to Dr Mulsow for drawing my attention to Wachter's use of Anne Conway.

Since this manuscript treatise attacks the Trinitarian views propounded in Petersen's *Geheimnisz der Wiederbringung aller Dinge*, it is conceivable that Wachter became acquainted with Anne Conway's book through Petersen. But he may equally have been motivated to read the book as a result of his conversations with Speeth. Whether or not Conway's *Principia philosophiae* was the precipitating factor in his revisionism, the episode is testimony to Anne Conway's success in removing what she calls 'offense' from the doctrine of the Trinity through her syncretist, ecumenist conflation of Christ with Adam Kadmon in her concept of Middle Nature. In her system, this doctrine serves to remove the danger of pantheism and Spinozism. In Wachter's application of it, however, it contributes to the vindication of Spinozism itself. With Wachter, then, the *fortuna* of Conway's *Principia* takes a philosophico-controversialist direction, and is absorbed within the broad stream of the free-thinking of the radical Enlightenment.

AFTERWORD: ANNE CONWAY TODAY

Many of the difficulties to be faced in trying to reclaim Anne Conway as a philosopher today are the same as those for all female philosophers of the past. Having dropped from view before the modern canon was established, they are inevitably assigned subordinate status as 'minor' figures. And in most cases the small size of their published output appears to confirm that minor status. It is, however, easy to forget that canon formation – that is, what determines the selection of particular aspects of philosophy as important – is itself historically contingent, and that the philosophical canon is not fixed for all time. Another way of talking about the 'minor' figures, both male and female, who are excluded from the canon, is as *unfamiliar* philosophers. The unknowns are, almost by definition, the philosophers for whom there is no interpretative tradition. Either for historical reasons (because they had no followers) or by neglect, they have not contributed to philosophical discourse as it has been practised at any given time after they lived. As a result we often do not have the interpretative tools for examining their writings, or we operate unawares, with the prejudices that accrue to a particular classification of philosophies and philosophical habits inculcated through acquaintance with a different sort of philosophy.

The account of Anne Conway's philosophical development that I have given is very much that of a woman thinker in contact with an intellectual world dominated by men. This is not surprising, given the fact that, in the seventeenth century, philosophy was very much a masculine preserve. In addition to which, the historical documentation of women's lives for this period yields very little information about the intellectual life of women. The absence of documentation does not necessarily mean that women had no life of the mind. No attempt to explain the nature of Anne Conway's philosophical activity and her achievement in that domain would be complete without some consideration of the feminine circumstances in which she wrote. First of all, there is the question of whether she was aware of other women, like herself, who were actively interested in science and philosophy. If it is possible to answer that question, we have some means of assessing whether her isolation as an invalid thinker was compounded by a sense of isolation as a female thinker. Then there is also the question of her relationship to her female public today. The formulaic genuflections to the woman-learned-beyond-her-sex which characterise the early modern accommodation of female philosophers have now been replaced by latter-day questions about the gendered character of philosophy and specifically female forms of philosophy. How, indeed, do we place Anne Conway in relation to feminist thought in the twenty-first century? Ancillary to these questions is the issue of canonicity: of how the criteria of selection have operated to the exclusion of women and whether, indeed, this situation can be rectified by returning them to visibility.

PHILOSOPHY IN THE FEMININE?

I have argued that Anne Conway may have been aware of women like Elizabeth of Bohemia, Katherine Ranelagh and Margaret Cavendish. But, distinguished constellation though they be, they hardly constitute a female intellectual milieu. Although they were certainly exceptional in being able to pursue their philosophical interests, any value they may have had as role models was limited. And there is no evidence of co-operative interaction with Anne Conway. On the contrary, Anne Conway seems to have kept Margaret Cavendish at a firm distance. On the evidence available, the context in which she studied and wrote philosophy was a private and domestic one. In this respect, her pursuit of philosophy was not unlike that of Damaris Masham, who mentions reading philosophy in the privacy of her closet.[40] Anne Conway was, furthermore, confined to her home by illness and therefore unable to participate in public intellectual life, had she wished to do so. In this domestic context she certainly had contact with intelligent and educated women – her library keeper, Sarah Bennet, her

[40] Hutton (1993).

companion, Elizabeth Foxcroft, and her Quaker maid, Priscilla Evans.[41] But she was dependent on sympathetic men for her contact with the world of ideas. The very conditions in which Anne Conway practised philosophy suggest that women did not figure on her philosophical horizon.

If there was no distinctively female context for Anne Conway in the seventeenth century, there have, nonetheless, been attempts in the twentieth century to set her within an identifiably female tradition. The best-known such attempt is by Carolyn Merchant, who, in *The Death of Nature*, argues that we may identify female characteristics in the type and content of the philosophy practised by women in the early modern period.[42] This essentialist approach is founded on a presumed opposition between two strands of seventeenth-century natural philosophy: Hermeticism and alchemy, on the one hand, and the new 'mechanical' natural philosophies of Descartes, Hobbes and the Royal Society, on the other. Merchant contrasts the mechanical model of the latter with what she perceives as the more organic thinking about the natural world to be encountered in Hermeticism and alchemy. She also perceives these latter as non-exploitative in their methods of investigating the natural world. Accordingly, Merchant classes the older forms of natural philosophy displaced by philosophical mechanism as more female-friendly. She locates Anne Conway's philosophy within this 'female' framework of natural philosophy, on account of her repudiation of Cartesian and Hobbist philosophy and her apparently holistic concept of substance. Conway's use of the conceptual vocabulary of alchemy appears to confirm the location.

Unfortunately, Carolyn Merchant's well-meant attempt to discuss Conway's thought in a historically nuanced way is flawed by its underlying assumptions. First of all, her view that Conway repudiated Descartes in entirety is unsustainable. Conway did not reject Cartesianism in its entirety, and the aspects of Descartes' philosophy that she retains included his account of the mechanical laws of local motion (in chapter IX). Secondly, Carolyn Merchant mistakenly aligns More with the Royal Society and the mechanists, and as an enemy of vitalism, on account of his controversy with the alchemist Thomas Vaughan. Yet More's philosophy of spirit has more in common with those against whom Merchant sets him. And, as I have argued, Conway's philosophical outlook has strong affinities with More's in spite of her criticism of him. Merchant regards Hermeticists and

[41] See above, p. 112. Priscilla Evans is described as 'a fair Latin scholar'. *Conway Letters*, p. 422.

[42] Merchant (1980). A recommendation of her approach is that it proposes a greater degree of historical specificity. In particular, she focuses on the currents of thought unfamiliar in philosophical history (Hermetic and alchemical thought).

alchemists as guardians of an organic philosophy of nature in contrast to seventeenth-century men of science who claimed to control nature. Yet exactly the same claims to mastery of nature are made by alchemists and Hermeticists.[43]

An alternative essentialist approach to female thinkers of the past posits a specifically female epistemology or epistemologies in contra-distinction to the perceived masculinity of philosophical epistemologies. In contemporary feminism most such attempts are stamped with the anti-rationalism of the post-modern age, with the result that it has become almost commonplace to identify Cartesian rationalism, and the dualism that it upholds, as unequivocally antithetical to women, and responsible for ensuring the 'masculinisation' of philosophy. Most famously, Susan Bordo identifies the masculine traits of Cartesian reason as 'detachment, clarity and transcendence of the body'.[44] Although Genevieve Lloyd concedes that Descartes offered a new egalitarianism in knowledge through a philosophical method accessible to all, including women, she nonetheless argues that, in practice, 'the sharpness of his separation of truth-seeking from practical affairs of everyday life reinforced already existing distinctions between male and female roles, opening the way to the idea of distinctive male and female consciousness'.[45]

Fortunately a number of important studies have begun to turn the tide on this view of Cartesianism. Recent work on early modern women's philosophy has challenged such interpretations on historical grounds,[46] while new work on Cartesianism, especially studies of Descartes' theory of the passions, is challenging the caricature image of Descartes as a mere rationalist.[47] The case of Anne Conway certainly complicates the anti-Cartesian assumptions of feminist historians of philosophy. In so far as her philosophical treatise contains a repudiation of Cartesian dualism, her philosophy appears to endorse their position. Nevertheless, her use of Cartesianism and the role of Cartesianism as a philosophical facilitator lend credence to the case of those who have sought to correct this picture. The grounds and philosophical purpose of Anne Conway's repudiation of Cartesian dualism are quite different from those by which twentieth-century feminists

[43] Tiles (1986).

[44] Bordo (1987), p. 8. See especially, Grimshaw (1982), Lloyd (1995), Hekman (1990). Attacks on Cartesian rationalism often entail simultaneous attacks on Baconian science, and an elision of the two to construct a '"super-masculinized" model of knowledge' (Bordo 1987, p. 8). Those who argue in this way usually draw on Merchant (1980) and Keller (1985).

[45] Lloyd (1995), pp. 49–50.

[46] Atherton (1993), O'Neill (1998). See also Duran (1991) and Lennon (1992).

[47] James (1997).

wish to divest themselves, and philosophy, from the hold of Cartesianism. Conway refuted Cartesian dualism, not in order to found a new feminine subjectivity, but in order to elaborate a science of nature more powerful in its explanatory theory than Descartes', and one which was compatible with the demands of Christian theism. Where modern feminists and modern philosophers in general focus on Descartes' *Meditations*, Anne Conway focused on his natural philosophy. Nor did she have any qualms about the value of philosophical reason. On the contrary, like Mary Astell and Elizabeth of Bohemia, she set a high valuation on reason, as is evident in the early stage of her correspondence, when she tells More, 'I professe it is an infinite pleasure I take in reading your letters; filled with a greate deale of reason they are alwaies'.[48] From the few indications she gives us in her treatise, it is evident that Anne Conway was an unrepentant rationalist, an innatist who never doubted the value of the geometrical method and who did not eschew a hypothetico-deductive mode of argument. Furthermore, although, as we have seen, she describes her philosophy as anti-Cartesian, she accepted Descartes' science of motion.

Nor was Cartesianism an impediment in her philosophical life. On the contrary, Cartesianism opened up the way to philosophy for her. And she was not alone in this. A fact of the historical record is that almost all the women who became interested in philosophy in the seventeenth century were interested in the *new* philosophies of the period.[49] The majority of these either came to philosophy via Descartes, or were interested in Cartesianism in one form or another. The list would include Princess Elizabeth of the Palatinate, Queen Christina of Sweden, Margaret Cavendish, Duchess of Newcastle, Mary Astell and the *salonistes*, Anne de la Vigne, Marie du Pré and Catherine Descartes, niece of the philosopher. It is not irrelevant to point out that, although their number was small, there were more female philosophers in the seventeenth century than in any previous century. Furthermore, it was on Cartesian grounds that Poulain de la Barre argued for the intellectual equality of women with men in his *De l'égalité des sexes* (1673) which was the first philosophically grounded defence of male and female equality.[50] Such a defence is by definition impossible within the framework of the Aristotelianism that dominated philosophy previously, where reason itself is a mark of sexual difference.[51]

[48] *Conway Letters*, p. 61.

[49] The exception is Anna Maria van Schurman, who was taught by Descartes' detractor, Gisbert Voet (Voetius), in Utrecht.

[50] See Desmond Clarke's introduction to his translation Clarke in Francois Poulain de la Barre, *The Equality of the Sexes*, trans. Desmond Clarke (Manchester: Manchester University Press, 1990).

[51] See Maclean (1980) and Horowitz (1976).

Contrary to the perceptions of feminist anti-Cartesians, the lesson of history is that Cartesianism offered opportunities for women to philosophise that the Aristotelianism it replaced did not.[52] We need to be mindful that the interpretative strategies of feminist anti-Cartesians have been honed to tackle issues besetting modernity and post-modernity. It is worth recalling Jean Grimshaw's caveat that 'attempts to identify any sort of characteristic male point of view in philosophy, a typically or essentially male metaphysic, or a male view of human nature, founder on the rock of historical complexity and difference'.[53] Early modernity cannot be subjected to modern categories without loss and distortion.[54]

The kinds of difficulty to be encountered when trying to claim Anne Conway for a female philosophical heritage are compounded when trying to place her in relation to feminism. To treat her as a proto-feminist is highly problematic. Although a woman, writing at a time when femininity and rationality were considered mutually contradictory,[55] she has nothing to say on politics, society or even the nature of woman. Unlike her contemporary Margaret Cavendish, she does not betray any concern about her position as a woman trying to do philosophy. She makes no comments about the impediments to education that women of her time had to face. Again, unlike Margaret Cavendish, she eschewed public profession of her philosophical interests. Indeed her public stance is consistently self-effacing. And, unlike her younger contemporary Mary Astell, Anne Conway offers no statement about the nature of woman or women's role in society. Nor does she display any consciousness of herself as a female subject in terms meaningful to twentieth-century feminists. She proposed no programme of social action and none can be extrapolated from her philosophical system. She was not a moral philosopher but a metaphysician. To this we might add that her use of the terms 'male' and 'female' is loaded with traditional sexist connotations of active and passive.

The apparent blankness of the page of Anne Conway's feminist credentials might suggest that the price of Conway's entry into philosophy was capitulation to a masculine philosophical order. However, before jumping to such a conclusion, we might pause to reflect on the distorting effect of modern categories. The fact of her not fitting those categories is certainly indicative of her difference from the present. Acknowledgement of that

[52] For the legacy of misogyny in Aristotelianism, see Maclean (1980).

[53] Grimshaw (1982), p. 70.

[54] A case in point is Harth (1992) which explains the use of reason by women of the early Enlightenment as a strategy of subversion.

[55] This is true within the Aristotelian tradition. See Maclean (1980).

difference perhaps offers us a key to a more positive interpretation. While Anne Conway cannot be called a feminist in the modern sense of the term, this does not mean that she has no place in the history of feminism, or that hers was not a female philosophical voice. I do not by that mean that she anticipates feminist positions in her philosophy. However, perhaps complexity and difference offer us a key. We do not, in her treatise, have a social agenda. Nor do we have a fully developed ethical system. But we do have a philosophy which incorporates a feminine principle as the counter-balance to a male principle in all things, including individual monads. These are, of course, not socially operative concepts. Nor does her philosophy lend itself to a political programme. Nevertheless, we have a philosophy which transcends the categories by which modern philosophy defines both self and other. Moreover, hers was, in its own day, a remarkably independent philosophical system.[56]

In the foregoing study I have attempted to set Anne Conway in historical and philosophical context in order the better to understand the nature of her philosophy and grasp the measure of her achievement. This inevitably throws into focus her difference from the present, but it offers a beginning point for giving her meaningful philosophical identity in the present. Whatever conclusions her modern readers may reach about her as a philosopher, to give her prominence in the annals of philosophical history unquestionably has symbolic value for women in philosophy today, whatever their area of philosophy. But Anne Conway is not the preserve of philosophers alone. Restored to visibility, she is a beacon to all women of today faced with a never-ending struggle for opportunity and recognition. For she was a woman who turned impediment to advantage, by practising her chosen pursuit in spite of restrictive social norms and the most inhospitable circumstances of ill health. There is much to support the judgement of Marjorie Nicolson, the remarkable woman scholar who did so much to recover her for the present, that she was 'the most remarkable woman . . . of that remarkable age'.[57]

[56] For a fuller discussion of this see Hutton (1997e).

[57] *Conway Letters*, p. xxxvi.

Bibliography

PRIMARY SOURCES, ANNE CONWAY

MANUSCRIPTS

Cambridge, Christ's College, MS 21 (letters of Anne Conway and Henry More).
London, British Library MS Additional
23,214 (letters from Anne Conway to her husband).
23,215 (letters to Anne Conway from John Finch and Thomas Baines).
23,216 (letters from Henry More and others).
23,217 (letters to Anne Conway from Quakers).
38,855, f. 108 (letter from John Finch to Anne Conway).
London, Friends' House, Box Meeting Accounts, 1681–1750 ('Lady Conaways legacy paid by van Helmott . . . ').

PRINTED SOURCES

Principia philosophiae antiquissimae & recentissimae de Deo, Christo & creatura id est de spiritu & materia in genere. Printed in *Opuscula philosophica quibus continetur, principia philosophiae antiquissimae & recentissimae ac philosophia vulgaris refutata quibus junctur sunt C.C. problemata de revolutione animarum humanorum*. Amsterdam, 1690.

The Conway Letters. The Correspondence of Viscountess Anne Conway, Henry More and their Friends, ed. S. Hutton and M. H. Nicolson, Oxford: Clarendon Press, 1992.

TRANSLATIONS

The Principles of the Most Ancient and Modern Philosophy: Concerning God, Christ, and the Creature; that is, concernng Spirit and Matter in General. English translation by 'J. C.' London, 1692.

The Principles of the Most Ancient and Modern Philosophy. English translation by Allison P. Coudert and Taylor Corse. Cambridge: Cambridge University Press, 1996.

Zasady Filozofii Najstrszej i Najnowsze. Dotyczace Boga, Chrystusa I Stworzenia Czyli o Duchu I Materii. Polish translation by Joanna Usakiewicz. Krakow: Arius, 2002.

MODERN REPRINTS

The Principles of the Most Ancient and Modern Philosophy. Modern reprint of the Latin and English printings, with introduction by P. Loptson, Dordrecht: Kluwer Academic Publishers, 1982.

The Principles of the Most Ancient and Modern Philosophy. Parallel text edition by Peter Loptson. Delmar, NY: Scholar's Facsimiles and Reprints, 1998.

EXTRACTS

A Dictionary of Philosophical Quotations, ed. A. J. Ayer and Jane O'Grady. Oxford: Blackwell, 1992.

Women Philosophers, ed. Mary Warnock. London: Dent, 1996.

Women Philosophers of the Early Modern Period, ed. Margaret Atherton. Indianapolis, IN: Hachette, 1995.

OTHER PRIMARY SOURCES

MANUSCRIPTS

Armagh, Armagh Robinson Library, MS g.III. 15 (Conway Library Catalogue).

Leicester, Leicestershire, Leicester and Rutland County Record Office. Finch papers, MS DG7 lit 9.

London, British Library, MS Sloane 35 (catalogue of Stubbe's books) and 530 ('Some Observations of Francis Mercury van Helmont' transcribed by Daniel Foote).

London, British Library, MS Stowe 205.

London, British Library, MS Additional 22,911 ('An Account of ye Master's Lodgings in ye College and of his private Lodge by itself').

London, British Library MS Additional 4,293 (Boyle on Greatrakes).

London, British Library, MSS Additional 4,280 and 4,278 (Pell–Cavendish letters).

London, Friends' House Library, Spence MS 378.

London, Public Record Office, SP 120/7 (list of Conway books) and Prob 11/160 ff. 503–5 (will of Sir Heneage Finch).

Oxford, Bodleian Library, MS Locke 17 (Adam Boreel poem on Lady Conway).

San Marino, California. Huntington Library. Hastings MSS (Correspondence of Edward, third Viscount Conway and Sir George Rawdon).

Wolfenbüttel, Herzog August Bibliothek. Cod. Guelf. Extrav. 30.4 (Correspondence of Knorr von Rosenroth).

PRINTED DOCUMENTS

Berwick, E. (ed). *The Rawdon Papers Consisting of Letters on Various Subjects, Literary, Political and Ecclesiastical to and from Dr John Bramhall, Primate of Ireland*, 3 vols. London, 1819.

Historical Manuscripts Commission, *The Manuscripts of His Grace the Duke of Portland Preserved at Welbeck Abbey*, ed. F. H. B. Daniels, 3 vols. London: HMSO, 1891–1923.

Report on the Manuscripts of Allen George Finch, Esquire, of Burley-on-the-Hill, Rutland. London: HMSO, 1913.

Report on the Manuscripts of the Late Reginald Rawdon Hastings Esq, ed. F. Bickley. London: HMSO, 1930.

The Parish Register of Kensington, co. Middlesex, from A.D. 1539 to A.D. 1675, ed. F. N. Macnamara and A. Strong Maskelyne. Publications of the Harleian Society Registers, vol. XVI, London, 1890.

Proceedings Especially in the County of Kent, in Connection with Parliaments Called in 1640, ed. Lambert B. Larkin. London: Camden Society, 1862.

PRINTED SOURCES

Abu Bakr ibn al-Tufail, known as Hai Ebn Yokdhan. *Philosophus autodidactus sive epistola Abi Jaafer Ebn Tophail de Hai Ebn Yokdhan, in qua ostenditur quo modo ex inferiorum contemplatione ad superiorum notitiam ratio humana contemplatione ad superiorum nonitiam ratio humana ascendere possit*. Oxford, 1671.

An Account of the Oriental Philosophy, shewing the Wisedom of some Renowned Men of the East, translated by Edward Pocock. No place of publication, 1674.

Agrippa, Henry Cornelius. *De occulta philosophia*. 1510.

Andrea, Johann Valentin. *Chymische Hochzeit*. 1616. English translation by Ezekiel Foxcroft, *The Hermetick Romance or the Chemical Wedding*. London, 1690.

Barclay, Robert. *Universal Love considered and established upon its Right Foundation*. N.P., 1677.

Reliquiae Barclaeanae. Correspondence of Col. David Barclay and Robert Barclay of Urie. London: Winter and Bailey, 1870.

An Apology for the True Christian Divinity. [Aberdeen], 1678.

Boyle, Robert. *Some Considerations Touching the Usefulnesse of Experimental Naturall Philosophy*. London, 1663.

The Origin of Forms and Qualities. London, 1666.

A Free Enquiry into the Vulgarly Conceived Notion of Nature. London, 1686. Modern edition, ed. E. B. Davis and M. Hunter, Cambridge: Cambridge University Press, 1996.

The Works of the Honourable Robert Boyle, 5 vols. London, 1772.

The Correspondence of Robert Boyle, ed. Michael Hunter, Antonio Clericuzio and Lawrence M. Principe, 6 vols. London: Pickering and Chatto, 2001.

Brucker, Jacob. *Historia critica philosophiae*. Lipsiae, 1742–67.

Burnet, Gilbert. *History of My Own Time*, ed. O. Airy, 2 vols. Oxford, 1897.

Cavendish, Margaret, Duchess of Newcastle. *Philosophical and Physical Opinions*. London, 1663 (first published 1655).

Philosophical Letters. London, 1664.

Charleton, Walter. *Ternary of Paradoxes*. London, 1650.

Physiologia Epicuro-Gassendo-Charletoniana. London, 1654.

[Conway, Edward]. *Exceeding Good Newes from Ireland being a perfect Relation of the great overthrow given to the Rebels, by the Forces of Ulster, under the command of col. Conoway and Lieut. Col Oconally*. London, 1646.

Covel, John. *Extracts from the Diary of Dr. John Covel, 1670–1679* in J. T. Bent (ed.), *Early Voyages and Travels in the Levant*. London: Hakluyt Society, 1893.

Croese, Gerard. *The General History of the Quakers*. London, 1696 (first published in Latin in 1695).

Cudworth, Ralph. *A Sermon Preached Before the Honourable House of Commons*. Cambridge, 1647. In C. A. Patrides (ed.), *The Cambridge Platonists*. Cambridge: Cambridge University Press, 1969; reprinted 1980, pp. 90–127.

The True Intellectual System of the Universe. London, 1678.

A Treatise Concerning Eternal and Immutable Morality, ed. S. Hutton. Cambridge: Cambridge University Press, 1996 (first published 1731).

Descartes, René. *Lettres de Mr Descartes*, ed. Claude Clerselier, 2 vols. Paris, 1657–9.

Oeuvres de Descartes, ed. Charles Adam and Paul Tannery, new presentation by B. Rochot. Paris: Vrin, 1974.

The Philosophical Writings of Descartes, 3 vols. trans. J. Cottingham, R. Stoothoff and D. Murdoch. Cambridge: Cambridge University Press, 1985.

Digby, Sir Kenelm. *Two Treatises. In the one of which, the nature of bodies; in the other, the Nature of mans soule; is looked into: in way of discovery, of the immortality of reasonable soules*. Paris, 1644.

Evans, Katherine and Sarah Cheevers. *A Short Relation of some of the Cruel Sufferings (for the truths sake) of K. E. and S. Chevers in the Isle of Malta*. London, 1662.

[Fabroni, A., ed.]. *Lettere indedite de uomini illustri*. Florence, 1773, pp. 261–70.

Fell, Margaret. *Women's Speaking Justified*. London, 1666.

[Fleming, Robert]. *Survey of Quakerism*. London, 1677.

Fox, George. *The Short Journal and Itinerary of George Fox*, ed. N. Penny. Cambridge: Cambridge University Press, 1925.

Gironnet, Jean. *Philosophia vulgaris refutata*, printed in *Opuscula philosophica*. Amsterdam, 1690.

Glanvill, Joseph. *Lux Orientalis*. London, 1662.

Plus Ultra: or, The Progress and Advancement of Knowledge Since the Days of Aristotle. London, 1668.

A Praefatory Answer to Mr Henry Stubbe, the Doctor of Warwick. Wherein Malignity, Hypocrisie, Falshood of his Temper, Pretences, Reports, and the Imperinency of his Arguings & Quotations in his Animadversions on Plus Ultra, are Discovered. London, 1671.

Sadducismus Triumphatus. London, 1688.

Glisson, Francis. *Tractatus de natura substantiae energetica*. London, 1672.

Greatrakes, Valentine. *A Brief Account of Mr Valentine Greatraks, and Divers of the Cures by him lately performed. Written by himself in a Letter Addressed to the Honorable Robert Boyle Esq*. London, 1666.

Helmont, Francis Mercury van. *Adumbratio kabbalae christianae, id est syncatabasis hebraizans, sive brevis applicatio doctrinae habraeorum cabbalisticae ad dogmata novi foederis; pro formanda hypothesi, ad conversionem judaeorum proficua*. Frankfurt am Main, 1684. Printed in *Kabbala denudata*, vol. II (1684).

A Cabbalistical Dialogue. London, 1684. Also printed in Latin in *Kabbala denudata*, vol. I (1677–8).

Two Hundred Queries Modestly Propounded Concerning the Doctrine of the Revolution of the Human Souls and its Conformity with the Truth of the Christian Religion. London, 1684.

Paradoxal Discourses of F.M. van Helmont Concerning the Macrocosm and Microcosm. London, 1685.

One Hundred and Fifty Three Chymical Aphorisms. London, 1688.

De revolutione animorum humanorum quanta stet istius doctrinae cum veritate. Christianae religionis conformitas problematum centuriae duae in *Opuscula philosophica* (1690). Latin version of *Two Hundred Queries.*

The Divine Being and its Attributes Philosophically Demonstrated from the Holy Scriptures and the Original Nature of Things according to the principles of F.M.B. of Helmont. Translated from Dutch version of Paulus Buchius by Benjamin Furly. London, 1693.

Seder Olam: or the Order, Series, or Succession of All Ages, Periods, and Times of the Whole World Theologically, Philosophically, and Chronologically Explicated and Stated, trans. J. Clark, MD. London: T. Hawkins, 1694.

The Spirit of Diseases or Diseases from the Spirit Laid open in some Observations Concerning Man, and His Deseases, Wherein is Shewed How much the Mind Influenceth the Body in Causing and Curing of Deseases. London, 1694.

Helmont, Jan Baptiste van, *Ortus medicinae, id est initia physicae inaudita, progressus medicinae novus in morborum ultionem ad vitam longam . . . edente authoris filio Francisco Mercurio van Helmont, cum ejus praefatio ex Belgico translata.* Amsterdam: Elzevir, 1648. German translation by Knorr von Rosenroth, *Aufgang der Artzeny-Kunst* (Sulzbach, 1683). English translation by John Chandler, *Oriatrike, or Physick Refined* (London, 1664). French translation by Jean Leconte, *Les oeuvres de Jean Baptiste van Helmont* (Lyons, 1670).

Kabbala denudata seu doctrina hebraeorum transcendentalis et metaphysica atque theologica opus antiquissimae philosophiae barbaricae variis speciminibus refertissimum. Trans. and ed. Christian Knorr von Rosenroth. 4 parts in 2 vols. Sulzbach, 1677–8, vol. II, 1684.

Keith, George. *Immediate Revelation, or Jesus Christ the Eternall Son of God, revealed in man and revealing the knowledge of God, and the things of his Kingdom immediately.* No publisher or place of publication, 1668.

Immediate Revelation . . . with an Appendix containing an Answer to some further Objections, second edition. n.p., 1675.

The Way Cast Up, and the Stumbling-blockes removed from before the feet of those who are seeking the way to Zion. n.p. [1677].

The Way to the City of God Described. n.p., 1678.

The Rector Corrected: of the Rector of Arrow Shooting his Arrow beside the Mark. London, 1680.

Knorr von Rosenroth, Christian. See *Kabbala denudata.*

Leibniz, Gottfried Wilhelm von. *Correspondance de Leibniz avec la Princesse Electrice Sophie de Brunswick-Lunebourg,* ed. O. Klopp, 3 vols. Hanover, London and Paris, n.d.

Die Philosophischen Schriften von G. W. Leibniz, ed. C. I. Gerhardt, 7 vols. Berlin, 1875.

Discourse on Metaphysics, in *Philosophical Papers and Letters*, trans. L. Loemker. Chicago: Chicago University Press, 1956.

New Essays on Human Understanding, ed. P. Remnant and J. Bennett. Cambridge: Cambridge University Press, 1981.

G. W. Leibniz's Monadology. An Edition for Students, ed. Nicholas Rescher. London: Routledge, 1991.

Locke, John. *A Treatise Concerning Human Understanding*. London, 1690.

Malpighi, Marcello. *The Correspondence of Marcello Malpighi*, 5 vols. Ithaca and London: Cornell University Press, 1975.

More, Henry. *Philosophical Poems*. Cambridge: R. Daniel, 1647. Includes *Psychozoia* first published as *Psychodia Platonica: or, a Platonicall Song of the Soul*. Cambridge: R. Daniel, 1643.

An Antidote against Atheisme: or, an Appeale to the Natural Faculties of the Minde of Man, whether there be not a God. London, 1653.

Conjectura cabbalistica: or, a Conjectural Essay of Interpreting the Minde of Moses According to a Threefold Cabbala, viz., Literal, Philosophical, Mystical. London: J. Flesher, 1653.

The Immortality of the Soul, so farre forth as it is Demonstrable from the Knowledge of Nature and the Light of Reason. London: J. Flesher; Cambridge: W. Morden, 1654.

Enthusiasmus triumphatus, or a Discourse on the Nature, Causes, Kinds and Cure of Enthusiasm. London: J. Flesher, Cambridge, W. Morden, 1656.

An Explanation of the Grand Mystery of Godliness; or, a True and Faithful Representation of the Everlasting Gospel of our Lord and Saviour Jesus Christ. London: J. Flesher; W. Morden, Cambridge, 1660.

A Collection of Several Philosophical Writings. London: J. Flesher; W. Morden, Cambridge, 1662.

Apology of Henry More (1664). Printed in *A Modest Enquiry*.

A Modest Enquiry into the Mystery of Iniquity. London, J. Flesher; Cambridge, W. Morden, 1664.

Enchiridion ethicum, praecipua moralis philosophiae rudimenta complectens. London: J. Flesher; Cambridge: W. Morden, 1667.

Divine Dialogues Containing Sundry Disquisitions and Instructions Concerning the Attributes of God in the World. London: J. Flesher, 1668.

An Exposition of the Seven Epistles to the Seven Churches. London, 1669.

Enchiridion metaphysicum. London: J. Flesher; Cambridge: W. Morden, 1671. Reprinted in *Opera omnia*.

A Letter from Dr More to J. G. giving him an account how M. Stubb belies him. Published with Glanvill's *Prefatory Answer*, 1671.

H. Mori Cantabrigiensis opera omnia, 3 vols. London: J. Maycock for J. Martyn and W. Kettilby, 1675–9. Comprising, vol. I, *Opera theologica* (London, 1675) and vols. II and III, *Opera philosophica* (London, 1679).

Epistola altera, quae brevem tractatus theologico-politici confutationem complectitur, in *Opera omnia*, vol. II, pp. 565–614.

Remarks upon Two Late Ingenious Discourses; the One, and Essay, Touching the Gravitation and Non-gravitation of fluid Bodies; the Other, Touching the Torricellian Experiment, so far forth as they may concern any passages in his Enchiridion Metphysicum. London, 1676.

Apocalypsis apocalpseos, or the Revelation of St John the Divine Unveiled. London, 1680.

A Plain and Continued Exposition of the Several Prophecies of the Prophet Daniel. London: M. Flesher for W. Kettilby, 1681.

Two Choice and Useful Treatises: the one Lux Orientalis; or an Enquiry into the Opinions of the Eastern Sages Concerning the Praeexistence of Souls [by Joseph Glanvill] . . . *The Other, A Discourse of Truth by the late Reverend Dr. Rust, Lord Bishop of Dromore in Ireland. With Annotations on them both* [by Henry More]. London: J. Collins, 1682.

An Illustration of Those Two Abstruse Books in Holy Scripture, The Book of Daniel and the Revelation of S. John. London: M. Flesher for W. Kettilby, 1685.

Paralipomena Prophetica: Containing Several Supplements and Defenses of Dr. Henry More his Expositions of the Prophet Daniel and the Apocalypse. London: W. Kettilby, 1685.

Discourses on Several Texts of Scripture. London: J.R. for B. Aylmer, 1692.

Letters on Several Subjects by the Life Pious Dr Henry More. London, 1694.

Descartes. Correspondence avec Morus et Arnauld. ed. and trans. G. Rodis Lewis. Paris, 1953.

The Poems of Henry More, ed. G. Bullough. Manchester, 1931.

Muggleton, Lodowick. *A Looking Glass for George Fox*. London, 1667.

Muggleton, Lodowick and John Reeve. *Joyful News from Heaven: or the Last Intelligence from our Gorify'd Jesus above the Stars, wherein is Infallibly Recorded How that the Soul dieth in the Body*. [London 1658?]

Nicholas of Cusa, *Ὀφαλμοσ Ἁπλουσ or the Single Eye, Entitled the Vision of God*, trans. Giles Randall. London, 1646.

The Idiot in Four Books, trans. John Everard. London. 1650.

Opera omnia, 19 vols. Hamburg: Meiner, 1932–.

Oldenburg, Henry. *The Correspondence of Henry Oldenburg*, ed. A. R. Hall and M. Boas Hall, 13 vols. Madison: University of Wisconsin Press, vols. I–IX; London: Mansell, vols. X–XI; London: Taylor and Francis, vols. XII–XIII, 1965–86.

Opuscula philosophica quibus continetur, principiae philosophiae antiquissimae & recentissimae ac philosophia vulgaris refutata quibus junctur sunt C.C. problemata de revolutione animarum humanorum. Amsterdam, 1690.

Origen (Origines Adamantius). *Origenes Contra Celsus libri octo*, trans. William Spencer. Cambridge, 1658.

On First Principles, trans. G. W. Butterworth. London, 1936.

Parker, Samuel. *An Account of the Nature and Extent of the Divine dominion & Goodnesse*. Oxford, 1666.

Free and Impartial Censure of the Platonick Philosophie. Oxford, 1666.

Penington, Isaac, *Letters of Isaac Penington*. London, 1828.
Penn, William. *The Papers of William Penn*, ed. Mary Maples Dunn and Richard S. Dunn, 5 vols. Philadelphia: University of Pennsylvania Press, 1981–7.
No Cross, No Crown. London: Society of Friends, 1930; first published 1669.
Petersen, Johann Wilhelm. *Μυστεριον Ἀποκαταστασεοσ Παντον, das ist: das Geheimnisz der Wiederbringung aller Dinge*, 3 vols. 1700–10.
Philo of Alexandria, *Philo in Ten Volumes*, ed. F. H. Colson and G. H. Whitaker. London and Cambridge MA: Harvard University Press, 1985 (first published 1932).
Poulain de la Barre, François. *The Equality of the Sexes*, trans. Desmond Clarke. Manchester: Manchester University Press, 1990.
Reeve, John. *See* Muggleton, Lodowick.
Reuchlin, Johannes. *De arte cabalistica*. Hagenau, 1517.
Rigge, Ambrose. *The Good Old way and Truth which the Ancient Christians many Ages and Generations ago witnessed unto in the World from Age to Age; even from the Days of Christ unto this very time, wherein the same Doctrine, Life and Practice is witnessed unto us who are in contempt called Quakers*. London, 1669.
Robertson, William. *The Gate or Door to the Holy Tongue*. London, 1653.
[Rust, George]. *A Letter of Resolution concerning Origen and the Chief of his Opinions*. London, 1661.
Rust, George, *A Funeral Sermon Preached at the Obsequies of the Right Reverend Father in God, Jeremy, Lord Bishop of Down*. London, 1670.
Sewel, W. *The History of the Rise, Increase and Progress of the Christian People Called Quakers*. London, 1725.
Spinoza, Baruch, *Opera quotquot reperta sunt*, ed. J. van Vloten and J. P. N. Land. The Hague: Nijhoff, 1964.
Sprat, Thomas, *The History of the Royal Society of London*. London, 1667.
Sterry, Peter. *Discourse of the Freedom of the Will*. London, 1675.
Stubbe, Henry. *The Miraculous Conformist; or, an account of several marvailous cures performed by the stroaking of the hands of Mr V. Greatarick, with a physical discourse thereupon, etc.* Oxford, 1666.
Campanella Reviv'd: or, An Enquiry into the History of the Royal Society. London, 1670.
A Censure upon Certain Passages Contained in A History of the Royal Society. London, 1670.
Legends No Histories: or, A Specimen of some Animadversions upon the History of the Royal Society. London, 1670.
Plus Ultra Reduced to a Non-Plus, or a Specimen of some Animadversions upon the Plus Ultra of Mr Glanvill. London, 1670.
A Letter to Dr Henry More in Answer to what he writ and printed in Mr Glanvil's Book. Oxford, 1671.
A Reply unto the Letter Written to Mr Henry Stubbe in Defense of the History of the Royal Society. Oxford, 1671.
Survey of Quakerism . . . by a Lover of the Truth. London, 1677.
Taylor, Jeremy. *The Whole Works*, ed. R. Heber, 10 vols. London, 1856.

Theologia Germanica. Or Mysticall Divinitie. A Little Golden Manuall briefly Discovering the Mysteries, Sublimity, Perfection and Simplicity of Christianity, trans. Giles Randall. London, 1646.

Tozetti, T. (ed.). *Atti e memorie inedite dell'Accademia del Cimento*. Florence, 1780.

Walpole, Horace. *The Yale Edition of Horace Walpole's Correspondence*, 41 vols., ed. W. S. Lewis. London: Oxford University Press, 1937–83.

Ward, John. *Diary of the Reverend John Ward, A.M., Vicar of Stratford-upon-Avon, extending from 1648–1679*, ed. C. Severn. London, 1839.

Ward, Richard. *The Life of the Pious and Learned Henry More*. London, 1710; new edition, ed. S. Hutton et al., Dordrecht: Kluwer, 2000.

Webster, John. *Vindiciae academiarum, or the Examination of the Academies*. London, 1654.

Whitehead, George. *The Glory of Christ's Light within Expelling Darkness*. [London], 1669.

The Way of Life and Perfection Livingly Demonstrated. N.p., 1676.

Whiting, John. *Persecution Exposed*. London, 1715.

Willis, Thomas. *De anima brutorum quae hominis vitalis ac sensitiva est exercitationes duae*. London, 1672. English version, *Two Discourses concerning the Soul of Brutes, which is that of the vital and Sensitive of Man*, in *The Remaining Medical Works of that Famous and Renowned Physician Dr. Thomas Willis*. London, 1683.

The Anatomy of the Brain and Nerves, ed. William Feindel. Montreal, 1965.

Thomas Willis's Oxford Lectures, ed. Kenneth Dewhurst. Oxford: Sandford, 1980.

Wilson, Thomas. *The Spirit of Delusion Reproved: or the Quakers Cause Fairly Heard, and Justly Condemned. Being an Answer to William Penn, George Fox, George Whitehead, George Keith, Edward Burroughs, and several other the most leading Men amonst them*. London, 1678.

Worthington, John. *The Diary and Correspondence of John Worthington*, ed. J. Crossley and R. C. Christie, 3 vols. Manchester: Chetham Society, 1847–86.

SECONDARY SOURCES

Abbott, G. F. (1920). *Under the Turk at Constantinople: A Record of Sir John Finch's Embassy, 1674–1681*. London: Macmillan.

Aiton, E. J. (1985). *Leibniz. A Biography*. Bristol and Boston: Adam Hilger.

Audi, Robert (ed.) (1995). *The Cambridge Dictionary of Philosophy*. Cambridge and New York: Cambridge University Press.

Atherton, Margaret (1993). 'Cartesian Reason and Gendered Reason', in Louise Antony and Charlotte Witt (eds.), *A Mind of One's Own: Feminist Essays on Reason and Objectivity*. Boulder, CO: Westview Press.

Baar, Miriam de, Machteld Löwenstyn, Marit Monteiro and A. Agnes Sneller (eds.) (1996). *Choosing the Better Part. Anna Maria van Schurman (1607–1678)*. Dordrecht: Kluwer.

Bailey, M. L. (1914). *Milton and Jacob Boehme. A Study in German Mysticism in Seventeenth-Century England.* New York: Oxford University Press.

Bailey, Richard (1992). *New Light on George Fox and Early Quakerism. The Making and Unmaking of a God.* San Francisco: Mellen Research University Press.

Baldi, M. (ed.) (1996). *'Mind Senior to the World'. Stoicismo e origenismo nella filosfia platonica del seicento inglese.* Milan: Francoangeli.

Becco, Anne (1978). 'Leibniz et François Mercure van Helmont: bagatelle pour des monades'. *Studia Leibnitiana*, Sonderheft 7: 119–42.

Berg, J. van den (1988). 'Continuity within a Changing Context. The Millenarian Concepts of Joseph Mede'. *Pietismus und Neuzeit*, 14: 189–200.

Birrell, T. A. (1991). 'Reading as Pastime: The Place of Light Literature in Some Gentlemen's Libraries of the Seventeenth Century', in R. Myers and M. Harris (eds.), *Property of a Gentleman.* N.p.: St Paul's Bibliographies.

Blau, J. (1944). *The Christian Interpretation of the Cabala in the Renaissance.* New York: Columbia University Press.

Bolton, F. R. (1958). *The Caroline Tradition of the Church of Ireland, with Particular Reference to Bishop Jeremy Taylor.* London: SPCK.

Bordo, Susan (1987). *The Flight to Objectivity. Essays on Cartesianism and Culture.* Albany, NY: State University of New York Press.

Braithwaite, W. C. (1919). *The Second Period of Quakerism*, London: Macmillan.

Brown, Stuart (1984). *Leibniz.* Brighton: Harvester.

(1990). 'Leibniz and Henry More's Cabbalistic Circle', in Hutton (1990), pp. 77–96.

(1997) 'F. M. van Helmont: His Philosophical Connections and the Reception of his Later Cabbalistical Philosophy', in M. A. Stewart (ed.), *Studies in Seventeenth Century European Philosophy*, Oxford: Clarendon Press.

Burns, Norman T. (1972). *Christian Mortalism from Tyndale to Milton.* Cambridge, MA: Harvard University Press.

Cassirer, Ernst (1953). *The Platonic Renaissance in England*, translation of *Die Platonische Renaissance in England* by J. P. Pettegrove. Edinburgh: Nelson.

Clericuzio, Antonio (2000). *Elements, Principles and Corpuscles. A Study of Atomism and Chemistry in the Seventeenth Century.* Dordrecht: Kluwer.

Clucas, Stephen (ed.) (2003). *Princely Brave Woman. Essays on Margaret Cavendish, Duchess of Newcastle.* London: Ashgate.

Colie, Rosalie (1957). *Light and Enlightenment. A Study of the Cambridge Platonists and the Dutch Arminians.* Cambridge: Cambridge University Press.

(1963). 'Spinoza in England, 1665–1730'. *Proceedings of the American Philosophical Society* 107: 184–5.

Copenhaver, B. P. (1980). 'Jewish Theologies of Space in the Scientific Revolution: Henry More, Joseph Raphson and Isaac Newton and their Predecessors'. *Annals of Science*, 37: 489–548.

Corns, T. N. and Loewenstein, D. (eds.) (1995). *The Emergence of Quaker Writing. Dissenting Literature in Seventeenth-Century England.* Portland, OR: Frank Cass.

Costello, W. T. (1958). *The Scholastic Curriculum at Early Seventeenth-Century Cambridge*. Cambridge, MA: Harvard University Press.

Coudert, Allison (1975). 'A Cambridge Platonist's Kabbalist Nightmare'. *Journal of the History of Ideas*, 36: 633–52.

(1976). 'A Quaker Kabbalist Controversy. George Fox's Reaction to Francis Mercurius van Helmont'. *Journal of the Warburg and Courtauld Institutes*, 39: 171–89.

(1990). 'Henry More and Witchcraft', in Hutton (1990), pp. 115–36.

(1992). 'Henry More, the Kabbalah and the Quakers', in Kroll et al. (eds.) (1992), pp. 31–67.

(1995). *Leibniz and the Kabbalah*. Dordrecht, Kluwer.

(1999). *The Impact of the Kabbalah in the Seventeenth Century. The Life and Thought of Francis Mercury van Helmont (1614–1698)*. Leiden: Brill.

(forthcoming), 'Judaizing in the Seventeenth Century. Francis Mercury van Helmont and Johann Peter Späth (Moses Germanus)', in M. Mulsow and R. H. Popkin (eds.), *Secret Conversions to Judaism in Early Modern Europe*.

Craig, Edward (ed.) (1998). *Routledge Encyclopedia of Philosophy*. London: Routledge.

Crino, A.-M. (1957). *Fatti e figure del seicento anglo-toscana. Documenti inediti sui rapporti letterari, diplomatici e culturali fra Toscana e Inghilterra*. Florence: Olschki.

(1968). *Un principe de Toscana in Inghilterra e in Irlanda nell 1669. Relazione ufficiale del viaggio di Cosimo de' Medici tratta dal 'Giornale' di L. Magalotti*. Rome: Edizione di Storia e Letteratura.

Cristofolini, Paolo (ed.) (1995). *L'hérésie spinoziste: la discussion sur le Tractatus Theologico-Politicus, 1670–1677*. Amsterdam and Maarssen: APA–Holland University Press.

Critchley, M. (1937). 'The Malady of Anne, Vicountess Conway', *King's College Hospital Gazette*, 16: 44–9.

Crocker, Robert (1990). 'Mysticism and Enthusiasm in Henry More', in Hutton (1990a), pp. 137–55.

(2003). *Henry More, 1614–1687. A Biography of the Cambridge Platonist*. Dordrecht: Kluwer.

Cromartie, Alan (1995). *Sir Matthew Hale, 1609–1676. Law, Religion and Natural Philosophy*. Cambridge: Cambridge University Press.

Cunningham, Andrew and O. Grell (eds.) (1996). *Religio Medici: Medicine and Religion in Seventeenth-Century England*. Aldershot: Scolar Press.

Darwall, Stephen (1995). *The British Moralists and the Internal Ought 1640–1740*. Cambridge: Cambridge University Press.

Debus, Alan (1977). *The Chemical Philosophy. Paracelsian Science and Medicine in the Sixteenth and Seventeenth Centuries*, 2 vols. New York: Science History Publications.

Dobbs, B. J. T. (1973–4). 'Studies in the Natural Philosophy of Sir Kenelm Digby', *Ambix* 18: 1–25; 20: 143–63; 21: 1–28.

Duran, Jane (1989). 'Anne Viscountess Conway: A Seventeenth-Century Rationalist'. *Hypatia: A Journal of Feminist Philosophy*, 4: 64–79.

(1991). *Towards a Feminist Epistemology*. Lanham, MD: Rowman and Littlefield.

Eales, Jacqueline (1990). *Puritans and Roundheads. The Harleys of Brampton Bryan at the Outbreak of the English Civil Wars*. Cambridge: Cambridge University Press.

Fichant, Michael (1991). *De l'horizon de la doctrine humaine. 'Αποκοταστασισ παντον (La restitution universelle)*. Paris: Vrin.

Fletcher, H. E. (1956). *The Intellectual Development of John Milton*. Urbana: University of Illinois Press.

Force, James E. and R. H. Popkin (eds.) (1994). *The Books of Nature and Scripture. Recent Essays on Natural Philosophy, Theology, and Biblical Criticism in the Netherlands of Spinoza's Time and the British Isles of Newton's Time*. Dordrecht: Kluwer.

Fordyce, C. J. and T. M. Knox (1936–9). 'The Books Bequeathed to Jesus College Library, Oxford, by Lord Herbert of Cherbury'. *Proceedings and Papers of the Oxford Bibliographical Society*, 5: 53–115.

Frank, Robert G. (1974). 'The John Ward Diaries: Mirror of Seventeenth-Century Medicine'. *Journal of Medical History*, 29: 147–79.

(1980). *Harvey and the Oxford Physiologists*. Berkeley: University of California Press.

Frankel, Lois (1991). 'Anne Finch, Viscountess Conway', in M. E. Waithe (ed.), *A History of Women Philosophers*. vol. III. Dordrecht, Kluwer, pp. 41–58.

Freeman, Arthur and Paul Grinke (2002). 'Four New Shakespeare Quartos? Viscount Conway's Lost English Plays'. *Times Literary Supplement*, 5 April, pp. 17–18.

Gabbey, Alan (1977). 'Anne Conway et Henry More. Lettres sur Descartes, 1650–1'. *Archives de Philosophie*, 40: 379–404.

(1982). '"Philosophia cartesiana triumphata", Henry More, 1646–71', in T. M. Lennon, J. M. Nicholas and J. W. Davis (eds.), *Problems in Cartesianism*. Kingston and Montreal: McGill–Queen's University Press, pp. 171–509.

Gascoigne, J. (1989). *Cambridge in the Age of Enlightenment. Science, Religion and Politics from the Restoration to the French Revolution*. Cambridge: Cambridge University Press.

Giglioni, Guido (1991a). 'La teoria dell'immaginazione nell "idealismo" biologico di Johannes Baptista van Helmont'. *La Cultura*, 29: 110–45.

(1991b). 'Il *Tractatus de natura substantiae energetica* di F. Glisson'. *Annali della Facoltà di Lettere e Filosofia del Università di Macerata*, 24: 137–79.

(1996). ' "Anatomist Atheist": The Hylozoistic Foundations of Francis Glisson's Anatomical Research', in Cunningham and Grell (1996), pp. 115–35.

Grafton, Anthony (1989). 'Protestant versus Prophet: Isaac Casaubon on Hermes Trismegistus', and 'The Strange Deaths of Hermes and the Sibyls', in A. Grafton, *Defenders of the Text. The Traditions of Scholarship in an Age of Science, 1450–1800*. Princeton: Princeton University Press.

Grell, Ole (1996). 'Plague, Prayer and Physic: Helmontian Medicine in Restoration England', in Cunningham and Grell (1998), pp. 204–27.

Grimshaw, Jean (1982). *Philosophy and Feminist Thinking.* Minneapolis: Minnesota University Press.

Gründer, K. and W. Schmidt-Biggemann (eds.) (1984). *Spinoza in der Frühzeit seiner Religiösen Wirkung.* Heidelberg: Verlag Lambert Schneider.

Hall, Rupert (1990). *Henry More. Magic, Religion and Experiment.* Oxford: Blackwell.

Hamilton, Alastair (1981). *The Family of Love.* Cambridge: James Clark.

Harris, Frances (1997). 'Living in the Neighbourhood of Science: Mary Evelyn, Margaret Cavendish and the Greshamites', in Hunter and Hutton (1997), pp. 198–217.

(2003). *Transformations of Love. The Friendship of John Evelyn and Margaret Godolphin.* Oxford: Oxford University Press.

Harrison, Peter (1993). 'Animal Souls, Metempsychosis, and Theodicy'. *Journal of the History of Philosophy,* 31: 519–44.

Harth, Erica (1992). *Cartesian Women.* Ithaca, NY: Cornell University Press.

Hekman, Susan (1990). *Gender and Knowledge. Elements of a Postmodern Feminism.* Oxford: Polity Press.

Henry, John (1982). 'Atomism and Eschatology. Catholicism and Natural Philosophy in the Interregnum'. *British Journal for the History of Science,* 15: 211–39.

(1986). 'A Cambridge Platonist's Materialism. Henry More and the Concept of the Soul'. *Journal of the Warburg and Courtauld Institutes,* 49: 172–95.

(1987). 'Medicine and Pneumatology: Henry More, Richard Baxter and Francis Glisson's *Treatise on the Energetic Nature of Substance*'. *Medical History,* 31: 15–40.

(1990), 'Henry More versus Robert Boyle: The Spirit of Nature and the Nature of Providence', in Hutton (1990).

Hervey, Helen (1952). 'Hobbes and Descartes in the Light of Some Unpublished Letters between Sir Charles Cavendish and John Pell'. *Osiris,* 10: 67–90.

Hobby, Elaine (1995). 'Handmaids of the Lord and Mothers in Israel: Early Vindications of Quaker Women's Prophecy', in Corns and Loewenstein (1995).

Hodge, Joanna (1988). 'Subject, Body and the Exclusion of Women from Philosophy', in Morwena Griffiths and Margaret Whitford (eds.), *Feminist Perspectives in Philosophy.* Basingstoke: Macmillan, pp. 152–68.

Horwitz, H. (1968a). 'The Work of Sir John Finch'. *Notes and Queries,* 213: 103–4.

(1968b). *Revolution Politics. The Career of Daniel Finch, Second Earl of Nottingham, 1647–1730.* Cambridge: Cambridge University Press.

Horowitz, M. C. (1976). 'Aristotle and Women'. *Journal of the History of Biology,* 9: 183–213.

Hull, W. I. (1933). *Willem Sewel of Amsterdam, 1653–1720: The First Quaker Historian of Quakerism.* Swarthmore, PA.

(1935). *William Penn and the Dutch Quaker Migration to Pennsylvania.* Swarthmore, PA.

(1941). *Benjamin Furly and Quakerism in Rotterdam.* Swarthmore, PA.

Hunter, Lynette (1997a). 'Women and Domestic Medicine: Lady Experimenters 1570–1620', in Hunter and Hutton (1997), pp. 89–107.

(1997b). 'Sisters of the Royal Society: The Circle of Katherine Jones, Lady Ranelagh', in Hunter and Hutton (1997), pp. 178–97.

Hunter, Lynette and Sarah Hutton (eds.) (1997). *Women, Science and Medicine 1500–1700. Mothers and Sisters of the Royal Society.* Stroud: Alan Sutton.

Hunter, Michael (1989). 'On Oldenburg and Millenarianism', in M. Hunter, *Establishing the New Science.* Woodbridge: Boydell.

(1995). *Science and the Shape of Orthodoxy. Intellectual Change in the Late Seventeenth Century.* Woodbridge: Boydell.

(1996). 'The Reluctant Philanthropist: Robert Boyle and the "Communication of Secrets and Receits in Physick"', in Cunningham and Grell (1996), pp. 247–72.

(1997). 'Boyle vs. the Galenists'. *Medical History,* 42: 322–49.

Hutton, Ronald (1989). *Charles II.* Oxford: Clarendon Press.

Hutton, Sarah (1984). 'Reason and Revelation in the Cambridge Platonists and their Reception of Spinoza', in Gründer and Schmidt-Biggeman (1984), pp. 181–200.

(ed.) (1990a). *Henry More (1618–1687): Tercentenary Studies.* Dordrecht, Kluwer.

(1990b). 'Henry More and Jacob Boehme', in Hutton (1990a), pp. 157–71.

(1992). 'Edward Stillingfleet and the Decline of Moses Atticus', in R. Kroll (ed.), *Philosophy, Science and Religion in England, 1640–1700.* Cambridge: Cambridge University Press, pp. 68–84.

(1993). 'Damaris Cudworth, Lady Masham: Between Platonism and Enlightenment'. *British Journal for the History of Philosophy,* 1: 29–54.

(1994). 'More, Newton and the Language of Biblical Prophecy', in Force and Popkin (1994), pp. 39–54.

(1995a). 'Henry More and the Apocalypse. *Studies in Church History,* Subsidia 10: 131–40.

(1995b). 'Anne Conway, critique de Henry More: substance et matière'. *Archives de Philosophie,* 58: 371–84.

(1995c). 'Henry Oldenburg and Spinoza', in Cristofolini (1995), pp. 106–19.

(1996a). 'Henry More and Anne Conway on Preexistence and Universal Salvation', in Baldi (1996), pp. 113–26.

(1996b). 'Lord Herbert of Cherbury and the Cambridge Platonists', in Stuart Brown (ed.), *British Philosophy in the Age of Enlightenment.* Routledge History of Philosophy, vol. V. London: Routledge, pp. 20–42.

(1996c). 'Of Physic and Philosophy. Anne Conway, Francis Mercury van Helmont and Seventeenth-Century Medicine', in Cunningham and Grell (1996), pp. 218–46.

(1997a). 'The Riddle of the Sphinx. Bacon and the Emblems of Science', in Hunter and Hutton (1997), pp. 7–28.

(1997b). 'Anne Conway, Margaret Cavendish and Seventeenth-Century Scientific Thought', in Hunter and Hutton (1997), pp. 218–34.

(1997c). 'Anne Conway', in Craig (1997), pp. 669–71.

(1997d). 'In Dialogue with Thomas Hobbes: Margaret Cavendish's Natural Philosophy'. *Women's Writing*, 4: 421–32.

(1997e). 'De alteriteit van der geschiedenis: over Anne Conway (1630–1679) en Mary Astell (1666–1731)', in J. Hermsen (ed.), *Het Denken ven der Ander.* Kampen: Kok Agora, pp. 39–55.

(1999a), 'More, Millenarianism and the Ma'aseh Merkavah', in J. E. Force and D. S. Katz (eds.), *Everything Connects. In Conference with Richard H. Popkin. Essays in his Honour*. Leiden: Brill, pp. 163–82.

(1999b). 'On an Early Letter by Anne Conway', in Pina Totaro (ed.), *Donne, filosofia e cultura nel seicento*. Rome: CNR, pp. 109–15.

(1999c).'Anne Conway and the Kaballah', in A. Coudert, S. Hutton and R. H. Popkin (eds.), *Judaeo-Christian Intellectual Culture in the Seventeenth-Century. A Celebration of the Library of Narcissus Marsh, in Dublin*. Dordrecht: Kluwer.

(2002). 'The Cambridge Platonists', in S. Nadler (ed.), *Blackwell Companion to Early Modern Philosophy*. Oxford: Blackwell.

(2003). 'Margaret Cavendish and Henry More', in S. Clucas (2003).

Iliffe, Robert (1994). '"Making a Shew": Apocalyptic Hermeneutics and the Sociology of Christian Idolatry in the Work of Isaac Newton and Henry More', in Force and Popkin (1994), pp. 55–88.

Isler, H. (1968). *Thomas Willis MD (1621–75), Doctor and Scientist*. New York: Hafner.

Israel, Jonathan (2001). *Radical Enlightenment. Philosophy and the Making of Modernity, 1650–1750*. Oxford: Oxford University Press.

Jacob, James R. (1983). *Henry Stubbe, Radical Protestantism and the Early Enlightenment*. Cambridge: Cambridge University Press.

Jacobsen, G. A. (1932). *William Blathwayt: A Late Seventeenth-Century English Administrator*. New Haven, CT: Yale University Press.

Jacquot, J. (1952). 'Sir Charles Cavendish and his Learned Friends'. *Annals of Science*, 8: 12–27.

James, Susan (1997). *Passion and Action. The Emotions in Seventeenth-Century Philosophy*. Oxford: Oxford University Press.

(1999). 'The Philosophical Innovations of Margaret Cavendish'. *British Journal for the History of Philosophy*, 7: 219–44.

Jordan, W. K. (1936–40). *The Development of Religious Toleration in England*, 4 vols. London: Allen and Unwin.

Jordy, A. de and H. Fletcher (1961). *A Library for Younger Schollers*. Illinois Studies in Language and Literature, vol. XLVIII. Urbana, IL: University of Illinois Press.

Kaplan, Barbara B. (1982). 'Greatrakes the Stroker: The Interpretations of his Contemporaries'. *Isis*, 73: 178–85.

Kaplan, Y., H. Mechoulan and R. H. Popkin (eds.) (1989). *Menasseh ben Israel and His World*. Leiden: Brill.

Katz, David (1990). 'Henry More and the Jews', in Hutton (1990), pp. 173–88.

Kearney, H. F. (1959). *Scholars and Gentlemen. Universities and Society in Pre-Industrial Britain 1500–1700*. London: Faber.

Keller, Evelyn Fox (1985). *Reflections on Gender and Science*. New Haven, CT: Yale University Press.

Koyré, A. (1957). *From the Closed World to the Infinite Universe*. Baltimore: Johns Hopkins University Press.

Kroll, Richard, R. Ashcraft and P. Zagorin (eds.) (1992). *Philosophy, Science and Religion in England, 1640–1700*. Cambridge: Cambridge University Press.

Lamprecht, S. P. (1935). 'The Role of Descartes in Seventeenth-Century England', in *Studies in the History of Ideas*, vol. III. New York: n.p., pp. 181–240.

Laudan, L. (1966). 'The Clock Metaphor and Probabilism: The Impact of Descartes on English Methodological Thought 1660–1685'. *Annals of Science*, 22: 73–104.

Lennon, T. M. (1992). 'Lady Oracle: Changing Conceptions of Authority and Reason in Seventeenth-Century Philosophy', in E. D. Harvey and K. Okruhlik (eds.), *Women and Reason*. Ann Arbor: Michigan University Press, pp. 39–61.

Lloyd, Genevieve (1995). *The Man of Reason. 'Male' and 'Female' in Western Philosophy*. London, Routledge (first published Methuen, 1984).

Loeber, Rolf (1981). *A Biographical Dictionary of Architects in Ireland, 1600–1722*. London: John Murray.

Lynch, Kathleen (1965). *Roger Boyle, First Earl of Orrery*. Knoxville, TN: University of Tennessee Press.

Mack, Phyllis (1992). *Visionary Women. Ecstatic Prophets in Seventeenth-Century England*. Berkeley: University of California Press.

Maclean, Ian (1980). *Renaissance Notion of Woman*. Cambridge, Cambridge University Press.

Maddison, R. E. W. (1969). *The Life of the Honourable Robert Boyle, FRS*. London: Taylor and Francis.

Malloch, T. A. (1917). *Finch and Baines: A Seventeenth-Century Friendship*. Cambridge: Cambridge University Press.

Merchant, Carolyn (1979). 'The Vitalism of Anne Conway: Its Impact on Leiniz's Concept of the Monad'. *Journal of the History of Philosophy*, 7: 255–69.

(1980). *The Death of Nature. Women, Ecology and the Scientific Revolution*. San Francisco: Harper and Row.

Mintz, Samuel (1962). *The Hunting of Leviathan. Seventeenth-Century Reactions to the Materialism and Moral Philosophy of Thomas Hobbes*. Cambridge: Cambridge University Press.

Moss, J. D. (1981). 'Godded with God: Hendrik Niclaes and his Family of Love'. *Transactions of the American Philosophical Society*, 71: 7–86.

Mullett, Charles F. (1938). 'A Letter by Joseph Glanvill on the Future State'. *Huntington Library Quarterly*, 4: 447–56.

Nicolson, Marjorie (1929). 'The Early Stages of Cartesianism in England'. *Studies in Philology*, 26: 356–74.

(1929–30). 'Christ's College and the Latitude Men'. *Modern Philology*, 27: 35–53.

(1930). 'George Keith and Cambridge Platonism'. *Philosophical Review*, 39: 36–55.

O'Neill, Eileen (1998). 'Disappearing Ink: Early Modern Women Philosophers and their Fate in History', in Janet A. Kourany (ed.), *Philosophy in a Feminist Voice. Critiques and Reconstructions*. Princeton: Princeton University Press, pp. 16–62.

Orio de Miguel, Bernadino (1993). 'Leibniz y la tradicion teosofico-kabbalistica: Francisco Mercurio van Helmont'. Dissertation, Universidad Complutense de Madrid.

Owen, G. R. (1937). 'The Famous Case of Lady Anne Conway'. *Annals of Medical History*, 9: 567–71.

Pacchi, Arrigo (1973). *Cartesio in Inghilterra da More a Boyle*. Bari: Laterza.

Pagel, Walter (1982). *Joan Baptista van Helmont. Reformer in Science and Medicine*. Cambridge: Cambridge University Press.

Passmore, J. A. (1951). *Ralph Cudworth, an Interpretation*. Cambridge: Cambridge University Press.

Petersson, R. T. (1956). *Sir Kenelm Digby. The Ornament of England, 1603–1665*. London: Jonathan Cape.

Plomer, H. R. (1904). 'A Cavalier's Library'. *The Library*, n.s. 5: 158–72.

Popkin, R. H. (1990). 'The Spiritualistic Cosmologies of Henry More and Anne Conway', in Hutton (1990), pp. 97–114.

(ed.) (1999). *The Columbia History of Western Philosophy*. New York: Columbia University Press.

Principe, Lawrence M. and Andrew Weeks (1989). 'Jacob's Divine Substance *Salitter*: Its Nature, Origin and Relation to Seventeenth-Century Science Theories'. *British Journal for the History of Science*, 22: 53–61.

Rattansi, P. (1989). 'The Helmontian–Galenist Controversy in Restoration England'. *Ambix*, 12: 1–23.

Rogers, G. A. J. (1985). 'Descartes and the English', in J. D. North and J. J. Roche (eds.), *The Light of Nature. Essays in the History and Philosophy of Science Presented to A.C. Crombie*. Dordrecht: Kluwer, pp. 281–302.

Rogers, G. A. J., J.-M. Vienne and Y.-C. Zarka (1997). *The Cambridge Platonists in Context*. Dordrecht: Kluwer.

Roy, Ian (1968). 'The Libraries of Edward, Second Viscount Conway, and Others. An Inventory and Valuation of 1643'. *Bulletin of the Institute of Historical Research*, 41: 35–46.

Runia, David T. (1986). *Philo of Alexandria and the Timaeus of Plato*. Leiden: Brill.

(ed.) (1995). *Philo and the Church Fathers. A Collection of Papers*. Leiden: Brill.

Russell, G. A. (1994). 'The Impact of the *Philosophus Autodictatus*: Pococke, John Locke and the Society of Friends', in G. A. Russell (ed.), *The 'Arabick' Interest of the Natural Philosophers in Seventeenth-Century England*. Leiden: Brill, pp. 224–65.

Rutherford, Donald (1995). *Leibniz and the Rational Order of Nature*. Cambridge: Cambridge University Press.

Salecker, R. (1931). *Christian Knorr von Rosenroth*. Leipzig: Mayer and Müller.

Sarasohn, Lisa T. (1984). 'Science Turned Upside-Down: Feminism and the Natural Philosophy of Margaret Cavendish'. *Huntington Library Quarterly*, 47: 289–307.

Saunders, David (1997). *Anti-Lawyers. Religion and the Critics of Law and State*. London: Routledge.

Schmitt, C. B. (1966). 'Perennial Philosophy from Agostino Steuco to Leibniz'. *Journal of the History of Ideas*, 27: 505–32.

Scholem, Gershom (1973). *Sabbatai Sevi, the Mystical Messiah, 1626–1676*. London: Routledge and Kegan Paul.

(1974). *Major Trends in Jewish Mysticism*. New York: Schocken Books. First published 1946.

(1984). 'Die Wachtersche Kontroverse über den Spinozismus und ihre Folgen', in Gründer and Schmidt-Biggeman (1984), pp. 15–25.

Secret, F. (1964). *Les kabbalistes chrétiens de la Renaissance*. Paris: Dunod.

Seidel, M. A. (1974). 'Poullain de la Barre's *The Woman as Good as the Man*'. *Journal of the History of Ideas*, 35: 499–508.

Shapin, S. and S. Schaffer (1985). *Leviathan and the Air Pump. Hobbes, Boyle and the Experimental Life*. Princeton: Princeton University Press.

Shapiro, Lisa (1999). 'Princess Elizabeth and Descartes: The Union of Soul and Body and the Practice of Philosophy'. *British Journal for the History of Philosophy*, 7: 503–20.

Sherrer, G. (1958). 'Philalgia in Warwickshire: F. M. van Helmont's Anatomy of Pain Applied to Anne Conway'. *Studies in the Renaissance*, 5: 196–206.

Smith, N. (1989). *Perfection Proclaimed: Language and Literature in English Radical Religion 1640–1660*. Oxford: Oxford University Press.

Soderland, Jean R. (1983). *William Penn and the Founding of Pennsylvania, 1680–84, A Documentary History*. Philadelphia: University of Pennsylvania Press.

Steneck, Nicholas (1982). 'Greatrakes the Stroker: The Interpretations of Historians'. *Isis*, 73: 161–77.

Stoesser-Johnston, A. (2000). 'Robert Hooke and Holland: Dutch Influence on his Architecture'. *Bulletin KNOB*, 99: 121–37.

Stranks, C. J. (1952). *The Life and Writings of Jeremy Taylor*. London: SPCK.

Thomas, K. (1978). *Religion and the Decline of Magic. Studies in Popular Beliefs in Sixteenth and Seventeenth-Century England*. Harmondsworth: Penguin.

Thune, N. (1948). *The Behemists and Philadelphians. A Contribution to the Study of English Mysticism*. Uppsala: Almquist and Wilksells.

Tiles, Mary (1986–7). 'Mathesis and the Masculine Birth of Time'. *International Studies in the Philosophy of Science: Dubrovnik Papers*, 1: 16–35.

Toomer, G. J. (1996). *Eastern Wisdom and Learning. The Study of Arabic in the Seventeenth Century*. Oxford: Oxford University Press.

Walker, D. P. (1964). *The Decline of Hell. Seventeenth-Century Discussions of Eternal Torment*. London: Duckworth.

(1972). *The Ancient Theology. Studies in Christian Platonism from the Fifteenth to the Eighteenth Century*. London: Routledge.

(1989). 'Medical Spirits in Philosophy and Theology from Ficino to Newton', in *Arts du spectacle et histoire des idées. Recueil offert en hommage à Jean Jacquot*. Tours: Centre d'Etudes Supérieures de la Renaissance, pp. 287–300.

Wall, Ernestine van der (1987). *De Mystieke Chiliast Petrus Serrarius (1600–1669)*. Dissertation, University of Leiden.

(1989). 'Petrus Serrarius and Menasseh ben Israel. Christian Millenarianism and Jewish Messianism in Seventeenth Century Amsterdam', in Kaplan et al. (1989), pp. 164–90.

Webster, Charles (1969). 'Henry More and Descartes, Some New Sources'. *British Journal for the History of Science*, 4: 359–77.

(1975). *The Great Instauration. Science, Medicine and Reform, 1626–1650*. London: Duckworth.

(1982). *From Paracelsus to Newton. Magic and the Making of Modern Science*. Cambridge: Cambridge University Press.

Weir, C. W. (1941). 'Francis Mercury van Helmont, his Life and his Position in the International Life of the Seventeenth Century'. Dissertation, Harvard University, Cambridge, Mass.

Whitebrook, J. C. (1911–12). 'Samuel Cradock, Cleric and Pietist (1629–1706) and Matthew Cradock, First Governor of Massachusetts'. *Congregational History Society Transactions*, 5: 181–91.

Wilcox, Catherine M. (1995). *Theology and Women's Ministry in Seventeenth-Century English Quakerism*. Lewisham, Queenstown and Lampeter: Edwin Mellen.

Wojcik, Jan W. (1997). *Robert Boyle and the Limits of Reason*. Cambridge: Cambridge University Press.

Wolfson, H. A. (1948). *Philo. Foundations of Religious Philosophy in Judaism, Christianity and Islam*, 2 vols. Cambridge, MA: Harvard University Press.

Yale, F. E. C. (1957–71). *Lord Nottingham's Chancery Cases*. London: Selden Society.

Yates, F. A. (1972). *The Rosicrucian Enlightenment*. London: Routledge and Kegan Paul.

Index